American Statesmen and Their Speeches
美国政治家及其演说述评

黄必康 /著

北京大学出版社
PEKING UNIVERSITY PRESS

图书在版编目(CIP)数据

美国政治家及其演说述评/黄必康著.—北京:北京大学出版社,2013.8
ISBN 978-7-301-23036-7

Ⅰ.①美… Ⅱ.①黄… Ⅲ.①政治家—演说—美国—高等学校—教材 Ⅳ.①K837.127

中国版本图书馆 CIP 数据核字(2013)第 190900 号

书　　　名：	美国政治家及其演说述评
著作责任者：	黄必康　著
责 任 编辑：	黄瑞明
标 准 书 号：	ISBN 978-7-301-23036-7/H·3364
出 版 发 行：	北京大学出版社
地　　　址：	北京市海淀区成府路 205 号　100871
网　　　址：	http://www.pup.cn　新浪官方微博：@北京大学出版社
电 子 信 箱：	zpup@pup.pku.edu.cn
电　　　话：	邮购部 62752015　发行部 62750672　编辑部 62754382
	出版部 62754962
印 刷 者：	北京大学印刷厂
经 销 者：	新华书店
	787 毫米×1092 毫米　16 开本　21.5 印张　450 千字
	2013 年 8 月第 1 版　2013 年 8 月第 1 次印刷
定　　价：	49.00 元

未经许可,不得以任何方式复制或抄袭本书之部分或全部内容。
版权所有,侵权必究
举报电话：010-62752024　电子信箱：fd@pup.pku.edu.cn

目录 / CONTENTS

1 写在前面 / FOREWORD

**第一章
殖民地的独立革命之声**

3 第一讲 约翰·温斯罗普(John Winthrop 1588—1649)
自由与权威
(On Liberty and Authority 1645)

11 第二讲 帕特里克·亨利(Patrick Henry 1736—1799)
不自由,毋宁死
(Give Me Liberty, or Give Me Death 1775)

19 第三讲 塞缪尔·亚当斯(Samuel Adams 1722—1803)
美利坚独立的决心
(Unshakable American Independence 1776)

26 第四讲 托马斯·杰斐逊(Thomas Jefferson 1743—1826)
美国独立宣言
(Declaration of Independence 1776)

**第二章
建国大业中的制宪分歧**

35 第五讲 本杰明·富兰克林(Benjamin Franklin 1706—1790)
美国宪法:有待完善的必然
(American Constitution: Imperfect but Necessary 1787)

42 第六讲 亚历山大·汉弥尔顿
(Alexander Hamilton 1755—1804)
论联邦政府和州政府的权力
(On the Power of Federal and the State Governments 1788)

51 第七讲 帕特里克·亨利(Patrick Henry 1736—1799)
走错一步,民主不再,共和消亡
(A Wrong Step Now and the Republic Will Be Lost Forever 1788)

59 第八讲 詹姆斯·麦迪逊(James Madison 1751—1836)
为联邦宪法一辩
(In Favor of the Federal Constitution 1788)

第三章
国家意识与民主法制建设

71　第九讲　乔治·华盛顿
（George Washington 1732—1799）（上）
第一任总统就职演说
（First Presidential Inaugural Address 1789）

79　第十讲　乔治·华盛顿
（George Washington 1732—1799）（下）
总统卸任告别演说
（Presidential Farewell Address 1796）

87　第十一讲　约翰·亚当斯（John Adams 1735—1826）
总统就职演说
（Presidential Inaugural Address 1797）

96　第十二讲　托马斯·杰斐逊（Thomas Jefferson 1743—1826）
第一任总统就职演说
（First Presidential Inaugural Address 1801）

第四章
和睦时代与平等主义民主

107　第十三讲　詹姆斯·门罗（James Monroe 1758—1831）
第一任总统就职演说
（First Presidential Inaugural Address 1817）

116　第十四讲　约翰·昆西·亚当斯
（John Quincy Adams 1767—1848）
总统就职演说
（Presidential Inaugural Address 1825）

124　第十五讲　安德鲁·杰克逊（Andrew Jackson 1767—1845）
第二任总统就职演说
（Second Presidential Inaugural Address 1833）

第五章
西部领土扩张的时代

135　第十六讲　詹姆斯·K.波尔克
（James K. Polk 1758—1831）
第一任总统就职演说
（First Presidential Inaugural Address 1845）

145　第十七讲　亨利·克莱（Henry Clay 1777—1845）
1850年妥协案演讲
（Speech on the Compromise of 1850）

154　第十八讲　西雅图酋长（Chief Seattle 1788—1866）
一个文明的失落：西雅图酋长演讲
（The Fall of a Civilization: Chief Seattle's 1854 Oration）

第六章
奴隶制与美国内战

165 第十九讲 约翰·C. 卡尔霍恩
(John C. Calhoun 1782—1850)
弗特山讲稿
(Fort Hill Address 1831)

175 第二十讲 约翰·布朗(John Brown 1800—1859)
法庭陈辞：为解放黑奴而献身
(To Mingle My Blood with the Blood of Millions of Black Slaves 1859)

181 第二十一讲 亚伯拉罕·林肯
(Abraham Lincoln 1809—1865)(上)
第一任总统就职演说
(First Presidential Inaugural Address 1861)

191 第二十二讲 亚伯拉罕·林肯
(Abraham Lincoln 1809—1865)(下)
第二任总统就职演说
(Second Presidential Inaugural Address 1865)

第七章
黑人为自由平等权利而斗争

201 第二十三讲 弗雷德里克·道格拉斯
(Frederic Douglass 1718?—1895)
7月4日美国独立日对黑人奴隶意味着什么？
(What to the Slave Is the Fourth of July? 1852)

210 第二十四讲 布克·T. 华盛顿
(Booker T. Washington 1857—1915)
亚特兰大博览会演讲
(Atlanta Exposition Address 1895)

220 第二十五讲 W. E. B. 杜波依斯
(W. E. B. Dubois 1868—1963)
告全国同胞尼亚加拉运动演讲
(Niagara Movement Address to the Nation 1906)

第八章
资本主义扩张中的改革和危机

231 第二十六讲 西奥多·罗斯福
(Theodore Roosevelt 1858—1919)
第二任总统就职演说
(Second Presidential Inaugural Address 1905)

239 第二十七讲 伍德罗·威尔逊
(Woodrow Wilson 1856—1919)
第二任总统就职演说
(Second Presidential Inaugural Address 1917)

248 第二十八讲 富兰克林·德拉诺·罗斯福
(Franklin Daleno Roosevelt 1882—1945)
第一任总统就职演说
(First Presidential Inaugural Address 1932)

**第九章
冷战与民权运动**

261 第二十九讲　约翰·F. 肯尼迪
（John F. Kennedy 1917—1963）
总统就职演说
（Presidential Inaugural Address 1861）

271 第三十讲　马丁·路德·金
（Martin Luther King, Jr. 1929—1968）
我有一个梦想
（I Have a Dream 1963）

282 第三十一讲　马尔科姆·X（Malcolm X 1925—1965）
选票，还是子弹
（The Ballot or the Bullet 1963）

**第十章
全球新秩序中的经济
危机和反恐战争**

295 第三十二讲　理查德·M. 尼克松
（Richard M. Nixon 1914—1994）
总统辞职演说
（Presidential Resignation Address 1974）

306 第三十三讲　罗纳德·W. 里根
（Ronald W. Reagan 1911—2004）
总统卸任告别演说
（Presidential Farewell Address 1989）

319 第三十四讲　乔治·W. 布什（George W. Bush 1946—　）
在美国西点军校毕业典礼上的演说
（Commencement Address at the United States Military Academy at West Point 2002）

331 **后记**/AFTERWORD

写在前面/FOREWORD

2004年，我在美国加州大学做富布赖特访学。当时正值美国大选，在任总统小布什和民主党候选人克里驴象大战正酣，媒体群起鼓噪，广告招贴满天，不亦乐乎。宁静的校园或有拉票的场子，引来师生参与和围观，台上的演说和台下的竞选口号汇成一股喧嚣的政治意识，台下观众或有争论，拉起了小圈子，你争我辩，互不相让。有中国留学生路过，一脸的茫然，也很少停下匆匆的脚步。他们在国内惯于复习考试，本来就不关心政治，美国的政治对他们来说更是陌生。况且，选美国总统与他们无关。这是长期对政治的冷漠造成的政治孤寂。当然，在美国，每次大选，也总有40%以上的合格选民选择不投票。

其实，如同语言一样，政治是人类存在本身。亚里士多德在其《政治学》里有一句名言："人是天生的政治动物。"马克思也说，人的本质就是"一切社会关系的总和"。这些经典之论都透视到人的本质存在问题。完全独立于政治以外的人不存在，一定要有，只能是以死表示"清白"，但却又无济于事，人类社会照样在政治、权力、利益的驱动下前行。作为身处政治社会的个体的人，要求自由、民主、解放、宽容、正义、身份、财产等无疑都是政治的诉求，都是离开了政治就毫无意义的空话，也都是离开了政治不可实现的东西。对于一个民族和国家，主权和领土、内务和外交、和平和战争、民族的复兴之梦等等都是与国际政治息息相关的。政治也是文化交流、国际交往和国际理解的共同话语。

美国的政治历史，即便追溯到"五月花号公约"为起点，也不到400年。比起中国5000多年漫长的文明进程，美国的政治历史以时间长度而论，也不过是中国两汉的更迭。但这却不是，也不应成为中国人盲目的民族自豪感和文化优越感的理由。辛亥革命以前中国的政治，在漫长的历史长河中滋生出各种政治思想萌芽，其中不乏以民为本，尊崇个人思想自由的精神火花，犹如在巨大的画布上散点分布的零星烛光。但是，它们都被强大的封建帝制的威权掐灭了。封建主义大一统的中央集权专制在"独尊儒术"的思想独裁中稳固确立，从此整整统治了中国1700多年，最终在辛亥革命建立共和以及护国起义反对帝制的枪声中分崩离析，被永远埋葬。相比之下，美国的政治思想及其社会实验极为集中，也是极见成效的。从早期清教殖民地自治民主和自由主义思想的发轫，经过启蒙主义的熏陶和独立革命时期欧陆自由主义政治思想的冲击，到费城制宪的奠基，美国民主共和政治体制的大厦在短短几十年的时间就基本建成。这个政治思想和体制在随后的领土扩张和大国博弈过程中得到鼓励，经历了奴隶制存废，内战分裂,反复的经济危机和社会危机的考验,在不断完善的过程中前行,一直支撑着美国走向现代和今天的强盛。可以说,抛开意识形态因素不论,这样的政治思想和体制在解释人类社会权力关系,限制权力腐败,促进社会发展,保护人民权利,维护社会正义各个方面都有可取之处,至今显示出了其旺盛的生命力。

冷战结束后,中国的崛起已成事实。在新的世界格局中,中美两国大国关系不断在战略伙伴和竞争对手之间蹉跎,在政治对峙和经济合作之间摇摆,在区域冲突危机和维护世界和平之间纠结,这更能让人感到两国加强政治互动理解和文化交流的迫切性。就中国而言,持续30多年的改革开放的进程逐渐走向深入,要进一步推动经济增长和民生改善,除了资源配置、经济体制、增长类型和科技创新诸多因素外,政治体制的改革和文化的传承和更新也愈来愈起到有效的推动作用。因此,在全球化过程加速;意识形态淡化和文化理解更为迫切的今天,提倡对美国政治历史有个全局的理解,从中借鉴有用的政治思想和实践,结合本国国情,探索出一条中国特色的社会主义发展道路,实现中华民族的伟大复兴,这对中美两国都有好处,也将是对世界和平的重大贡献。

当然,"橘生淮南则为橘,生于淮北则为枳"。照搬是没有出路的,政治上的教条主义在中外历史上都被证明是没有出息的。我们知道,任何的政治理念和实践都是在特定的历史环境中生成,又在实践中得以检验,得以完善的过程。在这个意义上,没有任何的"经世治国"之术能够原封不动地"放之四海而皆准"。没有什么政治理论和实践能够成为"普世"的真理,也没有任何一国的政治体制能够移植于他国的政治文化环境中而得以持续地兴盛。中国的封建专制能够维持其统治数千年,自有其自我调节和文化惯性的支撑,更重要的还在于农耕文化的封闭和自守造就的精神桎梏。古老帝国的政治体系一旦遭受全球现代性的无情冲击,必然土崩瓦解。美国的政治理念和体制脱胎于欧洲启蒙主义思想和各种联邦政体的政治实验,在美国从农业立国的理想和工业主义之间的张力中经受了多次的危机和考验,显示了其强大的生命力。然而,面对着冷战结束后世界多元的态势,面对着金融危机、恐怖主义的威胁和枪支泛滥等造成的社会心理危机,美国政治家所信奉的美国民主的"普世"价值也出现了颓势,它必须汲取新的思想成分,包容中国的思想智慧,方能得以进一步的完善。

还必须看到,政治话语是最诡谲的语言形式,政治家惯用的政治演讲更多的是意识形态的宣教。政治家们往往通过自己的演说来表达自己的政治主张,获得选民的支持。政治舞台上慷慨激昂的程式化语言往往掩盖了社会的矛盾,言之凿凿的承诺往往遮蔽了即将到来的危机。这种现象在大众传媒技术日益渗透到社会千家万户的今天,更是如此;而在美国政坛上,这一点尤其突出。成功的政治演说成了政客们在各级选举中先声夺人,走向权力巅峰的必由之路。美国政治家是深谙于此的。尤其是20世纪以来，美国总统选举在媒体科技的推动下愈发形成语言的狂欢化，造就了不少的"修辞总统"，民权运动的领袖们大多也以澎湃激情的演说著称，而奥巴马也是修辞演讲的高手，在一连串富有激情，言辞铿锵的演讲中走进了白宫。因此，我认为，研读美国政治历史中一些关键人物的政治演说，对于理解美国政治历史文化，将对一个人的阅读经验产生出意想不到的效果。了解了政治意识形态的虚妄和遮蔽作用，读者便可做到，听其言，知其意。透过政治话语的喧嚣，听到历史逻辑的在场。

同时，政治思想其实又是有趣的，我们在历史的镜框中展现出来的应该是一幅幅生动的人类政治关系演变的图画，而不是枯燥的理论和教条。我们没有时间隧道，不能回到历史真实，但我们却可以遵循人类社会发展的逻辑，根据一些历史现象，"重构"历史的场面，展示历史的图景，聆听历史的回声，从而在历史的形象中体会政治的抽象，增强自己的政治自觉和文化自觉。

基于以上认识和期待，笔者在本书中选取了34位美国历史上的重要政治人物分为10个章节加以评述，力图用生动具象的笔触，勾勒他们的历史形象和作用，总结他们的政治思想，从中烘托出一个时代的政治变迁。这些政治人物涵盖了美国从早期殖民地时期一直到9.11以后当代美国的各个关键的历史时期。同时，笔者选取了这些政治人物具有代表性的政治演说节选，以原文形式呈现，加以注释和重点评析，为有一定英文水平并愿意进一步提高英文水平的大学生和读者提供及时的学习辅导。每一讲之后提供阅读书目和讨论题目，为读者的后续学习提供了便利。

希望这本书像一座跨越美国300来年政治历史的长廊，让读者在观景式的轻松阅读过程中，翻看历史的场景，体会政治思想的意义，穿透政治演说修辞的语言外壳，享受阅读美国政治历史的乐趣。

黄必康
2013年8月1日识于
北京大学燕北园

第一章 ‖ 殖民地的独立革命之声

For we must consider that we shall be as a city upon a hill. The eyes of all people are upon us...

——John Winthrop

I know not what course others may take; but as for me, give me liberty, or give me death!

——Patrick Henry

We have no other alternative than independence, or the most ignominious and galling servitude.

——Samuel Adams

We hold these truths to be self-evident that all men are created equal.

——Thomas Jefferson

Preview Questions

01/

Who are puritans and why did they want to leave England to settle in the New World?

02/

What kind of "ideal" government did American colonists want to establish in North America?

03/

Aside from economic reasons, what are the political causes that lead to the American Revolution?

04/

What are some revolutionary ideals behind the colonial zeal for independence?

第一讲
约翰·温斯罗普(John Winthrop 1588—1649)

■ 政治历史评述

温斯罗普:山巅之城的清教统治者

16世纪初以来的美洲地理大发现,开启了人类新的欲望之门。大西洋彼岸神秘的大陆和丰腴的物产给危机四伏的欧洲注入了经济和文化的活力。此后不到半个世纪,西方征服者和殖民者,漂洋过海,纷至沓来,给美洲新大陆的原始文明带来毁灭性的灾难,也为欧洲各国带来新的财源和希望。人类纪元翻开了现代性进取和自毁新的一页。

约翰·温斯罗普就生长在这样一个社会动荡,欲望觉醒,人心思迁的时代。他出生于1588年,那年英国意外击败西班牙无敌舰队,成为海上霸主,是为大英帝国崛起的开端。但英国国内宗教改革造成的社会动荡余波尚烈。由于资本主义强势兴起,国内政治动荡,教派争端不断,经济不景气,物价飞涨,失业人口增加,英格兰人开始把视线投向海外,憧憬着新大陆的冒险乐园,盼望着西来的大洋潮汐给萎靡的生活注入新的活力。此时,冒险殖民者探险猎奇的故事源源不断传来,更诱惑人们向往着大洋彼岸异域崭新的生活图景。

1605年,寒冷的冬夜封锁着温斯罗普的家乡萨福克郡的爱德华斯通。人们围在大户人家的火炉旁,凝神屏气地听着教区牧师,航海旅行家塞缪尔·帕切斯(Samuel Parchus)讲述着海外猎奇。哥伦布的奇遇,披着熊皮的吃人生番和詹姆斯敦殖民地的遭遇,这一切都深深地吸引着这些渴望新生活,也向往着到远方传布基督福音和英格兰文化的新教教徒。青年温斯罗普就是这些故事最虔诚痴迷的听众之一,圣徒福音精神和美洲新大陆的召唤在他的心灵中深深地回响。此后些年,温斯罗普家道中落,曾思迁爱尔兰,但最终还是对美洲新大陆的渴望占了上风。面临着英格兰岛国民不聊生,日益衰败的颓势,清教徒温斯罗普忧心忡忡,似乎感到那是上帝对人类罪恶的惩罚,只有在新的领地以加尔文律法的严酷和自律的精神,才能在上帝之光的照耀下或得新生。于是,温斯罗普移居新英格兰心思愈重。一次与友人骑马外出,途中马失前蹄,温斯罗普坠入齐腰的泥潭,身体不断下沉,幸好脚底突然有物支撑,才免遭灭顶之灾。温斯罗普久思顿悟,认为那是上帝救赎的信号,从此坚定信念,说服家人,变卖家产,一心追寻1620年"五月花号"移居北美普利茅斯殖民地的航迹。正值马萨诸塞海湾公司拓展海外殖民地,温斯罗普被选为马萨诸塞海湾殖民地总督。1630年4月一个风高气爽的日子,温斯罗普登上"阿贝拉"号船,发表了他著名的"基督博爱之典范"的演说,号召殖民者们以上帝的契约律法和基督的博爱精神,以造物自然法的"公正"和上帝恩赐的"宽容",去建立"世界瞩目的山巅之城"。在人们的欢呼声和亲人离别的啜泣声中,"阿贝拉"号和其他满载900多名殖民者的船队缓缓驶离南安普顿港口,向茫茫大海驶去。

约翰·温斯罗普近来被一些史家称为被遗忘的美国建国之父,与乔治·华盛顿和托马斯·杰斐逊等国父相提并论。他憧憬的清教乌托邦"山巅之城"也一直是美国例外论和民族优越感的原型和象征。这个说法是有道理的,特别是考虑到思想意识的认识过程和社会政治组织形式的连续性和继承性,更是如此。

美国早期殖民地时期,除简短的"五月花号公约"所表现的契约自治社团精神和威廉·布雷德福的普利茅斯殖民地开发的原始叙事而外,较为成型的清教神权政治和管理体制的建立和实行,还应数新英格兰的马萨诸塞海湾殖民地最为完备。约翰·温斯罗普几乎连续但任该殖民地的总督长达20年,其间奉行清教地方自治的神权精英寡头专制,以神权社会的等级为基础,推行以上帝律法为本,行政长官权威和自由民绝对服从的自治政府模式,可称得上美国政治思想史和政治体制及社会实验的开端。表面看来,这些政治主张和自治模式与后来美国革命和建国时期的共和主义民主,平等和自由的观念和联邦体制格格不入,但是,温斯罗普带着清教乌托邦理想从英国旧体制和加尔文教中传承过来的神权家长制任意权利说,却为此后不断滋生的自由主义政治思想提供了直接的思想起点。可以说,温斯罗普的思想专制和政治上的不宽容,直接引发了马萨诸塞海湾殖民当局与罗杰·威廉、安妮·哈钦森、和托马斯·胡克等分离主义者和个人主义者之间不可调和的冲突,从而也导致了罗得岛和康狄涅格等殖民地的建立,使美国建国以前多元的民主政治意识有了发展的可能。从这个意义上说,温斯罗普堪称美国建国的思想起点和源泉。同时,他所代表的清教宿命论、上帝选民和自治主义的理想和实践,在"山巅之城"的隐喻中为以后美国盛行的"天定命运"观和孤立主义思潮提供了最原始的思想基础。

1645年,温斯罗普被控滥用职权,干预地方民团长官选举。法庭经过反复调查和审判,宣布他无罪。温斯罗普随后发表了简短演说,集中阐述了他的神权贵族任意权力说和管理思想。在这篇被称为"小言论"(Little Speech)的演说中,温斯罗普在表面温文尔雅的演说风格中,不容置疑地重申神权政府官员的绝对权威,规定了自由民所能享受自由的范围。在他看来,在等级制的社会里,政府官员一旦被有选举资格的少数教徒选出,就从上帝那里获得了绝对的权威。这是上帝与人类定下的契约,必须无条件地遵守,否则就会遭到上帝的严惩。人民必须相信,总督和其他官员对上帝的虔诚信仰和道德精神会引导他们公正地行使自己神圣的权力,为人民造福,而不会走向暴政。温斯罗普对当时开始冒头的商业自由主义精神忧心忡忡,在此以一种布道的方式对自由的观念作出严格的区分:本性的自由和公民的或曰道德的自由。前者是人的原始的、为所欲为的欲望冲动,它抵制任何权威制约,更可能走向邪恶和毁灭。后者是上帝与人类的契约规定下的自由,即社会制约,道德约束下的自由,也是社会权威监控下的社会自由。服从权威,遵守契约是这种自由的先决条件。文明社会每个公民都必须在服从权威的条件下才能享受这种公民的自由。不难看出,温斯罗普这里的权威即是自我合法化的权力,这样的权威观念也为权力的暴力作用预留了空间。

总之,温斯罗普是内心十分虔诚的清教徒,他在这篇演讲中表现出来的神权专制思想是他真实思想的流露,也是他长期管理马萨诸塞州海湾殖民地经验的总结。他提倡的是宗教精神和权威指引下的自由,而不是今天我们说的民主。历史学家也曾指责他思想趋于僵化,对新英格兰民主思潮进行了严酷的镇压。但我认为这只是脱离时代,不论个人思想发展过程的政治抽象,是对温斯罗普的苛责。这只能说明,在宗教精神和自由精神交织在一起的过程中,现代民主思想只能逐渐脱胎于宗教不宽容和封建专制的母体,在现实的,经济的发展过程中取得了自己的政治身份和地位,以在美国殖民地时期的生存环境和自治体制而论,更是如此。在这个意义上,托克维尔在其《美国的民主》中论及美国殖民地法律和习惯一节中的话,可谓一语中的:"初期移民的社会条件、宗教和民情,对他们新国家的命运无疑发生了巨大的影响。但是,新社会的建立并非起因于这些东西,因为社会的起点只存在于社会本身。任何人都不能同过去完全脱离关系,不管他们是有心还是无意,都会在自己固有的观念和习惯中混有来自教育和祖国传统的观念和习惯。"人类历史上,思想的超越者往往是冥思的哲学家,而伟大的哲学家永远不是杰出的政治家。

温斯罗普这篇演讲思想鲜明,结构严整,用词简练,颇有清教布道词的虔诚和热情,同时也表现了温斯罗普个人的清教理想主义的思想倾向和道德气质。温斯罗普喜欢读书,但读书不多。他写了大量的书信,其中表现出浓厚的清教道德意识和对社会政治的关切,表现了那个时代的宗教精神的指引下内敛思过,悲天悯人的文人气质。温斯罗普的宗教热情、多思的性格和惶惶的忧患意识在即席的演讲中也铸就了这种干练直白,同时又具有程式化的语言风格。当时的大学问家科顿·马瑟后来有一段总结清教主义文风的著名论断,在这能够恰当地说明温斯罗普这篇演说的语体特点:"关于文风,近来闹得沸沸扬扬,此时我必须表明对这个问题的看法。有这么一种写作风格,作者力图使读者在每一个段落中都可读到一些本质性的东西。不仅每个句子都读来有分量,而且整个段落视野广阔,新颖别致,其中一些甚至道出了言外之意。这类文章不拘泥于形式,也不热衷于引述他人,但默移潜化之间就让人读到了应该获得的意义。从文章表面看,作者似乎没有读过多少书,但是如果他没有大量阅读过当时的书籍,那是绝对写不出这样的文章。此类文章的谋篇布局不仅像一块金子织制的布料,而且上面还点缀着许多宝

石,有些像俄国外交使节身上穿的长袍。"(*Manuductio ad Ministerium*,1726)

　　这样的文章也是温斯罗普效仿的,谆谆的教诲是虔诚的表现,同时也是统治者心态的表达。只不过,对于马瑟用金子织制的布料和宝石做比喻,温斯罗普是不会苟同的。但是,我们在其中不难看出,新一代的殖民者及其后裔,已经开始对新世界的神奇充满了幻想。这一点连笃厚的老清教徒科顿·马瑟都无法抵御。此后,还是让富兰克林这样的伟人来为之正名吧。

■ 演讲文(节选)

On Liberty and Authority

John Winthrop

befallen: directed to
intermeddle: interfere with
proceedings: procedures

magistrates: officials

ordinance: law
eminently: clearly
vindicated: proved to be true
infirmities: weaknesses
censurers: critics

covenant: agreement; treaty; bond

furnish him with gifts: provide him with talents

I suppose something may be expected from me, upon this charge that is **befallen** me which moves me to speak now to you; yet I intend not to **intermeddle** in the **proceedings** of the court or with any of the persons concerned therein...

The great questions that have troubled the country are about the authority of the **magistrates** and the liberty of the people. It is yourselves who have called us to this office, and, being called by you, we have our authority from God, in way of an **ordinance**, such as hath the image of God **eminently** stamped upon it, the contempt and violation whereof hath been **vindicated** with examples of divine vengeance. I entreat you to consider that, when you choose magistrates, you take them from among yourselves, men subject to like passions as you are. Therefore, when you see **infirmities** in us, you should reflect upon your own, and that would make you bear the more with us, and not be severe **censurers** of the failings of your magistrates, when you have continual experience of the like infirmities in yourselves and others. We account him a good servant who breaks not his **covenant**. The covenant between you and us is the oath you have taken of us, which is to this purpose: that we shall govern you and judge your causes by the rules of God's laws and our own, according to our best skill. When you agree with a workman to build you a ship or house, etc., he undertakes as well for his skill as for his faithfulness, for it is his profession, and you pay him for both. But when you call one to be a magistrate, he doth not profess nor undertake to have sufficient skill for that office, nor can you **furnish him with gifts**, etc., therefore you must **run the hazard of** his skill and ability. But if he fails in faithfulness, which by his oath he is bound unto, that he must answer for. If it **fall out** that the case be clear to common apprehension, and the rule clear also, if he **transgress** here, the error is not in the skill, but in the evil of the will: it must be required of him. But if the case be doubtful, or the rule doubtful, to men of such understanding and parts as your magistrates are, if your magistrates should err here, yourselves must bear it.

For the other point concerning liberty, I observe a great mistake in the country about that. There is a twofold liberty, natural (I mean as our nature is now corrupt) and civil or **federal**. The first is common to man with beasts and other creatures. By this, man, as he stands in relation to man simply, hath liberty to do what he **lists**; it is a liberty to evil as well as to good. This liberty is **incompatible** and inconsistent with authority and cannot endure the least restraint of the most just authority. The exercise and maintaining of this liberty makes men grow more evil and in time to be worse than brute beasts: omnes sumus licentia deteriores (all superiority gets ruined). This is that great enemy of truth and peace, that wild beast, which all of the ordinances of God are **bent against**, to restrain and **subdue** it. The other kind of liberty I call civil or federal; it may also be termed moral, in reference to the covenant between God and man, in the moral law, and the politic covenants and **constitutions** amongst men themselves. This liberty is the proper end and object of authority and cannot **subsist** without it; and it is a liberty to that only which is good, just, and honest. This liberty you are to stand for, with the hazard (not only of your goods, but) of your lives, if need be. Whatsoever **crosseth** this is not authority but a **distemper** thereof. This liberty is maintained and exercised in a way of **subjection to** authority; it is of the same kind of liberty wherewith Christ hath made us free. The women's own choice makes such a man her husband; yet, being so chosen, he is her lord, and she is to be subject to him, yet in a way of liberty, not of bondage; and a true wife **accounts** her subjection her honor and freedom and would not think her condition safe and free but in her subjection to her husband's authority. Such is the liberty of the church under the authority of Christ, her king and husband; his **yoke** is so easy and sweet to her as a bride's ornaments; and if through forwardness or **wantonness**, etc., she shake it off, at any time, she is at no rest in her spirit, until she take it up again; and whether her lord smiles upon her and embraceth her in his arms, or whether he frowns, or **rebukes**, or **smites** her, she apprehends the sweetness of his love in all, and is

---

run the hazard of: take the risk of
fall out: turn out; happen
transgress: break (laws)

federal: civilized; socially organized
list: want; like
incompatible: not accord; resistant

bend against: firmly against
subdue: conquer; put under control
constitution: laws of government
subsist: live; survive
crossth = crosses: come against
distemper: bad temper; passionate will
subjection to: obedience to

account: consider...as

yoke: constraint or limit to freedom
wantonness: light and changeable behavior
rebuke: scold
smite: hit hard

dispensation:
offering,
exercising

brethren:
brothers

strive to: try
hard to

submit unto:
obey to

hearken:
listen carefully
preserve:
maintain, keep

refreshed, supported, and instructed by every such **dispensation** of his authority over her. On the other side, ye know who they are that complain of this yoke and say, Let us break their bands, etc.; we will not have this man to rule over us. Even so, **brethren**, it will be between you and your magistrates. If you want to stand for your natural corrupt liberties, and will do what is good in your own eyes, you will not endure the least weight of authority, but will murmur, and oppose, and be always **striving to** shake off that yoke; but if you will be satisfied to enjoy such civil and lawful liberties, such as Christ allows you, then will you quietly and cheerfully **submit unto** that authority which is set over you, in all the administrations of it, for your good. Wherein, if we fail at any time, we hope we shall be willing (by God's assistance) to **hearken** to good advice from any of you, or in any other way of God; so shall your liberties be **preserved** in upholding the honor and power of authority amongst you.

■ 重点述评与提示

1. The great questions that have troubled the country are about the authority of the magistrates and the liberty of the people.

   开宗明义，点明关键主词 authority 和 liberty 之间的矛盾，同时也隐隐道出了殖民地政治的危机，即神权专制和民主自由的矛盾。当时马萨诸塞海湾殖民地政府由总督 1 人和助理（magistrate）12 人组成，选民只限于少数有宗教教职的人。此处 country 一词并无国家之义，而是指殖民地政府自治管辖的区域。

2. We have our authority from God, in way of an ordinance, such as hath the image of God eminently stamped upon it, the contempt and violation whereof hath been vindicated with examples of divine vengeance.

   这是清教权力自我合法化的话语，权威来自上帝之戒律，虽与"君权神授"的封建专制意识有根本的区别，但却是政教合一的理论基石。这一思想后来经过民主派提倡"政教分离"的努力，逐步过渡到"权力来自人民"的理念。

3. We account him a good servant who breaks not his covenant. The covenant between you and us is the oath you have taken of us, which is to this purpose: that we shall govern you and judge your causes by the rules of God's laws and our own, according to our best skill.

   Covenant 是清教主义的一个关键词，来源于《圣经》旧约中上帝与之子民订立的

"契约"意识。《五月花公约》中也明确表示了契约自治的精神。根据上帝的律法,订立政府之法,以行使政府统治,这也是清教加尔文教的基本思想。

4. The other kind of liberty I call civil or federal; it may also be termed moral, in reference to the covenant between God and man, in the moral law, and the politic covenants and constitutions amongst men themselves.

　　这里有三层意思:上帝与人订立的契约是最根本的,一个社会应该有伦理的规约,公民个人都与政府有政治的约定。每个人都应把自己的自由限制在这三重的契约关系中。所谓 civil, federal 和 moral,都是一个意思,那就是"文明的,社会的",与 natural 相对。

5. This liberty is the proper end and object of authority and cannot subsist without it; and it is a liberty to that only which is good, just, and honest.

　　于是,在自由和权威的关系中,自由从属与权力,这样才能实现社会的正义。这是典型的权威主义与清教教义的结合,形成了政教合一的神权专制和宗教的不宽容。个人的自由和权利于是失去了现实的意义。good, honor, honest 也是美国一贯标榜的社会价值。

6. A true wife accounts her subjection her honor and freedom and would not think her condition safe and free but in her subjection to her husband's authority.

　　这是个比喻,以家庭夫妻关系谓个人自由应无条件服从政府权威,从而得到保护和自由,就像妻子应屈从丈夫的权威一样,但从中也看出马萨诸塞殖民地的夫权压迫亦不亚于神权专制.

7. But if you will be satisfied to enjoy such civil and lawful liberties, such as Christ allows you, then will you quietly and cheerfully submit unto that authority which is set over you, in all the administrations of it, for your good.

　　温斯罗普认为,与神权结合的政府权威只有通过有效的行政管理(administration)方能起到保护个人自由的作用。他本人也一直被历史学家誉为美国殖民地时期杰出的行政管理者(administrator)。

■ 思考及讨论题

1. How does Winthrop describe himself as a representative of God's authority over humankind?
2. What can be the difference between monarchical idea of "Divine Right" and

Winthrop's claim of absolute authority of the colonial magistrate?
3. According to Winthrop, how shall citizens judge the possible transgression of laws by their magistrates?
4. What can be the implications of Winthrop's theory of liberty to the idea of democracy and republican form of government?

■ 阅读书目

1. Bremer, Francis J. *John Winthrop: America's Forgotten Founding Father*. Oxford University Press, 2003.
2. Bremer, Francis J. *The World of John Winthrop: Essays on England and New England, 1588—1649* . Boston: Massachusetts Historical Society, 2005.
3. Crilly, Mark W. "John Winthrop: Magistrate, Minister, Merchant" in *The Midwest Quarterly*. Winter 1999.
4. Litke, Justin B. "Varieties of American Exceptionalism: Why John Winthrop Is No Imperialist" in *Journal of Church and State*. Volume, Spring 2012.

第二讲
帕特里克·亨利(Patrick Henry 1736—1799)

■ 政治历史评述

帕特里克·亨利:美国革命的激情喉舌

18世纪下半叶,英国在北美的十三州殖民地可谓山雨欲来风满楼。殖民地人民与英国议会的政治和经济矛盾演化到了公开武装冲突的境地。自从各殖民地建立以来,英国国内王位更替频繁,内外大事缠身,对海外殖民地疏于管理。1756年至1763年,英国为争夺殖民地,与法国进行了7年的战争。英王乔治三世骄横自负,战后执意在北美殖民地保持强大的驻军。当时英国已被战争拖得筋疲力尽,债台高筑,北美驻军的庞大军费自然需要各殖民地人民负担。筹款的最直接办法当然就是在当地征税。如果说,对于北美殖民地的人民来说,1651年以来英国议会颁布的一系列的《航海法》(Navigation Acts),甚至是1764年的《糖税法》(Sugar Act)都是宗主国为保护其海外贸易的立法措施,殖民地利益受到局部的行业损害,但是在大英帝国的旗帜下都能忍受的话,那么1765年的《印花税》(Stamp Act)却是赤裸裸为了政府的利益在民间的搜刮和对个人财产的剥夺行为,完全是暴政的压迫。而且,《印花税》的征收遍及社会各阶层行业,殖民地上下一切的社会活动和商业行为,无不受之影响。于是民怨四起,各地抗税风潮云涌,可想而知。殖民地人民提出"无代表权不纳税"(No taxation without representation)的口号,以捍卫自己的权利。震惊的英国议会对此虽有所妥协,1766年宣布取消《印花税》,但认定殖民者作为英国臣民,在英国议会具有"实际代表权"(virtual representation),必须无条件服从英国议会至高无上的征税立法权,此后又通过了《唐森德税法》(Townshend Duties),向殖民地部分商品征收进口税,引发新一轮的抗税风潮,也引发了所谓的"波士顿惨案",加重了对抗危机。更有甚者,英国议会为支撑濒于倒闭的东印度公司,通过《茶税法》(Tea Act)再次向殖民地征税。

1773年12月16日寒冷的冬夜,一批"波士顿自由之子"抵抗运动的成员化装成印第安人,潜入靠港的商船队,将324箱茶叶倾倒大海。这次"波士顿倾茶事件"震惊英国朝野,议会不久通过了一系列的《强制法案》(Coercive Acts),派军队进驻波士顿,关闭港口,实施了一系列政治和经济的弹压措施。在这样的局势下,各殖民地要求革命,要求独立的呼声高涨。1775年4月19日,美国独立战争的第一枪在列克星顿和康科德打响,消息传来,各州殖民地纷纷组织民军,以防不测。美国独立战争于是拉开了延迟已久的帷幕。

时势造英雄。正是在这风起云涌的独立革命潮流中,帕特里克·亨利脱颖而出,成为了美国至今公认的民族英雄。亨利以慷慨激昂,雄辩滔滔著称,在那群情激昂,热血沸腾的革命和独立声浪中,铿锵的辩才和煽情的演讲是掌握舆论,推动革命的最好武器,也是一个人成为政治领袖的最佳途径。亨利那篇"不自由,毋宁死"的讲演曾经激起多少美国青年的壮志豪情,至今也是每个美国中学生必读的经典之作。难怪亨利享有"美国革命的号角"的美誉,与乔治·华盛顿"美国革命的刀剑"和托马斯·杰斐逊"美国革命的笔墨"齐名,颇有美国革命"三剑客"的味道。

其实,今日观之,帕特里克·亨利也唯有充溢的激情和天才的演说能力方能在美国的政治历史中占有独特的一页。

帕特里克·亨利1736年生于弗吉尼亚一个普通苏格兰裔移民家庭。据说他早年常有吞吐山河之志,却不屑学业,视书本为畏途,但对垂钓狩猎却情有独钟,常常穿着邋遢,或游荡于山林之中,或蹒跚于湖畔河床之上,喜与山野之人为伍,对文明礼仪不屑一顾,全然是一个马克·吐温笔下的浑小子。后经父兄全力督促和协助,亨利略通希腊文和拉丁文,数学也算有不少长进。勉强毕业当地乡学。此后,他与兄长合伙经商,尽干贴本买卖,一年不到,资财散尽,却又疯狂爱上一个穷姑娘。俩人谈婚论嫁却一贫如洗,不得不求助于父母。经双方父母共同努力,就近找个小农场安顿了这一小对贫贱夫妻,指望他们能勤俭持家,一生无忧。殊不知亨利疏懒成性,两年之后,农场荒芜,只好典当出去,盘进一家店铺,重操经商旧业,以亨利之经商经验,往后如何,可想而知。看来,亨利浪子回头无望,从此该穷愁潦倒,默默无闻。但是,亨利从小的志向似乎终于找到了正途。1760年早春,亨利出现在弗吉尼亚首府,宣布参加律师资格考试。此举着实让大家吃惊不小。托马斯·杰斐逊后来对帕特里克·亨利曾有如下评判:"此公任何方面的知识都相当贫乏。既不读书,又无书可读。"如此的水平何以胜任律师之职?亨利的考试也果然差欠。四个考官中两个好好先生碍于情面,勉强签字通过,其余两人坚决不同意。亨利于是软磨硬泡,承诺日后加倍用功念书,终于获得二人签字,当上了律师。

1763年,已近而立之年的亨利当上弗吉尼亚议会议员。从此亨利激进的思想,天生的辩才和澎湃的激情有了用武之地,他巧辩法庭,步入政坛,又适逢美国独立战争和革命风暴的洗礼,终于以"革命的号角"傲立于世。

亨利这篇"不自由,毋宁死"的演讲带有强烈的传奇色彩,亨利当时没有书面的讲稿,演讲时也概无纪录,亨利生前也从未发表过这篇演讲。只是在 1816 年,也就是在演说发生后 41 年以后,这篇演讲才第一次出现在威廉·威尔特写的《帕特里克·亨利传》中。根据传记的记载,1775 年 3 月 23 日,弗吉尼亚州首府里士满市内圣·约翰教堂召开的州议会进行到第三天。帕特里克·亨利递交一份提案,提议立即宣布弗吉尼亚州处于紧急状态,招募民兵,向英国开战。当时有相当一部分人不愿与英国决裂,对英王乔治三世仍抱有幻想,还有些人采取静观其变的态度。为了让这部分人丢掉幻想,投票支持提案,坚决走独立之路,亨利走上讲坛,发表了这篇激动人心的旷世演讲。

亨利在演讲中应用排比句式和重叠同义表达,反复设问自答,调动听众的情绪,逐步推向义无反顾,死而后已的高潮。同时,亨利掌控演讲语气和节奏,从理性的平静到情绪的高昂,从低平的音调到声嘶力竭的呼喊,最终以"不自由,毋宁死"的绝句收煞全篇。据后来的在场人回忆,亨利讲到终场,"双臂上举,凌虚张开,怒目圆睁,脖子上青筋暴跳……讲到最后一句'不自由,毋宁死'时,紧握右拳击打左胸,似匕首刺入这位爱国者的心脏。"此时听众群情激昂,高呼"武装起来,血战到底"的口号。听众中有后来战死沙场的大陆军英雄卡林顿,当时不能自己,喟然长叹:"愿我葬于此地。"这也许是后人的传奇渲染,但亨利的演讲为后世传诵不断,足见其强大的思想感召力和修辞感染力。

帕特里克·亨利一生除一些书信外很少写作,他的思想也未有系统地梳理,但从其政治表现可见,他笃信个人的独立与自由高于一切,崇拜言论自由。他对政府权力,尤其是集中的权力持极不信任的态度,这在他后来极力反对弗吉尼亚州批准美国联邦宪法这件事中表现得十分充分。这其中可能有个人性格不从约束和外在表现欲等方面的原因。

也许正是读书不多,没有沉重"传统知识"的羁绊,才使得帕特里克·亨利这样的人充满反叛的思想意识和革命的决心和勇气。多思的气质往往由浓厚的书卷气熏陶而成,决而起行的个性却往往是天生和时势的产物。从某种意义上说,所谓"秀才造反十年不成",正好反衬了亨利思想的轻快和直截了当的革命先锋精神。至于轰轰烈烈的革命之后,如何进行思想重建和更新,如何创建民主共和的现代国家,这就不是亨利之所能了。

■ 演讲文

Give Me Liberty, or Give Me Death

Patrick Henry

Mr. President:

patriotism: faith and loyalty to one's homeland (here: Virginia)

entertaining: consider (an idea) and argue for it
ceremony: courtly politeness
proportion: similar degree
magnitude: bigness; size; degree
keep back: hold back; reserve
treason: betrayal of one's country
revere: respect; honor
illusion: false belief or unreal vision
siren: singing woman devil who misleads sailors
be disposed to: be willing to
salvation: delivery from sin (Puritanical notion)
anguish: great pain

solace: comfort; think for the better
insidious: tend to be evil

No man thinks more highly than I do of the **patriotism**, as well as abilities, of the very worthy gentlemen who have just addressed the House. But different men often see the same subject in different lights; and, therefore, I hope that it will not be thought disrespectful to those gentlemen, if, **entertaining** as I do opinions of a character very opposite to theirs, I shall speak forth my sentiments freely and without reserve.

This is no time for **ceremony**. The question before the House is one of awful moment to this country. For my own part I consider it as nothing less than a question of freedom or slavery; and **in proportion to** the **magnitude** of the subject ought to be the freedom of the debate. It is only in this way that we can hope to arrive at truth, and fulfill the great responsibility which we hold to God and our country. Should I **keep back** my opinions at such a time, through fear of giving offense, I should consider myself as guilty of **treason** towards my country, and of an act of disloyalty towards the majesty of heaven, which I **revere** above all earthly kings.

Mr. President, it is natural to man to indulge in the **illusions** of hope. We are apt to shut our eyes against a painful truth, and listen to the song of that **siren**, till she transforms us into beasts. Is this the part of wise men, engaged in a great and arduous struggle for liberty? Are we **disposed** to be of the number of those who, having eyes, see not, and having ears, hear not, the things which so nearly concern their temporal **salvation**?

For my part, whatever **anguish** of spirit it may cost, I am willing to know the whole truth—to know the worst and to provide for it. I have but one lamp by which my feet are guided; and that is the lamp of experience. I know of no way of judging of the future but by the past. And judging by the past, I wish to know what there has been in the conduct of the British ministry for the last ten years, to justify those hopes with which gentlemen have been pleased to **solace** themselves and the House?

Is it that **insidious** smile with which our petition has been lately received? Trust it not, sir; it will prove a snare to your feet. Suffer not yourselves to be betrayed with a kiss. Ask yourselves how this gracious reception of our petition **comports** with these warlike preparations which cover our waters and darken our land. Are fleets and armies necessary to a work of love and **reconciliation**? Have we shown ourselves so unwilling to be reconciled that force must be called in to win back our love? Let us not deceive ourselves, sir. These are the implements of war and **subjugation**—the last arguments to which kings **resort**. I ask gentlemen, sir, what means this **martial array**, if its purpose be not to force us to submission? Can gentlemen assign any other possible motives for it? Has Great Britain any enemy, in this quarter of the world, to call for all this accumulation of navies and armies?

No, sir, she has none. They are meant for us; they can be meant for no other. They are sent over to bind and **rivet** upon us those chains which the British ministry have been so long forging. And what have we to oppose to them? Shall we try argument? Sir, we have been trying that for the last ten years. Have we anything new to offer on the subject? Nothing.

We have held the subject up in every **light** of which it is capable; but it has been all in vain. Shall we resort to entreaty and humble **supplication**? What terms shall we find which have not been already exhausted? Let us not, I **beseech** you, sir, deceive ourselves longer.

Sir, we have done everything that could be done to **avert** the storm which is now coming on. We have **petitioned**; we have **remonstrated**; we have supplicated; we have **prostrated** ourselves before the throne, and have **implored** its interposition to arrest the tyrannical hands of the ministry and Parliament.

Our petitions have been slighted; our remonstrances have produced additional violence and insult; our supplications have been disregarded; and we have been **spurned**, with contempt, from the foot of the throne. In vain, after these things, may we indulge the fond hope of peace and reconciliation. There is no longer any room for hope.

If we wish to be free—if we mean to preserve **inviolate** those inestimable privileges for which we have been so long contending—if we mean not basely to abandon the noble struggle in which we have been so long engaged, and which we have **pledged** ourselves never to abandon until the glorious object of our contest shall be obtained, we must fight! I repeat it, sir, we must fight! An **appeal** to arms and to the God of Hosts is all that is left us!

They tell us, sir, that we are weak—unable to cope with so

---

comport: behave
reconciliation: peace despite differences
subjugation: slavery
resort: use
martial array: military preparation

rivet: fix forcefully

light: aspect; perspective
supplication: pray for favor
beseech: beg
avert: avoid
petition: pray humbly for favor
remonstrate: protest against
prostrate: to lie or kneel down
implore: beg emotionally
spurn: kick

inviolate: complete and perfect
pledge: swear; take an oath
appeal: call for help

formidable: very powerful **adversary:** enemy, rival	**formidable** an **adversary**. But when shall we be stronger? Will it be the next week, or the next year? Will it be when we are totally disarmed, and when a British guard shall be stationed in every house? Shall we gather strength by irresolution and inaction? Shall we acquire the means of effectual resistance, by lying **supinely** on our backs, and hugging the **delusive phantom** of hope, until our enemies shall have bound us hand and foot?
supinely (lying) on one's back **delusive:** formless **phantom:** ghost	
	Sir, we are not weak, if we make a proper use of the means which the God of nature hath placed in our power. Three millions of people, armed in the holy cause of liberty, and in such a country as that which we possess, are **invincible** by any force which our enemy can send against us. Besides, sir, we shall not fight our battles alone. There is a just God who presides over the destinies of nations, and who will raise up friends to fight our battles for us.
invincible: not to be defeated	
vigilant: careful, watchful, alert **clanking:** loud, heavy sound made by metal objects	The battle, sir, is not to the strong alone; it is to the **vigilant**, the active, the brave. Besides, sir, we have no election. If we were base enough to desire it, it is now too late to retire from the contest. There is no retreat but in submission and slavery! Our chains are forged! Their **clanking** may be heard on the plains of Boston! The war is inevitable—and let it come! I repeat it, sir, let it come!
extenuate: lessen the seriousness **gale:** sudden and rushing wind	It is in vain, sir, to **extenuate** the matter. Gentlemen may cry, "Peace! Peace!"—but there is no peace. The war is actually begun! The next **gale** that sweeps from the north will bring to our ears the clash of resounding arms! Our brethren are already in the field! Why stand we here idle? What is it that gentlemen wish? What would they have? Is life so dear, or peace so sweet, as to be purchased at the price of chains and slavery? **Forbid** it, Almighty God! I know not what course others may take; but as for me, give me liberty, or give me death!
forbid: stop	

■ 重点述评与提示

1. This is no time for ceremony. The question before the House is one of awful moment to this country. For my own part I consider it as nothing less than a question of freedom or slavery

　　这三个简短有力的陈述句与开篇的客套拖沓形成鲜明的对照，既说明形势紧迫，不容置疑，又点破问题的实质，为以下的重叠的铺陈定下了基调。

2. Should I keep back my opinions at such a time, through fear of giving offense, I

should consider myself as guilty of treason towards my country, and of an act of disloyalty towards the majesty of heaven, which I revere above all earthly kings.

此时弗吉尼亚还有半数以上的人不赞成独立,或采取观望态度,因为他们对英王乔治三世还抱有幻想。注意 treason, disloyalty 和 earthly kings 这样的措辞。此前,亨利的反对者攻击他是叛国者。亨利在此话中有话,把矛头指向了乔治三世,这也是他下文中力劝听众丢掉幻想,拿起武器的一个主要支点。

3. Is this the part of wise men, engaged in a great and arduous struggle for liberty? Are we disposed to be of the number of those who, having eyes, see not, and having ears, hear not, the things which so nearly concern their temporal salvation?

反诘是亨利演说的惯用手法。此处他似褒实贬,双重设问,极力隐射那些反对独立的议员闭目塞听,鼠目寸光,不知大厦之将倾。temporal salvation 意为信奉上帝,以基督的精神救赎现世中上帝的子民,区别于少数上帝选民向往的 eternal salvation 和福音派带有慈善性质的 social salvation。

4. Is it that insidious smile with which our petition has been lately received? Trust it not, sir; it will prove a snare to your feet. Suffer not yourselves to be betrayed with a kiss.

设问自答以增强说服力和鼓动性。insidious smile 指英王乔治三世召见使者时常面带微笑,但却笑里藏刀,惯设骗局。这也是此处说的 betray with a kiss:基督就是被犹大的一吻而出卖的。

5. Sir, we have done everything that could be done to avert the storm which is now coming on. We have petitioned; we have remonstrated; we have supplicated; we have prostrated ourselves before the throne, and have implored its interposition to arrest the tyrannical hands of the ministry and Parliament.

当时弗吉尼亚有相当一部分人对英王仍抱有幻想,希望他出面干预,阻止英国议会对殖民地的压迫。为了打消这部分人的幻想,亨利意在表明,殖民地人民已经极尽努力,但却屡遭拒斥,已经忍无可忍。为了渲染这一点,这里连用 petition, remonstrate, supplicate, prostrate, implored 五个近义词,利用每个词的动作在程度上的差别,层层递进地表现出殖民地人民从请愿抗议到忍辱负重的过程。具体形象生动,令听众痛心而愤然。

6. There is no retreat but in submission and slavery! Our chains are forged! Their clanking may be heard on the plains of Boston! The war is inevitable—and let it come! I repeat it, sir, let it come!

连续的惊叹,句子短促而有力,观念清晰,意象生动,演说至此已经达到高潮。此时的亨利声情并茂,显示出其演员般的演讲风格。

7. Is life so dear, or peace so sweet, as to be purchased at the price of chains and slavery? Forbid it, Almighty God! I know not what course others may take; but as for me, give me liberty, or give me death!

   设问中再次点明演说的主题,把自由与奴役的二项对立推向逻辑极端,然后断然否定贪生而受辱,顺势呼出这句让人热血沸腾的口号:不自由,毋宁死!

■ 思考及讨论题

1. What could be the viewpoints of those "worthy gentlemen" as Henry calls them?
2. What is the main evidence with which Henry dispels the illusions of hope on the part of many Virginians?
3. Before Henry spoke, did it seem that he was in the majority? Why? Why not?
4. To what extend Henry is exaggerating the whole thing?
5. Why Patrick Henry was later venerated as a revolutionary hero?

■ 阅读书目

1. Mayo, Bernard. *Myths and Men: Patrick Henry, George Washington, Thomas Jefferson.* Athens: University of Georgia Press, 1959.
2. Tyler, Moses Coit, *Patrick Henry.* Boston: Houghton Mifflin, 1898.
3. Kidd, Thomas S. *Patrick Henry: First Among Patriots.* New York: Basic Books, 2011.
4. Eddlem, Thomas R. "Liberty's Son of Thunder: Patrick Henry's Words Were His Most Potent Weapons. Americans Sacrificing for Their Country Today Still Echo His Thunderous Cry, 'Give Me Liberty or Give Me Death! '" in The New American, November 3, 2003.

第三讲
塞缪尔·亚当斯(Samuel Adams 1722—1803)

■ 政治历史评述

塞缪尔·亚当斯:美国独立半途而废的革命家

　　1775年4月19日午夜,夜黑风高。马萨诸塞的剑桥,驻波士顿英军司令盖奇将军精心挑选的850名士兵整装待发,他们将在弗兰西斯·史密斯中校的率领下长途奔袭,直扑波士顿西北50英里以外的康科德和列克星顿,夺取殖民地反叛分子藏在那里的军火库。而且,据密探报告,这些大逆不道的叛逆者的首领塞缪尔·亚当斯和约翰·汉考克就躲藏在列克星顿小镇。与此同时,波士顿银匠,自由之子保罗·里维尔正快马加鞭,单骑向列克星顿飞奔。他要在英军到来之前告知同伴们在老诺斯教堂(Old North Church)挂上两个红灯预警。同时他还必须立刻赶到列克星顿,通知亚当斯等人迅速撤离。

　　一阵急促的敲门声把亚当斯从睡梦中惊醒,当他被告知英军迫近,武装冲突一触即发的消息,兴奋之情,溢于言表。这是他们为了波士顿和整个北美英属殖民地人民的自由而奋斗多年所希望看到的景象,他们知道,此时当地的民兵都已经严阵以待,准备以战斗来捍卫自己神圣的权利和自由。这将是美国独立战争的第一枪,它将推动各州殖民地议会向英国宣战,最终走向与大英帝国彻底决裂,建立独立自主的共和国。这两位"自由之子"抵抗组织的领导人匆匆离开列克星顿,听着身后渐远的小镇上传来的枪声,亚当斯禁不住内心的喜悦,转身对汉考克说:"今晨星光灿烂!"

　　这就是被誉为"美国革命之父"的塞缪尔·亚当斯。他生于波士顿这个政治气氛浓厚的城市,从小目睹父亲聚众谈论政治,成立党团俱乐部,建立土地银行,为民请命。在这样的政治氛围中长大,亚当斯对英国议会的殖民地政策疑心重重,对强化殖民地自治,保障公民的自由和自然权利情有独钟。早在1743年,21岁的亚当斯就在哈佛大学硕士考试的规定提问中明确提出:在英联邦的统治无法维持的状况下,人民根据自己的自然权利,起来反对至上的王权是完全合法的。这样的思想来自英国哲学家洛克,亚当斯当时针对美国殖民地的状况表述了这样的思想,比杰斐逊1776年的《独立宣言》整整早了33年。固然,亚当斯没有美国建国大业,制定宪法的赫赫功名,但他却是一个天才的革命运动组织者和领导者,是美国建国的先驱者。他奔走于波士顿政治团体,社会帮派之间,混迹于作坊酒馆,与劳动阶级打成一片,赢得他们的支持。亚当斯是制造革命舆论的大家。他组织"自由之子"抵抗运动,成了波士顿平民党的领袖和马萨诸塞州议会的书记议员,他不停地呐喊,在《波士顿公报》发表一系列政论,鼓吹公民自然权利和财产不受侵犯,唤起民众的民族独立意识,捍卫殖民地人民的自由和权利。他首次提出"无代表权

不纳税"的主张,并坚决否认英国议会有向殖民地征税的至上权利,坚持殖民地有权自己征税;他也是革命的行动家,不失时机地利用英国议会对北美殖民地的一次次征税危机,鼓动此起彼伏的抗议浪潮,甚至酿成过激的暴力行为。这些抗议行动迫使英国议会决定派军进驻波士顿,以镇压"不轨之徒"。此后,在"波士顿惨案"后平民党和"自由之子"抵抗组织处于十分不利的情况下,又是亚当斯借机制造和操控革命舆论,重起独立呼声,酿成"倾茶事件",逼迫英国派遣远征军"平叛",终于造成双方剑拔弩张,彻底决裂的态势。同时,亚当斯还具有革命的预见,看到美国的独立必须对各州都具有普遍意义,因此,在他极力促成下,十三州殖民地成立了通讯委员会,达成共识,为发表统一的独立宣言和战后签署《邦联条约》奠定了基础。

这是一个行动中的革命党人的形象,他对打破美国殖民者对英国的亲缘情结,促成美国独立的作用是怎么强调也不为过的。他的政治影响和声望在当时比后来的美国建国之父们都毫不逊色。1775年,追捕他的英国军官惊呼:"难以置信,从纽约到佐治亚,这么辽阔的大陆完全被一个出身平凡卑微,家境捉襟见肘的家伙运于股掌之间。"无怪乎他的敌人咒骂他是"大煽动家","现代的马基雅维里",指责他为了政治目的,不择手段,甚至置道德和名誉于不顾。无怪乎英军受命全力追捕亚当斯。欲置之死地而后快。也无怪乎美国第二届总统约翰·亚当斯有句名言这样描述他的这位表亲:"天生锻造的钢铁锲子,劈裂开北美连接在大英帝国身上的生死结。"

1774年至1781年间塞缪尔·亚当斯代表马萨诸塞州参加大陆会议。在诸多的委员会中不知疲倦地工作,是公认的"台柱"人物。亚当斯在此期间最重大的贡献就是促进大陆会议力排异议,早日通过著名的《独立宣言》。1776年,北美殖民地自抵制《印花税法》,闹独立风潮已经十年有余。但以来自宾夕法尼亚的约翰·迪金森为代表的一些与会代表对宗主国仍然抱有幻想。他们极力反对最终与英国决裂,主张和平和妥协,部分代表采取观望政策。这也难怪,殖民地与英国母国在政治和经济上矛盾可以是你死我活,但深层的历史和文化纽带和情感联系却是骨肉相连,难舍难分的。况且,双方国力和军力如此悬殊,一旦撕破脸,各殖民地的前途可是凶多吉少。正因为此,独立战争第一枪虽然一年前已经打响,此后邦克战役的规模和伤亡也令双方震惊,华盛顿也就任大陆军总司令,光复了波士顿,但美国独立却迟迟没有成为政治上的事实。亚当斯对此甚为忧虑。他向会议大声质问:"交战的双方还能互为依靠吗?美国难道还没有独立吗?为什么不宣告独立呢?"

1776年6月28日,大陆会议独立宣言起草委员会在大会上宣读《独立宣言》草稿,经

过几天的辩论,大会于 7 月 4 日以 9 票赞成的多数,正式通过了《独立宣言》。8 月 1 日,亚当斯在费城议会里发表了有关美国独立的最后的演讲。第二天,大陆会议主席约翰·汉考克在《独立宣言》正本上签署了自己的名字,其他成员依次代表自己的州庄重地写下了自己的名字,这标志着美利坚合众国的正式诞生。可以看出,在促进《独立宣言》的政治过程中,除了有托马斯·潘恩的小册子《常识》对大众政治、国家独立意识的影响外,主要也得归功于亚当斯的执著与协调精神。

亚当斯在这篇演讲中阐明大势,反复申明:各殖民地除了联合行动,宣布独立,已无路可走。英国狼已经被牢牢套住,如不一鼓作气拔掉其凶残的狼牙,日后必后患无穷。他使用"美国人"这个称谓,强调各殖民地的团结一致,指出英国的腐败与没落,指出美国的独立不仅是美国人民为了自由而斗争的结果,也是为整个人类建立自由庇护所的开始。一如亚当斯革命鼓动家的风格,整个演讲充满了夸张的言辞和比喻,在激昂的意识形态宣泄中长自己的志气,掩盖了美国大陆军军纪不整,将才不用,弹药匮乏的劣势。亚当斯在演讲中还善用痛苦的意象,渲染殖民地人民在英国军队铁蹄下的苦难,以激励"美国人民"别无选择,奋起战斗的决心。

1780 年始,亚当斯从美国政坛逐渐淡出,终究没有积极参与杰斐逊、麦迪逊等人的建国大业。这是与他地方主义的局限分不开的。他缺乏美国整体大局的关怀。对联邦政府权力的怀疑导致他专注于本州利益的得失。他不懂军事,不谙外交,不善交际,与盟友交恶,甚至缺乏发展眼光,卷入颠覆华盛顿的活动中。此外,作为清教徒的亚当斯在宗教意识和共和政治二者之间难持平衡:对简朴的生活过分的追求

使他坚持认为自由的先决条件是个人的简朴和德操。他的生活和视野与时代的发展格局格格不入,在坚信个人拥有自然法赋予的权利和自由的同时,却不知时代不仅要求实施个体的自由和民主,而且开始寻求"平等"的精神。在多数政治家开始看到共和国前景的时候,亚当斯的眼光却过多地停留在过去。可以说,克己复礼正好是他的晚年行为的最好注解。他是旧体制的破坏者,却不是新秩序的建构者。在时代进步和变革的风雨中,这位波士顿政治风云时代的革命家最后的归宿还是一位裹足不前的清教道德家。是的,塞缪尔·亚当斯是一位天生的革命家,但他没有能够挣脱怀旧的情绪和宗教传统的束缚,却不是一位与时俱进,彻底的革命家。

演讲文(节选)

Unshakable American Independence

Samuel Adams

...

Sir, we are now on this continent, to the astonishment of the world, three millions of souls united in one cause. We have large armies, well disciplined and appointed, with commanders inferior to none in military skill, and superior in activity and **zeal**. We are furnished with **arsenals** and stores beyond our most **sanguine** expectations, and foreign nations are waiting to crown our success by their alliances. There are instances of, I would say, an almost astonishing Providence in our favor; our success has **staggered** our enemies, and almost given faith to **infidels**; so we may truly say it is not our own arm which has saved us.

The hand of Heaven appears to have led us on to be, perhaps, humble instruments and means in the great providential **dispensation**, which is completing. We have fled from the political **Sodom**; let us not look back, lest we perish and become a monument of infamy and **derision** to the world. For can we ever expect more unanimity and a better preparation for defense; more **infatuation** of counsel among our enemies, and more valor and zeal among ourselves? The same force and resistance, which are sufficient to **procure** us our liberties will secure us a glorious independence and support us in the dignity of free, **imperial** states. We cannot suppose that our opposition has made a corrupt and **dissipated** nation more friendly to America, or created in them a greater respect for the rights of mankind. We can therefore expect a restoration and establishment of our privileges, and a compensation for the injuries we have received, from their **want of** power, from their fears, and not from their virtues. The unanimity and valor, which will effect an honorable peace, can **render** a future contest for our liberties unnecessary. He who has strength to chain down the wolf is a madman if he let him loose without **drawing** his teeth and **paring** his nails.

We have no other **alternative** than independence, or the most **ignominious** and **galling servitude**. The legions of our enemies thicken on our plains; **desolation** and death mark their bloody career; whilst the **mangled** corpses of our countrymen seem to cry out to us as a voice from Heaven.

Our union is now complete; our constitution composed,

---

zeal: passion
arsenal: factory of arms
sanguine: hopeful; confident

stagger: surprise
infidel: nonbeliever

dispensation: handling of things
Sodom: (biblical) city of evil
derision: scorn, mockery
infatuation: intensive love
procure: secure
imperial: noble and dignified

dissipated: separated

want of: lack of

render: make
draw: pull out
pare: cut smooth
alternative: choice
ignominious: shameful
galling: bitter
servitude: slavery
desolation: total destruction
mangled: ruined and bloody

established, and approved. You are now the guardians of your own liberties. We may justly address you, as the **decemviri** did the Romans, and say: "Nothing that we propose can pass into a law without your consent. Be yourselves, O Americans, the authors of those laws on which your happiness depends."

You have now in the field armies sufficient to repel the whole force of your enemies and their base and **mercenary auxiliaries**. The hearts of your soldiers beat high with the spirit of freedom; they are animated with the justice of their cause, and while they grasp their swords can look up to Heaven for assistance. Your adversaries are composed of **wretches** who laugh at the rights of humanity, who turn religion into derision, and would, for higher wages, direct their swords against their leaders or their country. Go on, then, in your generous **enterprise**, with gratitude to Heaven for past, success, and confidence of it in the future. For my own part, I ask no greater blessing than to share with you the common danger and common glory. If I have a wish dearer to my soul than that my ashes may be mingled with those of a **Warren** and a **Montgomery**, it is that these American States may never cease to be free and independent.

> **decemviri**: executive official of ancient Romans
>
> **mercenary**: army paid to fight
> **auxiliary**: subordinate force
>
> **wretch**: villain; rogue; evil man
> **enterprise**: mission; venture; undertaking
> **J. Warren, R. Montgomery**: American generals killed in 1775, in the battlefields

■ 重点述评与提示

1. Sir, we are now on this continent, to the astonishment of the world, three millions of souls united in one cause. We have large armies, well disciplined and appointed, with commanders inferior to none in military skill, and superior in activity and zeal.

   开篇即现革命鼓动家的风格,慷慨激昂的语气掩盖的正好是相反的事实。当时实际的情形是,各殖民地二百万余万人口中,赞成独立的死党只占 25% 左右,其他多为观望者和保皇派。新近由十三州地方民兵拼凑起来的大陆军 2 万人,军纪松散,军官大多为当地有名望的狂热革命者充任,除了为美国独立献身的牺牲精神外,军事素质普遍低下,军中武器低劣短缺,补给困难,前景十分堪忧。

2. We have fled from the political Sodom; let us not look back, lest we perish and become a monument of infamy and derision to the world. Sodom,

   圣经里描写的罪恶之城,被上帝用烈火毁灭。清教徒亚当斯此处用这一典故,既述说了英国社会罪孽深重,又表明了清教徒逃离英国的幸运,同时还暗示抛弃旧世界,在新大陆建立上帝之城的前景。

3. He who has strength to chain down the wolf is a madman if he let him loose without drawing his teeth and paring his nails.

    这里把英国议会比作恶狼,虽已被套住,但如不拔除其爪牙而放生,则后患无穷,比喻意象栩栩如生,为的是打消有些人最后的幻想,立刻宣布彻底脱离英国。

4. We have no other alternative than independence, or the most ignominious and galling servitude. The legions of our enemies thicken on our plains; desolation and death mark their bloody career; whilst the mangled corpses of our countrymen seem to cry out to us as a voice from Heaven.

    这是宣传鼓动家在演说中惯用的夸张和具象手法。Ignominious 意指心灵的屈辱和痛苦,galling 尤指肉体的痛苦,加上英军嗜血成性,同胞血肉模糊的尸体的悲鸣,如此种种,都可刺激感官,削弱理智。实际上,此时邦克山战役已经结束,英军伤亡 1 千余人,美军伤亡 400 余人。

5. Our union is now complete; our constitution composed, established, and approved. ... You have now in the field armies sufficient to repel the whole force of your enemies and their base and mercenary auxiliaries.

    亚当斯在此又做夸张鼓动。1772 年他倡导成立了 13 州通讯委员会,1774 和 1775 年,第一届和第二届大陆会议在费城分别召开。但 13 州殖民地基本还是各行其是,真正的政治联盟,要等到 1881 年 13 州正式批准《邦联条约》,才算基本完成。而这份可称为美国第一部宪法的文件此时尚未起草。mercenary autxiliaries 指英军中的德国雇佣军。

6. If I have a wish dearer to my soul than that my ashes may be mingled with those of a Warren and a Montgomery, it is that these American States may never cease to be free and independent.

    所谓生命诚可贵,愿为自由和独立而抛。亚当斯在此用了 American States 的说法,这是此前未有过的,可见萌发了统一的国家意识。Joseph Warren,大陆军上校,身先士卒,率队冲锋,战死在不久前的邦克山战役中;Richard Montgomery 大陆军准将,率军挺进加拿大,新近战死在魁北克战役。

■ 思考及讨论题

1. To what extent do we take Samuel Adams as a revolutionary and a forgotten finding father of the United States of America?
2. What is the main argument of this high-pitched speech?

3. What is the main rhetoric scheme used by Samuel Adams in this speech?
4. Why Boston became largely the centre of anti-British demonstrations and the first battlefield of the War for Independence?

■ 阅读书目

1. Irvin, Benjamin H. Samuel Adams: *Son of Liberty, Father of Revolution*. New York: Oxford University Press, 2002.
2. Hosmer, James K. *Samuel Adams*. Boston: Houghton Mifflin, 1888.
3. Countryman, Edward. "The Creation of America: Through Revolution to Empire" in *The Virginia Magazine of History and Biography*, April 1, 2001.
4. Eddlem, Thomas R. "Father of the American Revolution: Pious, Principled, and Passionate for Liberty, Samuel Adams Championed the Cause of Independence with His Unique Ability to Communicate, Motivate, and Organize" in *The New American*, July 29, 2002.

第四讲
托马斯·杰斐逊（Thomas Jefferson 1743—1826）

■ 历史评述

美国《独立宣言》[①]：革命的理论和时代的心声

"我们认为下述真理是不言而喻的：人人生而平等，造物主赋予每个人一些不可剥夺的权利，其中包括生存权、自由权和追求幸福的权利。"

著名美国民主共和思想家托马斯·杰斐逊在《独立宣言》中写下的这一句名言，经过了几个世纪的非语境化话语反复和建构，今天似乎已经成为社会弱势群体、边缘化人群或"受压迫者"争取自由与权利的标牌语。如果我们将之重新置于历史语境，剖析其政治思想和哲学渊源，这应该是解读《独立宣言》这篇影响深远的政治历史文献的最佳起点。

要说美国《独立宣言》就必须先说英国哲学家和政论家约翰·洛克，因为他是公认的美国《独立宣言》的思想先驱。这位1632年出生的牛津才子对哲学，教育，医学，自然科学都有浓厚的研究兴趣并取得成果，34岁就入选英国皇家协会。他1690年发表的《人类理智论》否定人类生而知之，认为人类的知识都是后天通过经验的积累和认识取得的。这一思想开英国经验主义的先河。同年发表的《政府论》（上下篇）矛头直指根深蒂固的"君权神授"论，为1688英国光荣革命建立以议会为主导的君主立宪制政府张目，系统地论述了社会契约论的思想。特别是在《政府论》（下篇）中，洛克一反英国哲学家托马斯·霍布斯有关人性恶的观点，认为自然状态下的人类具有平和善良的天性和乐观向上的理性，他们生来就拥有自然法所赋予的生存权和追求自由和私人财产的权利。为了组成有效的社会以保护这些权利，人民把一部分权利让与政府。政府必须取得人民的认同和批准才能合法地行使权力。如果政府被少数既得利益者控制，实行专制暴政或不能有效地履行保护人民的职责，那么人民有权推翻现存的国家机器，组建新的政府。也就是说，在当时的语境中，洛克认为王权并非神圣不可动摇，人民为了捍卫自己的权利，起来反抗甚而颠覆王权统治，是完全合法的。这就是美国《独立宣言》的思想来源。

其实，洛克在美国名声鹊起，那还是1765年英国向其美洲殖民地征收印花税以后的事，而且这是洛克的反对派一手促成的。洛克一向不重名分，为人低调。一直默默无闻。

[①] 杰斐逊等人起草的《美国独立宣言》，并未在大陆会议上进行演讲，因而不是严格意义上的演讲文。但与其在美国政治历史上的重要性，权且作为演讲文列此。杰斐逊生平在第十二讲中有介绍，此处从略。

在英国本土,有关社会契约论的思想在洛克之前已有不少表述。比起他的政治思想,他的哲学认识论思想受到更多的关注,甚至他的教育思想都受到更多的尊重。

当然,在意识形态领域,洛克的《政府论》直接号召人民革命,显得更激进,更具颠覆性,因而显得更危险。洛克在《政府论》(下)第二章里这样说道:"同物种之生物,以及其他杂质物种,既生而共享大自然中相同之有利条件,且同样具有运用其心智之能力,则应相互平等,彼此不分主从尊卑……,这是再明白不过的道理。"这是自然法则(natural law)规定的真理,也是美国《独立宣言》直接承继的"不言而喻"(self-evident)的真理。这一"人人生而平等"的思想直接否定了人类社会等级与生俱来的观念,提供了追求个人自然权利和私有财产的前提,直接威胁到英国乃至欧洲君主封建社会赖以生存的精神基石,因此一定受到维护现行制度统治阶层的压制。英国托利党指谪洛克是叛逆者的后台,无政府主义的煽动家,狂热的共和分子(commonwealth-man),妄图颠覆基督教的无神论者,甚至把洛克与领导清教革命,推翻查理一世的奥利弗·克伦威尔相提并论。1710年一份托利党报纸刊载一幅漫画,攻击辉格党政论家本杰明·豪德利。画中豪德利端坐写字台后,身后的书架上,洛克的《政府论》赫然在目。豪德利的肩上站立着手握弑君之斧的克伦威尔。然而,保皇党对洛克的愤怒攻击正好帮了倒忙。洛克作为政治理论家在英国的名声大震。同时,托利党有时对洛克主要论点进行生搬硬套的指责,反

倒使大众对这些论点耳熟能详。比如,托利党女权主义者玛丽·阿斯泰尔曾攻击洛克罢黜了君主暴政,却完整地保留了夫权暴政:"如果人人生而平等,为什么所有女人却生而为奴?"于是,"人人生而平等"之声广为社会传播。

18世纪中叶,美国革命已现端倪,洛克的政治思想自然成了托马斯·杰斐逊,约翰·亚当斯,詹姆斯·麦迪逊等美国政治领袖反抗暴政,追求独立的思想武器。他们把洛克视为"革命原则"的源泉,为反抗英国议会乃至国王的暴政提供合法化理论基础。洛克被尊为自由主义的奠基者,自由观念的哲学家。自然法则面前"人人生而平等"的观念,人民主权的意识,社会契约论的理想,政府分权的思想,个人财产不可剥夺的原则,宗教自由的主张等等都被广为接受并传播开来,形成时代的主流社会意识。这种社会政治意识形态的传播经过了爱国主义的强化和在新英格兰已经开始的武装冲突的催化,最终在托马斯·杰斐逊起草的美国《独立宣言》中以文字的形式凝聚成北美十三州殖民地共同的政治纲领。可以说,《独立宣言》是当时社会意识的理性表达。正如弗吉尼亚大学历史学家梅里厄·彼得森在其巨著《托马斯·杰斐逊和一个崭新的国家》中所说:"《独立宣言》表达的思想属于每一个人,但又不属于某一个具体的人。在1776年,这些思想是当时公众舆论的组成部分,就像整个社会通行的硬通货,在美国爱国者之间广泛流

通。"杰斐逊本人虽然极力为《独立宣言》思想的原创性辩护,公开申明他"没有照搬此前任何人的具体著述。但他也必须承认他起草《独立宣言》的目的是"用适当的语气和时代召唤的精神表达出美利坚人的心声。"

《独立宣言》以18世纪典型的逻辑三段式文章格局构成,文字表达简洁清晰,高贵中透出理性的雅正,克制中流露出情绪的愤然,通篇既统筹于杰斐逊学者型思辨的理性,又回响着托马斯·潘恩《常识》通俗的激越。

第一部分为前言,表述宣告独立的政治思想基础,其中到处都可以看到洛克《政府论》的思想印迹。杰斐逊在这一部分中用"追求幸福"取代了洛克关于人的自然权利,包括拥有"健康"和"财产"的权利,显示了在殖民地生存环境中强调个人主观能动的个性。因为杰斐逊认为,财产权也是基于自然法的,而不是神权的赋予。特别是殖民者基于自己的劳动,在本来是空闲的土地上开拓出自己的种植园,英国国王没有为追求这些财产付出劳动,因而无权处置这些劳动成果。财产只有在人的主动追求中才成其为人的权利。这显然是在高度的归纳中对洛克的思想做出了美国式的注解。杰斐逊的草稿呈送大陆会议辩论后对此部分没有做大的修改,可见与会代表思想的一致性。

第二部分以简短的前提表述为引导,说明任何政府的存在应该具有一定稳定性,人民只有在向政府反复申述无效的情况下才有可能起来造反。这既说明殖民地人民已经到了忍无可忍的地步,为下文述说殖民地宣布脱离大英帝国的种种原因提供逻辑前提,又对欧洲各国政府做出一种温和姿态:当时法国中产阶级已经蠢蠢欲动,大革命已在酝酿之中。美国革命大有可能成为法国革命推翻路易十六君主统治可资借鉴的先例。在此部分中,杰斐逊把矛头直指英王乔治三世,列举英王专制立法,违宪司法,压制海外贸易,强行征税和驻军等28条罪状。在当时国内舆论鼎沸,北方战端已开的紧迫形势下,大陆会议对此部分的内容更为关注。因为长期以来,十三州殖民地,特别是中部各州的

大多数与会代表把宣布独立看成是大逆不道的举动,不到万不得已不可铤而走险。由于保守派、激进派和动摇派争论不休,第二次大陆会议在是否直接指控乔治三世这一点上也具有妥协性。甚至在1776年邦克战役后,杰斐逊还在大陆会议的授意下与保守派迪金森共同起草的了一份号召殖民地武装起来的宣言,同时向英王示好,呼吁和平解决争端。而《独立宣言》把最后一层纸捅破,其内容轻重和措辞语

气,在当时的形势下是极为敏感,必须慎之又慎的事。大陆会议的集体讨论对这一部分做了不少的修改,删去了一些针对英国国王本人的过激之辞,突出了王权对地方议会立法横加干涉这一主题。在南卡罗来纳州和佐治亚州的动议下,大会全部删除了杰斐逊

原稿中指控乔治三世鼓励奴隶贩运,"残酷践踏人性的战争"的段落,此举既是为缓和口气,也是为保护南北殖民地在奴隶贸易中的既得利益。同时,这也为近一个世纪后美国南北冲突的大悲剧埋下了种子。值得一提的是,杰斐逊在《独立宣言》草稿中抨击奴隶制并对大陆会议删除此节一直耿耿于怀,但本人却拥有数百的奴隶,至死都在从事奴隶买卖而维持家业。此知行分离,难免一直被后世诟病。

《独立宣言》的第三部分是结论。大会经过讨论,大幅度精简了杰斐逊草稿中的文辞,以昭示天下的文告语体,宣告以人民的名义行使美利坚合众国国会的职责,正式彻底脱离大英帝国,独立行使国家权力。这标志着一个崭新的国家的诞生。

■ 《独立宣言》(节选)

Declaration of Independence

Thomas Jefferson

When in the Course of human events, it becomes necessary for one people to dissolve the political **bands** which have connected them with another, and to **assume** among the powers of the earth, the separate and equal station to which the Laws of Nature and of Nature's God entitle them, a **decent** respect to the opinions of mankind requires that they should declare the causes which **impel** them to the separation.—We hold these truths to be self-evident, that all men are created equal, that they are **endowed** by their Creator with certain **unalienable** Rights, that among these are Life, Liberty and the pursuit of Happiness.—That to secure these rights, Governments are **instituted** among Men, deriving their just powers from the **consent** of the governed,—That whenever any Form of Government becomes destructive of these ends, it is the Right of the People to alter or to abolish it, and to institute new Government, laying its foundation on such principles and organizing its powers in such form, as to them shall seem most likely to **affect** their Safety and Happiness.

Prudence, indeed, will **dictate** that Governments long established should not be changed for light and **transient** causes; and accordingly all experience hath shown, that mankind are more disposed to suffer, while evils are sufferable, than to right themselves by abolishing the forms to which they are accustomed. But when a long train of abuses

band: association tie; affiliation
assume: take the responsibility of
decent: suitable, dignified
impel: force; press
endow: grant allow
unalienable: not to be taken away; permanently attached
instituted: established
consent: agreement

effect: bring good result to
prudent: rational and cautious judgment
dictate: demand; require
transient: momentary, insignificant

usurpation: violation; taking sth. unlawfully
evince: show
despotism: dictatorship
constrain: enforce; compel

candid: openly justified
representative: people elected to speak for the populace
rectitude: virtue; uprightness
solemnly: seriously; honestly
allegiance: loyalty

levy: officially declare and enforce
divine: holy
pledge: promise by swearing
sacred: holy; blessed

and **usurpations**, pursuing invariably the same Object **evinces** a design to reduce them under absolute **Despotism**, it is their right, it is their duty, to throw off such Government, and to provide new Guards for their future security.—Such has been the patient sufferance of these Colonies; and such is now the necessity which **constrains** them to alter their former Systems of Government. The history of the present King of Great Britain is a history of repeated injuries and usurpations, all having in direct object the establishment of an absolute Tyranny over these States. To prove this, let Facts be submitted to a **candid** world...

We, therefore, the **Representatives** of the United States of America, in General Congress, Assembled, appealing to the Supreme Judge of the world for the **rectitude** of our intentions, do, in the Name, and by Authority of the good People of these Colonies, **solemnly** publish and declare, That these United Colonies are, and of Right ought to be Free and Independent States; that they are Absolved from all **Allegiance** to the British Crown, and that all political connection between them and the State of Great Britain, is and ought to be totally dissolved; and that as Free and Independent States, they have full Power to **levy** War, conclude Peace, contract Alliances, establish Commerce, and to do all other Acts and Things which Independent States may of right do.—And for the support of this Declaration, with a firm reliance on the protection of **Divine** Providence, we mutually **pledge** to each other our Lives, our Fortunes and our **sacred** Honor.

■ 重点述评与提示

1. We hold these truths to be self-evident, that all men are created equal, that they are endowed by their Creator with certain unalienable Rights, that among these are Life, Liberty and the pursuit of Happiness.

   自然法则之内人生而平等，人人具有平等的权利，这是洛克政治思想的起点。他用了较长的篇幅阐明这一点，其中把生存、自由和住宅统统归纳为财产权。这里，杰斐逊在紧贴洛克思想的同时作了美国式的注解，加入了"追求幸福"的权利，排除了英国对殖民地的财产权。在起草过程中，本杰明·富兰克林斟酌再三，采用"self-evident"（不言而喻，自明）一词，精当地概括了自然法则毋须人为规约的真理性，这是点睛之笔。

2. That to secure these rights, Governments are instituted among Men, deriving their just powers from the consent of the governed,—That whenever any Form of Government becomes destructive of these ends, it is the Right of the People to alter or to abolish it, and to institute new Government...

   政府的合法性来自人民的允准,这既是社会契约的核心,也是共和政府的基石。殖民地人民漂洋过海来到新大陆,既对暴政记忆犹新,对新的政府的建立也是满腹狐疑,唯恐政府形成新的权力中心,滋长腐败,催生新的暴政。《独立宣言》规定人民有权利推翻违背人民意愿的政府,建立新的政体,既是洛克思想的表达,也可赢得广大的民心。

3. Prudence, indeed, will dictate that Governments long established should not be changed for light and transient causes; and accordingly all experience hath shown, that mankind are more disposed to suffer, while evils are sufferable, than to right themselves by abolishing the forms to which they are accustomed.

   prudence 这个词在杰斐逊时代更多地指杰出人物的一种智慧和秉性,有点"现实策略"的意思。《独立宣言》宣布人民有权推翻不良政府,本是独立革命的需要。但对此权利不做现实的策略考虑,则"民主"泛滥,暴民产生。当时法国中产阶级势力渐盛,革命呼声愈高,政府人心惶惶。美国独立既指望法国相助,说话自然不能太绝,否则有号召法国革命推翻政府之嫌。这是外交的姿态和策略。同时,这也是现实的文本策略,为下文说明殖民地人民忍无可忍,不得已而推翻英国统治进行了铺垫。如此,把矛头直指英王乔治三世,历数其暴行,也就自然而然,易于为大多数殖民地人民接受了。

4. The history of the present King of Great Britain is a history of repeated injuries and usurpations, all having in direct object the establishment of an absolute Tyranny over these States.

   如此在正式文件中公然把矛头直指大英帝国国王,前所未有,是叛国罪。据说乔治三世竟然不戴眼镜就看清楚了头号叛国者,大陆会议主席汉考克在《独立宣言》文本上签下的大名,大怒之中把全部签署者列入应该绞死的叛国者名单。大多数签署人也因此抱有不成功便成仁的心理准备,无怪乎富兰克林在《独立宣言》上签下大名之后说道:"We must all hang together, or assuredly we shall all hang separately."(我等必须团结一致,否则必将被分别吊死。)

5. And for the support of this Declaration, with a firm reliance on the protection of Divine Providence, we mutually pledge to each other our Lives, our Fortunes and our sacred Honor.

   此刻,《独立宣言》一旦签署,将标志着北美英属殖民地正式与大英帝国彻底决裂。会议代表们都知道这意味着什么。前途未卜,生死攸关。这是严酷的现实,不再有激昂的口号,不再有英雄的气概,只有默默的祈祷,愿上帝护佑每个参与者的生命、财产和荣誉。

■ 思考及讨论题

1. To what extent can we say that American independence is a revolution?
2. What are some major causes of American Revolution?
3. What is the Law of Nature? Why it is essential to justify the American colonists separation from the Great Britain?
4. According to the Declaration of Independence, where does a government take its power and why such a government is necessary?
5. In what way do we perceive a historical dimension in this important document?

■ 阅读书目

1. Eicholz, Hans L. *Harmonizing Sentiments: The Declaration of Independence and the Jeffersonian Idea of Self Government*. New York: Peter Lang, 2001.
2. Dumbauld, Edward. *The Declaration of Independence and What It Means Today*. Norman: University of Oklahoma Press, 1950.
3. Locke, John. *Second Treaties of Government*. Cambridge University Press, 1988.
4. Stuart, Leibiger. "Jefferson's Declaration of Independence: Origins, Philosophy and Theology" in *The Virginia Magazine of History and Biography*, 1998.

第二章 ‖ 建国大业中的制宪分歧

Thus I consent, Sir, to this Constitution because I expect no better, and because I am not sure, that it is not the best.
——Benjamin Franklin

It is undeniable that there must be a control somewhere. Either the general interest is to control the particular interests, or the contrary.
——Alexander Hamilton

If a wrong step be now made, the republic may be lost forever.
——Patrick Henry

Ambition must be made to counteract ambition... If men were angels, no government would be necessary.
——James Madison

Preview Questions

01/

What was the economic and political situation when the War for Independence was ended?

02/

What are the primary weaknesses of the *Articles of Confederation*?

03/

What are the main propositions of Federalists, and that of the Antifederalists?

04/

According to the American Constitution, how is the federal government structured? For what purposes?

第五讲
本杰明·富兰克林(Benjamin Franklin 1706—1790)

■ 政治历史评述

本杰明·富兰克林:实用理性和中庸精神的智者

  1785年9月14日早晨,潮汐初起,微风拂煦。本杰明·富兰克林搭乘的客轮于7月28日离开法国后经过49天横跨大西洋的航行,终于到达了目的地费城。富兰克林曾经先后8次横渡大西洋,这是他最后一次跨洋航行,再次回到阔别的故土。已近80岁高龄的富兰克林站在甲板上,注视着愈近眼底的费城,心中百感交集,颇有英国诗人史蒂文森的名诗句"水手飘海兮,魂归故里"(Home is the sailor, home from the sea!)的感叹。此时,美国独立战争结束不到两年,百废待兴,美国国父们正致力于建设"一个更完善的联邦",富兰克林的到来,也使这项建国大业增添了智慧和经验的象征。海港码头,前来欢迎富兰克林的人群簇拥着他们心目中的圣贤,欢呼声此起彼伏,一直把他送到家门。不久,已经79岁的富兰克林被选为宾夕法尼亚州行政会议主席,代表本州参加在费城举行的制宪会议。

  这就是富兰克林在新生的美利坚人民心中的形象:一个为公共事务不知疲倦,思想永不枯竭的美国智者和实干家。他被称为"第一个美国人","扬基人的鼻祖","多重性的美国人"。他对新教伦理的体认和发扬培养了美国早期中产阶级的市场意识和开拓精神,他对社会公共事业的关心和贡献促进了美国城镇文化的建设,他的科学研究精神和技术发明也令欧洲人对美国刮目相看。在他的身上,体现着美国文化多样性和实用主义精神的基本价值观:务实精明、勤奋刻苦、克己节俭、独立自信。富兰克林白手起家,自学成才,无师自通的成功故事昭示的是美国之梦的雏形和一个机会均等的社会。经过200多年社会和历史意识的不断塑造,富兰克林就这样成了大众心目中几近圣人的精神文化偶像。这种造神意识可以说在富兰克林生前就有了政治性的导向。华盛顿当年在致富兰克林的信中就赞扬他具有超乎生命的"哲学心灵","仁爱之德使人敬仰;睿智之才让人称羡;爱国之情令人尊敬;慈善之心受人爱戴"。虽然,美国第二届总统约翰·亚当斯对此溢美之辞不以为然,认为富兰克林的名声是美国革命非常时期的夸张结果,但是,在美国一直需要精神偶像的过去,政治意识形态的评判却不能阻止公共话语的精神建构及其在历史上持续的影响。今天,美元百元大钞上的富兰克林神态安详,慈祥和蔼的目光中闪烁着智慧和乐观,这本身就是很好的现代象征:物质的成功、人性善和启蒙理性的结合。在一副新英格兰清教徒和教友派的面孔下展示的是美国实用主义的起源和原始范例。

对于新生的美利坚合众国,富兰克林始终是爱国者。与当时其他美国政治家相比,他的爱国情怀有更为宽广的内涵。他的政治根基是北美殖民地,但是他关心的则是大西洋两岸的英国人乃至全人类的命运。他曾经是大英帝国利益的拥戴者,幻想在大英帝国一统的政治格局中最大限度地实行民主政治,保障个人的自然权利,促进社会文明的进步和物质的繁荣。1757年始,他作为北美殖民地的使者和事实上的外交代表常驻英国,倡导理性,和平地解决双边的争端。富兰克林在目睹了英国议会对其北美殖民地的强制税收和高压政策后,重新成为一个坚定的为殖民地利益呐喊的共和主义者。这也因为他虽然侵染在英

国贵族议会政治的漩涡之中,但骨子里仍然回旋着平民主义和道德主义的理想,在英国贵族议会的弊端体制中却感到了内心深处的共和主义的呼唤。于是在1775年美国独立战争前夕,他谢绝豪尔勋爵的高官许愿,毅然卷起铺盖,重回故土的怀抱并积极投身于其争取自由和独立的斗争中。

在第二届大陆会议中,富兰克林等人协助杰斐逊起草《独立宣言》,并在他70岁这一年(1776年)签署了这份文件。尽管如此,在启蒙思想和人性善信念的促动下,他始终认为人类的知识,智慧和经验,可以最终解决政治和经济利益争端。1783年下半年,独立战争即将以美军的胜利而宣告结束。富兰克林对9月3日巴黎和约的签署充满期望,但对战争造成的创伤不无遗憾。7月27日,他在致英国皇家协会主席约瑟夫·邦克斯的信中这样写道:"我希望和平能持久不衰。人类既然自称是有理性的动物,就应该具有足够的理性和智慧最终解决他们的争端,而毋须彼此割断对方的喉咙;因为在我看来,天下没有什么好的战争或坏的和平!"可见,富兰克林的思想中有种超越政治的人文关怀,一种道德与自由同一的观念。在他的视野中,总是有人类整体命运的走向,他的爱国的意识也似乎带有一定某种政治强迫性。由此观之,富兰克林晚年成为一名彻底的废奴主义者并最终解放了他自己仅有的两名奴隶,这并非是偶然的。

富兰克林在政治上具有中庸精神,在政治甚至军事冲突面前一直力图保持中立,两面斡旋。希望冲突双方做出妥协和让步。这种精神在1787年美国制宪会议上也表现得十分突出。富兰克林参加制宪会议时已经81岁高龄,他的参与实际上是一个新生的共和国具有世界眼光的象征。与会的代表们虽然有备受海内外尊重的乔治·华盛顿,也有托马斯·杰斐逊,詹姆斯·麦迪逊这样的饱学之士,但对于建立新的国家体制,代表们都缺乏先例和经验,在政治上和国际外交事务中也多有惶恐,显得底气不足。富兰克林的参与给制宪会议增加了政治砝码和文化厚重感。他受到与会代表普遍的尊敬,尽

管他的诸多提议都在普遍的赞扬声中被束之高阁。其实,富兰克林在制宪会议的作用更多的还是化解分歧,达到妥协。在为期近 4 个月的制宪会议中,仅仅就在国会的议员名额分配问题,即大州和小州的平等代表权问题就用了近 2 个月的时间才达到基本的妥协,可见当时利益关系和意见纷争到了何等程度。每每如是,富兰克林总是从中斡旋,两面调停,以长者之谆谆,语重心长的说明求同存异的道理。富兰克林经常以他喜爱的寓言方式,劝喻代表们悬置分歧,朝着共同的既定目标携手共进。他告诉弗吉尼亚的代表,制宪会议就像一条饥渴难耐的双头蛇,正朝着大河爬行。但如果一个蛇头坚持往东,另一个蛇头执意往西,那么它们永远不能达到河边,它们共同的躯体只会枯死半途。正是富兰克林这样的中庸意识和妥协的精神,还有他本人的影响力,在很大程度上促进了制宪会议的日程,使之最终在 9 月 17 日产生并通过了这部约 4000 字组成的纲领性的美国宪法。

富兰克林的妥协和顾全大局的精神虽然为美国宪法的诞生起到重要的催生作用,但是他本人对依据此宪法建立权力相对集中的联邦政府却还是疑虑重重。在制宪会议代表们签字通过宪法之前,富兰克林要求向大会做简短演讲。在这篇演说中,富兰克林表达了自己对宪法的双重态度,也表述了自己一贯的思想:其一,人类的知识积累和思想的形成是一个不断完善的过程,犹如启蒙思想家所相信的那样,是一个不断试验,不断进步,不断走向完美的过程;其二,人类在道德和自由的指引下,可以通过思想的碰撞和协商,也就是通过不断的思想实验,找的一种适合社会发展的政治体制和政府形式;其三,现实社会是不可能完美的,也不可能通过等待而获得完美,等待只会丧失一次次的机会,只有决而起行,把思想付诸实践行动,才能使自由和道德中的个体的人组织起来并适应社会,共同创造未来。

富兰克林这篇演说中无不展现他的文化智者的形象和历史的厚重感,其中也不乏对人性深入的剖析和对具体事例的说明。这种娓娓道来却又不乏思智的修辞风格不是富兰克林刻意的自我塑造,而是他一贯崇尚启蒙理性,提倡实践检验真理的科学的思想方法,是一种化入他本人个体思维范式的风格。比起汉弥尔顿和麦迪逊等人的《联邦党人》,比起那种号召美国人民接受新生的联邦宪法的滔滔辩词,富兰克林这种既老成持重,又不乏诙谐的文风要有力得多。不难想象,富兰克林在美国人心目中先贤智者的形象本身就有巨大的说服力,对此后各州为批准宪法的辩论起到了难以估量的积极作用。

■ 演讲文

American Constitution: Imperfect but Necessary

Benjamin Franklin

Mr. President,

I confess that there are several parts of this constitution which I do not at present approve, but I am not sure I shall never approve them: For having lived long, I have experienced many instances of being **obliged** by better information, or fuller consideration, to change opinions even on important subjects, which I once thought right, but found to be otherwise. It is therefore that the older I grow, the more **apt** I am to doubt my own judgment, and to pay more respect to the judgment of others. Most men indeed as well as most **sects** in Religion, think themselves in possession of all truth, and that wherever others differ from them it is so far error. Steele a Protestant in a **Dedication** tells the Pope, that the only difference between our Churches in their opinions of the certainty of their **doctrines** is, the Church of Rome is **infallible** and the Church of England is never in the wrong. But though many private persons think almost as highly of their own infallibility as of that of their sect, few express it so naturally as a certain French lady, who in a dispute with her sister, said "I don't know how it happens, Sister, but I meet with no body but myself, that's always **in the right**—*Il n'y a que moi qui a toujours raison*."

In these **sentiments**, Sir, I agree to this Constitution with all its faults, if they are such; because I think a general Government necessary for us, and there is no form of Government but what may be a blessing to the people if well administered, and believe farther that this is likely to be well administered for a course of years, and can only end in **Despotism**, as other forms have done before it, when the people shall become so corrupted as to need despotic Government, being incapable of any other. I doubt too whether any other **Convention** we can obtain, may be able to make a better Constitution. For when you **assemble** a number of men to have the advantage of their joint wisdom, you inevitably assemble with those men, all their **prejudices**, their passions, their errors of opinion, their local interests, and their selfish views. From such an assembly can a perfect production be expected? It therefore **astonishes** me, Sir, to find this system approaching so near to perfection as it does; and I think it will astonish our enemies, who are waiting with confidence to hear that our **councils** are **confounded** like those of the **Builders** of **Babel**; and that our States are on the point of separation, only to meet hereafter for the purpose of cutting one another's throats. Thus I consent, Sir, to this Constitution because I expect no better, and because I am not sure, that it is not the best. The opinions I have had of its errors, I sacrifice to the public good. I have never whispered a syllable of them abroad. Within these walls they were born, and here they shall die. If every one of us in returning to our **Constituents** were to report the objections he has had to it, and endeavor to gain **partisans** in support of them, we might prevent its being generally received, and thereby lose all the **salutary** effects and great advantages resulting naturally in our favor among foreign Nations as well as among ourselves, from our real or apparent **unanimity**. Much of the strength and efficiency of any Government in procuring and securing happiness to the people, depends, on opinion, on the general opinion of the goodness of the Government, as well as of the wisdom and **integrity** of its Governors. I hope therefore that for our own sakes as a part of the people, and for the sake of **posterity**, we shall act heartily and unanimously in recommending this Constitution (if approved by Congress and confirmed by the Conventions) wherever our influence may extend, and turn our future thoughts and endeavors to the **means** of having it well administered.

On the whole, Sir, I can not help expressing a wish that every member of the Convention who may still have objections to it, would with me, on this occasion doubt a little of his own infallibility, and to **make manifest** our unanimity, put his name to this instrument.

council: political meeting
confound: chaotic, end roughly as failure
Babel: (from Bible) the Tower of Babel, built by humans with the intention to make it reach the heaven
constituent: voters in the community
partisan: members with same political views
salutary: favorable
unanimity: unity; oneness; total agreement
integrity: honesty; uprightness; virtue
posterity: later generations
means: ways; methods
make manifest: make it clear; make it appear clearly

■ 重点述评与提示

1. Most men indeed as well as most sects in Religion, think themselves in possession of all truth, and that wherever others differ from them it is so far error.

   指出人性盲目自大的弱点,同时批评宗教派别排除异己,唯我独尊,以此劝喻各位与会代表以发展的眼光和妥协的精神对待新生的宪法。这是富兰克林的基本态度,其底蕴是启蒙主义的基本前提:即人类能够通过理性克服自身弱点,不断进步,趋向完美。

2. But though many private persons think almost as highly of their own infallibility as of that of their sect, few express it so naturally as a certainFrench lady, who in a dispute with her sister, said "I don't know how it happens, Sister, but I meet with nobody

but myself, that's always in the right—Il n'y a que moi qui a toujours raison."

  富兰克林行文的特点和幽默,严肃的话题中来点插科打诨市的风俗场景。这里,法国贵妇目光短浅,自以为是的特点跃然纸上。富兰克林曾常驻法国多年,宫廷上下,情场内外出尽风头,在此来点小幽默,既可讽刺人性弱点,也可展示其经验阅历。文如其人。

3. I think a general Government necessary for us, and there is no form of Government but what may be a blessing to the people if well administered, and believe farther that this is likely to be well administered for a course of years, and can only end in Despotism...

  富兰克林在此认为,通过制宪成立中央政府只是权宜之计,政府良好的运作可以为民谋利,但从长远的观点看问题,权力的集中必然导致腐败,导致专制。显然,富兰克林的启蒙主义建立在人性善和抽象民主的基础上,在这一点上他缺乏麦迪逊的政治远见。

4. Thus I consent, Sir, to this Constitution because I expect no better, and because I am not sure, that it is not the best. The opinions I have had of its errors, I sacrifice to the public good.

  这里集中体现了富兰克林的中庸妥协精神,也表达了他对实体联邦政府的怀疑。

5. If every one of us in returning to our Constituents were to report the objections he has had to it, and endeavor to gain partisans in support of them, we might prevent its being generally received, and thereby lose all the salutary effects and great advantages resulting naturally in our favor among foreign Nations as well as among ourselves, from our real or apparent unanimity.

  为了避免因猜测引起的州际和党派纷争,制宪会议始终对外界保密,以显现新独立的十三州人民安定团结,一致对外。富兰克林这里表达的正是这个愿望。但是,这是一个幼稚的愿望。民主制宪立国不可能没有人民的参与。在随后批准宪法的全国大辩论中,各州利益,党派集团的观点和分歧得到充分的表达,这在美国政治历史上未必不是好事。

6. Much of the strengthand efficiency of any Government in procuring and securing happiness to the people, depends, on opinion, on the general opinion of the goodness of the Government, as well as of the wisdom and integrity of its Governors.

  这是富兰克林对民主政治的理解,与《独立宣言》中表达的人民主权思想是一致的。但是,把廉洁的政府和人民的福祉建立在当权者的"智慧和品德"之上,却未脱离古典民主意识的窠臼。

■ 思考及讨论题

1. What role did Benjamin Franklin largely play in the Constitutional Conventsion?
2. What was Franklin's attitude toward the American Constitution?
3. For what reasons did Franklin recommend the Constitution with all its possible faults?
4. How do you understand Franklin's thoughts on government and democracy?

■ 阅读书目

1. Franklin, Bejamin. *The Autobiography of Benjamin Franklin*. New York: Macmillan, 1914.
2. Dull, Jonathan R. *Benjamin Franklin and the American Revolution*. Lincoln: University of Nebraska Press, 2010.
3. Cohen, I. Bernard. *Benjamin Franklin: His Contribution to the American Tradition*. Indianapolis: Bobbs-Merrill, 1953.
4. Hedgepeth, Julie William. "Benjamin Franklin's Printing Network, Disseminating Virtue in Early America" in *Journalism History*, Spring 2006.

第六讲
亚历山大·汉弥尔顿
（Alexander Hamilton 1755—1804）

■ 政治历史评述

亚历山大·汉弥尔顿：现代美国的先行者

美国东部，哈德逊河畔，纽约与新泽西州交界处有一个风光秀丽的小镇名叫威哈肯（Weehamken）。18世纪，纽约的贵族和名人凡有不解之夙仇，都喜好相约到威哈肯决斗，以捍卫各自的荣誉和名节。久之，威哈肯城边高地的树林空地几乎成了公认的决斗专用场地。1804年7月11日，美国原财政部长，政治思想家亚历山大·汉弥尔顿不顾友人劝阻，匆匆赶往威哈肯。他将在那与时任美国副总统的阿伦·伯尔也上演一场生死决斗，了结两人多年的夙仇。这是一桩政治公案。其中最令伯尔耿耿于怀的是，汉弥尔顿常在公众场合，口无遮拦，对他进行措辞激烈的攻讦。而且一再拒绝道歉。更有甚者，汉弥尔顿在1800总统选举中把关键的一票投向自己的政治宿敌托马斯·杰斐逊，使伯尔的总统梦完全破灭。在汉弥尔顿看来，这是两害取其轻，因为伯尔是更危险的政敌，一个"蛊惑人心的政客"。汉弥尔顿随后还极力挫败伯尔竞选纽约州长的企图。伯尔一怒之下，向汉弥尔顿提出决斗挑战。此时，伯尔和他的支持者已先期到达，正清理场地，步量距离，确定决斗双方站立点。汉弥尔顿及友人和随行医生随后到达，双方站好位置，等候仲裁人发信号。汉弥尔顿持枪立定，等候命运的裁决。他一向对以决斗的方式解决私人争端极为反感，认为那是人类"无知，迷信和中世纪野蛮的残余"。决斗前夕他在给妻子最后一封信中说提到这场决斗，认为"作为基督徒，我的良知决定我一定会把我自己的生命置

之度外，也不愿承担夺取他人生命的罪名"。而且，汉弥尔顿的儿子菲利普三年前也是在同一地点决斗而死。但是，名誉胜过理性，思想屈从时代。汉弥尔顿最终选择决斗场。但

他决定不开一枪,以此来表白他对决斗习俗的不赞同态度。结果,伯尔一枪击中汉弥尔顿,子弹穿过肝脏和脊椎。第2天,医生宣布亚历山大·汉弥尔顿不治身亡。美国政坛的新星划过光彩夺目的轨迹,就此匆匆陨落。

汉弥尔顿在其短暂的政治生涯中为后人留下了丰富的遗产。这位1755年生于西印度群岛的年轻人1772年移居纽约,心中充满了对未来的想象。作为生于美国本土以外的外乡人,汉弥尔顿在纽约毫无人脉。但他天资聪明,勤奋进取,常常读书学习到午夜,凌晨又在住地附近的墓地徘徊,思考安排新的一天的学习内容。来到纽约的第二年,汉弥尔顿进入纽约的王家学院。在学期间喜好偏科听课,争锋好辩。不久,他一反王家学院效忠英王和英国教会的政治倾向,公开演讲,发表号召革命的文章。在1776年美国独立革命的风潮中,这样一个激进思想的学生很快就成为革命军中马前卒,在华盛顿的大陆军中担任炮队队长。行军和战斗间歇,汉弥尔顿仍手不释卷,埋头于历史,政治,经济书籍之中。1777年,独立战争战事不利,华盛顿司令部急缺既有爱国热情和军事经验,又能言善辩,刀笔犀利的知识型参谋人员。于是,汉弥尔顿成为华盛顿总司令的随从参谋,鞍前马后,立下汗马功劳,直至1781年战争结束。在此期间,汉弥尔顿不仅形成了自己干练的军事和政治管理能力,更重要的还是获得了一种透过局部地方利益,驾驭全局的观念和视野,这为他日后担任华盛顿的财政部长期间推行中央集权,鼓励国家信贷和产业经济的政策奠定了管理实践的基础。

1789年,汉弥尔顿就任美国财长,当务之急是处理国家的债务,重铸国家信贷形象。当时美国政府和各州政府欠债总额高达5000万美元,其中大约1200万为欠法国,西班牙等国的外债,其余的4000万为国债。汉弥尔顿向国会提交公共贷款报告提案,要求由联邦政府统筹债务,甚至接管各州欠下的债务,如数偿还。此举目的在于以联邦政府的国家权力整合财政运算,使美国的经济运行于国家权力的掌控之中。

汉弥尔顿的思想深受英国传统的影响,他赞同大卫·休谟的人性论,接受托马斯·霍布斯建立国家强权的主张,对普通人民大众缺乏信心,认为人类由贪婪的欲望驱使,追逐利益,在无政府状态下加速堕落。只有国家权力才能统筹社会经济生活,才能使新生的国家发展和强盛。国家必须依靠掌握经济命脉的实业家,商人,律师等阶层,保护他们的经济利益,使他们积极地参与国家信贷,共同促进国家的经济发展。为此,汉弥尔顿进一步向国会提出著名的制造业报告,主张国家鼓励制造业,以工业最大的利润为国家的最大利益,提出建立国家银行,使财富和资本集中于有能力推动工商业经济发展的精英手中。同时,中央集权化的联邦政府可名正言顺地利用国家权力这一工具,提高关税,保护本国资本运作和国内市场,补贴工业产品的开发,鼓励发明和提高产品质量。同时,汉弥尔顿认为,在欧洲帝国争霸的世界格局中,美国不能指望通过发展农业,出口农产品而立于不败之地。有强大的中央集权的国家支持的工商业不仅不会削弱农业的发展,反而会促进土地的使用和资本化。

在汉弥尔顿看来,从政治经济的角度看问题,国家权力充分运作和工业经济繁荣的环境是社会公正和个人自由和民主权利的保障。而他的反对者杰斐逊和麦迪逊对此的看法正好相反:强大的政府必然走向专制和独裁,少数人获利的工业经济必然导致大多数人的贫困和民主权利的丧失,最终使共和政治体制衰亡。

18世纪最后的15年是汉弥尔顿思想多产的时期。他对美国宪政思想的历史贡献集中表现在他与詹姆斯·麦迪逊和约翰·杰伊1787—1788年间共同撰写的《联邦党人文集》中。这部文集旨在全面阐述美国宪法的政治思想及联邦政府构成机制,劝导各州及时批准联邦宪法。严格说来,《联邦党人文集》也是美国联邦政府形成过程中围绕着宪法最激烈的思想辩论的杰出产物。1787年9月17日,费城的制宪会议经过数月的争论和妥协,终于落下帷幕,各位代表终于松了口气,联邦宪法呼之欲出。

与此同时,反对批准宪法的呼声也不绝于耳。反对派旗帜鲜明,自称反联邦党人,在著名民主自由斗士帕特里克·亨利和理查·亨利·李的率领下,展开声势浩大的抵制宪法运动。在他们看来,联邦宪法没有明确的保障公民权的条款,这部宪法建立并扶持一个中央集权政府,与美国独立革命和自由共和的精神背道而驰,公民的自由和权利将随着各州权力的削弱而被无情地剥夺。这样针锋相对的意识形态对峙使新获得独立的美国走到了思想分裂,分崩离析的边缘。当时有位马萨诸塞州的代表拒绝签字,十分担心地预测这场思想论战可能最终会酿成一场你死我活的内战。

此时,汉弥尔顿在纽约州扛起联邦党人的大旗,邀约了麦迪逊和杰伊向公众鼓吹宪法,写成这部《联邦党人文集》并独自撰写了其85篇政论中的51篇。在这些政论中,汉弥尔顿展示了作为政治理论家和思想家的思辨精神,历数美国独立后州权大于邦联国会,政治上无所适从,经济上各行其是的混乱局面,力陈宪法所规定的分权原则对于保证共和政体的必要性,廓清联邦政府权利与州权的互相依存关系。这些努力为近一年后联邦宪法获得多数州的通过并正式生效起到了关键的作用。而且,《联邦党人文集》在美国政治历史上的许多案例中都被引用,时至今日,其影响仍经久不衰。

汉弥尔顿也是杰出的演说家。为争取关键的纽约州批准联邦宪法,他在制宪会议和纽约州宪法批准会议上发表了一系列的演讲,出色地阐述了《联邦党人文集》中的制宪思想和联邦政治体制原则。1788年6月,纽约州的宪法辩论进入了关键的时刻。参加制宪会议的三个来自纽约的代表中有两个宣布退出,拒绝签署宪法,彻底退出立宪会议。纽约州州长乔治·克林顿是老谋深算的州权主义者,纽约的反联邦党人的强大后台。看来,纽约州批准宪法的可能不大。而该州作为人口大州,对联邦宪法实际的生效至关重要。汉弥尔顿不得不独立支撑危局,连续9天在讨论宪法的会议上滔滔不绝地演讲。在6月24日的演说中,汉弥尔顿为了赢得纽约州批准宪法,不惜修饰强硬的态度,以设问劝导的语气,循循善诱的修辞文体,说明州权直接享有民众广泛的代表性的优越性,它的存在是必然的,与联邦权力互为依存,同时申明只有联邦主权才能形成排除地方偏见和局部利益的统一制约力量。在他看来,参议院是保证州权得以充分发挥作用的立法机构;一个政府稳定机制的政策将会消除地方的偏见和人为的偶然因素,只有国家的统一意志才能保证社会的长治久安和子孙后代的幸福。汉弥尔顿的努力没有白费。终于,在这篇演讲的第二天,纽约州议会以 30 票赞成 27 票反对的微弱多数批准了联邦宪法。美国作为一个独立的国家从此走上了宪政民主共和的发展道路。

也许,汉弥尔顿的早逝正是历史命运的安排。他对美国独立、宪政建国和社会经济发展的历史作用已在他去世前的 15 年中达到顶点。他提倡的强化国家权力的政治思想和资本主义工业主导的国家发展模式注定只属于美国的未来。1800 年,主张扩大州权,地方民主自治和小农自由经济的托马斯·杰斐逊登上美国总统宝座,汉弥尔顿的精英国家主义和资本主义经济思想失去了联邦政府权力的依托,也就失去了大张旗鼓地实际运作的机会。但是,作为一种政治经济思想形态,它已浸入美国社会意识,与其他的思想主流在美国社会和经济发展的历史过程中此消彼长,持续地彰显自己的存在,成为当今美国现代工业和现代资本主义信贷经济的重要思想来源。在这个意义上,我们完全可以说,亚历山大·汉弥尔顿是现代美国的先行者。

■ 演讲文(节选)

On the Power of Federal and the State Governments

Alexander Hamilton

...

Gentlemen indulge too many unreasonable **apprehensions** of danger to the State governments; they seem to suppose that the moment you put men into a national **council**, they become corrupt and tyrannical and lose all their affection for their fellow citizens. But can we imagine that the Senators will ever be so insensible of their own advantage as to sacrifice the **genuine** interest of their constituents? The State governments are essentially necessary to the form and spirit of the general system. As long, therefore, as Congress has a full **conviction** of this necessity, they must even upon principles purely national, have as firm an attachment to the one as to the other. This conviction can never leave them, unless they become madmen. While the Constitution continues to be read and its principle known, the States must by every rational man be considered as essential, **component parts** of the Union; and therefore the idea of sacrificing the former to the latter is wholly **inadmissible**.

The **objectors** do not **advert** to the natural strength and resources

apprehension: worry, anxiety
council: a group of people chosen to make laws, rules or decisions
genuine: real; true; of one's true feeling and knowledge
conviction: very strong belief or opinion
component parts: parts that are necessary to the whole
inadmissible: not to be accepted
objector: opponent
advert: mention

of State governments, which will ever give them an important superiority over the general government. If we compare the nature of their different powers, or the means of popular influence which each possesses, we shall find the advantage entirely on the side of the States. This consideration, important as it is, seems to have been little attended to. The **aggregate** number of representatives throughout the States may be two thousand. Their personal influence will, therefore, be proportionably more extensive than that of one or two hundred men in Congress. The State establishments of civil and military officers of every description, infinitely **surpassing** in number any possible correspondent establishments in the general government, will create such an extent and complication of attachments as will ever secure the **predilection** and support of the people. Whenever, therefore, Congress shall **meditate** any **infringement** of the State Constitutions, the great body of the people will naturally take part with their domestic representatives. Can the general government **withstand** such a united opposition? Will the people suffer themselves to be **stripped of** their privileges? Will they suffer their Legislatures to be reduced to a shadow and a name? The idea is shocking to common sense.

From the circumstances already explained and many others which might be mentioned, results a complicated, **irresistible** check, which must ever support the existence and importance of the State governments. The danger, if any exists, flows from an opposite source. The probable evil is that the general government will be too dependent on the State Legislatures, too much governed by their prejudices, and too **obsequious** to their **humors**; that the States, with every power in their hands, will make **encroachments** on the national authority till the Union is weakened and dissolved.

Every member must have been struck with an observation of a **gentleman from Albany**. Do what you will, says he, local prejudices and opinions will go into the government. What! shall we then form a Constitution to cherish and strengthen these prejudices? Shall we confirm the **distemper** instead of remedying it? It is undeniable that there must be a control somewhere. Either the general interest is to control the particular interests, or the contrary. If the former, then certainly the government ought to be so framed as to **render** the power of control efficient to all intents and purposes; if the latter, a striking **absurdity** follows; the controlling powers must be as numerous as the varying interests, and the operations of the government must therefore **cease**; for the moment you accommodate these different

---

aggregate: total amount of

surpass: better or greater than
predilection: favor; liking
mediate: negotiate
infringement: break of rules

withstand: resist; stand up to
stripped of: taken off by force; remove
irresistible: too strong and powerful to be stopped
obsequious: humble; servile
humor: willful or thoughtless decisions
encroachment: invasions; taking gradually as one's own possessions
gentleman from Albany: John Lansing (1754—1829), an Anti-federalist
distemper: infectious disease

render: make; use
absurdity: ridiculous consequence

cease: stop

interests, which is the only way to set the government in motion, you establish a controlling power. Thus, whatever constitutional **provisions** are made to the contrary, every government will be at last driven to the necessity of subjecting the partial to the **universal** interest. The gentlemen ought always in their reasoning to distinguish between the real, genuine good of a State and the opinions and prejudices which may **prevail** respecting it; the latter may be opposed to be sacrificed; the former is so involved in it that it never can be sacrificed.

There are certain social principles in human nature from which we may draw the most solid conclusions **with respect to** the conduct of individuals and of communities. We love our families more than our neighbors; we love our neighbors more than our countrymen in general. The human affections, like the solar heat, lose their **intensity** as they depart from the center and become **languid** in proportion to the expansion of the circle on which they act. On these principles, the attachment of the individual will be first and forever secured by the State governments; they will be a mutual protection and support. Another source of influence, which has already been pointed out, is the various official connections in the States. **Gentlemen** endeavor to **evade** the force of this by saying that these offices will be insignificant. This is by no means true. The State officers will ever be important, because they are necessary and useful. Their powers are such as are extremely interesting to the people; such as affect their property, their liberty, and life. What is more important than the administration of justice and the **execution** of the civil and criminal laws? Can the State governments become insignificant while they have the power of raising money independently and without control? If they are really useful, if they are **calculated** to promote the essential interests of the people, they must have their confidence and support. The States can never lose their powers till the whole people of America are robbed of their liberties. These must go together; they must support each other, or meet one common fate. On the gentleman's principle we may safely trust the State governments, **tho** we have no means of resisting them; but we can not confide in the national government, tho we have an effectual constitutional guard against every encroachment. This is the essence of their argument, and it is false and **fallacious** beyond conception.

With regard to the **jurisdiction** of the two governments I shall certainly admit that the Constitution ought to be so formed as not to prevent the States from providing for their own existence; and I

---

provision: term; article; statement

universal: general; national

prevail: becoming popular; overwhelm

with respect to: concerning to; regarding to

intensity: strength
languid: slow and lazy; inactive

Gentlemen: anti-federalist who spoke against the Constitution
evade: avoid; not to talk about

execution: carrying out; performance; implementation
calculated: carefully planned

tho: though; even if

fallacious: proved untrue; unreasonable
jurisdiction: the right to use official power to make legal decision

concede: admit **in the next breath**: immediately after **retract**: withdraw **concurrent**: existing at the same time **subordinate**: secondary; unimportant; attached **sophistry**: ways to make it seemingly true in order to deceive people **clashing**: conflict; contradiction **maxim**: proverb or well-known saying; brief statement of wisdom **pervert**: change to make it harmful **wander**: walking aimlessly **conjecture**: guessing; speculation **transgress**: to go beyond against the rules or laws	maintain that it is so formed, and that their power of providing for themselves is sufficiently established. This is **conceded** by one gentleman, and **in the next breath** the concession is **retracted**. He says Congress has but one exclusive right in taxation—that of duties on imports; certainly, then, their other powers are only **concurrent**. But to take off the force of this obvious conclusion, he immediately says that the laws of the United States are supreme and that where there is one supreme there can not be a concurrent authority; and further, that where the laws of the Union are supreme those of the States must be **subordinate**, because there can not be two supremes. This is curious **sophistry**. That two supreme powers can not act together is false. They are inconsistent only when they are aimed at each other or at one indivisible object. The laws of the United States are supreme as to all their proper constitutional objects; the laws of the States are supreme in the same way. These supreme laws may act on different objects without **clashing**, or they may operate on different parts of the same common object with perfect harmony. Suppose both governments should lay a tax of a penny on a certain article; has not each an independent and uncontrollable power to collect its own tax? The meaning of the **maxim**, there can not be two supremes, is simply this—two powers can not be supreme over each other. This meaning is entirely **perverted** by the gentlemen. But, it is said, disputes between collectors are to be referred to the Federal courts. This is again **wandering** in the field of **conjecture**. But suppose the fact is certain, is it not to be presumed that they will express the true meaning of the Constitution and the laws? Will they not be bound to consider the concurrent jurisdiction; to declare that both the taxes shall have equal operation; that both the powers, in that respect, are sovereign and coextensive? If they **transgress** their duty we are to hope that they will be punished. Sir, we can reason from probabilities alone. When we leave common sense and give ourselves up to conjecture, there can be no certainty, no security in our reasonings.

■ 重点述评与提示

1. But can we imagine that the Senators will ever be so insensible of their own advantage as to sacrifice the genuine interest of their constituents? The State governments are essentially necessary to the form and spirit of the general system.

　　重申州权是联邦政府存在的必然组成部分。这里强调的是,国会不会因权力的高度集中而腐败,各州的参议员数量相等,他们代表的是各州人们的切身利益,受到人民的监督,州政府的权力没有被联邦宪法削弱或取代。

2. If we compare the nature of their different powers, or the means of popular influence which each possesses, we shall find the advantage entirely on the side of the States.

  这里的潜台词是,如何理解权力属于人民这个命题。双方争执的焦点也在此。宪法的表述是"美利坚人民",联邦政府代表着全体人民,反联邦党人坚持的是"各州人民",即人民归属各州的权力。汉弥尔顿这里意在调和此根本分歧,采取迂回策略,试图用各州议会代表的数量说明各州在代表性问题上比联邦政府更占优势。而且,人民更关心自己在各州的切身利益。

3. The probable evil is that the general government will be too dependent on the State Legislatures, too much governed by their prejudices, and too obsequious to their humors; that the States, with every power in their hands, will make encroachments on the national authority till the Union is weakened and dissolved.

  一语道破汉弥尔顿内心深深的忧虑:如果任州权坐大,地方利益和偏见膨胀,那么联邦政府将名存实亡,重新回到"邦联条约"政令不出公门,各州各行其是的无政府状态。这里连用三个排比,dependent, governed, obsequious 语义递降,直至衰弱和消亡,起到良好的修辞效果。

4. Either the general interest is to control the particular interests, or the contrary. If the former, then certainly the government ought to be so framed as to render the power of control efficient to all intents and purposes; if the latter, a striking absurdity follows; the controlling powers must be as numerous as the varying interests, and the operations of the government must therefore cease.

  此前,退出制宪会议的纽约州代表,反联邦党人约翰·朗辛在辩论发言中曾断言:"联邦政府中将完全可能充斥着地方利益,局部观点和偏见,只是程度有所不同而已。"(It is entirely probable that local interests, opinions, and prejudices, will ever prevail in the general government, in a greater or less degree.)。汉弥尔顿在这里针锋相对,指出联邦宪法就是对此的制约,否则国将不国。

5. There are certain social principles in human nature from which we may draw the most solid conclusions with respect to the conduct of individuals and of communities. We love our families more than our neighbors; we love our neighbors more than our countrymen in general.

  人性自私褊狭,只顾眼前利益而缺乏远见,这本是汉弥尔顿集权国家主义政治思想的逻辑起点。在此用来安抚州权主义的反联邦党人,在汉弥尔顿是权宜之计,而在今天看来,不无讽刺意味。

6. On the gentleman's principle we may safely trust the State governments, tho we have no means of resisting them; but we can not confide in the national government, tho we have an effectual constitutional guard against every encroachment.

汉弥尔顿把对手的论点推至逻辑极点:各州权力无制约机制但可绝对信任;联邦权力有法可依而让人不放心。由此喻示分权制衡原则的失效,凸现对手的谬误和荒唐。

7. The meaning of the maxim, there can not be two supremes, is simply this—two powers can not be supreme over each other.

宪法是国家的根本大法,这是基本原则。但各州主权自治,与联邦主权并行不悖,这也是美国联邦宪法的根本特点。汉弥尔顿在此重申了这一点。

■ 思考及讨论题

1. Why a general system of government is ever necessary?
2. According to the Anti-federalists, what dangers are imposed by the Constitution?
3. Why did Hamilton say that the power of the State governments is superior to that of the general government?
4. What did Hamilton worry about in terms of the relationship between the State governments and the Federal government?
5. How do you understand the claim that both the State and the Federal governments are the supreme powers?

■ 阅读书目

1. Murray, A. Joseph. *Alexander Hamilton: America's Forgotten Founder*. New York: Algora Publishing, 2007.
2. Hacker, Louis M. *Alexander Hamilton in American Tradition*. New York: McGrow-Hill, 1957.
3. Miller, John C. *Alexander Hamilton: Portrait in Paradox*. New York: Harper & Brother, 1959.
4. Brook, Allan. "Alexander Hamilton: the Enlightened Realist" in *The Hudson Review*, Autumn 2004.

第七讲
帕特里克·亨利(Patrick Henry 1736—1799)

■ 政治历史评述

帕特里克·亨利:自由斗士,反宪何急?

又必须提到著名的民主自由斗士帕特里克·亨利(其生平已在第二讲中简述),因为他在1787年美国宪法大论辩中反对宪政,捍卫个体公民的自由和权利,维护州权和地方自治的表演太鲜活,在光荣的失败中衬托了美国"建立一个更完善的联邦"的理想。

美国宪法是美国人的荣耀。美国建国240多年来,政党纷争,内战分裂,权力更迭,而宪法的基本原则保持不变。历史的演进和社会的变迁,都能够以修正案的形式在宪法的基本框架内得到法律的表达和包容,也许这也印证了美国宪法开篇所表达的理想:"建立一个更完善的联邦"。宪政立法,以维护国家稳定、社会正义和个人的幸福,这是一个不断演进的历史过程。只要地球存在,人类完善自我的历史就不会终结,美国宪法也应如此,与时俱进,不断完善。

我们无从预测未来。我们今天看到美国人对自己国家的宪法的推崇和自豪,不免会把目光投向其诞生的历史瞬间,发现它的诞生也不是一帆风顺的。18世纪最后的10多年,那是一个不乏对统一强国的希望和自信,同时也充满了对国家权力疑惑甚至敌视的时代。独立革命的风暴过去,自由的空气吹来的却也有怀旧的思绪;松散的13州邦联政体难以聚集人气,各州以地方利益为重,互相推诿,相互抵制,甚至出现一州否决,全局瘫痪的政治局面。《独立宣言》营造出来的美利坚统一国家意识尚未成型,随着独立自由的实现,独立自治的地方主义和州权至上的思想又开始蔓延。在此形势下,美国宪法力图强化国家权力和意志,建立民选代议,权力制衡的国家机器。它的出现,强化了上述两种政治意识,使之震荡重组,迅速形成两种旗鼓相当,势不两立的意识形态阵营。

1787年9月17日,费城制宪会议终于落幕,宪法既出,举国哗然,以亚历山大·汉弥尔顿和詹姆士·麦迪逊为首的立宪势力拉起联邦党人的大旗,鼓吹建立实体的国家政体,为宪法的最终批准生效而努力;帕特里克·亨利则鼓起自己一生最后的政治能量。毫不犹豫地在弗吉尼亚州扯起反对宪法的大旗,号召人们站在反联邦主义的旗帜下,为捍卫个体公民的自由和权利,维护州权和地方自治而战。双方动员各自的政治资源,在全国上下掀起一场波及社会各阶层的大辩论,一场批准宪法或拒绝宪法的大论战。

在这场围绕着宪法合法性问题的大辩论中,帕特里克·亨利占有举足轻重的地位。

按照费城制宪会议的规定,宪法通过以后必须得到13州中9个州的批准方可正式生效。此时,在1787年9月17日宪法在制宪会议上通过后的9个月内,先后有8个州批准了宪法。在剩下的5个州中,弗吉尼亚的立场至关重要。而亨利这位在美国独立革命中以"不自由,毋宁死"的激昂演讲而著名的政治家在弗吉尼亚州有着广泛的政治影响。在联邦党人看来,宪法是否最终获得批准生效,很大程度上取决于亨利的态度和立场,或者说,取决于他反对宪法的程度。早在制宪会议结束后,华盛顿就匆匆回到弗吉尼亚家中,立即寄给好友亨利一信并附上宪法抄本,试探其立场。亨利的答复是迅速的,坚决的:"我本人对所提议之联邦宪法无论如何不能苟同,伏乞见谅"。不久,麦迪逊在写给杰斐逊的信中表达了对亨利立场的极度关注:"弗吉尼亚方面的消息极为不妙……,亨利先生的态度此间暂不得知,成败与否很大程度上看他如何表态了。"其实,亨利已经发表宣言,制造舆论,旗帜鲜明地反对批准宪法。几个月过去,弗吉尼亚州反联邦党势力大增。形势对联邦党人极为不利。

1788年6月初,弗吉尼亚州批准宪法会议终于召开。来自各地民选的170名代表云集州府里士满最大的会议厅,对是否批准宪法展开辩论,投票表决。来自弗吉尼亚各地甚至其他州的民众也拥蜂而至,争先目睹决定命运的一刻。美国民众的政治关注度历来很高,18世纪末这场关系到宪法存亡的辩论也许是美国有史以来最为空前的。

可想而知,这正是亨利期待看到的热烈场面。如此群情激昂的政治舞台可以启迪亨利的政治灵感,开启知识和智慧之门,把他特有的滔滔辩才发挥到淋漓尽致的地步。而且,这是亨利政治生命中最后一次耀光,此后他将淡出政治历史舞台,在默默无言中旁观美国政坛的风云变幻。亨利饱含激情,全力投入到这场宏大的政治戏剧中。在23天的大会辩论中,亨利有18天都在发表主题演讲。有几天他一天之内三次上台演说,有一天发表了五次演讲,另有一天竟然发表了八次演说。在一次演说中,他整整站立七个小时,滔滔不绝,毫无倦容!政治的执着,语言的狂欢,到此地步,可谓极致。

亨利对宪法的攻击是全方位的。归纳起来,大致有以下三点。

首先,制定宪法本身不合法。13州联合体的政治基础是1776年大陆会议通过的《邦联条约》,那是以各州的独立主权为基础而组成的政治盟约。任何各州的联合政治行为都必须在这个条约的基础上施行。条约可以修改完善,但不能对之采取革命性转变。费城制宪会议无权完全抛开这个政治联盟而代之以一个权力集中的实体政府。换言之,制宪者无权以各州全体人民的名义号令天下。宪法开篇即说"我们,美利坚合众国的人民",而不是说"我们,美利坚的各州",这实际上就表明了对各州主权的剥夺,对共和理想的颠覆。可以看出,在亨利的思想意识中,共和体制建立在公民意志和州权基础上。在现代国家意识逐渐增长的时代,亨利小国寡民式的自由社会显得十分地苍白无力。革命后获得的自由惯性把他推向地方主义的死角,使他不能获得新的政治视角和远见。

其次,建构一个权力集中,高于各州主权的实体政府将对公民的自由、权利和幸福构成直接的威胁。亨利虽然对此表现得痛心疾首,但却语焉未详,未能具体说明宪法是如何威胁到个体公民的自由与权利。这也是在辩论中联邦党人抓到的软肋。但在亨利反复的强调和呼吁中,我们可以看到,在亨利的意识中有一种本能的对国家权力的警觉或恐惧。在他看来,权力的本性就是压迫,特别是对弱势群体的压迫。压迫就意味着个人的自由和社会权力的丧失。美国独立革命推翻了英国议会权力的压迫,人民获得了独立和自由,此时宪法不能构建新的国家权力来毁灭革命的成果。而且,宪法在构建国家权力的同时没有对个体公民的自由和权利提供任何的保障,这更显示了国家权力的本来面目。宪法后来最终增补了完整的"权利法案",这不能说不与亨利的大声疾呼有关。

第三,权力的集中和实体运作必将导致专制和暴政。亨利此论的前提是权力的个人化。政府的行政长官集军政大权于一身,如果其本身道德堕落和欲望无度,则不可逆转地走向独裁和暴力。而人民没有任何渠道对其行为进行遏制或惩戒,其结果就是君临天下的结局。可以看出,亨
利对新的宪法中体现的人民主权,代议民主和权力制衡的观念不甚理解,他的思想中因果单一,缺乏现代国家意识的自觉,特别是缺乏英国和欧陆启蒙主义关于契约论和国家法制理念的熏陶。这也是亨利最终不能阻止弗吉尼亚州批准宪法的重要原因之一。

亨利最终失败了。高亢的语言和饱满的激情未能阻止冷峻理性和时代前进的步伐。弗吉尼亚州议会以微弱优势批准了宪法,但同时也申明保留除了明确授于联邦政府的权力以外的一切州权,并有权在必要时向联邦国会提出任何的宪法修正案。在这里,亨利的反对意见已经得到了肯定的表述。

所幸,亨利和反联邦党人没有走得太远。他们保留了反对立场,但未做出实际行动分裂联邦。这也是亨利在这场意识形态论战中的底线。大会辩论伊始,他曾反复申明,坚决反对分裂邦联的行为。大会投票表决之前,亨利自知大势已去,向大会发言保证将平静地保留立场,决不诉诸暴力。为了人民的安宁,自由和幸福将"以宪法的方式,全身心地追寻可能失去的自由,并祛除政体中产生的弊病"。以此姿态宣布失败,亨利虽败犹荣。他的高贵气质引起人们的敬重;他对自由的热爱,对公民权利的捍卫赢得了人们的理解,他饱含激情的滔滔辩才经年回荡在一代代人的脑海。

后世一位史家用以下诗意的语言描述了1788年6月25日昂首站在弗吉尼亚州会议厅的亨利:"亨利展现了他的天性,和善友爱,毫无恨意。风暴过去,晨光初曦,亨利犹如海上一道微澜，撞击着坚硬的悬崖峭壁，然后，波光粼粼中，悄然退回自己的家园。"的确，当今美国宪法经受了240多年的历史风浪，在不断完善中履行着自己的历史职责，而帕特里克·亨利正是为这一辩证的历史进程提供了原初的推动。比起19世纪美国内战的硝烟和20世纪经济大萧条的苍凉，其力微不足道，但它却见证着美国宪政历史发展的逻辑起点。

■ 演讲文（节选）

A Wrong Step Now and the Republic Will Be Lost Forever

Patrick Henry

Mr. Chairman,

The public mind, as well as my own, is extremely uneasy at the proposed change of Government. **Give me leave** to form one of the number of those who wish to be thoroughly **acquainted** with the reasons of this **perilous** and uneasy situation—and why we are brought **hither** to decide on this great national question. I consider myself as the servant of the people of this Commonwealth, as a **sentinel** over their rights, liberty, and happiness. I represent their feelings when I say, that they are **exceedingly** uneasy, being brought from that state of full security, which they enjoyed, to the present **delusive** appearance of things. A year ago the minds of our citizens were at perfect **repose**. Before the meeting of the late Federal Convention at Philadelphia, a general peace, and a universal tranquility prevailed in this country—but since that period they are exceedingly uneasy and **disquieted**. When I wished for an appointment to this Convention, my mind was extremely **agitated** for the situation of public affairs. I **conceive** the republic to be in extreme danger. If our situation be thus uneasy, **whence** has arisen this fearful **jeopardy**? It arises from this fatal system—it arises from a proposal to change our government—A proposal that goes to the utter **annihilation** of the most solemn engagements of the States. A proposal of establishing nine States into a confederacy, to the eventual exclusion of four States. It goes to the annihilation of those solemn treaties we have formed with foreign

---

Give me leave: allow me
acquainted with: know about
perilous: dangerous
hither: here
sentinel: guard; watcher; defender
exceedingly: extremely
delusive: uncertain; dreamy
repose: rest

disquieted: anxious

agitated: disturbed
conceive: think
whence: from where
jeopardy: danger
annihilation: total destruction

nations. The present circumstances of France—the good offices rendered us by that kingdom, require our most faithful and most **punctual adherence** to our treaty with her.

We are in alliance with the Spaniards, the Dutch, the Prussians: Those treaties bound us as thirteen States, confederated together—Yet, here is a proposal to **sever** that confederacy. Is it possible that we shall abandon all our treaties and national engagements? —And for what? I expected to have heard the reasons of an event so unexpected to my mind, and many others. Was our civil polity, or public justice, endangered or **sapped**? Was the real existence of the country threatened—or was this **preceded** by a mournful progression of events? This proposal of altering our Federal Government is of a most alarming nature: Make the best of this new Government—say it is composed by anything but **inspiration**—you ought to be extremely cautious, watchful, jealous of your liberty; for instead of securing your rights you may lose them forever. If a wrong step be now made, the republic may be lost forever. If this new Government will not **come up to** the expectation of the people, and they should be disappointed—their liberty will be lost, and tyranny must and will arise. I repeat it again, and I beg Gentlemen to consider, that a wrong step made now will **plunge** us into misery, and our Republic will be lost. It will be necessary for this Convention to have a faithful historical detail of the facts, that preceded the session of the Federal Convention, and the reasons that **actuated** its members in proposing an entire alteration of Government—and to demonstrate the dangers that awaited us: If they were of such awful magnitude, as to **warrant** a proposal so extremely perilous as this, I must assert, that this Convention has an absolute right to a thorough discovery of every circumstance relative to this great event. And here I would make this enquiry of those **worthy characters** who composed a part of the late Federal Convention. I am sure they were fully impressed with the necessity of forming a great consolidated Government, instead of a confederation. That this is a consolidated Government is demonstrably clear, and the danger of such a Government, is, to my mind, very **striking**. I have the highest **veneration** for those Gentlemen, —but, Sir, give me leave to demand, what right had they to say, We, the People. My political curiosity, exclusive of my anxious **solicitude** for the public welfare, leads me to ask, who authorized them to speak the language of, We, the People, instead of We, the States? States are the characteristics, and the soul

punctual adherence: accurate duty; observation

sever: tear apart; cut to pieces; end the relationship with

sap: weaken
precede: happened before in series

inspiration: sudden thought or feeling; wonderful ideas

come up to: satisfy; meet

plunge into: throw into

actuate: motivate; activate

warrant: need; deserve

worthy characters: honorable gentlemen

striking: strange; shocking
veneration: great respect; honor
solicitude: care; concern

agent: member; contributor; doer
compact: formal agreement

testimonial: formal letter of thanks and praise

that illustrious man: George Washington who was good friend of Henry
were he here: if he were here

insurrection: uprising; rebellion
tumult: disturbance
notwithstanding: in spite of
inflammatory: excited and passionate
resentment: hard feeling
amend: make up for
delegated: represented

of a confederation. If the States be not the **agents** of this **compact**, it must be one great consolidated National Government of the people of all the States. I have the highest respect for those Gentlemen who formed the Convention, and were some of them not here, I would express some **testimonial** of my esteem for them. America had on a former occasion put the utmost confidence in them: A confidence which was well placed: And I am sure, Sir, I would give up anything to them; I would cheerfully confide in them as my Representatives. But, Sir, on this great occasion, I would demand the cause of their conduct.—Even from **that illustrious man**, who saved us by his valor, I would have a reason for his conduct—that liberty which he has given us by his valor, tells me to ask this reason,—and sure I am, **were he here**, he would give us that reason: But there are other Gentlemen here, who can give us this information. The people gave them no power to use their name. That they exceeded their power is perfectly clear. It is not mere curiosity that actuates me—I wish to hear the real actual existing danger, which should lead us to take those steps so dangerous in my conception. Disorders have arisen in other parts of America, but here, Sir, no dangers, no **insurrection** or **tumult**, has happened—everything has been calm and tranquil. But **notwithstanding** this, we are wandering on the great ocean of human affairs. I see no landmark to guide us. We are running we know not whither. Difference in opinion has gone to a degree of **inflammatory resentment** in different parts of the country—which has been occasioned by this perilous innovation. The Federal Convention ought to have **amended** the old system—for this purpose they were solely **delegated**: The object of their mission extended to no other consideration. You must therefore forgive the solicitation of one unworthy member, to know what danger could have arisen under the present confederation, and what are the causes of this proposal to change our Government. ...

■ 重点述评与提示

1. I consider myself as the servant of the people of this Commonwealth, as asentinel over their rights, liberty, and happiness.

    commonwealth 即指在《邦联条约》下十三州组成的松散的政治联盟，亨利自诩是这个"州际间友谊的联盟"(league of friendship between states)的倡导者,因而也是独立革命后人民权利、自由和幸福的守望者。

2. Before the meeting of the late Federal Convention at Philadelphia, a general peace, and a universal tranquility prevailed in this country;—but since that period they are exceedingly uneasy and disquieted.

亨利不能与时俱进,囿于地方主义的狭窄视野,不能超越单纯的独立自由革命的理想,看不到独立战争后国会财政亏空,经济衰落,债券贬值,土地价格飞涨,官逼民反的重重危机,这是他缺乏国家意识的表现。然而,制宪会议引起的思想分裂和大辩论也的确是他感到忧心忡忡的局面。

3. Make the best of this new Government—say it is composed byanything but inspiration —you ought to be extremely cautious, watchful, jealous of your liberty; for instead of securing your rights you may lose them forever.

这是亨利反对宪法的主要观点:个人在中央集权的实体国家权力的压迫下,人民将丧失自己通过独立革命获得的自由和权利。

4. Sir, give me leave to demand, what right had they to say, We, the People. My political curiosity, exclusive of my anxious solicitude for the public welfare, leads me to ask, who authorized them to speak the language of, We, the People, instead of We, the States?

美国宪法开篇第一句就说,"We, the people of the United States",表明联邦政府主权来自全美国人民总体。以此不同,1781年签订的《邦联条约》开篇第就申明的"各州拥有主权、自由、独立、司法权",表明主权在州。这一改变引起了亨利的警觉,认为这是联邦政府消化州权,走向集权统治,压制个人自由和权利的信号。

5. Even from that illustrious man, who saved us by his valor, I would have a reason for his conduct—that liberty which he has given us by his valor, tells me to ask this reason,—and sure I am, were he here, he would give us that reason.

这里,亨利把矛头直指制宪会议的主席乔治·华盛顿,这是需要勇气的。华盛顿当时名望极高,是人们心中的民族英雄,对亨利也是礼遇有加。亨利演讲起来,顾不了许多,足见这位"自由斗士"为民请命的精神。

6. Difference in opinion has gone to a degree of inflammatory resentment in different parts of the country—which has been occasioned by this perilous innovation.

亨利可能有些夸张,局势尚未到达此剑拔弩张的地步。但是可以说,18世纪末这场关系到宪法存亡的辩论的激烈程度也许是美国有史以来最为空前的。美国民众的政治关注度历来很高,也许起始与此?

■ 思考及讨论题

1. What could the word "people" mean to Patrick Henry?
2. How does Henry's confederation differ from the Federalist's federal system?
3. Why did Henry say that the Constitution would lead to the death of liberty?
4. Comment on Henry's speech style in contrast to that of Hamilton's.

■ 阅读书目

1. George, Bancroft. *History of the Formation of the Constitution of the United States of America*. 2 vols. New York: D. Appleton and Company, 1882.
2. Jonathan, Elliot.*The Debates in the Several State Conventions, On the Adoption of the Federal Constitution, etc*. 5 vols. Philadelphia: J.B. Lippincott & co., 1876
3. Wooton, David. *The Essential Anti-federalist and Federalist Papers*. Indianapolis: Heckett, 2003.
4. Bordon, Morton.ed. *The Federalist Papers*. East Lansing: Michigan State University Press, 1965.

第八讲
詹姆斯·麦迪逊(James Madison 1751—1836)

■ 政治历史评述

詹姆斯·麦迪逊:美国宪法之父

在美国早期宪政的奠基者和践行者中,麦迪逊可称为现代意义上的第一位美国政治思想家,他以其善思博学,思辨缜密而著称,以其对民主政体和共和思想的研究而受到普遍的尊敬,以其对人性的社会和政治分析而令人信服,以其制定美国宪法的重大贡献而当之无愧地被誉为"美国宪法之父"。

麦迪逊 1751 年生于弗吉尼亚州一个乡镇农场主家庭。他身材矮小羸弱,沉默寡言,说话低声细语,一生不善交际。在当时身材魁梧,高谈阔论的美国国父和其他诸多政治活动家中,麦迪逊并不引人注目。他当过弗吉尼亚州议员,代表弗吉尼亚州参加大陆会议,1800 年被胜选的好友托马斯·杰斐逊总统提名为美国国务卿。最终于 1808 年被选为美国第 4 任总统,而且借第二次对英战争之后高涨的爱国热情和联邦党人覆亡之大势连任总统大任。

但麦迪逊不是一个政治活动家。历届州立法会议活动中,甚至在费城制宪会议的初期辩论中,他都洗耳恭听,不言不语。在一群慷慨激昂,妙语连珠的与会代表中,麦迪逊表现得不善言辞,默默无闻。但他却善于观察,用心思考,捕捉当下的政治和社会的关键问题来印证,补充和阐释头脑中逐渐成形的政治思想理论体系和国家形式的构想;为日后制定美国宪法奠定理论和实践两方面的充实基础。时至今日,他对制宪会议辩论的全程笔录都是研究美国宪政的最珍贵的第一手资料。

麦迪逊也称不上是位强势胜任的政治领袖人物。在担任美国总统期间,麦迪逊缺乏领导统筹能力,使国会长期不和,对外政策刚柔不济。他延续前任总统杰斐逊的贸易禁运和削减财政开支的政策,致使国防力量不堪一击。1812 年第二次对英战争战端即开,他又优柔寡断,用人不当,导致北部战线连连失利,直至英军长驱直入,占领首府华盛顿,麦迪逊总统仓促逃离,站在波多马克河对岸眼睁睁地看着总统府(今日的白宫)被英军付之一炬。多亏美国弱小的海军在海上屡屡偷袭得手,加上"老胡桃"安德鲁·杰克逊率兵在新奥尔良占据有利地形,以逸待劳,以几十人伤亡的代价,打得骄横一时的 2000 多英军尸横遍野,几乎全军覆没,不然总统麦迪逊在与英国的和谈前后可能会大失脸面,也不会有麦迪逊总统虽败犹荣的历史形象。

然而,真正杰出的政治思想家的作用是超然于国家政务和业绩之上的。国家的兴衰取决于远见实干的政治领袖,外交得失需要精明睿智的头脑,战场上的输赢也靠智勇双全的将才,而在一个爱国热情激荡,国计民生百废待兴的新生国家,只有少数的头脑能够在静思的理性中决定着这个国家的未来。换言之,政治思想家的思想成果和政治理论建树决定着这个国家的政治体制和国家功能的根本形式和走向,是一个国家是否能够长治久安,人民是否能够自由安宁的根本保障。而这正是麦迪逊作为政治思想家能够担负起来的历史重任。这也是麦迪逊在美国政坛上的影响持续不衰的原因。

詹姆斯·麦迪逊的这种学者型的政治家形象是他早年在新泽西学院(后来的普林斯顿大学)的刻苦攻读的必然结果。他18岁进入这所学院,校方鼓励知识占有,克己自律。麦迪逊在此两方面都堪称楷模。他对知识如饥似渴,每天睡眠仅4—5小时,在普林斯顿近3年,刻苦学习逻辑学和多种语言,博览群书。他精通拉丁文,背诵西塞罗的《演说术》和维吉尔的长诗,研读李维的《罗马史》;用希腊文阅读亚里士多德的《政治学》和《逻辑学》,修昔底斯的《伯罗奔尼撒战争史》,普鲁塔克的《希腊罗马名人传》。最重要的是,麦迪逊受到导师威特斯布恩的指导,大量阅读18世纪的一些道德和政治哲学家,其中对大卫·休谟和约翰·洛克的思想多有吸纳,对他日后的国家政治理论的形成多有内在的影响。同时,麦迪逊与18世纪启蒙认识论思想保持一致,对人性具有现实和乐观的认识,认为自由的人类主体的认知趋于无穷,因此任何政治权力和国家形式都必须容纳多种思想意识和宗教信仰的参与,从中获得权力的合法性。有此坚实的历史政治知识基础,国家理论思考,才能使麦迪逊在后来的制宪会议和批准宪法的辩论中起到不可替代的理论中坚作用。

麦迪逊的国家政治理论首先是建立在对历史上诸多政治体制的研究基础上的。1787年费城制宪会议前一年,麦迪逊把自己关进书房,整整几个月悉心研究分析了自14

世纪以来至17世纪在希腊,比利时,瑞士和德国等地区产生的一些城邦联盟政治体制,发现了这些城邦联盟宗教专制,缺乏宽容,联盟内部缺乏实体权力中心,导致这些联盟国家内忧外患,分崩离析的政治局面。这些研究坚定了他在美国以国家宪法的形式建立国家权力,规约人性欲望的信心。在此研究基础上,麦迪逊研究了英国哲学家大卫·休谟的国家学说并借鉴美国邦联国会失败教训,认为在较大的政治社会范围之内建立一个具有实际权力的联邦共和体制是可能的,也是必须的。麦迪逊正是在这一点上看到人类自我的欲望与政府权力之间的关系。与富兰克林等深受启蒙思想影响的思想家不同,麦迪逊认为人性趋向无休止的自我追求与实现,必然由于利益和兴趣的异同而组合成不同的党派和利益集团。这是历史上任何形式的国家和社会都不可避免的。麦迪逊对党派和利益集团虽然也持否定态度,但他也看到,人人虽然生而平等,但在人的欲望的驱动下,在物质社会发展的现实中这种平等意识一定会被打破。承认社会人的不同生存和意识状况,是民主共和的国家政治学的基本前提。麦迪逊坚持认为,在一个大范围的共和体制内,随着社会多元利益的变化和发展,党派和利益团体也会不断发生改变,其边界趋于不确定,各党派和利益集团之间会产生制约关系,防止某派系权力膨胀,形成专制,对共和社会和人的自由造成威胁。同时,人民也在这一关系中通过参与不断变化的政治党派和利益集团,获得共和体制下最大的民主与自由。这就是所谓"权欲制约权欲"(ambition against ambition)的国家权力策略。国家主权政府操控各政治派系的斗争,从中行使国家权力的有效作用。这就是麦迪逊力图建立民主共和法制体系的理论基础。这一思想后来在其《联邦党人文集》第10篇中再次得以重申。

理论既已廓清,剩下的问题就是如何制定一部各党派或利益集团都认可的国家宪法,并以其原则建立美国政治体制和的联邦政府。这个联邦政体应该能够承认并包容最大限度的社会利益派系和鼓励人的自我实现,既不能重蹈《邦联条约》软弱国会的覆辙,也不能重演十三州或各行其是,或采取"多数的暴政"策略使国家权力名存实亡。麦迪逊为此殚精竭虑,最终写出"弗吉尼亚方案"作为宪法的最初文本,供来自各州的与会代表讨论。这个宪法的原初文本明确权力制衡,分权治国的原则,提出建立一个由立法,司法和行政三个部门的实体联邦政府,其中国会为立法机关,由民选的众议院和由各州提名并由众议院指定的参议院组成,总统由参众两院提名选举,领导行政当局,司法部门由最高法院和一个司法审查委员会组成。值得注意的是,经过制宪会议数月的激烈辩论和一系列的妥协方案,最终获得通过的美国宪法保留麦迪逊最初的"弗吉尼亚方案"的整体框架和主要的内容。从以上看,麦迪逊后来被誉为"美国宪法之父"是当之无愧的。

麦迪逊在弗吉尼亚州批准宪法会议上与反联邦主义领袖帕特里克·亨利进行了针锋相对的辩论,其中可窥视到麦迪逊思想的理性锋芒。亨利年长麦迪逊15岁,是弗吉尼亚政治元老,也可算是麦迪逊的政治长辈。当年26岁的麦迪逊初出道,1777年被选为弗吉尼亚州议员,从偏僻的家乡蒙特皮尔来到首府州议院,对身为州长和议长的亨利自然十分地恭敬。而今11年过去,麦迪逊在政坛的实力和名声已今非昔比。他虽然生性内向,不善演讲,但经过多年的政治决策参与和思考,加之学养深厚,思辨缜密,对付激情有余,思想不足的亨利可谓绰绰有余。会议辩论前,弗吉尼亚的联邦党人对亨利的政治威望和澎湃的辩才深感忧虑,唯恐与会的170余名代表中的多数人在对宪法本身未作细致理解和分析判断之前被亨利反对宪法的激情演说所蛊惑,因而把希望寄托在麦迪逊身上,希望他能够以自己对宪法的深刻理性和洞察能够一举击败以亨利为首的反联邦党人。麦迪逊不负众望,制定了与具体的辩论方案,意欲
避开亨利对制宪合法性和对宪法的总体进行的攻击,而是就宪法本身进行逐条逐句的具体辩论。

亨利并非等闲之辈,在会议一开始就识破了联邦党人逐条辩论的策略,借机发动强大的攻势。亨利在会议的第3天发表了数小时演说,以其独特的,声情并茂的演说风格,从根本上质疑制宪的权力合法性,谴责以此宪法组建的实体联邦政府与民主共和的原则相悖,最终走向专制和暴政,削弱甚至完全取消州权立法,从而剥夺公民的自由和权力。亨利的演讲回旋着一种英国议会辉格党人的批判意识和为民请命的献身精神,在与会代表中引起了很大的反响,联邦党人对此深感不安。如果按亨利的思路进行回应,则正中其下怀,宪法的具体内容将会被悬置,大多数与会代表对宪法将投反对票。

在此情势人,联邦党人不约而同地将目光投向麦迪逊,指望他能力挽狂澜,把会议辩论重新拉回到对宪法内容进行逐条辩论的正确轨道。第二天早会,麦迪逊起身第一个发言,开门见山,要求会议对宪法内容本身的优劣进行研究和评判。他注视着在场的亨利,明确指出,玩弄语言辩术,发表主观的断言和感论于事无补,对宪法进行冷静的理性分析才是做出正确的取舍判断的正确途径。麦迪逊进而要求亨利对宪法做具体的分析,拿出证据表明公民的权力是如何受到了宪法的威胁,宪法中的哪一条会导致集权和暴政。麦迪逊也指出了亨利演说中的逻辑不连贯现象,更反衬了他的理性批判精神。同时,麦迪逊指出亨利对宪法中规定的实体联邦政府性质的曲解,向与会代表细致说明宪法规定的联邦政府与《邦联条约》国会的权力来源不同,指明州权的性质和范围。

麦迪逊的通篇演讲虽然音调不高,缺乏感染力,但却立论鲜明,逻辑连贯,言之有物,与亨利演讲的随意和空乏形成了鲜明的对照,为联邦党人最终赢得弗吉尼亚州批准宪法起到中流砥柱的作用。可以说,在这个意义上,詹姆斯·麦迪逊对美国宪政的历史地位更加显赫,更无愧于美国宪法之父的美名。

■ 演讲文(节选)

In Favor of the Federal Constitution

James Madison

merit: good quality and feature; advantage
aptitude: ability capability; quality
address: try to deal with a problem
rational: objective thinking of reason
assertion: definite statement

We ought, sir, to examine the Constitution on its own **merits** solely. We are to inquire whether it will promote the public happiness; its **aptitude** to produce this desirable object ought to be the exclusive subject of our present researches. In this pursuit, we ought not to **address** our arguments to the feelings and passions but to those understandings and judgments which were selected by the people of this country, to decide this great question by a calm and **rational** investigation.

I hope that gentlemen, in displaying their abilities on this occasion, instead of giving opinions and making **assertions**, will

condescend to prove and demonstrate by a fair and regular discussion. It gives me pain to hear gentlemen continually **distorting** the natural construction of language; for it is sufficient if any human production can stand a fair discussion. Before I proceed to make some additions to the reasons which have been **adduced** by my honorable friend over the way, I must take the liberty to make some observations on what was said by another **gentleman**.

He told us that this Constitution ought to be rejected because it endangered the public liberty, in his opinion, in many instances. Give me leave to make answer to that **observation**. Let the dangers which this system is supposed to be **replete with** be clearly pointed out. If any dangerous and unnecessary powers be given to the general legislature, let them be plainly demonstrated; and let us not rest satisfied with general assertions of danger, without examination. If powers be necessary, apparent danger is not a sufficient reason against **conceding** them. He has suggested that **licentiousness** has seldom produced the loss of liberty, but that the tyranny of rulers has almost always affected it. Since the general civilization of mankind I believe there are more instances of the **abridgment** of the freedom of the people by gradual and silent encroachments of those in power than by violent and sudden **usurpations**; but, on a **candid** examination of history, we shall find that turbulence, violence, and abuse of power, by the majority **trampling on** the rights of the minority, have produced **factions** and commotions which, in republics, have more frequently than any other cause, produced despotism. If we go over the whole history of ancient and modern republics we shall find their destruction to have generally resulted from those causes. If we consider the peculiar situation of the United States, and what are the sources of that diversity of sentiment which **pervades** its inhabitants, we shall find great danger to fear that the same causes may terminate here in the same fatal effects which they produced in those republics. This danger ought to be wisely guarded against...

I must confess I have not been able to find his usual **consistency** in the gentleman's argument on this occasion. He informs us that the people of the country are at perfect repose; that is every man enjoys the fruits of his labor peaceably and securely, and that everything is in perfect **tranquility** and safety. I wish sincerely that this were true. If this be their happy situation, why has every state acknowledged the contrary? Why were deputies from all the states sent to the general convention? Why have complaints of national and individual **distresses**

---

condescend: kind enough
distort: change the natural order of things
adduce: proved with evidence
gentleman: (here) Patrick Henry

observation: opinion; viewpoint
replete with: fill up with; full of

concede: admit; allow; grant
licentiousness: selfish and wicked desire
abridgment: cut to make it short
usurpation: revolt; rebellion
candid: sincere; honest
trample on: oppress
faction: small group of interests

pervade: spread widely over

consistency: logic agreement of ideas from the beginning to the end
tranquility: peacefulness

distress: anxiety; misery; grief

been echoed and reechoed throughout the continent? Why has our general government been so shameful disgraced and our Constitution violated? Wherefore have laws been made to authorize a change, and wherefore are we now assembled here? A federal government is formed for the protection of its individual members. Ours has attacked itself with **impunity**. Its authority has been disobeyed and despised.

I think I perceive a **glaring** inconsistency in another of his arguments. He complains of this Constitution because it requires the consent of at least three-fourths of the states to introduce **amendments** which shall be necessary for the happiness of the people... In the first case, he asserts that a majority ought to have the power of altering the government when found to be inadequate to the security of public happiness. In the last case, he affirms that even three-fourths of the community have not a right to alter a government which experience has proved to be **subversive** of national **felicity**! Nay, that the most necessary and urgent alterations cannot be made without the absolute unanimity of all the states! Does not the thirteenth article of the Confederation expressly require that no alteration shall be made without the unanimous consent of all the states? Should anything in theory be more **perniciously improvident** and injudicious than this submission of the will of the majority to the most trifling minority? Have not experience and practice actually manifested this theoretical inconvenience to be extremely **impolitic**?...

Give me leave to say something of the nature of the government and to show that it is safe and just to **vest** it with the power of taxation. There are a number of opinions, but the principal question is whether it be a federal or a consolidated government. In order to judge properly of the question before us, we must consider it **minutely** in its principal parts. I conceive myself that it is of a mixed nature; it is in a manner unprecedented; we cannot find one express example in the experience of the world. It stands by itself. In some respects it is a government of a federal nature; in others, it is of a consolidated nature. Even if we attend to the manner in which the Constitution is investigated, **ratified**, and make the act of the people of America, I can say, notwithstanding what the honorable gentleman has **alleged**, that this government is not completely consolidated, nor is it entirely federal. Who are parties to it? The people-but not the people as composing one great body, but the people as composing thirteen **sovereignties**. Were it, as the gentleman asserts, a consolidated government, the assent of a majority of the people would be sufficient for its establishment; and, as a majority have adopted it already, the remaining states would be bound by the act of the majority, even if they unanimously rejected it. Were it such a government as is suggested it would be now binding on the people of this state without their having had the privilege of **deliberating** on it. But, sir, no state is bound by it, as it is, without its own consent. Should all the states adopt it, it will be then a government established by the thirteen states of America, not through the intervention of the legislatures, but by the people at large. In this particular respect the **distinction** between the existing and the proposed governments is very material. The existing system has been derived from the dependent **derivative** authority of the legislatures of the states; whereas, this is derived from the superior power of the people....

I wish this government may answer the expectation of its friends and **foil** and apprehension of its enemies. I hope the patriotism of the people will continue and be a sufficient guard to their liberties. I believe its tendency will be that the state governments will **counteract** the general interest and ultimately **prevail**. The number of the representative is yet sufficient for our safety and will gradually increase; and if we consider their different sources of information, the number will not appear too small.

deliberate on: *willingly intend to do*

distinction: *marked difference*
derivative: *obtained or acquired from other sources*
foil: *make it worse*
counteract: *respond; act as opposition*
prevail: *prove superior; succeed*

■ 重点述评与提示

1. In this pursuit, we ought not to address our arguments to the feelings and passions but to those understandings and judgments which were selected by the people of this country, to decide this great question by a calm and rational investigation.

    麦迪逊的理性风格,不是以夸张的修辞,激昂的演讲见长,而是以冷峻的理性,客观具体的分析取胜。其中用词清正,句式整一,与亨利的程式化典雅和语义拖延形成了鲜明的对照。

2. If powers be necessary, apparent danger is not asufficient reason against conceding them.

    这里表面上是对亨利有关权力导致专制这一论断的反驳,实质上是在坚持权力制约人类欲望的必要。这也是麦迪逊思想与汉弥尔顿相通的地方。

3. ... but, on a candid examination of history, we shall find that turbulence, violence, and abuse of power, by the majority trampling on the rights of the minority, have produced factions and commotions which, in republics, have more frequently than any other cause, produced despotism.

麦迪逊对历史上的联盟政体颇有研究,在辩论中显示出极大的优势:历史上所谓的民主大多数情况下是暴民政治,是多数的暴政(tyranny of majority),其结果是帮派纷争,社会动荡,最终导致专制极权。这是针对亨利提倡州权和个人自由的有力反驳,传达出来的是霍布斯利维坦式的权力意识。

4. If this be their happy situation, why has every state acknowledged the contrary?

麦迪逊在此问之后连珠炮般地连发五问,用事实充分揭示了亨利对形势的误判,进而说明了建立实体联邦政府以保护每个公民权利的必要性和紧迫性。巧用修辞设问排比,在辩论中可产生类似拳击中组合拳的功效。

5. Should anything in theory be more perniciously improvident and injudicious than this submission of the will of the majority to the most trifling minority?

少数服从多数,以决定国家、公共和集体事务是共和政体中的一项重要原则。亨利否定此原则,要求各州全体一致通过才能批准宪法,这是倒退回各州互不相让,一盘散沙的邦联国会。注意麦迪逊用词的精当和连贯:improvident 的语义集"愚蠢"和"短视"为一体,导致判断和决策的 injudicious (不明智),这对民主共和政体是 pernicious (极为危险)的。

6. I conceive myself that it is of a mixed nature; it is in amanner unprecedented; we cannot find one express example in the experience of the world. It stands by itself.

麦迪逊在此说明,比起欧洲历史上的一些联盟政体,美国宪法显示出独特的优势,是一场政治的实验。依此建立的联邦政府既是由拥有主权,独立自治的各州组成的联邦体系,同时又是具有统一征税等具体实权的实体权力机构,后文也表明,联邦政府的权力来源于各州人民,代表着全体人民的利益和福祉。

7. In this particular respect the distinction between the existing and the proposed governments is very material. The existing system has been derived from the dependent derivative authority of the legislatures of the states; whereas, this is derived from the superior power of the people....

区分这一点十分地重要,为后来的联邦司法解释提供法理基础:邦联国会产生于各州议会的参与,而联邦政府却享有各州总体的人民主权。马歇尔大法官在1819年马卡罗诉马里兰州案中发挥了此说,进一步明确了联邦人民主权大于州权,并拥有"隐含主权"的原则。

■ 思考及讨论题

1. What is the main idea of Madison's famed claim that "ambition must be made against ambition"?
2. How much do you understand James Madison as the "father of American Constitution"?
3. How shall we understand the idea that the general government of the United States is a mixture of federal system and consolidate government?
4. Discuss about Madison's speech style in contrast to that of Patrick Henry's.

■ 阅读书目

1. Morgan, Rober J. *James Madison on the Constitution and the Bill of Rights*. New York: Greenwood Press, 1988.
2. Samples, John. *James Madison and the Future of Limited Government*. Washington D. C.: Cato Institute, 2002.
3. Barlo, Jackson J. *The American Founding: Essays on the Formation of American Constitution*. New York: Greenwood Press, 1988.
4. Farrand, Max. *The Framing of the Constitution of the United States*. New Haven: Yale University Press, 1913.

第三章 ‖ 国家意识与民主法制建设

The name of American, whichbelongs to you in your national capacity, must always exalt the just pride of patriotism more than any appellation derived from local discrimination
　　　　　　　　　　　　　　　　　——George Washington

Democracy never lasts long. It soon wastes, exhausts and murders itself. There has never been a democracy yet that did not commit suicide.
　　　　　　　　　　　　　　　　　——John Adams

Though the will of the majority is in all cases to prevail..., the minority possess their equal rights, which equal law must protect, and to violate would be oppression.
　　　　　　　　　　　　　　　　　——Thomas Jefferson

Preview Questions

01/

To what extent does the American Constitution contribute to the shaping of American national identity?

02/

What are the significances of the War of 1812 in American political and economic history?

03/

What are the opposing views between Thomas Jefferson and John Adams?

04/

What were the main issues in the US foreign policy during the Adams's and Jefferson's administration?

第九讲

乔治·华盛顿（George Washington 1732—1799）（上）

■ 政治历史评述

乔治·华盛顿：独立战争的功臣，不情愿的美国总统

乔治·华盛顿1732年2月22日出生于弗吉尼亚州一个殷实的农场主家庭，少年接受过当地最基础的教育，当过土地测量员，通过婚姻继承了弗农山庄和大片的土地。他精于经营，锱铢必较，成为当地远近有名，颇具财力的农场主。华盛顿为人敦厚，处事沉稳，他视诚实正直，个人荣誉为生命之品格，颇有英国绅士气质。华盛顿的教育程度不算高。他初识拉丁文和基础数学运算，也读过一点英国文学。受当时绅士阶层价值观的熏陶，年幼的华盛顿善于骑射，向往军旅。20岁那年，华盛顿在军中谋得副官的职位，21岁就晋升少校军衔。

1753年英法北美战端即开，年轻气盛的华盛顿带领一队民军和一群印第安盟友一路北进，被法军团团围困在一个叫做尼塞西提的孤立据点。盟友印第安人见势不妙，一声唿哨做了鸟兽散。华盛顿苦守一天，自料不敌，率部向法军投降。法国人为了宣传的目的，让缴械后的华盛顿带队返回弗吉尼亚。华盛顿对此次战败屈辱倒还坦然，反称这是一次象征性的胜利。他在写给兄长的信中这样描述自己的战场感受："我听到子弹在耳边呼啸而过。想想看，我真觉得那声音中带有些许美妙的乐感。"那姿态颇有几分胜败乃兵家常事的大将风度。世事晦暗，焉知非福。据说英王乔治三世在伦敦听到华盛顿上述感言后，不无揶揄地说："这个华盛顿，他如果耳边听到的子弹飞得多了，也就不会说那是音乐了。"于是华盛顿的大名在英国朝野无人不知。

话说回来，也许正是这血气方刚，不论输赢的闯劲和经历锻造了华盛顿在21年后独立战争的逆境中屡败屡战，百折不挠的精神。1775年5月的一天，华盛顿戎装出席在费城第二届大陆会议上，显然是志在军权。会上经过约翰·亚当斯的力荐提名和代表们的一致响应，华盛顿被任命为美国大陆军总司令。7月3日，华盛顿来到波士顿城外，面对着各州组织起来的近15000名民兵，宣布正式行使大陆军总司令之职，这一天正好是21年前他在北方领地战败，向法国军队投降的日子。波士顿城内的英军约7000人，指挥官盖奇将军是华盛顿20年前的老长官。那时华盛顿不过是个中级军官，在盖奇手下做一名普通参谋。此时两军对垒，华盛顿除局部的兵力超过英军而外，并不占优势。相反，大陆军由各地组织起来的民兵拼凑而成，军纪废弛，缺乏训练，毫无正规作战经验。

军中几乎没有建立像样的指挥系统,南北将领各行其是,缺乏统一调度,每次战役都没有预备队和统一的炮火支援。更糟糕的是,后勤得不到保障;军中缺少帐篷,军毯和统一的军服,更谈不上药品,给养和弹药补充,就连军饷也成了问题。每次战斗遇挫,士兵成群结队开小差。在此状况下,华盛顿以即将签署的《独立宣言》鼓舞士气。仍以其优势兵力围困波士顿,凭借爱将亨利·诺克斯将军历尽艰辛,在雪地里从几十英里以外拖运过来的43门大炮轰击波士顿,迫使英军弃城撤退。但好景不长,英军得到兵力增援,进攻纽约,直逼费城。华盛顿的大陆军节节败退,一直被英军撑过特拉华河,所剩几千残兵在新泽西的雪地里忍饥挨饿,怨声载道。大陆军士气低落,逃兵成群,部队几近解散。但作为军中统帅,华盛顿并未丧失信心,他重整旗鼓,亲率哀兵,在圣诞节之夜越过冰封的特拉华河,向河对岸的2000余英军发动突袭。正在轻歌曼舞,酒酣梦沉的英军德国雇佣兵来不及组织像样的抵抗,大部做了俘虏。华盛顿取得空前胜利,在军中威信大增,于是乘胜一鼓作气,重创英军于普林斯顿。此关键两战稳住了大陆军的阵脚,双方处于胶着状态,这正合了华盛顿坚持持久战和游击战的心意。经过数年的艰苦转战,历尽挫败的悲哀的胜利的喜悦,华盛顿终于抓住战机,在约克顿赢得了最后的胜利。从此,华盛顿的声名更是日照中天,无与伦比。当时马里兰州的一家报纸模仿莎士比亚赞颂由法国凯旋的英王亨利五世的笔法这样赞美凯旋的战神华盛顿:

你曾想想,欢呼声浪冲破门窗,	You would thought the very windows spoke,
门框间人们不分长幼争先恐后,	So many greedy looks of young and old
投出急切的目光争睹他的仪容;	Through casements darted their desiring eyes
全城涂彩的街墙同声发出呼喊:	Upon his visage; and that all the walls,
上帝保佑赐福予你啊,华盛顿!	With painted imagery, had said at once,
	God save thee, GEORGE WASHINGTON!

这就是美国人心目中为美国的独立和自由赢得战争的传奇英雄。在当时万众仿佛获得新生,向往独立政体的年代,华盛顿赫赫的声名把他推到国家权力的顶峰。当制宪的辩论落幕,宪法批准已成定局之后,华盛顿毫无悬念地被一致推选为第一届美国总统。

其实,华盛顿并非神人,他对此深有自知之明:中外历史上,大凡社会动荡,官逼民反,总有人登高一呼,众人揭竿而起。英雄辈出之中,偶尔也会出现才学品德双全,文韬武略皆备之士,以文治武功之大业名留青史,但大多数情况下也都是文才运筹帷幄,将军决胜千里之外。美国独立和早期宪政的国父们大多也不出此例:革命舆论,独立宣言,制宪文章,皆出自亚当斯、杰斐逊、麦迪逊等旷世文才,而华盛顿将军一生戎马,

掌权治国未必是他的强项。因此,在 1783 巴黎和约签定,英国正式承认美国独立之后,华盛顿即发表声明,辞去大陆军总司令之职,向大陆会议交回委任状,迫不及待地解甲归田,返回弗农山庄颐养天年,同时声明今后不再谋求任何公职。可想而知,当得知自己不可避免地将赴任总统之职,华盛顿心里充满矛盾和感慨,更多的是不情愿。他一生对个人的名誉视为生命,就连当年大陆会议任命他为大陆军总司令,他都对此任职可能引起他的名誉损失忧心忡忡,曾悄悄对身边的帕特里克·亨利说:"我指挥美国大陆军之日,即是我注定失败之时和名誉扫地之日。"此时的他,凭借 8 年坚韧的信心和命运的眷顾,历尽艰难打赢了战争,却不料随着这份新的荣誉到来的却是新的,更大的责任的挑战。

1789 年 4 月,身居弗农山庄的华盛顿知道自己就任美国第一届总统也是众望所归,不可推卸,正等待着国会的最后通知。他对身边的心腹爱将亨利·诺克斯说道:"此去政府任职,心里感到就好像一名罪犯赶赴刑场。我对此是何等的不情愿:此生已近黄昏,为公操劳大半生,但此时仍须离开这温馨宁静的农庄,去面对大海般无穷无尽的困难。我对政治,既无能无策,又无心思,何以掌舵领航!我深知,此次出海我肩负着国民的重托和我自己的荣誉。但是结果如何,唯有天知!"无奈之情,溢于言表。

华盛顿此番无奈的心境和归隐之愿在公开正式的政治场合,也表达得淋漓尽致。

1789 年 4 月 30 日,在首届总统就职演说中,华盛顿面对着国会议员和众多的听众,身着国产礼服,配饰将军佩剑,在礼炮和鸣枪声中,用 18 世纪典型的高雅委婉,回旋着清教布道调的文体,一语三返,曲折回荡,反复地表达了这种矛盾的心情,其中每每想起田园晚年生活,是那么的深情向往,提到国民的期待和国家的召唤,又显得那么的义不容辞,想到总统责任的重大,又是那么的惶恐谦卑。这些都是他两难心情的真实表白。华盛顿任两届总统,期间多为外交内务所困,心力交瘁。直至 1797 年第二届总统任期满,华盛顿才如释重负,他那归田园居,颐养天年的夙愿终得实现,但是,此时的他已体弱多病,垂垂老矣,生命留给他的时间也只有短短的三年。1799 年 12 月 12 日,一个风雪交加的夜晚,华盛顿在弗农山庄溘然长逝,年仅 68 岁。

First Presidential Inaugural Address

George Washington

Fellow-Citizens of the Senate and of the House of Representatives,

Among the **vicissitudes** incident to life no event could have filled me with greater anxieties than that of which the notification was **transmitted** by your order, and received on the 14th day of the present month. On the one hand, I was summoned by my Country, whose voice I can never hear but with **veneration** and love, from a **retreat** which I had chosen with the fondest **predilection**, and, in my flattering hopes, with an **immutable** decision, as the **asylum** of my declining years—a retreat which was rendered every day more necessary as well as more dear to me by the addition of habit to **inclination**, and of frequent interruptions in my health to the gradual waste committed on it by time. On the other hand, the magnitude and difficulty of the trust to which the voice of my country called me, being sufficient to awaken in the wisest and most experienced of her citizens a distrustful **scrutiny** into his qualifications, could not but overwhelm with **despondence** one who (inheriting inferior **endowments** from nature and unpracticed in the duties of civil administration) ought to be peculiarly conscious of his own deficiencies. In this conflict of emotions all I dare **aver** is that it has been my faithful study to collect my duty from a just appreciation of every circumstance by which it might be affected. All I dare hope is that if, in executing this task, I have been too much **swayed** by a grateful remembrance of former instances, or by an affectionate sensibility to this **transcendent** proof of the confidence of my fellow citizens, and have thence too little consulted my incapacity as well as **disinclination** for the weighty and untried cares before me, my error will be **palliated** by the motives which mislead me, and its consequences be judged by my country with some share of the **partiality** in which they originated...

No people can be bound to acknowledge and **adore** the **Invisible Hand** which conducts the affairs of men more than those of the United States. Every step by which they have advanced to the character of an independent nation seems to have been distinguished by some token of providential agency; and in the important revolution just accomplished in the system of their united government the tranquil **deliberations** and voluntary consent of so many distinct communities from which the event has resulted can not be compared with the means by which most governments have been established without some return of **pious** gratitude, along with an humble anticipation of the future blessings which the past seem to **presage**. These reflections, arising out of the present crisis, have forced themselves too strongly on my mind to be suppressed. You will join with me, I trust, in thinking that there are none under the influence of which the **proceedings** of a new and free government can more auspiciously commence.

By the article establishing the executive department it is made the duty of the President "to recommend to your consideration such measures as he shall judge necessary and **expedient**." The circumstances under which I now meet you will **acquit** me from entering into that subject further than to refer to the great constitutional charter under which you are assembled, and which, in defining your powers, designates the objects to which your attention is to be given. It will be more consistent with those circumstances, and far more **congenial** with the feelings which **actuate** me, to substitute, in place of a recommendation of particular measures, the **tribute** that is due to the talents, the **rectitude**, and the patriotism which adorn the characters selected to devise and adopt them. In these honorable qualifications I behold the surest **pledges** that as on one side no local prejudices or attachments, no separate views nor party **animosities**, will misdirect the comprehensive and equal eye which ought to watch over this great assemblage of communities and interests, so, on another, that the foundation of our national policy will be laid in the pure and immutable principles of private morality, and the **preeminence** of free government be exemplified by all the attributes which can win the affections of its citizens and command the respect of the world. I **dwell on** this prospect with every satisfaction which an ardent love for my country can inspire, since there is no truth more thoroughly established than that there exists in the **economy** and course of nature an indissoluble union between virtue and happiness; between duty and advantage; between the genuine **maxims** of an honest and magnanimous policy and the solid rewards of public prosperity and **felicity**; since we ought to be no less persuaded that the **propitious** smiles of Heaven can never be expected on a nation that disregards the eternal rules of order and right which Heaven itself has **ordained**;

deliberation: wise thoughts

pious: faithful
presage: good signs for some future events

proceeding: scheduled operation

expedient: urgent, emergent
acquit: make it not as the duty of

congenial: fit; accord
actuate: activate
tribute: praise
rectitude: virtue; uprightness
pledge: swear; vow
animosity: hatred; hard feeling

preeminence: greatness; outstanding characters
dwell on: trust in; look forward to
economy: order; good arrangement
maxim: principle
felicity: happiness
propitious: favorable
ordain: order (as laws)

	and since the preservation of the sacred fire of liberty and the destiny of the republican model of government are justly considered, perhaps, as deeply, as finally, **staked on** the experiment entrusted to the hands of the American people.
stake on: depend on; supported by	
	Besides the ordinary objects submitted to your care, it will remain with your judgment to decide how far an exercise of the occasional power delegated by the fifth article of the Constitution is rendered expedient at the present **juncture** by the nature of objections which have been urged against the system, or by the degree of **inquietude** which has given birth to them. Instead of undertaking particular recommendations on this subject, in which I could be guided by no lights derived from official opportunities, I shall again give way to my entire confidence in your **discernment** and pursuit of the public good; for I assure myself that **whilst** you carefully avoid every alteration which might endanger the benefits of an united and effective government, or which ought to await the future lessons of experience, a **reverence** for the characteristic rights of freemen and a regard for the public harmony will sufficiently influence your deliberations on the question how far the former can be **impregnably fortified** or the latter be safely and advantageously promoted....
juncture: critical moment; **inquietude**: uneasiness; disturbance **discernment**: insight; ability to tell the difference of; **whilst**: while **reverence**: great respect; veneration **impregnably**: firmly; **fortify**: strengthen; reinforce **sentiment**: thought **resort**: seek for the help of **supplication**: asking for	
	Having thus imparted to you my **sentiments** as they have been awakened by the occasion which brings us together, I shall take my present leave; but not without **resorting** once more to the benign Parent of the Human Race in humble **supplication** that, since He has been pleased to favor the American people with opportunities for deliberating in perfect tranquility, and **dispositions** for deciding with unparalleled unanimity on a form of government for the security of their union and the advancement of their happiness, so His divine blessing may be equally **conspicuous** in the enlarged views, the temperate consultations, and the wise measures on which the success of this Government must depend.
disposition: arrangement **conspicuous**: clear; obvious	

■ 重点述评与提示

1. Among the vicissitudes incident to life no event could have filled me with greater anxieties than that of which the notification was transmitted by your order, and received on the 14th day of the present month.

开篇就用否定强调加比较级的句式，用以突出一种严肃庄重的语气。anxiety 一词为本段主题词,表达了因为要听从国家使命的召唤而不能归园田居的无奈。句中用词庄重典雅,属18世纪典型的公文体。整个句子对本段下文中以重叠从句表达的矛盾心情做出准确的概括。

2. In this conflict of emotions all I dare aver is that it has been my faithful study to collect my duty from a just appreciation of every circumstance by which it might be affected.

  这不是客套话。作为第一届总统,华盛顿面临的是组建一个概无先例可参照的联邦政府行政当局。既然是勉为其难,本段下文的话语自然也就多有谦辞。

3. No people can be bound to acknowledge and adore the Invisible Hand which conducts the affairs of men more than those of the United States.

  华盛顿在此为以后的美国总统就职演说开了一个先例,那就是必定要表达"天佑美国"的观念。这一信念追溯到清教徒上帝契约的"山巅之城"(City on the Hill),经过形成于19世纪中叶大规模西进扩张过程中的"天定命运观"(Manifest Destiny)的强化,形成当今美国民主政体的优越感(或世界霸权)。

4. ...on one side no local prejudices or attachments, no separate views nor party animosities... so, on another, that the foundation of our national policy will be laid in the pure and immutable principles of private morality...

  基于地缘政治和利益形成的党派纷争是华盛顿一直担心却在其总统任内不断出现的现象。这是因为他尚未认识在民主政治中政党对个人权欲的钳制作用,而把联邦政府的清廉和高效建立在参与执政者的个人道德操行的基础上。

5. ...since the preservation of the sacred fire of liberty and the destiny of the republican model of government are justly considered, perhaps, as deeply, as finally, staked on the experiment entrusted to the hands of the American people.

  这既是对美国独立革命和宪政建国的夸耀,又是对"美国例外论"的原初宣扬。此后的美国总统无不在其演说中重复着这一观念:世界的和平和美好都取决于美国民主政体的实验和传播。近180年后肯尼迪总统在其就职演讲中说"我们是美国第一场革命的后代……(神圣的)火炬已经传递给了新一代的美国人。"可见政治的互文。

6. ... a reverence for the characteristic rights of freemen and a regard for the public harmony will sufficiently influence your deliberations on the question how far the former can be impregnably fortified or the latter be safely and advantageously promoted....

  既要保持国家的稳定,又要保证个人的自由和权利,这是华盛顿面临的重大问题。独立后的美国社会经济不振，金融混乱，税赋沉重，物价飞涨，频频引发动乱。此时华盛顿就职总统，1786 年 8 月历经半年的谢斯起义仍历历在目，提请国会注意解决或平衡这一问题，是理所当然的事。

■ 思考及讨论题

1. Explain why George Washington was the first and only president of the United States to be elected unanimously by the electoral college?
2. What were the main problems facing George Washington as the president of the country?
3. Why was Washington so reluctant to be the president of the United States?
4. From the stately style of Washington's first inaugural speech, what do we learn about the man?

■ 阅读书目

1. Towne, Edward, C. B. A. *Life and Time of Washington*. New York: Belcher Publishing Co, 1903.
2. Wrong, George M. *George Washington and His Comrade in Arm: A Chronicle of the War of Independence*. New Haven: Yale University Press, 1921.
3. Wahlke, John C. *The Cause of American Revolution*. Boston: D. D. Heath, 1962.
4. Henriques, Peter R. "An Imperfect God: George Washington, His Slaves and the Creation of America" in *The Virginia Magazine of History and Biography*, October, 2003.

第十讲

乔治·华盛顿（George Washington 1732—1799）（下）

■ 政治历史评述

乔治·华盛顿：个人崇拜的牺牲品，孤立主义的始作俑者

乔治·华盛顿的生平在上一讲中有过概述，此讲着重其对美国政治历史的贡献和意义。

华盛顿是美国18世纪独立建国初期美国国家意识萌芽状态下英雄崇拜意识的产物，是人们心中传奇的将军英雄。那时，美国人的个人崇拜意识丝毫不比东方国家的差。这也难怪，1786年，八年艰苦卓绝的独立战争终于以胜利告终，美国人民在欢庆胜利的喜悦之中把目光投向心中的英雄华盛顿。他们看到的是一位战神，一位胜利之神。于是，英雄偶像崇拜的社会意识开始聚敛，在独立爱国情结的驱动下不断衍生，变形，叠加，形成造神意识形态，在社会历史中留下永恒的印记。华盛顿的画像，书信集，日记集，回忆录层出不穷，当时有关华盛顿的专文，小册子，演说辞，赞美诗比比皆是。这一切在现实基础的舞台上造就出一位头顶各种耀眼光环的传奇人物。有的文人宣称，如果说英国对人类的最大贡献是莎士比亚，那么美国对世界的贡献就是华盛顿。文化的造神意识甚至延伸到家庭伦理意识中。有人甚至宣布：华盛顿之所以没有自己嫡出的后代，就是因为上帝显灵，指派他做美国人民的父亲。宗教话语也加入这场夸张的赞美诗会，以一种既神秘又权威的语气把华盛顿塑造成人人顶礼膜拜的半神。1783年耶鲁的一位牧师在教堂里以典型的布道腔调宣布："您（华盛顿）的名声散发着芬芳，远胜过阿拉伯的香料；聚神聆听的天使将捕获到您名声的缕缕暗香，广洒布施于苍穹，使这广袤的天宇洋溢着您的香泽。"在宗教的圣坛上高声赞美一位政治和军事人物，几乎与万能的上帝同享权力和尊严，这在美国历史上绝无仅有的。今天看来，坐落在美国首府中心，高达555英尺的华盛顿纪念碑高耸入云，是英雄崇拜的时代象征，它纪念的是一位半神半人的救星。尽管当今有些所谓"修正派"历史学家开始对华盛顿颇有微词，但是这却掩盖不了这样的事实：华盛顿的大名已经永久地铭刻在美国的政治文化中。

其实，华盛顿盛名之下，却有自知：将军马背上打下江山，未必有下马治国的方策和能力，但他必须勉为其难，尽管这意味着他所看重的名誉受到损害。华盛顿8年的任期也是新生美国的内外交困的多事之秋：内政方面，战后国库空虚，物价飞涨，国债外债累累，老兵难以妥善安置，发动了有名的谢斯起义。此外，制定宪法引起党争不断，内阁里矛盾重重，财长汉弥尔顿和杰斐逊国务卿的矛盾不断激化，联邦党人和共和党人势不两立。外交方面,英国人心有不甘,欧洲列强对其北美利益仍虎视眈眈,不断制造边界事端。为了避免与英国再次的全面战争,华盛顿密派特使杰伊与英国谈判,签订的"杰伊"条约,却引起到了全国的抗议高潮,谴责联邦政府丧权辱国。华盛顿本人也声望大跌,示威人群举着华盛顿被送上绞架的漫画,高呼口号,甚至弗吉尼亚州的大陆军退役老兵都呼喊"华盛顿将军速速就死。"这似乎就是历史嘲弄。华盛顿注定只能在政治的漩涡中忍受八年的煎熬。他在第二任总统就职演说称自己是"主事治安官"(Chief Magistrate)而不是通称的"最高行政长官"(Chief Executive),宣称如果他个人任内的行为有违宪法条款,将甘愿接受法律和人民的制裁云云,几句话匆匆带过,草草了事。全篇演说仅135字,足见其心力交瘁,无可奈何之心境。直至1796年第二届总统任期满,华盛顿将军才如释重负,终于可以回归自我,以建国长者心态,谆谆告诫国民,认真总结历史经验,展望共和国的未来。

华盛顿1796年9月发表向全国人民告别演说。此文从未公开当众宣讲,而是在他卸任前夕发表在一家报纸上并迅速得以转载。当时欧洲的媒体立即做出反应,称这是"一位父亲留给子女最丰富的遗产。"这篇长篇"演讲"此后一个近两个世纪一直被公认是阐明美国立国的政治原则的开山之作,与林肯的第二次就职演说一起分别被奉为美国政治圣经的旧约和新约。华盛顿在这篇演说中以明晰简洁的语言,以长者之谆谆,语重心长地告诫美国人:美利坚国家的统一和团结是美国独立和自由的根本保证,是美国民富国强,长治久安的守护神,是每个美国人个人安全和生活幸福的源泉。每个美国人都应该摒弃党派之争和集团利益,捍卫国家的统一,防止任何分裂国家的可能的行为,甚至不惜为此付出生命的代价。华盛顿在两届总统任期内深感以汉弥尔顿为首的联邦党人和杰斐逊的民主共和党人的纷争给统一的联邦国家造成的危害。他由此认为,政党是联邦统一,安定团结的最危险的敌人,是少数野心家为

了私利或小团体利益不惜损害大众利益,颠覆国家的政治手段和谋略,应该永久地加以防范和限制。华盛顿在告别演说中提出了"外交中立和不结盟"的原则,此后一个世纪一直被奉为美国外交政策的基石,也是美国孤立主义的源头。华盛顿总结了任内八年美国在欧洲大国,特别是英法两国的势力范围之间持平衡,求生存的历史经验,认为美国和欧洲各国有着不同的利益需求,美国"外交行为的重要准则"就是尽可能地与欧洲各国建立贸易往来,但是尽量避免与之建立政治的联盟。因为,美国若卷入欧洲列强尔虞我诈,唯利是图的政治和宗教纷争,不仅将一无所获,而只会搅乱美国国内的和平和稳定,阻碍美国的发

展和繁荣。

综而观之，华盛顿一生为了美国的独立，自由和发展有两个八年的独特贡献。头八年独立战争的军事生涯为他赢得了他向往的荣誉，其中充满了艰辛和磨砺，也不乏胜利的满足和喜悦。后八年的政治经历却是一场不情愿的政治战争，其中充满了个人内心的挣扎和无奈，但客观上也为美国政治历史的进程奠定了基础，写下了重要的篇章。

历史就是这样的无情，个人的自由和选择在社会意识的惯性作用下显得那么的不足道，但正是历史的选择使得个人的存在和行为获得了永恒的意义。华盛顿虽未更多留下自己思想的记载，但他的生命和行为对美国人民却具有特殊的，永久的意义。

■ 演讲文（节选）

Presidential Farewell Address

George Washington

Friends and Fellow Citizens,

The period for a new election of a citizen to administer the executive government of the United States being not far distant, and the time actually arrived when your thoughts must be employed in designating the person who is to be **clothed with** that important trust...

The unity of government which **constitutes** you one people is also now near to you. It is justly so, for it is a main pillar in the **edifice** of your real independence, the support of your tranquility at home, your peace abroad, of your safety, of your prosperity, of that very liberty which you so highly prize.

But as it is easy to foresee that from different causes and from different quarters much pains will be taken, many **artifices** employed, to weaken in your minds the conviction of this truth, as this is the point in your political fortress against which the **batteries** of internal and external enemies will be most constantly and actively (though often **covertly** and **insidiously**) directed, it is of infinite moment that you should properly estimate the immense value of your national union to your collective and individual happiness; that you should cherish a cordial, habitual, and immovable attachment to it; accustoming yourselves to think and speak of it as the **Palladium** of your political safety and prosperity; watching for its preservation with

---

clothed with: empowered
constitute: group; make parts to the whole
edifice: huge building or structure

artifice: trick; scheme; plot
battery: gun; cannon; artillery
covertly: secretly
insidiously: dangerously in the future
Palladium: god of wisdom who provides protection

jealous anxiety; **discountenancing** whatever may suggest even a suspicion that it can in any event be abandoned, and **indignantly** frowning upon the first **dawning** of every attempt to alienate any portion of our country from the rest or to **enfeeble** the sacred ties which now link together the various parts.

The name of American, which belongs to you in your national capacity, must always **exalt** the just pride of patriotism more than any **appellation** derived from local discriminations. With slight shades of difference, you have the same religion, manners, habits, and political principles. You have in a common cause fought and triumphed together. The independence and liberty you possess are the work of joint **councils** and joint efforts, of common dangers, sufferings, and successes....

In **contemplating** the causes which may disturb our Union it occurs as matter of serious concern that any ground should have been furnished for characterizing the parties by geographical discriminations-Northern and Southern, Atlantic and Western-**whence designing** men may endeavor to excite a belief that there is a real difference of local interests and views. One of the expedients of party to acquire influence within particular districts is to **misrepresent** the opinions and aims of other districts. You cannot shield yourselves too much against the jealousies and **heartburnings** which spring from these misrepresentations; they tend to render alien to each other those who ought to be bound together by **fraternal** affection...

To the **efficacy** and permanency of your union a government for the whole is indispensable. No alliances, however strict, between the parts can be an adequate **substitute**. They must inevitably experience the **infractions** and interruptions which all alliances in all times have experienced. Sensible of this momentous truth, you have improved upon your first **essay** by the adoption of a Constitution of government better calculated than your former for an intimate union and for the **efficacious** management of your common concerns. This government, the off-spring of our own choice, uninfluenced and **unawed**, adopted upon full investigation and mature **deliberation**, completely free in its principles, in the distribution of its powers, uniting security with energy, and containing within itself a provision for its own amendment, has a just claim to your confidence and your support. Respect for its authority, **compliance** with its laws, **acquiescence** in its measures, are duties **enjoined** by the fundamental maxims of true liberty.

---

discountenance: stop; discourage
indignantly: angrily
dawning: appearance
enfeeble: weaken

exalt: reinforce by praising
appellation: name; title

council: discussion; negotiation
contemplate: think about; consider
whence: from where
designing: having evil purpose; tricky
misrepresent: misunderstand; express wrongly
heartburning: envy

fraternal: brotherly
efficacy: effect; achievement
substitute: replacement
infraction: law-breaking violation;
essay: try; experiment
efficacious: effective
unawed: not to be feared
deliberation: examination; consideration

compliance: obey
acquiescence: silently agree
enjoin: order; enforce

第十讲 | George Washington

The basis of our political systems is the right of the people to make and to alter their constitutions of government. But the constitution which at any time exists until changed by an explicit and authentic act of the whole people is sacredly **obligatory** upon all. The very idea of the power and the right of the people to establish government **presupposes** the duty of every individual to obey the established government...

I have already intimated to you the danger of parties in the state, with particular reference to the founding of them on geographical discriminations. Let me now take a more comprehensive view, and warn you in the most solemn manner against the **baneful** effects of the spirit of party generally....

The alternate domination of one faction over another, sharpened by the spirit of revenge natural to party **dissension**, which in different ages and countries has **perpetrated** the most horrid **enormities**, is itself a frightful despotism. But this leads at length to a more formal and permanent despotism. The disorders and miseries which result gradually incline the minds of men to seek security and **repose** in the absolute power of an individual, and sooner or later the chief of some **prevailing** faction, more able or more fortunate than his competitors, turns this disposition to the purposes of his own elevation on the ruins of public liberty....

Observe good faith and justice towards all Nations; cultivate peace and harmony with all. ... In the execution of such a plan, nothing is more essential, than that permanent, **inveterate antipathies** against particular Nations, and passionate attachments for others, should be excluded; and that, in place of them, just and **amicable** feelings towards all should be cultivated. The Nation, which indulges towards another a habitual hatred, or a habitual **fondness**, is in some degree a slave. It is a slave to its **animosity** or to its affection, either of which is sufficient to lead it **astray** from its duty and its interest. Antipathy in one nation against another **disposes** each more readily to offer insult and injury, to lay hold of slight causes of **umbrage**, and to be haughty and **intractable**, when accidental or trifling occasions of dispute occur. Hence frequent collisions, **obstinate**, **envenomed**, and bloody contests. ... So likewise, a passionate attachment of one Nation for another produces a variety of evils. Sympathy for the favorite Nation, facilitating the illusion of an imaginary common interest, in cases where no real common interest exists, and infusing into one the **enmities** of the other, betrays the former into a participation in the

---

obligatory: having obligation
presuppose: imply; include the meaning of

baneful: harmful

dissension: differences in opinion
perpetrate: commit (crime)
enormity: great sin and crime
repose: rest; relaxation
prevailing: advantageous; triumphant

inveterate: deeply rooted
antipathy: unpleasant feeling
amicable: friendly
fondness: love
animosity: hatred
astray: go away from the right path
dispose: tend to
umbrage: anger
intractable: stubborn
obstinate: uncontrollable
envenomed: poisoned

enmity: hatred; hostility

quarrels and wars of the latter, without adequate **inducement** or justification. It leads also to **concessions** to the favorite Nation of privileges denied to others, which is apt doubly to injure the Nation making the concessions; by unnecessarily parting with what ought to have been retained; and by exciting jealousy, ill-will, and a disposition to **retaliate**, in the parties from whom equal privileges are withheld....

Our detached and distant situation invites and enables us to pursue a different course. If we remain one people, under an efficient government, the period is not far off, when we may **defy** material injury from external annoyance; when we may take such an attitude as will cause the neutrality, we may at any time resolve upon, to be **scrupulously** respected; when **belligerent** nations, under the impossibility of making **acquisitions** upon us, will not lightly hazard the giving us **provocation**; when we may choose peace or war, as our interest, guided by justice, shall counsel....

The duty of holding a neutral conduct may be inferred, without anything more, from the obligation which justice and humanity impose on every nation, in cases in which it is free to act, to maintain **inviolate** the relations of peace and **amity** towards other nations....

inducement: motive, cause
concession: admit; agreement
retaliate: strike back; take revenge
defy: confront, challenge; face
scrupulous: careful, cautious
belligerent: warring, militant
acquisition: gain; benefit
provocation: challenge; invasion
inviolate: not to be harmed; defended
amity: friendship

■ 重点述评与提示

1. The unity of government... is a main pillar in the edifice of your real independence, the support of your tranquility at home, your peace abroad, of your safety, of your prosperity, of that very liberty which you so highly prize.

   联邦政府统一的权威是这篇演说中最重要的主题：没有联邦的统一，就没有美国真正的独立。这里用支撑大厦的立柱的明喻十分准确而形象，此后连用四个排比，奠定了美国意识形态的基石。

2. ...you should cherish a cordial, habitual, and immovable attachment to it; accustoming yourselves to think and speak of it as the Palladium of your political safety and prosperity...

   一反以往老派贵族的修辞文体，以谆谆教诲的语气，教导美国人民把联邦权威的统一视为美国国家安全和社会繁荣的保护神，将此观念化为日常生活行为的习惯，对当时美国现代国家观念和国民身份的形成起到重要作用。

3. One of the expedients of party to acquire influence within particular districts is to misrepresent the opinions and aims of other districts... they tend to render alien to each other those who ought to be bound together by fraternal affection...

　　为了联邦的统一，就必须抵制各州权地方主义的偏见。华盛顿指出了基于地方利益的党派互相歪曲对方观点所造成的危害，但他的着眼点还是旧的邦联条约所提倡的各州和平共处，兄弟情谊的理想。下文虽然号召各州遵循宪法，接受约束，但由于对政党在共和体制中的作用缺乏认识和估计，不免流于空泛。

4. The very idea of the power and the right of the people to establish government presupposes the duty of every individual to obey the established government...

　　这句颇有哲理的语句表达出来的是18世纪欧洲启蒙主义的政治哲学观念，其中有洛克的共和政府论，也有霍布斯利维坦国家主义的回声。肯定权力和人民主权也就意味着个人对政府应尽的服从义务。

5. The alternate domination of one faction over another, sharpened by the spirit of revenge natural to party dissension, which in different ages and countries has perpetrated the most horrid enormities, is itself a frightful despotism.

　　华盛顿在两届总统任内深受内阁党派纷争之苦，因而把政党一律视为褊狭自私的小集团。他看不到在宪政权利制衡的体制中政党做能扮演的积极作用。政党通过共和体制的选举轮流执政，这实际上也是政治权力相互制衡的表现，这是经过历史证明是可行的。

6. The Nation, which indulges towards another an habitual hatred, or an habitual fondness, is in some degree a slave. It is a slave to its animosity or to its affection, either of which is sufficient to lead it astray from its duty and its interest.

　　在欧洲列强争霸世界的战争中采取中立主义和不结盟政策，这是华盛顿这篇演说中的又一重大主题，构成美国外交政策的基石，也是美国孤立主义的源头。当时新生的美国尚弱，不足与英法等争雄，中立主义是现实的需要，同时也是美国独立革命意识的延伸。华盛顿在这里通过奴隶依附关系的比喻生动地表现了这一点。

7. The duty of holding a neutral conduct may be inferred, without anything more, from the obligation which justice and humanity impose on every nation,...

　　华盛顿在上文中分析了国家间结盟的危害和中立主义将给美国带来的好处后，得出这句结论式的概括，美国的中立和不结盟于是具有了普遍意义，成了每个国家主持正义和尊重人性的不二法门。这是典型的意识形态宣教。其实，美国的中立主义理想不久就遭受了一系列的挑战，在经历了1897年的美法危机和杰斐逊任内的禁运政策之后，终于在1812年的对英战争中基本破灭。

■ 思考及讨论题

1. Why this "Farewell Address" by Washington is said to be the "old testament" of American political bible?
2. What happened during Washington's administrations that made him so anxious about the unity of the nation and of the government?
3. Why Washington's warning against the evil of political parties was largely ignored by later politics?
4. To what extent is it true to say that Washington's proposition of neutrality was idealistic?

■ 阅读书目

1. Peterson, William D. *George Washington: Foundation of Presidential Leadership and Character*. Westport CT: Praeger, 2001.
2. Fenwick, Charles G. *American Neutrality, Tial and Failure*. New York: New York University Press.
3. Dawson, Mathew Q. *Partisanship and the Birth of America's Second Party 1796—1800 Stops the Wheel of Government*. Westport CT. Greenwood Press, 2000.

第十一讲
约翰·亚当斯(John Adams 1735—1826)

■ 政治历史评述

约翰·亚当斯:民主法治国家的倡导者

2008年5月,新上任的英国外交大臣大卫·米里邦德(David Miliband)在美国华盛顿的战略与国际研究中心(CSIS)面对一些研究外交政策的专家发表演说,声称美国的国父们一开始就向美国人民灌输了对民主观念深深的怀疑意识。米里邦德说,美国独立革命的急先锋,后来的第二届美国总统约翰·亚当斯在1814年这样写道:"民主从来都不能持久生存。民主产生后不久就会衰退,枯竭,最终自行消亡。从古到今,任何民主都注定逃脱不了自我扼杀的命运。"米里邦德认为这些话已经被历史证明是"赫然醒目地不真实",因为民主忍受了美国建国初期的阵痛,经历了美国内战的血腥考验,在废除奴隶制,保障民权和争取妇女选举权的历史进程中不断经历改革,保持了旺盛的生命力。20世纪,民主政治走向了整个拉丁美洲和非洲,而且在冷战结束后,民主进程推进到整个中欧和东欧。这里,我们暂且不论密里邦德这番话传达出来的冷战思维意识和意识形态偏见,就以对"民主"的理解来论,这种无视社会历史时空和语境的意识形态宣教必然导致对亚当斯民主观念的曲解,也就更无从理解他在美国建国初期力图建构法治国家的思想和实践。

其实,民主是一个历史范畴。在亚里士多德的政治学体系里,"民主"几乎就是"暴政"的同义词。西方现代意义的民主观念,即共和代议政府体制,代表选举制,言论和结社自由,是19世纪后半叶政治演进的产物。亚当斯时代的美国,大多数清教徒殖民者和欧洲各地携家带口迁徙而来的人们远离欧洲旧世界的政治权力,经济危机和社会传统,在美洲新大陆如获新生,他们梦想独立自主的崭新生活,视个人自由的权利和选择为生存的首要保障。他们对权力抱有本能的怀疑和否定。在他们的思想意识中,政治体制从来都是对个体自由的限制和威胁。宗教信仰的力量足以统筹社会意识,而政府的必要性只是在个体生存受到自然和社会的威胁时才有意义。当时,欧洲的启蒙思想对于大多数殖民者的生存现实相距甚远,洛克等人的政府契约论只在少数的文化精英中引起思想共鸣,现代意义上的共和政体离现实还相当遥远。在这样的政治文化中,一旦权力加强其统筹力度,即是对个人自由的压迫,必然引起群起而攻之。当时蜂起的抗议英国国会向北美殖民地征税的运动就集中地反映了这一社会思想现实。抗议者们呼喊着反抗议会独裁,要求代表权与民主,实际上正表达了反抗压迫,捍卫自由的心声。民主实际上是自由的同义词。在约翰·亚当斯看来,这样的民主如不加以启蒙理性和法制观念的引导,必然走向其反面,民主政治的愿望将堕落成暴民政治的现实,民主将在大众声嘶力竭的呼喊声中,在打家砸室,涂柏油粘羽毛,游街示众和绞刑的暴力中耗尽自己的能量。托马斯·杰斐逊曾对亚当斯说:"常青之自由之树须用暴君和爱国者的鲜血时常浇灌。"亚当斯闻之感到十分震惊,这一根本的政治分歧使得两人结束友谊,分道扬镳,此后成了长期的政治宿敌。而在亚当斯的政治生涯中,我们可以看

到,民主的观念是与实体联邦国家权力和建设法制公民社会的理想相生相伴,共同产生意义的。当然,这一观点的形成与亚当斯的家庭出身和教育,在哈佛的教育背景,学习政治法律和他作为知名律师在社会下层长期不知疲倦的工作分不开的。

约翰·亚当斯1735年5月生于新英格兰一个名叫布伦垂的乡村里。父母亲都是老实巴交的农民。少年约翰曾一度厌学,对书本和文字完全失去兴趣。他告诉父亲,他不想上大学,就想一辈子当个农民。老亚当斯不甘心,让儿子转学到一家附近的私立小学。校长马契对学生严格要求又循循善诱,亚当斯果然变得十分用功,成绩扶摇直上。第二年,15岁亚当斯的获哈佛奖学金。开学典礼辩论会上,亚当斯作为前三名辩手,正方回答了"民权政府是否对人类社会有绝对的必要性?"这一问题,这也是他往后一生都在回答的问题。在少年亚当斯的脑海里,政府的权威和律制对于人性从善的作用是不可替代的。政府依法治国以保证大多数人民的权利和幸福,这一原则贯穿了亚当斯一生的政治生涯。

1759年11月,亚当斯在当时著名的律师杰雷米尔·格雷德列(Jeremiah Gridley)的办公室参加律师资格考试,在连续几个小时的面试中,格雷德烈详细考问了亚当斯对政治历史和法律的阅读和理解,末了语重心长地劝诫他要"追求法律之学,不受法律之利。"此等警示直言对当时24岁的亚当斯自然是如雷贯耳,座右之铭。而且,对于法律的热爱一开始就与人类社会的命运紧密相连。亚当斯后来这样写道:"一个人如能深刻理解法律并游刃有余地运用法律,援助孤立无援的弱者,拒斥无法无天的傲慢者,为含冤者伸张正义,促进公民权利,申明并保障自由和德行,遏止并消灭暴政和罪孽,试问人间还有什么知识比法律更具有崇高的目标和伟大的品格?"在亚当斯往后的国家政治思考和践行中,这种"法律至上"的思想得以持续的表现,甚至被当时的民主派政敌斥为"君主权威意识"和国家专制主义的表现。

1765年3月,英国议会通过法案,向北美殖民地征收印花税。消息传来,立即引起暴力倾向的抗税浪潮。8月的一天,波士顿愤怒的抗议者向征税官的家投掷石块,此后又砸了总督哈钦森的家。亚当斯当时已是一名颇有名气的律师,他在支持抗税运动的同时目睹暴力升级也感到忧心忡忡,他在当地报纸上匿名无题发表了一篇与当时的革命口号相悖的政论文章。文中只字未提印花税,也没有号召武装起来进行暴力革命,而是

论述了殖民地人民的自由不是必须争取而得的理想,而是英国法律早已规定的一种不可剥夺的权利,也是祖祖辈辈美利坚人民奋斗而已经获得的权利。真正的危险在于殖民地人民对自己的自由权利的无知和失语。文章号召人们运用知识,独立思考,以领悟并保障自己与生俱来的神圣权利。

在亚当斯的律师生涯中,最能体现他法律不受政治约束的原则的,莫过于他为"波士顿惨案"中的英军官兵进行法庭辩护这一轰动一时的事件。1768年,英国议会向殖民地开始新一轮的征税,同时派英军进驻波士顿。市民与英军冲突时而发生,双方气氛紧张,一触即发。1770年3月5日,波士顿漫天大雪,市区积雪深达英尺。晚上9点,在海

关站岗的一名英军士兵遭到一群市民的围攻,不久引来几百人群的加入和围观。不久,8名英军赶来增援。愤怒的人群大声诅咒叫骂,向英军雨点般地投去雪球冰块,石头棍棒。混乱中一名英军受伤倒地,同时枪声骤响,人群惊恐逃散之后,雪地里留下了5具中枪死去的尸体和6名受伤者。波士顿自由之子领导人立即谴责英军的暴行,称之为"对无辜平民的血腥屠杀"。波士顿"自由之子"快马驰报各地,引起各殖民地舆论大哗,群情激昂。

事件发生第二天,保皇党派人请约翰·亚当斯为肇事英军官兵法庭辩护。亚当斯毫不推辞,立即接手这件冒天下之大不韪的工作。在他看来,在自由的国度,政治立场的取舍在法律面前没有任何意义,对任何人的审判都应由法律提供公正的判决。作为律师,他甘愿自己的公众名誉受损,甘愿承受社会舆论的巨大压力,决意本着献身法律,追求社会公正的精神,以事实证据为依据,履行自己神圣的法律职责。在法庭上,亚当斯明确指出:"事实是最顽强的东西,不论我们的希冀和意图如何,也不论我们情感的表现如何,都不能改变事实和证据。"根据亚当斯掌握的事实证据,认定英军士兵是在一伙暴民反复的暴力攻击,生命遭到严重威胁的情况下自卫过当而造成这场悲剧。自卫是每个自由人保护自己生命不受伤害的自然合法权利。英军官兵也是受害者,是英国议会在波士顿驻军这一错误的政策的受害者。陪审团经过反复合议,最终判决6名英军士兵无罪,2名有罪,刑当拇指烙印。当然,对于统治者来说,政治的利益高于一切,几年之后,亚当斯的名字赫然列在英国国王的黑名单上,成了必须立即绞死的头号叛国者。

10多年后,当亚当斯就职美国总统后,他倡导的法制民主国家的基本理念与杰斐逊倡导的小政府大民主的自由主义国家观念必然产生严重对立。在杰斐逊的民主共和党看来,亚当斯政府实行的完全是一条敌视人民,压制民主的专制主义的路线。他签署的《移民归化法》和《惩治叛乱法》是对个人自由选择,言论和结社自由等民主信条最赤裸裸的压制。但是,亚当斯的强硬国家权威主义也为美国的强大赢得了时间。他在任内坚持政治独立和外交中立,审慎处理了XYZ事件,化解了与法国的危机,避免了战争,同时也

建立了美国的海军优势,为 1812 年第二次对英战争积蓄了力量。但是,在当时个人主义和自由主义盛行的时代,他基于人性恶的斗争策略多少显得有些独断专行;他把希望建立在少数精英领袖的行政能力和道德品质上的法制国家理念显得有些不合时宜;他虽然大力提倡对年轻的一代和社会底层人群进行法制教育,但在当时普遍彰显个人自由和权利的社会意识环境中,这样的呼吁却带有更多的理想主义色彩。因此,亚当斯虽竭尽全力,却未能连任,于 1800 年被杰斐逊的民主共和党赶下了政治历史舞台,成了夹在两任总统华盛顿和杰斐逊之间的"被遗忘的美国总统"。

亚当斯生性外向,能言善辩,得意时喜形于色,失意时怒发冲冠,阐述政治立场鞭辟入里,言之凿凿;情寄家书柔肠百回,多情浪漫,全然是性情中人的形象,与华盛顿的老谋深算,汉弥尔顿的刚愎自用,杰斐逊的独往独行和麦迪逊的书生意气形成鲜明的对照。然而,政治对个性的制约作用是巨大的。这表现在亚当斯的总统就职演说中。

亚当斯有很高的文字修辞能力。他在哈佛接触的第一本书是罗马修辞演说家西塞罗的《修辞术》。他对这本书爱不释手,诵读不倦。因其口才出众,在独立战争期间被派遣出使法国和荷兰,战后又到英国办外交,没有参加制宪会议。1796 年回国与杰斐逊竞选总统险胜,成为第二届美国总统。在其就职演说中,亚当斯表现得异常地谨慎小心,避免使用他一贯倡导的法制治国理念。他既没有华盛顿的威望,有没有杰斐逊撰写《独立宣言》的声名,长期在国外的经历也使得许多听众心存疑虑。他必须阐明自己对宪法的了解和态度,甚至必须表白自己不是倾向贵族政治的"君主派"。因此,亚当斯的就职演说以一种十分庄重的语体,表明自己的爱国情怀和政治能力,其中叙述美国革命和建国的艰辛,颂扬美国人民坚忍不拔的精神,赞美宪法的伟大。这些都为后来的就职演说设立了套路,成了美国政治神话和身份的最初内容。在明确阐明本届政府的施政纲领时,亚当斯还特意写出了一句包含 724 个字,重复从句结构的长句子,以表明自己的政治行政能力。整篇演说试图多用稳定平衡的长句子,排比,重复,面面俱到地让听众相信,本届政府依据宪法,包容全局,为人民谋利。这就是作为政治家的亚当斯必须采用的意识形态策略。

■ 演讲文(节选)

Presidential Inaugural Address

John Adams

…
When it was first perceived, in early times, that no middle course for America remained between unlimited **submission** to a foreign

| **submission**: obedience |

legislature and a total independence of its **claims**, men of reflection were less **apprehensive** of danger from the **formidable** power of fleets and armies they must determine to resist than from those contests and dissensions which would certainly arise concerning the forms of government to be **instituted** over the whole and over the parts of this extensive country. Relying, however, on the purity of their intentions, the justice of their cause, and the **integrity** and intelligence of the people, under an overruling Providence which had so signally protected this country from the first, the representatives of this nation, then consisting of little more than half its present number, not only broke to pieces the chains which were **forging** and the rod of iron that was lifted up, but frankly cut **asunder** the ties which had bound them, and launched into an ocean of uncertainty. ...

Negligence of its regulations, inattention to its recommendations, if not disobedience to its authority, not only in individuals but in States, soon appeared with their melancholy consequences—universal **languor**, jealousies and rivalries of States, decline of navigation and commerce, discouragement of necessary manufactures, universal fall in the value of lands and their produce, contempt of public and private faith, loss of consideration and credit with foreign nations, and at length in discontents, animosities, **combinations**, partial conventions, and **insurrection**, threatening some great national **calamity**.

In this dangerous crisis the people of America were not abandoned by their usual good sense, presence of mind, resolution, or integrity. Measures were pursued to **concert** a plan to form a more perfect union, establish justice, insure domestic tranquility, provide for the common defense, promote the general welfare, and secure the blessings of liberty. The public **disquisitions**, discussions, and deliberations issued in the present happy Constitution of Government.

Employed in the service of my country abroad during the whole course of these **transactions**, I first saw the Constitution of the United States in a foreign country. Irritated by no literary **altercation**, animated by no public debate, heated by no party animosity, I read it with great satisfaction, as the result of good heads **prompted** by good hearts, as an experiment better adapted to the genius, character, situation, and relations of this nation and country than any which had ever been proposed or suggested. In its general principles and great outlines it was conformable to such a system of government as I had ever most esteemed, and in some States, my own native **State** in particular, had contributed to establish. ...

---

claim: demands
apprehensive: worried
formidable: very strong; powerful
instituted: established

integrity: honesty; dignity; virtue

forge: made; mode manufacture; cast
asunder: into pieces

negligence: carelessness; indifference
languor: laziness; inactiveness

combination: league; faction organization
insurrection: rebellion; uprising
calamity: disaster
concert: negotiate; coordinate
disquisition: speech with a specified topic

transaction: event; incident; happening
altercation: quarrel, strife
prompt: motivate; urge; inspire

State: (here) the state of Massachusetts

Returning to the bosom of my country after a painful separation from it for ten years, I had the honor to be elected to a **station** under the new order of things, and I have repeatedly laid myself under the most serious obligations to support the Constitution. The operation of it has equaled the most **sanguine** expectations of its friends, and from an habitual attention to it, satisfaction in its administration, and delight in its effects upon the peace, order, prosperity, and happiness of the nation I have acquired an habitual attachment to it and veneration for it.

What other form of government, indeed, can so well deserve our esteem and love?

There may be little **solidity** in an ancient idea that **congregations** of men into cities and nations are the most pleasing objects in the sight of superior intelligences, but this is very certain, that to a **benevolent** human mind there can be no spectacle presented by any nation more pleasing, more noble, majestic, or **august**, than an assembly like that which has so often been seen in this and the other Chamber of Congress, of a Government in which the Executive authority, as well as that of all the branches of the Legislature, are exercised by citizens selected at regular periods by their neighbors to make and execute laws for the general good. Can anything essential, anything more than mere **ornament** and decoration, be added to this by **robes and diamonds**? Can authority be more amiable and respectable when it descends from accidents or institutions established in remote **antiquity** than when it springs fresh from the hearts and judgments of an honest and enlightened people? For it is the people only that are represented. It is their power and majesty that is reflected, and only for their good, in every **legitimate** government, under whatever form it may appear. The existence of such a government as ours for any length of time is a full proof of a general **dissemination** of knowledge and virtue throughout the whole body of the people. And what object or consideration more pleasing than this can be presented to the human mind? If national pride is ever justifiable or **excusable** it is when it springs, not from power or riches, grandeur or glory, but from conviction of national innocence, information, and benevolence.

In the midst of these pleasing ideas we should be unfaithful to ourselves if we should ever lose sight of the danger to our liberties if anything partial or **extraneous** should **infect** the purity of our free, fair, virtuous, and independent elections. If an election is to be determined by a majority of a single vote, and that can be **procured** by a party

---

station: position, (here) referring to his vice-presidency of the country
sanguine: warm; confident; optimistic

solidity: hardness; firmness; validity
congregation: crowd (of people)
benevolent: kind; warm-hearted; charitable
august: grand; magnificent

ornament: outward show of beauty
robes and diamonds: (here) the power of kings
antiquity: ancient times and places
legitimate: lawful

dissemination: transmission; circulation

excusable: explainable with good reasons

extraneous: unrelated;
infect: affect like disease
procure: obtain

artifice: cheat; trick; manipulation **suffrage**: the right to vote **menace**: threat **fraud**: cheating **intrigue**: trick **venality**: corruption **candid**: honest and just **lot**: luck	through **artifice** or corruption, the Government may be the choice of a party for its own ends, not of the nation for the national good. If that solitary **suffrage** can be obtained by foreign nations, by flattery or **menaces**, by **fraud** or violence, by terror, **intrigue**, or **venality**, the Government may not be the choice of the American people, but of foreign nations. It may be foreign nations who govern us, and not we, the people, who govern ourselves; and **candid** men will acknowledge that in such cases choice would have little advantage to boast of over **lot** or chance....
entertain: hold; have;	With this great example before me, with the sense and spirit, the faith and honor, the duty and interest, of the same American people pledged to support the Constitution of the United States, I **entertain** no doubt of its continuance in all its energy, and my mind is prepared without hesitation to lay myself under the most solemn obligations to support it to the utmost of my power.

■ 重点述评与提示

1. ...men of reflection were less apprehensive of danger from the formidable power of fleets and armies they must determine to resist than from those contests and dissensions which would certainly arise concerning the forms of government to be instituted over the whole and over the parts of this extensive country.

   美国独立革命的胜利固然辉煌,但更为重要的是排除各州偏见和分歧,统一思想,解决国家的政治体制问题,这是亚当斯演说开篇的主题,也是他的思想优势。因此他对独立战争一笔带过,而在下文中着意描述独立战争后邦联国会旧体制下的社会矛盾和问题,以突出宪政建国的决定性意义。

2. Negligence of its regulations, inattention to its recommendations, if not disobedience to its authority, not only in individuals but in States, soon appeared with their melancholy consequences.

   本句中的"it"指的是1781以后的邦联国会政体,亚当斯在这里极力铺陈其权力羸弱,形同虚设,令行不止,导致各州乃至个人各行其是,帮派林立,民不聊生,国将不国的晦暗局面。为的是在下文颂扬宪法。赞美联邦分权而立的政体。

3. Irritated by no literary altercation, animated by no public debate, heated by no party animosity, I read it with great satisfaction, as the result of good heads prompted by good hearts, as an experiment better adapted to the genius, character, situation, and

relations of this nation and country than any which had ever been proposed or suggested.

　　亚当斯的政敌曾攻击他是贵族派,是反共和主义者,对此他必须通过表明对宪法的赞美而做出回应。1787年,亚当斯身在欧洲,并未得以参与制宪会议。此时他在演说中刻意进行自我形象塑造,表明自己能够置身于制宪辩论其外而对宪法有较为客观公正的评判。这是亚当斯不得已的聪明。

4. Can anything essential, anything more than mere ornament and decoration, be added to this by robes and diamonds?

　　此处连用两个修辞设问句,把自己对宪法和人民主权的共和政体的赞扬态度推向高潮。句中使"ornament""decoration"与比喻君主权威的"robes and diamonds"产生语义关联,从而也回应了政敌对他是"君主贵族派"的指责。

5. For it is the people only that are represented. It is their power and majesty that is reflected, and only for their good, in every legitimate government, under whatever form it may appear.

　　亚当斯历来对人性从善和"民主"观念表示怀疑,认为必须用权力和法律来规约人性的欲望,引导"民主"的正能量。这里对人民在共和政府中的决定作用如此强调,不能不说是一种自我表白,同时亦是政治需要使然。

6. In the midst of these pleasing ideas we should be unfaithful to ourselves if we should ever lose sight of the danger to our liberties if anything partial or extraneous should infect the purity of our free, fair, virtuous, and independent elections.

　　又是自我表白!亚当斯在总统选举中得到了华盛顿的表态支持,而且由于汉弥尔顿的操纵失效反而帮了他的大忙,但他却仅以选举团人3票的优势击败对手杰斐逊。面子上自然有些过不去,此时宣誓就职总统大位,理应为这场自由公正,诚信独立的选举正名。

■ 思考及讨论题

1. Why John Adams was praised as "Colosus of Independence" by Thomas Jefferson?
2. What is John Adams's view of "democracy" and the power of government?
3. Why was John Adams accused by his political opponents as an anti-constitutional monarchist?
4. What did Adams do during his administration to make this accusation seemingly so?

5. Why Adams used in this speech mostly the well-balanced long sentences?

■ 阅读书目

1. Ellis, Joseph J. *Passionate Sage: The Character and Legacy of John Adams*. New York: W. W. Norton and Company, 2001.
2. McCullough, David. *John Adams*, Simon and Schuster, 2001.
3. Adams, Charles Francis. *The Works of John Adams: With a Life of the Author, Notes and Illustrations*. Little Brown, 1851.
4. Morrison, James, "John Adams Wrong" in *Washington Times*, May 23, 2008.

第十二讲
托马斯·杰斐逊(Thomas Jefferson 1743—1826)

■ 政治历史评述

托马斯·杰斐逊:百科全书式的知识分子,多面理想的政治思想家

　　托马斯·杰斐逊是闻名遐迩的《美国独立宣言》的作者,是美国伟大的思想家、政治家、美国民主自由,共和政治的奠基者和捍卫者。他担任过华盛顿总统的国务卿,创立了民主共和党,后来成为两任总统,为早期政党和政治体制的运作,经济的独立和领土的扩展做出了重要贡献。杰斐逊式的民主成为美国政治生活取之不尽的思想来源,后世不论是安德鲁·杰克逊的民主党,约翰·克莱的辉格党还是林肯的共和党,都宣称继承了杰斐逊民主的精华。杰斐逊是一位杰出的,既坚持思想原则性又不乏现实策略的灵活性的政治家。除此之外,杰斐逊还是学者,是以教育为本,传播文化的启蒙思想家。这些都是政治意识形态宣示的杰斐逊的正统形象。

　　但是,杰斐逊的形象和意义不止于此。读过杰斐逊的传记和他浩繁的书信,我们可以发现,比起华盛顿,汉弥尔顿和麦迪逊等同时代的政治家,杰斐逊多了一些理想与现实互相制约,互相妥协的成分。他有点像不断变位中的多棱镜投影:光彩夺目,叠像环生,喻示出这位大人物的多元气质和知行迷误。

　　我们看到,他是通识人文教育的典范,百科全书式的启蒙学问家,一位误入政途的理想主义者。他的内心渴望独居内省的田园生活,却必定为了推翻暴政,抑制贵族,实现民主自由的理想而在喧嚣的政坛上耗尽大半生的时光。他早年在威廉—玛丽学院专攻法律,却喜爱博览杂书,乐于游历,探索人类总体知识的关联与贯通;他立志当一名律师,通晓其当代政治律制,也对人类知识有全景式的观照:自然科学、数学、哲学、经济学、历史学、文学艺术,无所不知,高雅建筑艺术,实用测量技术,考古鉴别,无所不晓;他精通拉丁语和希腊语,能用多种欧洲语言直接获取西方各国的政治历史文化;他既推崇语言力量,偏好逻辑与修辞,谙熟古典文章修辞,却又低调怯场,不善演说。他倡导人人生而平等自由的信念,抨击奴隶制,言之凿凿:"命运之书大写着:黑人和妇女必须得到自由",却在自己的农庄深筑高墙,蓄役300多名黑人奴隶,苦心经营祖传家业,直到1826年临终时才签署文书,解放其中3名黑奴。他在生活中既表现出弗吉尼亚偏僻山居乡绅的朴实无华,又显现了精英知识阶层特立独行的名士派头;他崇尚知识理性,对宗教若即若离,既不信奉基督上帝,也不完全听从自然神的喻示前行;在政治上,他既抵制国家权力集中,维护州权和个人权利,又在总统任内推行国家意志,强力执行海外禁运,甚而使用国家权力镇压敢于抵制禁运的新英格兰商人；他既厉行节俭,消减政府和军费开支,又甘冒违宪风险,越过国会廉价购买路易斯安娜领地,加重了联邦政府的债务负担,同时也为他一贯反对的工业和商业资本主义的发展提供了基本的物质条件；他提倡小国寡民的理想,却热衷于刘易斯和克拉克向西部的探险,为自己不愿看到的美国西部领土扩张充当先锋；他倡导农业立国,弱权政府,却也痛感工业落后就会受强国欺凌的现实可能,主张同时发展工业和农业,引导美国进入世界强国之列。

总之,托马斯·杰斐逊充分表现出一代伟人丰富的主体性和文化矛盾,同时也展示出自己平凡中见奇的独特个性和风采。也许,杰斐逊为自己写下的墓铭志正好指引着后世人去理解他的一生:"此处安息着托马斯·杰斐逊:《独立宣言》的起草人,弗吉尼亚宗教自由法案的作者,弗吉尼亚大学之父。"显然,政治独立自由以求分权共和,民主治国；宗教自由以高扬主体意识自由和多元；崇尚教育以利人类启蒙和知识传播。这三个方面也许正是杰斐逊极力想让后人记住的精神遗产。这也正是美国大众意识中应该记住的杰斐逊精神和风格。著名杰斐逊研究专家梅里厄·皮特森可谓一语中的:"美国人崇敬华盛顿；爱戴林肯,不忘杰斐逊。"

的确,美国人忘不了杰斐逊,忘不了他所倡导的美国民主共和思想,重农自主经济的理想主义和自然经济的社会图景。尤其是在21世纪科技发达,物质丰腴,生态恶化,全球资本无孔不入,经济金融危机四伏和恐怖主义威胁的今天,杰斐逊式的民主和小国寡民式的农业理想国更能显现出一种遥远乌托邦的魅力。

杰斐逊的民主思想建立在启蒙主义自然法,人类自主理性和道德至上的基础上。他坚持自然法则状态下人人独立自由平等的权利,他反复强调,"大多数人的意愿和每个社会的自然法则,是人类权利唯一的确切保障"。以此原则建立的政府是执行全体人民意愿的机构,本身并不产生权力,也不应具有对人民的压迫性,因为,"保护人民生活和幸福,而非破坏人民的生活和幸福,是好的政府首要的唯一合法的目标。"在此视野中,资本积累,国家银行,金融体系和大工业制造以少数人追求最大利益为特征,必然产生以特权等级和精英阶层为主的国家机器,对大多数人的自由和权利造成直接的危害,直接威胁到以农业个体自然经济为基础的美国民主共和制度,同时,城市人口的聚集,物欲的膨胀必然导致权力腐败和人性堕落。在杰斐逊看来,这些权力的弊端都在汉弥尔顿的国家集权主义以及约翰·亚当斯政府的贵族倾向和扩军行为中得到展示。特别是亚当斯总统任内通过了《外侨法》和《惩治煽乱法》,在杰斐逊的民主共和党看来,这更是对公民的平等权利,结社和言论自由的赤裸裸的践踏。杰斐逊要做的就是反其道而行之。他创建民主共和党,竞选总统,把1800年的选举看成是通过政党政治和民主选举的手段推翻联邦党人贵族政治,恢复美国共和主义和民主自由的一场革命。在1799年初竞选

前的书信中,杰斐逊明白无误地表明,一旦当选,他的政府将放权于州,精简政府,节俭自律,保护普通人的民主和自由:

> 我反对将各州的一切权力都让渡予联邦政府,也反对联邦政府将其所有权力都赋予行政机关。我主张政府部门厉行节俭,所有公共税收都用于偿还国债,而不是用于增设官位,发放薪金,鼓励党争。……我主张宗教自由,反对为了建立合法的统治地位,打压异己教派而采取的任何形式的操控手段;我主张言论自由,反对违反宪法,采取强制的,而不是理性的手段制止公民对政府部门的怨言或批评,尽管这些怨言或批评不一定有道理……

在这些民主政治立场的背后,回响着反对贵族政治和精英文化,提倡简约政府和个人自然权利的声音,而节俭和素朴的品质则是遵循自然法则的必然结果,也是杰斐逊时代的经济形式和社会特征。沃侬·帕灵顿在《美国思想史》中简练准确地勾勒出杰斐逊民主政治产生的社会历史根源:"杰斐逊时代的美国是带有朴素的国内经济的一个朴素世界。人口90%以上是乡野村夫,大多数是土地保有者,以传统方式处理地方事务。没有贫穷的两极分化,没有严密的阶级组织。"深受弗吉尼亚乡土农耕文化熏陶的杰斐逊也自然在其政治思想和行为中表现了对权力仪式的不屑和对大多数普通人思想和生活方式的认同。可以说,杰斐逊民主思想外在的形式就是他称之为的"共和式的简约原则"。简朴应体现在美国社会和政治生活的方方面面。

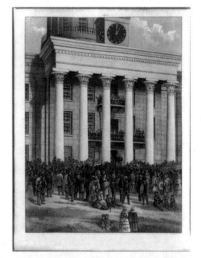

1801年3月4日早晨,杰斐逊出现在新建首都华盛顿举行的新总统就职仪式上。他一反前任总统华盛顿和亚当斯就职时炫耀张扬的贵族做派,执意不肯佩戴总统佩剑,不乘坐仪仗马车,坚持身着布衣,从旅店步行穿过简易铺设的街道,到尚未落成的国会大厦宣读就职演说,然后平静地步行返回住宿旅店。此举当时令人吃惊而费解。现在看来,这既是杰斐逊特立独行的名士派头展现,更是他信奉的自由民主精神和小政府主张的体现。有了这样的理解,我们就不难想象,杰斐逊后来当总统独特而随和的作风:作为堂堂大国的总统,杰斐逊有一次竟然身穿睡衣,脚履拖鞋,在刚建成不久的总统府(后来的白宫)接见衣冠楚楚的大英帝国公使! 他也曾一再阻止支持者为他举行生日庆典,宣称"我唯一庆祝的生日就是7月4日,那就是美国《独立宣言》的生日。"以其一贯的思想作如是观,这样的政治话语也就不言而喻了。

文如其人。杰斐逊简约近民的思想和风格也显现在他最有名的第一任总统就职演说词中。这篇演说是一篇杰作,它宣示了民主共和体制的重新确立,也为后世各任美国总统就职演说提供了典范。杰斐逊认为,"诚实的心灵"和"知识的头脑"是任何政治演讲的根本,而政治家成功的公众形象并不取决于支离破碎的激情和天马行空的想象,而应该是实事求是,言之有物的内容。与同时代的大多数政治家一样,杰斐逊受过严格的修辞训练,他认为强有力的演说内容,简明生动的形式表达,逻辑修辞的能力是共和民主政体中启蒙理性的显现,是政治哲学必不可少的学习内容。只不过，比起华盛顿刻意的古典、麦迪逊严谨的逻辑和亚当斯恣肆夸张的典雅，杰斐逊的就职演说多了一些冷峻的简洁、实在的修辞力度和平易的现实

风格。如是，杰斐逊的这篇就职演说中用表现出简洁平易、形象生动的修辞风格，表达了爱国的情怀，预示了美国的崛起，重新阐述了民主共和政体的少数服从多数的原则立场，同时强调政治宽容，保护少数人的权利。杰斐逊还在演说中号召政治和解，营造统一的政治局面，明确表达了民主共和党提倡小政府大自由，充分尊重个人自由和权利，以农为本，发展个体经济的施政主张。

有趣的是，杰斐逊并不算一个现代意义上成功的政治演讲家。他擅长写作，沉于思考，却不善于面对观众发表演讲，厚重而又多彩的思想往往缺乏富有感染的即兴话语表现力。这也许是那个时代饱学之士的通病。但思想的力量却由语言符号载负，经久不衰，流传以远。在1801年3月那个初暖乍寒的日子里，杰斐逊在总统就职仪式上，面对听众神情紧张，声音短促而微弱，机械地宣读着精心准备、两面都写满文字的讲稿。现场的听众几乎全然没有听出杰斐逊总统在说什么，但这不重要，思想在物化的形式中将得到永久的保存和流传。这篇演讲在总统就职仪式之前就已刊载在美国的报刊上，这意味着的民主共和原则和社会理想将在美国大众心中驻留，它的影响将持续久远。同时，这篇演讲平易谦和的文风和简洁有力的语言风格也为之赢得声誉，被公认为美国政治文化中"及时和永恒"（timely and timeless）的杰作。

■ 演讲文（节选）

First Presidential Inaugural Address

Thomas Jefferson

Friends and Fellow Citizens,

Called upon to undertake the duties of the first **executive** office of our country, I **avail myself of** the presence of that portion of my fellow citizens which is here assembled to express my grateful thanks for the favor with which they have been pleased to look toward me, to declare a sincere consciousness that the task is above my talents, and that I approach it with those anxious and awful **presentiments** which the greatness of the **charge** and the weakness of my powers so justly inspire. A rising nation, spread over a wide and fruitful land,

executive: administrative
avail myself of: make use of
presentiment: foresight; provision
charge: duty; task

traversing all the seas with the rich productions of their **industry**, engaged in commerce with nations who feel power and forget right, advancing rapidly to destinies beyond the reach of mortal eye—when I **contemplate** these **transcendent** objects, and see the honor, the happiness, and the hopes of this beloved country committed to the issue, and the **auspices** of this day, I shrink from the contemplation, and humble myself before the magnitude of the **undertaking**. Utterly, indeed, should I despair did not the presence of many whom I here see remind me that in the other high authorities provided by our Constitution I shall find resources of wisdom, of virtue, and of zeal on which to rely under all difficulties. To you, then, gentlemen, who are charged with the **sovereign** functions of legislation, and to those associated with you, I look with encouragement for that guidance and support which may enable us to **steer** with safety the **vessel** in which we are all embarked amidst the conflicting elements of a troubled world.

During the contest of opinion through which we have passed the **animation** of discussions and of **exertions** has sometimes worn an aspect which might impose on strangers unused to think freely and to speak and to write what they think; but this being now decided by the voice of the nation, announced according to the rules of the Constitution, all will, of course, arrange themselves under the will of the law, and unite in common efforts for the common good. All, too, will bear in mind this **sacred** principle, that though the will of the majority is in all cases to **prevail**, that will to be rightful must be reasonable; that the minority possess their equal rights, which equal law must protect, and to **violate** would be oppression. Let us, then, fellow citizens, unite with one heart and one mind. Let us restore to social **intercourse** that harmony and affection without which liberty and even life itself are but **dreary** things. And let us reflect that, having **banished** from our land that religious intolerance under which mankind so long bled and suffered, we have yet gained little if we **countenance** a political intolerance as despotic, as wicked, and capable of as bitter and bloody persecutions. During the **throes** and **convulsions** of the ancient world, during the agonizing **spasms** of **infuriated** man, seeking through blood and slaughter his long-lost liberty, it was not wonderful that the agitation of the **billows** should reach even this distant and peaceful shore; that this should be more felt and feared by some and less by others, and should divide opinions as to measures of safety. But every difference of opinion is not a difference of principle. We have called by different names **brethren** of the same principle. We

traversing: spread over; going across
industry: mode of production
contemplate: think of
transcendent: grand; splendid; superb
auspice: protection responsibility
undertaking: task; obligation
sovereign: highest; top; supreme
steer: guide; direct; control; manage
vessel: boat; (here) the United States
animation: energy; liveliness
exertion: effort

sacred: holy; of the highest honor
prevail: win; dominate
vilate: go against
intercourse: communication
dreary: miserable
banish: reject; dismiss; outlaw
countenance: admit; accept as possible
throe: sudden pain
convulsion: (here) social unrest
spasm: recurrent pain
infuriated: restless with anger and rage
billow: huge wave

bretheren: brother

are all Republicans, we are all Federalists. If there be any among us who would wish to dissolve this Union or to change its republican form, let them stand **undisturbed** as monuments of the safety with which error of opinion may be tolerated where reason is left free to **combat** it. I know, indeed, that some honest men fear that a republican government can not be strong, that this Government is not strong enough; but would the honest **patriot**, in the full tide of successful experiment, abandon a government which has so far kept us free and firm on the **theoretic** and **visionary** fear that this Government, the world's best hope, may by possibility want energy to preserve itself? I trust not. I believe this, on the contrary, the strongest Government on earth. I believe it the only one where every man, at the call of the law, would fly to the standard of the law, and would **meet** invasions of the public order as his own personal concern. Sometimes it is said that man can not be trusted with the government of himself. Can he, then, be trusted with the government of others? Or have we found angels in the forms of kings to govern him? Let history answer this question.

Let us, then, with courage and confidence pursue our own Federal and Republican principles, our attachment to union and representative government. Kindly separated by nature and a wide ocean from the **exterminating havoc** of one quarter of the globe; too high-minded to endure the **degradations** of the others; possessing a chosen country, with room enough for our descendants to the thousandth and thousandth generation; **entertaining** a due sense of our equal right to the use of our own faculties, to the **acquisitions** of our own **industry**, to honor and confidence from our fellow citizens, resulting not from birth, but from our actions and their sense of them; enlightened by a **benign** religion, professed, indeed, and practiced in various forms, yet all of them **inculcating** honesty, truth, temperance, gratitude, and the love of man; acknowledging and adoring an overruling Providence, which by all its **dispensations** proves that it delights in the happiness of man here and his greater happiness **hereafter**—with all these blessings, what more is necessary to make us a happy and a prosperous people? Still one thing more, fellow citizens—a wise and **frugal** Government, which shall restrain men from injuring one another, shall leave them otherwise free to regulate their own pursuits of industry and improvement, and shall not take from the mouth of labor the bread it has earned. This is the sum of good government, and this is necessary to close the circle of our **felicities**.

---

undisturbed: not bothered; permitted
combat: fight

patriot: one who love his/her country
theoretic: unrealistic
visionary: imaginary

meet: face; fight back; challenge

exterminating: totally destructive
havoc: chaos; disaster
degradation: corruption; downfall
entertain: hold; have
acquisition: obtaining; gaining
industry: diligence
benign: kind; warm-hearted
inculcate: instruct; advocate
dispensation: arrangement; distribution
hereafter: in the future
frugal: inexpensive; economical

felicity: happiness

■ 重点述评与提示

1. A rising nation, spread over a wide and fruitful land, traversing all the seas with the rich productions of their industry, engaged in commerce with nations who feel power and forget right, advancing rapidly to destinies beyond the reach of mortal eye.

    这是总统就职演说的套路,表达爱国情怀,赞美自己的国家,同时也自谦一番,顺势对国会两院表达敬意。杰斐逊借此机会预示美国是一个正在崛起的国家,与欧洲的大国贸易往来,同时也含蓄指责这些国家恃强凌弱,没有大国的责任。此时的美国正在英法海上争霸的夹缝中求发展。

2. I look with encouragement for that guidance and support which may enable us to steer with safety the vessel in which we are all embarked amidst the conflicting elements of a troubled world.

    别忘了杰斐逊是一位谙熟多种语言,具有理想主义气质的思想家。此处比喻美国犹如一艘航船,大家同舟共济,安全地航行在世界的风浪之中。话语中既号召国内统一意志,稳定与团结,又表明了美国难守中立,举步维艰的外交困境,可谓妙笔。

3. All, too, will bear in mind this sacred principle, that though the will of the majority is in all cases to prevail, that will to be rightful must be reasonable; that the minority possess their equal rights, which equal law must protect, and to violate would be oppression.

    这是这篇演讲的核心内容:党争之后在宪法的原则下团结起来,重申共和主义少数服从多数的原则。更为重要的是,着重提出法律保护少数人的意见和平等权利,杜绝权力压迫,巩固宗教宽容,提倡政治宽容,这也是杰斐逊民主的精髓。

4. If there be any among us who would wish to dissolve this Union or to change its republican form, let them stand undisturbed as monuments of the safety with which error of opinion may be tolerated where reason is left free to combat it.

    这是总统选战后号召国内政治和解的一段精辟之言,其中以庄重的语气表达了保护少数人的民主权利和言论自由的理性主义原则:反对派的主张无论多么错误和极端(甚至瓦解联邦,改变共和政体),都不可使用国家机器实施镇压,而应由理性来加以克服。这才是能够长治久安的政府。

5. Sometimes it is said that man can not be trusted with the government of himself. Can he, then, be trusted with the government of others? Or have we found angels in the forms of kings to govern him? Let history answer this question.

    麦迪逊和汉弥尔顿在《联邦党人文集》第51篇中有名言:"如果人类是天使,就不需要任何政府。"可见联邦党人强调民权政府的必要和作用。痛恨暴政的杰斐逊当然不相信君主制中有天使,但人类组成的任何政府是否能有效地进行社会管理,为个人提供安全感,这是个问题,有待历史来回答。

6. ...a wise and frugal Government, which shall restrain men from injuring one another, shall leave them otherwise free to regulate their own pursuits of industry and improvement, and shall not take from the mouth of labor the bread it has earned.

　　这是杰斐逊的名言,他相信人类的理性可以正确引导自己的行为,毋须政府的制约。因此节俭和智慧的政府是最好的政府,"管得最少的政府就是最好的政府"。增加税收,从个体"劳动者口中获取其劳动所得的面包",当然是有违民权政府保护公民这一根本原则的。这也是典型的杰斐逊民主的理想主义表述。

■ 思考及讨论题

1. What are the essential principles of Jeffersonian Democracy?
2. Why did Jefferson say that his election as the President of US in 1800 was the victory of a "real revolution in the principles of our government"?
3. How shall we understand the statement that "Government is the best that governs least"?
4. To Jefferson, what could be the moral problems of industrialization and commercialization?

■ 阅读书目

1. Jefferson, Thomas. *Autobiography of Thomas Jefferson*. New York: Capricorn Books, 1959.
2. Cogliano, Francis D. *Thomas Jefferson: Reputation and Legacy*. Edingburg: Edinburg University Press.
3. Brodie, Fawn M. *Thomas Jefferson: An Intimate History*. New York: W. W. Norton, 1974.
4. Ellis, Joseph J. *American Sphix: The Character of Thomas Jefferson*. Alfred A. Knopf, inc., 1997.

第四章 ‖ 和睦时代与平等主义民主

At no period of our political existence had we so much cause to felicitate ourselves at the prosperous and happy condition of our country.

—James Monroe

The best guarantee against the abuse of power consists in the freedom, the purity, and the frequency of popular elections．

—John Quincy Adams

I know what I am fit for. I can command a body of men in a rough way; but I am fit to be President.

—Andrew Jackson

Preview Questions

01/

Why James Monroe's eight years of presidency (1817—1825) was labeled "The Era of Good Feeling"?

02/

What was "the Compromise of 1820" and how was it reached?

03/

What are the characteristics of the "Jacksonian Democracy" and why is it said to be an ambiguous term?

04/

What is the "Market Revolution" that characterizes the period between 1815—1848?

第十三讲

詹姆斯·门罗(James Monroe 1758—1831)

■ 政治历史评述

詹姆斯·门罗:和睦时代美国外交政策的里程碑

美国第六任总统约翰·昆西·亚当斯曾说,1816—1825年詹姆斯·门罗总统任期是美国历史上的"黄金时代"。当时的美国报纸也为这个相对安定和谐的时代贴上了"和睦时代"(The Era of Good Feeling)的标签。美国独立建国至1816年近半个世纪,经历了一系列的国内外危机,此时似乎开始走出建国时期意识形态纷争的低谷,缓解了在欧洲列强压力下的生存问题,开始考虑这个国家在世界权力格局中一些实际的发展问题。政治上,杰斐逊的民主共和党包容了革命时期独立和爱国意识,在联邦党人规划的政府权力格局中发挥基于个人权利的民主作用;联邦党人在对法国战与和问题上发生分裂,后来又随着汉弥尔顿和亚当斯相继淡出政治舞台,在杰斐逊和麦迪逊的民主共和党面前显得一蹶不振。1812年第二次对英战争中联邦党人又站在英国人一边,彻底失去公众支持,战后渐行消亡。政党纷争平息,使得麦迪逊政府战后能够放手加强国内基础建设,征收关税以振兴工业并再次建立了国家银行;民主共和党人亨利·克莱提出"美国体制计划",虽未获国会多数支持,却也为美国经济的振兴起到推波助澜的作用。美国民族身份感和自信心和国家意识普遍高涨。美国开始经历了40年未遇之政局平稳,社会和谐之景象。当然,这个所谓"和睦时代"由于有了1814年战后民族主义和国家意识的兴起以及门罗的亲民形象和下层民主意识的觉醒被夸大了。其实,门罗的时代也是新的美国政治经济和社会矛盾的酝酿阶段。1819年的经济危机和1820年有关奴隶制建州的密苏里妥协案都是被约翰·昆西·亚当斯称为的美国"大部头悲剧的小小前奏"。

詹姆斯·门罗一生,并无太多的传奇色彩。他于1758年4月28日出生于弗吉尼亚州一个下层农场家庭。门罗16岁进入威廉-玛丽学院,时年1774,独立革命的风云已经在北美殖民地激荡,康科德和列克星敦的枪声不久打破了校园的宁静,学生们热血沸腾,成群投笔从戎。门罗也不例外,不久参加大陆军。他在战役中曾身负重伤,立下战功。华盛顿曾对他有过如下的评价:"此人在任何时候都保持着一个军人勇武力行,明断进退的精神。"战后,门罗得到杰斐逊的指导,学习法律,步入政界。他32岁被当选国会参议员,9年后当选弗吉尼亚州州长。在政治上,他一直是杰斐逊的追随者,在政府中担任过外交官,低调行事,但颇有成绩,特别是与拿破仑谈判,以极低廉的价格购进了法国在北美的路易斯安那领地,使美国领土增加了将近一倍。1812年对英战争打响,门罗在麦迪逊内阁担任国务卿兼防长,战后也有了些声名,积累了不少的政坛人气。

总之,门罗30多年来一直在美国政坛时隐时现。论地位,他算是小字辈,一直身处国父们巨大的身影之中,他生性内向,读书不多,思想迟滞,甚至有些木讷,有时还显得有些莫名的敏感。但是,长期的政府行政经历也为他积累了政治经验,形成了稳健的行政风格。他遇事稳沉,判断准确,知人善任,领导目的明确,有条不紊,在联邦政府行政部门中注入了一种讲求实效的实用风格,由此竟成了竞选总统的热门候选人,在1816年的总统竞选中一鼓作气,几乎全票当选。

门罗正值"和睦时代"的历史机遇当选美国总统,在第一次就职演说中宣称这时的美国是一个具有"共同兴趣爱好的大家庭",决心以其稳健的行政领导能力促进建设"与共和政府的原则一致的和谐社会"。但以其平和低调的领导风格,8年任期内可圈可点的政绩并不多见。

詹姆斯·门罗的名字在美国历史上之所以那么赫然醒目就在于那份150多年以来一直影响了美国外交政策的《门罗宣言》。这是一份在美国孤立主义的"中立"外交政策外壳包装下彰显美国划分全球势力范围,谋求地区霸权乃至全球霸主地位的宣言。它诞生于美国国家意识和民族意识逐渐增强,欧洲殖民主义衰落,南美民族国家兴起的关键时期,此后适应了美国领土扩张的需要而成为美国外交政策主要参照的坐标。同时,150多年以来,门罗主义也因历史时代条件和美国国家利益的需要,在美国的外交事务中不断变幻其外在形式,增改内容,为美国在西半球乃至全世界的意识渗透和扩张鸣锣开道。犹如中国京剧的脸谱,同一场上演员,根据场上剧情和人物需要,甩袖之间变换各种脸谱,以表达剧中人不同的情感和愿望。

著名的《门罗宣言》1823年出台,绝非偶然。此时的美国,领土扩张,人口剧增,市场拓展,已经有了大西洋两岸分立,划分东西半球势力范围的战略构想。与拉美国家相同的殖民地传统和争取独立的经历,使美国认为自己是拉美独立国家当之无愧的盟主;逐

渐抬头的民族身份感和西部扩张的憧憬也促动了美国外交的主动和自信,开始有了与欧洲英法和西班牙等殖民大国平起平坐的冲动。1823年12月2日,门罗总统以书面的形式在给国会的年度国情咨文中发表了这份被称为"美国外交政策的里程碑"的《门罗宣言》,以不容置疑的语气宣布:"作为关系到美利坚合众国的权利和利益的原则,此时适于声明,南北美洲大陆已获得并保持其自由和独立之状态,从今以后不应被任何欧洲大国视为进一步推行殖民之对象。"门罗强调说,美国从未加入大西洋彼岸欧洲大国之间的事务和战争,也从未干预,未来也绝不会干预欧洲各国的海外殖民现状和独立性。美国自然与西半球的拉美国家和人民有更紧密的联系,因此必须申明,任何欧洲大国试图单方面"在此半球的任何地区推行他们的制度都将被视为

是对我们国家的和平和安全的危害。"美国不会对此坐视不管。这就是《门罗宣言》的两个核心观念。这是自美国建国半个世纪从未有过之外交强硬姿态,是美国"中立"外交政策和孤立主义在更大的政治地缘层次上的强权主义表述。有了这一划分势力范围,建立地区霸权的理据,美国开始步入大国之列,此后经过不到一个世纪的发展,终于成就了世界霸主之地位。

美国历届政府在制定外交政策方面都以门罗主义为出发点,在谋求美国国家利益的先决条件下对之进行解读和发挥,使《门罗宣言》不断翻新变脸。1845年,美国总统詹姆斯·波尔克在国会直接抛出《门罗宣言》,以其两个核心理念为根据,声称北美洲西海岸和俄勒冈领土都是美洲人的事务,美国对之有不可争议的领土权力,警告英国和欧洲不可插手。以此

为借口,波尔克理直气壮地兼并得克萨斯,夺取新墨西哥,吞并加利福尼亚和俄勒冈,成为美国历史上最成功的领土扩张总统。1904年12月6日,西奥多·罗斯福总统在美国国会发表了他对《门罗宣言》的新阐释,这就是著名的"罗斯福推论"。按照罗斯福的说法,如果拉美任何地区发生动荡和危机,引来欧洲国家的干预,都必然迫使美国在该地区采取实际措施,以保护该地区保持秩序和稳定,免受外来势力的危害。罗斯福对此辩称,美国对拉美任何地区没有领土要求,之所以如此定策,都是为了拉美国家的稳定和繁荣。实际上,这是与罗斯福提出美国应当充任"国际警察"角色和在亚洲地区挥舞"大棒"的帝国主义政策一脉相承的。在"罗斯福推论"的支撑下,美国政府怂恿中央情报局对拉美主权国家大肆开展渗透活动,在巴拿马,古巴,尼加拉瓜,海地和多米尼加共和国,格林纳达等地进行了赤裸裸的武装侵略和干涉。具有讽刺意味的是,20世纪80年代英国不惜血本,派遣特混舰队远征南美阿根廷,争夺马尔维纳斯群岛主权。美国总统里根一方面延续门罗主义思维,劝告英国息兵罢战,谈判解决争端,同时也摆出美洲国家"老大哥"的架子,要阿根廷放弃武力对峙。另一方面,里根在遭到阿根廷的拒绝后,转而公开宣布将尽力协助英军作战,对阿根廷采取经济制裁,支持英国重新占领马岛。阿根廷全国感到被美国出卖,美国门罗主义的实质由此彰显无遗。

由此观之,外交政策是一个国家政治意识形态最灵活,最狡黠的话语形式,同时也是国家之间国力角逐和权力制衡的晴雨表。大国兴衰,合纵连横之时,方显统观天下大势,谋划优胜劣汰之睿智和精明。美国今天的强大,一方面是其经济实力的体现,也有国际力量对比和冲突所提供的机遇原因,另一方面也是美国基于地缘优势和软实力,逐渐拓宽国际视野的结果。在这一过程中,国家政治体制的形式和有效运作固然起到一定作用,而更重要的则是一个国家领袖的政治素质所决定的全球战略眼光及其在外交领域的开放性表达。美国的《门罗宣言》以及此后形成的门罗主义对此是一个极好的说明。

在全球化进程加速的今天,世界政治和文化多元多极共生的局面也同时存在,现代交通和通讯技术开始遮蔽西方主义和殖民化的文化余声,门罗主义一类的国家政治意识已成明日黄花。所幸的是,门罗总统军旅一生,不善辞令,当年也未在国会演说发表《门罗宣言》,此时保持永久的沉默,也是对门罗主义最终命运的最佳注解。

1817年3月4日,门罗宣誓就任美国第5届总统。由于白宫在战争中被英军焚烧,此时尚在恢复中,就职仪式改在最高法院外的台阶上举行。门罗在就职演说中宣称这时的美国是一个具有"共同兴趣爱好的大家庭",决心以其稳健的行政领导能力促进建设"与共和政府的原则一致的和谐社会"。这篇演讲充满了对美国政体和建国40年来成就的溢美之词,鼓吹美国经济和社会的发展来源于人民执政,同时也回顾了美国1812年对英战争的原因和结果,以进一步加强国民的自尊心和自豪感。演讲文中反复出现"幸福"、"繁荣"、"和平"、"和谐"、"福祉"、"享受欢乐"等等语汇,句式多用比较级和最高级来突出表达社会的安定和繁荣。在说到个人政治自由,财产保障和宗教自由时,门罗用了一连串的反问,然后自豪地点明这些都是美国人已经尽情享受过的福祉。此类手法在演说中反复出现,在修辞的慷慨之余反倒显得有些空洞,有点权力自我标榜之嫌。但是,我们知道,门罗一上台后就先后自费巡视全国4个月之久,大力塑造与民同乐的亲民总统形象。由此观之,这种自我标榜和对话式的演说手法也就不足为奇了。从这个意义上,如果说门罗代表着美国从知识精英民主政治到杰克逊市平民民主的过渡,亦不为过。这是一个时代在门罗身上赋予的意义。

■ 演讲文(节选)

First Presidential Inaugural Address

James Monroe

commencement: beginning; start
elapse: pass of time

object: (here) issue; aspect
felicitate: cheer, congratulate
institution: (here) political system

...

From the **commencement** of our Revolution to the present day almost forty years have **elapsed**, and from the establishment of this Constitution twenty-eight. Through this whole term the Government has been what may emphatically be called self-government. And what has been the effect? To whatever **object** we turn our attention, whether it relates to our foreign or domestic concerns, we find abundant cause to **felicitate** ourselves in the excellence of our **institutions**. During a period fraught with difficulties and marked by very extraordinary events the United States have flourished beyond example. Their citizens individually have been happy and the nation prosperous.

Under this Constitution our **commerce** has been wisely regulated with foreign nations and between the States; new States have been admitted into our Union; our territory has been enlarged by fair and honorable treaty, and with great advantage to the original States; the States, respectively protected by the National Government under a mild, **parental** system against foreign dangers, and enjoying within their separate spheres, by a wise **partition** of power, a just proportion of the sovereignty, have improved their **police**, extended their settlements, and attained a strength and maturity which are the best proofs of **wholesome** laws well administered. And if we look to the condition of individuals what a proud spectacle does it exhibit! On whom has oppression fallen in any quarter of our Union? Who has been **deprived of** any right of person or property? Who restrained from offering his vows in the mode which he prefers to the **Divine Author** of his being? It is well known that all these blessings have been enjoyed in their fullest extent; and I add with peculiar satisfaction that there has been no example of a **capital punishment** being **inflicted** on anyone for the crime of high treason.

Some who might admit the competency of our Government to these beneficent duties might doubt it in **trials** which put to the test its strength and efficiency as a member of the great community of nations. Here too experience has **afforded** us the most satisfactory proof in its favor. Just as this Constitution was put into action several of the principal States of Europe had become much agitated and some of them seriously **convulsed**. Destructive wars **ensued**, which have of late only been terminated. In the course of these conflicts the United States received great injury from several of the **parties**. It was their interest to stand **aloof** from the contest, to demand justice from the party committing the injury, and to cultivate by a fair and honorable conduct the friendship of all. **War** became at length inevitable, and the result has shown that our Government is equal to that, the greatest of trials, under the most unfavorable circumstances. Of the virtue of the people and of the heroic **exploits** of the Army, the Navy, and the militia I need not speak.

Such, then, is the happy Government under which we live—a Government adequate to every purpose for which the social **compact** is formed; a Government elective in all its branches, under which every citizen may by his merit obtain the highest trust recognized by the Constitution; which contains within it no cause of discord, none

---

commerce: business and trade

parental: protective
partition: division
police: political rule and administration
wholesome: healthy
deprived of: taken away by force

Divine Author: holy creator of the universe
capital punishment: death sentence
inflict: enforce with pain

trial: difficult times
afford: offer; show
convulse: disorder; chaos
ensue: follow
parties: (here) warring nations of the Europe

aloof: away; clear
War: (here) the War of 1812

exploit: action; effort; fight

compact: community; organization

to put at **variance** one portion of the community with another; a Government which protects every citizen in the full enjoyment of his rights, and is able to protect the nation against injustice from foreign powers. ...

In explaining my **sentiments** on this subject it may be asked, What raised us to the present happy state? How did we accomplish the Revolution? How remedy the defects of the first **instrument** of our Union, by **infusing** into the National Government sufficient power for national purposes, without **impairing** the just rights of the States or affecting those of individuals? How **sustain** and pass with glory through the **late war**? The Government has been in the hands of the people. To the people, therefore, and to the faithful and able **depositaries** of their trust is the credit due. Had the people of the United States been educated in different principles, had they been less intelligent, less independent, or less virtuous, can it be believed that we should have maintained the same steady and consistent career or been blessed with the same success? While, then, the **constituent** body retains its present sound and healthful state everything will be safe. They will choose competent and faithful representatives for every department. It is only when the people become ignorant and corrupt, when they **degenerate** into a **populace**, that they are incapable of exercising the sovereignty. **Usurpation** is then an easy attainment, and an usurper soon found. The people themselves become the willing instruments of their own **debasement** and ruin. Let us, then, look to the great cause, and endeavor to preserve it in full force. Let us by all wise and constitutional measures promote intelligence among the people as the best means of preserving our liberties. ...

It is particularly **gratifying** to me to enter on the discharge of these duties at a time when the United States are blessed with peace. It is a state most **consistent with** their prosperity and happiness. It will be my sincere desire to preserve it, so far as depends on the Executive, on just principles with all nations, claiming nothing unreasonable of any and **rendering** to each what is its due.

Equally gratifying is it to witness the increased harmony of opinion which **pervades** our Union. Discord does not belong to our system. Union is recommended as well by the free and **benign** principles of our Government, extending its blessings to every individual, as by the other **eminent** advantages attending it. The American people have encountered together great dangers and sustained **severe** trials with success. They constitute one great family

---

variance: difference (in opinion)

sentiment: consideration

instrument: (here) 1781 Article of Confederation
infuse: input
impair: damage
sustain: hold up
late war: (here) the War of 1812
depositary: agent; representative

constituent: people who have right to vote

degenerate: morally decay
populace: unorganized mass
usurpation: rebellion
debasement: corruption; reduce of dignity and honor
gratify: feel great

consistent with: accord; go hand in hand

render: offer, give

pervade: spread over
benign: kind; friendly
eminent: outstanding

severe: serious

with a common interest. Experience has enlightened us on some questions of essential importance to the country. The progress has been slow, **dictated** by a just reflection and a faithful regard to every interest connected with it. To promote this harmony in accord with the principles of our republican Government and in a manner to give them the most complete effect, and to advance in all other respects the best interests of our Union, will be the object of my constant and zealous **exertions**.

Never did a government commence under **auspices** so favorable, nor ever was success so complete. If we look to the history of other nations, ancient or modern, we find no example of a growth so rapid, so gigantic, of a people so prosperous and happy. In **contemplating** what we have still to perform, the heart of every citizen must expand with joy when he reflects how near our Government has approached to perfection; that in respect to it we have no essential improvement to make; that the great object is to preserve it in the essential principles and features which characterize it, and that is to be done by preserving the virtue and enlightening the minds of the people; and as a security against foreign dangers to adopt such arrangements as are **indispensable** to the support of our independence, our rights and liberties. If we **persevere** in the career in which we have advanced so far and in the path already traced, we can not fail, under the favor of a gracious Providence, to attain the high destiny which seems to await us....

dictate: manage; control; master

exertion: endeavor; effort
auspice: good prediction; kind protection

contemplate: consider

indispensable: absolutely necessary
persevere: hold fast; insist on

■ 重点述评与提示

1. ... new States have been admitted into our Union; our territory has been enlarged by fair and honorable treaty, and with great advantage to the original States.
   截止门罗就任总统,共有6个新建的州加入了联邦。大多数新州的建立都伴随着对原住民印第安人的杀戮和驱赶。此后,杰克逊20年代末的"印第安驱逐法案"更是印第安人的灾难和白人至上西进建州的根据之一。门罗的演说意在营造和谐,树立合法性,必须掩盖这些残酷的事实。

2. On whom has oppression fallen in any quarter of our Union? Who has been deprived of any right of person or property? Who restrained from offering his vows in the mode which he prefers to the Divine Author of his being?
   一连串的反问,标榜了美国政治体制的优越:政治上没有压迫,尊重个人权利和财产,宗教的宽容和自由。此句下文提到这些年从未对任何人判过死刑,即便犯了叛国大罪也不例外。这也许指美国副总统伯尔。此人在决斗中杀死了前财长汉弥尔顿,又密谋分裂联邦,在西部和南方另立帝国。但最高法院审理时以罪证不足而宣判无罪。

3. It was their interest to stand aloof from the contest, to demand justice from the party committing the injury, and to cultivate by a fair and honorable conduct the friendship of all.

重申华盛顿的中立和不结盟外交政策,但经过了1812年的战争,这时已经是官样文章,已经显得有些底气不足了。如是反弹,才有后来《门罗宣言》对欧洲各国的强硬态度。

4. Such, then, is the happy Government ... which contains within it no cause of discord, none to put at variance one portion of the community with another.

此话有些绝对,也是意识形态宣教的必然。其实,这一时期联邦政府一直面临着州权之争,激进的北方联邦党人分裂联邦,联邦出资改善国内基础设施是否违宪,重建国家银行分歧等一系列的问题。

5. The Government has been in the hands of the people. To the people, therefore, and to the faithful and able depositaries of their trust is the credit due.

门罗虽然秉承华盛顿等人的贵族作风,却是一位以亲民形象著称的总统,上任伊始即自费巡视全国达4个月之久,一路与普通人一起乘驿车,来到美国边远村镇与民同乐。有此经历,此话应该少了一些抽象,多了一些诚意。这是美国大众平等主义民主的进步。

6. It is only when the people become ignorant and corrupt, when they degenerate into a populace, that they are incapable of exercising the sovereignty.

门罗树立了亲民形象,同时也看到对人民进行文明教育和民主教育对于国家政体的重大意义,这在当时也是难能可贵的。

7. In contemplating what we have still to perform, the heart of every citizen must expand with joy when he reflects how near our Government has approached to perfection; that in respect to it we have no essential improvement to make.

这是受到所谓"和睦时代"意识鼓舞的一番话。实际上,当时的美国政府正在走向重重的危机:1819年的经济恐慌,奴隶制问题,1820年的密苏里妥协案使南北分裂初见端倪,资本主义市场扩张带来阶级分化等等。而国会也在围绕合宪与违宪的一些问题纠缠不清。

■ 思考及讨论题

1. Why Monroe was called the last of the "Virginian Dynasty"?
2. What are some achievements made during Monroe's two terms of administration?
3. What happened during the Panic of 1819 and how did it start?
4. What is the influence of the "Missouri Compromise" on the issues of slavery?
5. What is the "Monroe Doctrine" and why was it honored as the blueprint of US foreign policies for the following decades?

■ 阅读书目

1. Renehan Fr., Edward J. *The Monroe Doctrine: The Cornerstone of American Foreign Policy*, Chelsea Publishing House, 2007
2. Unger, Harlow Giles. *The Last Founding Father: James Monroe and a Nation's Call to Greatness*. Da Capo Press, 2009.
3. Avarez, Alejandro. *The Monroe Doctrine, Its Importance in the International Life of the States in the New World*. New York: Oxford University Press, 1924.
4. Perkins, Dexter. *A History of Monroe Doctrine*. Boston: Little Brown, 1955.
5. Renehan, Edward J., Jr. *The Monroe Doctrine: The Cornerstone of American Foreign Policy*, Chelsea Publishing House, 2007.

第十四讲
约翰·昆西·亚当斯
(John Quincy Adams 1767—1848)

■ 政治历史评述

约翰·昆西·亚当斯:孤僻的外交家,学院派的总统

美国政坛上不乏特立独行的政治人物。托马斯·杰斐逊当年超凡脱俗的名士派头算是出名的。约翰·昆西·亚当斯也算得是一个性格孤僻内敛,独往独来的人物了。昆西18岁始在哈佛攻读法律,一次,同学们都要到附近的邦克山开烤肉派对,以庆祝新大桥的竣工开通,唯有他拒绝参与,认为这是亵渎了当年独立战争中为自由而战的烈士的英灵。这位独善其身,不苟言笑的政治家在1825年58岁时当上了第6任美国总统,仍旧不与人交往,离群索居。据说,昆西·亚当斯总统喜好晨泳,春夏每日凌晨起床,必定独步到距离白宫2公里以外的波多马克河游泳。有一次衣服被人拿走,总统不能裸奔回府,只好湿淋淋地在野地里苦等,直到有牧童路过,方嘱其到白宫报信,让侍从带来衣服接回。昆西一生严于律己内省,他在日记中是这样评论自己的性格的:"我是一个性格内向,冷峻威严的人。我的政敌说我是一个阴郁的恨世者,恨我的人说我是个不合群的野人。我自知此性格缺陷,却无变通纠正之意。"

昆西·亚当斯这样的性格与之家庭教育有关。他1767年出生在一个笃诚的清教徒家庭,父亲约翰·亚当斯善于读书思考,是为美国独立奔走的爱国者,后来成为第二届美国总统。昆西童年时代耳边听到的都是父亲的独立革命和自由的言论;母亲阿比盖尔是一位吃苦耐劳,并极具政治头脑的人,家教甚严,每天晚上都要儿子大段朗诵古典文章方能睡觉。当年波士顿民兵与英军首战邦克山,阿比盖尔为了让8岁的儿子从小立志为国,竟然带着他登上附近的山坡,耳边听着嗖嗖飞过的子弹,亲眼目睹硝烟弥漫的战场。老亚当斯1778年奉命出使法国,决定带着11岁的儿子昆西行万里路,见大世面。几年间,父子二人先到法国、英国、荷兰、瑞士、丹麦、德国和俄国。昆西随父出没于各国宫廷官场和上层社交圈,又得与富兰克林,杰斐逊等大人物接触,一时眼界打开,自然也就胸怀大志,到法国不久就开始日记,七十余年不曾间断,在巴黎的学校,他不仅学习各种古典课程,同时也选修各种人文艺术课程,对数学几何也保持极大的兴趣。1871年,14岁的昆西进入荷兰莱顿大学,热衷于学习欧洲各国语言,除了必备的拉丁文和希腊文外,掌握了法语、荷兰语、西班牙语、德语和俄语。他写的书信已初见文笔和议事之锋芒,展示了对经济学和政治学的兴趣。此时的昆西,浸淫于老欧洲的语言和文化,却未敢沉涵其中。为了对欧洲文化保持距离，坚守一个"美国人"的身份，昆西于1785年坚持回国，考入哈佛大学，其间严谨治学，博览群书，同时开始学习法律。如是观之，昆西·亚当斯的教育背景可谓既宽而杂：少年的欧洲阅历和观察为日后从政奠定了基础；对知识和语言的兴趣促成了今后的外交业绩；对美国身份和独立传统的坚持为未来的美国领土扩张和国内建设和发展提供了驱动。

昆西毕业后子承父业，成为律师，其间嗜书如命，几乎陷于现实生存与真理追求的两难境地中不能自拔。其时正遇到法国大革命的冲击，昆西于是写政论，笔锋犀利，颇有见地，由此受到高层注意。1794年华盛顿总统看好昆西，把他派往荷兰任美国常驻代表，期间他恪尽职守，在外交界开始崭露头角。1797受父亲总统约翰·亚当斯之命，昆西赴柏林任美国驻普鲁士大使，1801年奉命回国，两年后被马萨诸塞州议会选为国会参议员。从政后的昆西加入联邦党阵营，但对联邦党党派利益高于联邦利益的立场渐渐保持了距离。而联邦党在英国咄咄逼人的政策面前一味妥协忍让，终把反英派昆西·亚当斯推向了其反面。他坚持美国对英采取强硬立场，提倡独立发展美国经济，对杰斐逊的禁运政策投了赞成票，于是被联邦党占多数的州议会压迫，不得不1808辞去国会参议员职位，回到他喜爱的文学生涯之中，重操哈佛大学博伊尔斯顿讲席教鞭，教授修辞和演讲术。但是，昆西既心怀大志，又处政治漩涡之中，欲弃政从文，却是身不由己。一年之后，他接到任命担任驻俄国大使。1814年第二次对英战争结束，他在比利时根特代表美方主持和平谈判，站在民族主义立场，不卑不亢，挫败了英国人设立密西西比河和西北边界中立区的遏制政策。根特和约签署后，他又回到伦敦做大使，此后。1817年7月，昆西·亚当斯奉命回国做门罗总统的国务卿，基本结束了外交官的生涯，稳步在国内政坛上走向总统宝座。

外交家昆西·亚当斯做国务卿也颇有业绩。他立足美国未来大国的安全与发展，先是与英国讨价还价，稳固确立了西北边界，后来又借杰克逊将军南下的军事优势，逼西班牙人签订城下之盟，获得了佛罗里达大片的领土。他是著名的《门罗宣言》的始作俑者：凭借多年在欧洲的游学和外交经历，对法国大革命后欧洲组成"神圣联盟"的局势做出正确判断，力排众议，坚持撇开英国，单独宣布美国支持南美独立，以前所未有的强硬态度反对欧洲列强殖民美洲。可见，作为国务卿，昆西·亚当斯具有世界战略的眼光，在世界纷乱后重组的大势中，首先考虑为美国未来的生存、发展和扩张开辟道路。在他的心目中，美国即是世界的帝国观念似乎开始萌生。

当然，由于自信过度，说话尖刻，不近下层等性格特征，昆西·亚当斯虽以贵族风范当选

总统,却业绩不佳。他力主联邦出资大规模兴修国内交通建设,却未能在州权和联邦关系的平衡点,加之不能与时俱进,孤僻刻板,不善权变,因而实效不济。他受父母影响太深,对法制和权威抱有极大信心,同时也相信人性改善的可能。他的道德意识强大,但对大众的现实需要了解不多,因而虽积极倡导人的平等,但其奴隶立场太接近废奴主义,未能像林肯那样有折中的睿智和策略,因此民众对此呼应不多。直到他去世,人们才意识到他心灵中那种源于古典意识和宗教伦理以及现代天赋人权的人文关怀,也才有了从华盛顿市区到波士顿铁路沿线万众送行之壮观。19世纪美国,只有林肯的逝世才有过如此的景象。

说到昆西·亚当斯的政治演说功力之深,毋须赘言。这位哈佛毕业的才子一向以自己的语言才能感到自豪,认为"演说修辞的能力是人类所有进步的源泉","杰出的辩才就是力量"。他14岁就成段背诵莎士比亚名篇,19岁翻译亚里士多德的《修辞学》,用英语,法语和拉丁语阅读西塞罗、昆蒂里尔、柏拉图和其他大量古典作家的修辞文章;他是哈佛博伊尔斯顿讲席教授,是美国历史上唯一出版修辞学书的总统。

但是,在政治舞台上,除了修辞文章的精彩外,还有现实的需求,妥协和权变。昆西·亚当斯精致的语言表述旨在发掘传统的文气和古典伦理,而不是发扬一个国家现实的活力和道德精神。他带有西塞罗风格的文采和严谨的语言注定敌不过安德鲁·杰克逊蓬勃的人气。他像父亲老亚当斯一样,在自我表白和自我证明的心态和表述中熬过了一届总统任期,就被他称之为"自己的名字都几乎不会拼写的野蛮人"杰克逊取而代之了。

■ 演讲文(节选)

Presidential Inaugural Address

John Quincy Adams

...

compass: scope, period
covenant: agreement
unfold: execute

revenue: government income by taxes
judiciary: legal system

In the **compass** of thirty-six years since this great national **covenant** was instituted a body of laws enacted under its authority and in conformity with its provisions has **unfolded** its powers and carried into practical operation its effective energies. Subordinate departments have distributed the executive functions in their various relations to foreign affairs, to the **revenue** and expenditures, and to the military force of the Union by land and sea. A coordinate department of the **judiciary** has expounded the Constitution and the laws, settling in harmonious coincidence with the legislative will numerous weighty questions of construction which the imperfection of human language had **rendered** unavoidable. The year of **jubilee** since the first formation of our Union has just **elapsed**, that of the declaration of our independence is at hand. The **consummation** of both was effected by this Constitution.

Since that period a population of four millions has multiplied to twelve. A territory bounded by the Mississippi has been extended from sea to sea. New States have been admitted to the Union in numbers nearly equal to those of the first Confederation. Treaties of peace, **amity**, and commerce have been concluded with the principal **dominions** of the earth. The people of other nations, inhabitants of regions acquired not by conquest, but by **compact**, have been united with us in the participation of our rights and duties, of our burdens and blessings. The forest has fallen by the ax of our woodsmen; the soil has been made to **teem** by the **tillage** of our farmers; our commerce has **whitened** every ocean. The dominion of man over physical nature has been extended by the invention of our artists. Liberty and law have marched hand in hand. All the purposes of **human association** have been accomplished as effectively as under any other government on the globe, and at a cost little exceeding in a whole generation the expenditure of other nations in a single year.

Such is the unexaggerated picture of our condition under a Constitution founded upon the republican principle of equal rights. To admit that this picture has its **shades** is but to say that it is still the condition of men upon earth. From evil—physical, moral, and political—it is not our claim to be **exempt**. We have suffered sometimes by the visitation of Heaven through disease; often by the wrongs and injustice of other nations, even to the extremities of war; and, lastly, by **dissensions** among ourselves—dissensions perhaps inseparable from the enjoyment of freedom, but which have more than once appeared to threaten the dissolution of the Union, and with it the overthrow of all the enjoyments of our present **lot** and all our earthly hopes of the future. The causes of these dissensions have been various, founded upon differences of **speculation** in the theory of republican government; upon conflicting views of policy in our relations with foreign nations; upon jealousies of partial and sectional interests, **aggravated** by prejudices and **prepossessions** which strangers to each other are ever apt to entertain.

It is a source of gratification and of encouragement to me to observe that the great result of this experiment upon the theory of

---

rendered: made
jubilee: great joy in celebration
elapse: pass
consummation: perfect completion

amity: friendship
dominion: territory
compact: treaty, agreement

teem: fertile, rich
tillage: plough
whiten: covered by (white) sails
human association: social activity

shade: defect; shortcoming

exempt: except; stay away

dissension: quarrel over different ideas

lot: fortune; fate

speculation: thoughts; opinion
aggravated: made worse
prepossession: ideas that stay long and hard

crown: achieve
sanguine: hopeful; promising

human rights has at the close of that generation by which it was formed been **crowned** with success equal to the most **sanguine** expectations of its founders. Union, justice, tranquility, the common defense, the general welfare, and the blessings of liberty—all have been promoted by the Government under which we have lived. Standing at this point of time, looking back to that generation which has gone by and forward to that which is advancing, we may at once indulge in grateful **exultation** and in cheering hope. From the experience of the past we derive instructive lessons for the future. Of the two great political parties which have divided the opinions and feelings of our country, the **candid** and the just will now admit that both have contributed splendid talents, spotless integrity, ardent patriotism, and **disinterested** sacrifices to the formation and administration of this Government, and that both have required a liberal indulgence for a portion of human **infirmity** and error. The revolutionary wars of Europe, **commencing** precisely at the moment when the Government of the United States first went into operation under this Constitution, excited a collision of **sentiments** and of sympathies which kindled all the passions and embittered the conflict of parties till the nation was involved in war and the Union was shaken to its center. This time of trial **embraced** a period of five and twenty years, during which the policy of the Union in its relations with Europe constituted the principal basis of our political divisions and the most arduous part of the action of our Federal Government. With the **catastrophe** in which the wars of the French Revolution terminated, and our own subsequent peace with Great Britain, this **baneful** weed of party strife was uprooted. From that time no difference of principle, connected either with the theory of government or with our **intercourse** with foreign nations, has existed or been called forth in force sufficient to sustain a continued combination of parties or to give more than **wholesome animation** to public sentiment or legislative debate. ...

exultation: great happiness
candid: honesty; straightforwardness
disinterested: selfless; disregard of material interests
infirmity: weakness
commencing: beginning
sentiment: view, opinion

embrace: include; last

catastrophe: disasters; great traded
baneful: poisonous
intercourse: communication
wholesome: healthy
animation: excitement;
speculative: thoughtful

The collisions of party spirit which originate in **speculative** opinions or in different views of administrative policy are in their nature transitory. Those which are founded on geographical divisions, **adverse** interests of soil, climate, and modes of domestic life are more permanent, and therefore, perhaps, more dangerous. It is this which gives inestimable value to the character of our Government, at once federal and national. It holds out to us a perpetual **admonition** to preserve alike and with equal anxiety the rights of each individual

adverse: opposing

admonition: warning; precaution

State in its own government and the rights of the whole nation in that of the Union. Whatsoever is of domestic **concernment**, unconnected with the other members of the Union or with foreign lands, belongs exclusively to the administration of the State governments. Whatsoever directly involves the rights and interests of the federative **fraternity** or of foreign powers is of the **resort** of this General Government. The duties of both are obvious in the general principle, though sometimes perplexed with difficulties in the detail. To respect the rights of the State governments is the **inviolable** duty of that of the Union; the government of every State will feel its own obligation to respect and preserve the rights of the whole.

concernment: affaires; interests

fraternity: brotherhood
resort: business

inviolable: not to be violated or invaded

■ 重点述评与提示

1. The year of jubilee since the first formation of our Union has just elapsed, that of the declaration of our independence is at hand. The consummation of both was effected by this Constitution.

   亚当斯开篇照例对美国建国以来的历史做一番赞美回顾。这两句话紧凑严整，逻辑清晰，展示了修辞家驾驭语言的功力，其中联邦是铺垫，独立是重点，宪法是保障。这里的 has just elapsed 和 is at hand 形成对比，重心在后者，尤显表达的独到和精细。亚当斯在7月14日美国国庆日发表过长篇演说，重点阐述美国独立的外交政策，"独立"是他一生从政的基本立场。

2. The forest has fallen by the ax of our woodsmen; the soil has been made to teem by the tillage of our farmers; our commerce has whitened every ocean.

   这一排比句式中意象清晰，如见其形，可感到亚当斯的文学冲动。尤其是 whitened every ocean，直让听者想起莎士比亚的 Enrobe the roaring waters with my silks 的诗句。亚当斯少年时代就是莎士比亚迷，可想而知。

3. To admit that this picture has its shades is but to say that it is still the condition of men upon earth. From evil—physical, moral, and political—it is not our claim to be exempt.

   在亚当斯的思想构成中，洛克的自然法则和人性从善是主流，他也不赞同霍布斯的政治集权观念，但却汲取了其人性论观点。因此，亚当斯一直提倡人自身的道德自律，坚持对权力的道德约束，坚持统治者的道德义务，坚持法律对政府的监管。美国史家历来把他划为政治道德保守主义者之列。

4. Union, justice, tranquility, the common defense, the general welfare, and the blessings of liberty—all have been promoted by the Government under which we have lived.

   以西塞罗式的重尾句式,重申美国政治的传统核心价值,言简意赅。也是对前届政府的礼节性赞誉。

5. Of the two great political parties...both have contributed splendid talents, spotless integrity, ardent patriotism, and disinterested sacrifices to the formation and administration of this Government, and that both have required a liberal indulgence for a portion of human infirmity and error.

   总统选战结束,亚当斯的当选被反对派指责为卑劣的政治交易的结果。此时他力图重建政治平衡,延续所谓"和睦时代"的政治氛围,于是就有了这一番抚慰之言。句末言政治宽容,不忘表明自己的政治哲学理念:人性永恒的弱点需要永恒的自制。

6. With the catastrophe in which the wars of the French Revolution terminated, and our own subsequent peace with Great Britain, this baneful weed of party strife was uprooted.

   这里展示了亚当斯的国际视野:法国大革命和美英第二次战争是国内政治纷争的主要根源之一,这也说明美国不可能无视欧洲事务而自立。当然,把国内政党斗争简约为外交政策,也只是一厢情愿的想法。

7. Those which are founded on geographical divisions, adverse interests of soil, climate, and modes of domestic life are more permanent, and therefore, perhaps, more dangerous.

   随着美国领土的扩大和人口的增长,亚当斯目睹1821年"密苏里妥协案",称之为"大部头悲剧的小小前奏",此后奴隶制问题不断发酵,他忧心忡忡地预见到南北最终分裂的危险,这也许也是他担任总统后大力推行国内交通建设,坚持反对奴隶制的原因。

■ 思考及讨论题

1. What is the "first party system" and how was it ended after the War of 1812?
2. What were the major diplomatic achievements by J. Q. Adams?
3. Why Jacksonians accused J. Q. Adams of stealing the presidency with a "corrupt bargain"?

4. What were some major political prepositions by J. Q Adams after he left his presidency?

■ 阅读书目

1. Nagel, Paul C. *John Quincy Adams: A Public Life, A Private Life*. New York: Alfred A. Knopf, 1997.
2. Mattie, Sean. "John Quincy Adams and American Conservatism" in *Modern Age*. Volume: 45. Issue: 4, 2003.
3. Crowell, Thomas Y. *John Quincy Adams: His Theory and Ideas*. New York: Kessinger Publishing LLC. 1950.
4. Lindgren, James. "Rating the Presidents of the United States, 1789—2000: A Survey of Scholars in Political Science, History, and Law" in *Constitutional Commentary*. Winter 2001.

第十五讲
安德鲁·杰克逊（Andrew Jackson 1767—1845）

■ 政治历史评述

安德鲁·杰克逊：草根将军总统，大众平等主义的偶像

1828年11月，来自西部的牛仔式将军安德鲁·杰克逊在总统大选中以选举人团178票对83票的压倒多数，击败满腹经纶，老谋深算的在任总统约翰·昆西·亚当斯，堂而皇之地入主白宫，这标志着美国社会和经济转型中一个礼仪时代，精英政治的终结，同时也预示着美国杰克逊式大众平等主义民主的开端。

与杰斐逊1800年的"思想革命"有所不同，这个开端是充满原始民主形式和戏剧性的大众狂欢。1829年3月4日，杰克逊在国会山举行就职仪式。成千上万呼喊着平等主义口号的普通美国人从全国各地涌进首府华盛顿，争睹这位平民总统的真容。他们中大多数是来自南部和西部边远地区的拓荒者，小农生产者，村野鄙夫，退役老兵，爱尔兰移民，城市里的工人和小城镇的书报编辑。有些人硬是赶了几百英里的路程，为的就是看一眼大众的总统，自己心中的偶像。那情形就好像是"高贵的罗马城涌进了北方野蛮人的洪流"。一向典雅高贵，彬彬有礼的首府华盛顿充斥着喜怒笑骂形于色的下层外乡人。就职仪式这一天，杰克逊身穿黑色丧服，脸色阴沉地出现在总统就职仪式上。他的夫人拉切尔不久前忍受不了两党竞选的政治攻讦和谩骂，突发心脏病去世。杰克逊虽然胜选，但心中郁结不散。此时他面对沸腾的群众欢呼却表情漠然，显然还沉浸在丧妻的悲痛之中。在杰克逊草草念过事先写好的总统就职演说之后，激动的人群开始踏上国会山的台阶，涌向主席台。每个人都想与新任总统握手留念。杰克逊哪见过这阵势，他慌忙挤过涌动的人群，好不容易才骑

上马，朝白宫转移，身后跟随着长长一串热情洋溢，载歌载舞的人流。在白宫举行的招待会也成了精英高雅文化和低俗大众民主象征性冲突的场所。人们从四面八方涌入这幢被认为是典雅社会象征的白宫，有些急不可待的人甚至从洞开的窗户翻越入室。一时之间，白宫内人头攒动，美酒佳肴碰翻在地，地毯上威士忌酒和烟汁斑斑。这些边远地区来的大老粗也顾不上会摔坏墙壁上的艺术珍品和壁炉上供赏的古玩，拽过红木椅子，泥泞的长靴毫不顾忌地踏上精致昂贵的彩色饰垫，为的是居高看一眼心中的"老胡桃"英

雄。杰克逊也受用不起这般模样的平等和民主，慌不择路，从后门溜之大吉。白宫工作人员苦于这帮乌合之众久据白宫不散，急中生智，宣布在白宫外大草坪上有大桶果酒招待大家，人人有份，大伙一听，把老英雄杰克逊扔到脑后，一哄而出喝酒去。工作人员这才松口气，急忙用门闩顶住大门，可惜窗外如画的大草坪已被狂欢的人们践踏得泥泞不堪。这是平等主义的胜利，大众的庆典，一幅下里巴人参与政治的狂欢图。

在这场闹哄哄的政治狂欢中，尽管当中有不少人是来向杰克逊请功要官的，但就对美国民主的长远意义来看，这是平民社会意识的觉醒，是大众真正参与政治的表现，是平等主义的民主意识积蓄了多年能量后的一次爆发。它是"人人生而平等"的教条的一次实现。英国人为了达到这一境界，从1215年的大宪章到1688年的光荣革命，国王权威和民主势力经历了数百年的斗争，才达到君主立宪的妥协，在法国，启蒙思想的自由平等思想经历了法国大革命血与火的洗礼才得以初步实现。而在美国，平等主义的民主自由的理念在现代国家宪政的框架内，经历了1800年杰斐逊民主共和主义的思想革命到1828年杰克逊民主平等主义的现实狂欢，不到30年的时间就完成了它的现实转换，并深入美国政治生活，成为美国社会的政治共识。这不能不说是美国人的福分。正是在这个意义上，托克维尔才说："美国人所占的最大便宜，在于他们是没有经历民主革命而建立民主制度的，以及他们是生下来就平等而不是后来才变成平等的。"而且，依我看，所谓杰克逊式的美国民主对于此后100多年美国政治文化的积极意义正在于此。

另外，杰克逊式的民主也是美国当时社会变革和经济转型时代的必然产物。1812年战争后的美国，短暂的国家主义的和睦社会理想被1819年的经济恐慌和政治动荡无情地击破。社会经济在有所复苏之后，迎来了社会转型与变革，阶级矛盾加剧，祸福相依的痉挛时代。这是美国大众民主的时代，是建立在白人至上意识基础上的平等主义时代，但同时又是传统坍塌，法制废止，社会动乱，暴力横行的时代。如同上世纪60和70年代的中国文化大革命，大众宣泄的是集体无意识的平等主义冲动，在蔑视甚而打倒精英文化特权阶层的同时又树立起新的绝对统治权威并对之顶礼膜拜。正如历史学家霍夫斯塔特指出的：杰克逊时代"表达的是一个飞速发展国家的病态：对制约机制的抵制；不称职的政治领袖的专权；对权威的不耐烦。这个社会被自身的多元杂质文化弄得着魔混乱，根本上说，也被奴隶制这个古老而阴郁人类错误所诅咒"。

同时，这也是现代资本主义在美国发展的关键时代，由于交通运输和通讯技术的逐渐改善和进步，国内市场基本形成，东部的工业有了大的发展，开始出现了现代意义上的产业工人；惠特尼轧棉机的发明和使用，大规模地促进了南部的棉花经济生产；同时，西部开发运动开始逐渐冒头，广袤廉价的土地的诱惑，密西西比下游印第安人地区发现的金矿，都吸引着大量移民举家往西拓荒。美国人的自由概念得到了物质生存的证实和促动，走向了实用主义的方向。此外，这一时期大众媒体，报纸杂志，邮局，公共社会的影响日盛，还有大规模的群众参与的政党政治等社会因素都为杰斐逊式的民主注入了新的，实用的含义。科技进步和经济生活的改变于是引发了社会思想的变革。社会下层社会的劳动阶级自我意识逐渐觉醒，他们不再盲从少数政治精英的政治体制建构和社会解决方案，而是积极参与社会变革，向精英阶层和富有阶级叫板，要求废除选举权的财产资格，实行平等的政治和社会地位以及公民的权利。在这场美国历史上最为壮观的平等主义运动中,美国原始的种族优越感和经典的独立爱国意识合流,反联邦主义的社会能量和杰斐逊培育起来的个人主义和州权共和思想杂交汇合,产生了一系列要求平等的政治诉求:其中有对联邦政府内部机构体系的改革和分享要求,对大众普选和扩大选举权的呼声,也伴随着白人至上的种族自恋与对黑人奴隶和印第安人的种族压迫。而这一切纷然杂陈的社会和经济能量似乎都集中体现在一个草莽英雄安德鲁·杰克逊身上。

那么,杰克逊何许人?竟以一人之鲜活个性遮蔽久远的贵族精英传统,成就一个特定的民主时代?

杰克逊1767年3月15日生于北卡南部一个爱尔兰移民家庭,父亲在他未出生前就已去世。母亲从小培养杰克逊独立自主,自强不息的奋斗精神。少年杰克逊没有父亲的管束,又没有上过几天学,成天以印第安人为假想敌,自制矛刀和弓箭,出没于山林之中,酒坊之间,染上一身的匪气。他脾气暴躁,凶狠好斗,睚眦必报,成了远近闻名的江湖恶少。以此经历看,杰克逊后来对印第安部落大开杀戒,毫不手软,决斗场上视死如归,战场上死拼硬打,政坛上为我独尊,动辄兵戎相见等等这些鲁莽硬汉的个性也是环境和性格的必然。独立战争打响,13岁的杰克逊参加南卡民兵,1781年杰克逊被俘,一个英国军官命令他为自己擦皮鞋,倔强的杰克逊誓死不从,结果被这个英国军官用短剑在他的头上和手上留下了深深的伤痕,同时也在杰克逊心中种下了对英国军人深深的仇恨。1783年战争结束,杰克逊成了16岁的独立战争老兵,未来迷茫,不知所往。他先游手好闲于查尔斯顿,此后北迁来到北卡罗来纳谋点正事。他先给法官当听差。几年浸染在法律事务中,加上平时肯动点脑子,竟然在1786年9月通过了律师考试,成了一名开业律师。1788年10月,经官场朋友提携,杰克逊来到田纳西的纳什维尔镇当个检察官,成家立业,开办律师事务,购买奴隶经营店铺和农场,还热衷土地投机,成了远近闻名的检察官和实业家。1796年6月,杰克逊被选为田纳西州唯一的联邦众议员,不久被选为联邦参议员。可是,杰克逊生性粗莽,习惯了大胆想象,决而起行的务实作风,在参议院与那些带有些贵族做派,夸夸其谈的各州参议员为伍,形同异类。不到半年,杰克逊决定不再忍受,干脆一走了之,回到纳什维尔做了田纳西州大法官和军队统帅。1812年,第二次对英战争打响,年近50岁的杰克逊终于有了用武之地,率领训练有素的田纳西民军和部分正规军南下新奥尔良,在密西西比河岸泥泞沟堑阵地上和浓浓的晨雾中以坚忍的意志对垒英军的优势,击毙了英军名将帕克汉姆,以21人伤亡的极小代价歼灭英军2000余人,取得了闻名的新奥尔良大捷。杰克逊在欢呼声中几乎一夜之间成了美国的大英雄。

此后些年,杰克逊可谓是所向披靡:横扫佐治亚地区的塞米诺印第安部落,不顾国会禁令,长驱直入西属佛罗里达,推翻西班牙人的统治,为美国争得大块地盘。杰克逊的军事生涯到了登峰造极的地步:士兵们亲切地称他"老胡桃",印第安人敬畏地称他"利刀老杰克逊",西班牙人说他简直就是"丛林里的拿破仑"。1824年,杰克逊突然宣布竞选总统,赢得西部和南部下层社会广泛拥戴,支持率节节攀升,后因为未获得肯塔基参议员亨利·克莱关键的一票,杰克逊才饮恨败北。不料他4年之后卷土重来,竟以绝对优势登上总统宝座。

可见,这是一个思想单一,性情粗犷和我行我素的美国拓荒者形象。他崇尚权力意志,偏爱本真自然的个人能力,对后天学习获得的能力嗤之以鼻。西部土地的召唤造就了他的粗犷笃行和对印第安人的专横;南部的庄园和黑奴催生了他的爱国情怀和白人至上的优越感;东北部的工业城市和市场塑造了他对精英政治的鄙夷和对大多数平民的关怀。他生在南部小镇农庄,长在西部边疆,成于东部政坛的生活轨迹,几乎就是美国崇尚本真自由,不断进取开拓,追求大众民主的民族性格的象征。

杰克逊这种代表着美国不同地域大众性格的鲜明个性和平等主义意识与当时逐渐固化的美国行为习惯中的个人主义和自由主义一拍即合,铸成了影响一个时代并潜化于美国社会政治意识中杰克逊式的民主运动。

正是在这种白人至上的平等主义民主意识的驱动下,杰克逊才能在总统任内大刀阔斧地进行改革。他首创"政党分赃制",用人不论出身地位,把大批政府职位授予那些支持他的政党赢得选举的下层人士;他以代表大多数人利益的名义多次否决国会立法,常常对国会的立法案置之不理,10天之后自动否决;他废除定期内阁会议的繁文缛节,提倡少数内阁成员非正式的碰头会,随意讨论政府内外政策;他撤销第二特许美利坚中央银行,反对联邦政府组织的内务建设项目,认为这些都是以牺牲大多数人的利益,为少数银行家,企业家,既得利益者和政客聚敛财富的手段;他为大多数白人拓荒者开辟廉价的西部土地,对印第安人各部落领地巧取豪夺,最终采取暴力手段在寒冬向西驱赶印第安人2400多公里,留下了印第安人尸骨累累的"血泪之路",成为美国联邦政府犯下的种族主义罪行的永久见证;他把当时已经冒头的奴隶制问题看成是对大多数美国白人和联邦政府权威的潜在威胁,极力压制废奴主义运动,通缉逃奴,维护奴隶制的合法性。凡此种种,都是杰克逊式民主在政府层面上的集中表现。今天看来,杰克逊式民主的社会政治影响虽然在50年代被奴隶制争端和随后的南北战争所冲淡,但这些旨在推动大多数白人权利的平等主义改革和权力运作所造成的后果却沉淀下来,潜入现代美国社会意识,成为美国政治历史中最为鲜活的一页。

杰克逊的演说风格也别具一格。这位草民总统几乎没有受过像样的正规教育。既然当了总统,免不了登台演讲,时常让台下的幕僚为其捏一把汗。第一次总统就职演说时就出尽了洋相。当时杰克逊因夫人新丧,演说不在状态,加之听众欢呼声此起彼伏,让他十分紧张。握着讲稿的手不听使唤,一个劲地颤动,十分地尴尬。台下心情澎湃的听众指望他们的大英雄说出一些响当当的豪言壮语,但杰克逊略有爱尔兰口音的念白低沉微弱,没有人听到他在说什么。

但是,杰克逊的优势也是那些受过良好古典教育的精英派演说家所不具备的。他没有文化堆砌的沉重包袱,以其鲜明的个性和精神气质,有时直抒胸臆,无拘无束,更显自然豪放。在第二任总统就职演说中,杰克逊说到联邦统一的重要性时情不自禁,显出长者的语重心长:"我为国效力有些经验,加之人近老年,略有人生阅历。这些都能够证实我心中长期蕴含的信念,……";在任期届满时的告别演说中,杰克逊忍不住以父亲的口气谆谆告诫人民:"我的人生旅途已近终点…… 感谢上帝让我在自由的土地上渡过此生,是上帝给了我一颗对祖国的儿子般的爱心。此时我心中充满感激之情,感谢你们经久不衰和矢志不渝的热情支持,就此向你们表达我永久真诚的道别。"读到这样的文字,我们不禁会想起杰克逊从小就没有父爱的凄凉,也可以隐隐约约感受到他作为征服者让各族印第安部落酋长称呼他为"父亲"时的那份满足和无奈。

1833年,杰克逊的民望空前。这一年他巡视马萨诸塞州,应邀访问哈佛大学。哈佛一贯以学术独立,藐视政治著名,但该校校董们竟然投票一致赞同授予杰克逊法学名誉博士学位。当时校董之一的前总统昆西·亚当斯拒绝出席学位授予仪式,表示说,他"不愿看到敬爱的母校哈佛自贬如此,把博士学位授予一个自己的名字都几乎不会拼写的野蛮人。"亚当斯自小受过良好的古典教育,在哈佛也写过一本有关演说修辞的书。对于出身草莽的杰克逊自然是嗤之以鼻。但是,这位精英知识政治家似乎不明白,成功的演说家大致分为两类:一类以知识和逻辑见长,立论高远,引经据典,文辞雅正而不失迂阔,让人深感知识的丰富和真理的正义;另一类则以个人独特的性格和精神气质取胜,这类演说源于大众生活,基于个人经验,不拘一格的言辞背后无不闪动着普通大众心灵中共通的人生体验。而杰克逊无疑是属于后者。至于那些能够把知识和个性融为一体的演说家则是大师的风采了。

■ 演讲文(节选)

Second Presidential Inaugural Address

Andrew Jackson

Fellow-Citizens:

...

So many events have occurred within the last four years which have necessarily **called forth**—sometimes under circumstances the most delicate and painful—my views of the principles and policy which ought to be pursued by the General Government that I need on this occasion but **allude** to a few leading considerations connected with some of them.

The foreign policy adopted by our Government soon after the

call forth: bring to the surface; remind of;

allude: mention

formation of our present Constitution, and very generally pursued by successive Administrations, has been **crowned** with almost complete success, and has elevated our character among the nations of the earth. To do justice to all and to submit to wrong from none has been during my Administration its governing **maxim**, and so happy have been its results that we are not only at peace with all the world, but have few causes of **controversy**, and those of minor importance, remaining unadjusted.

In the domestic policy of this Government there are two objects which especially deserve the attention of the people and their representatives, and which have been and will continue to be the subjects of my increasing **solicitude**. They are the preservation of the rights of the several States and the **integrity** of the Union.

These great objects are necessarily connected, and can only be attained by an **enlightened** exercise of the powers of each within its appropriate sphere in conformity with the public will constitutionally expressed. To this end it becomes the duty of all to **yield** a ready and patriotic submission to the laws constitutionally enacted and thereby promote and strengthen a proper confidence in those institutions of the several States and of the United States which the people themselves have **ordained** for their own government.

My experience in public **concerns** and the observation of a life somewhat advanced confirm the opinions long since **imbibed** by me, that the destruction of our State governments or the **annihilation** of their control over the local concerns of the people would lead directly to revolution and anarchy, and finally to **despotism** and military domination. In proportion, therefore, as the General Government encroaches upon the rights of the States, in the same proportion does it **impair** its own power and **detract** from its ability to fulfill the purposes of its creation. Solemnly impressed with these considerations, my countrymen will ever find me ready to exercise my constitutional powers in arresting measures which may directly or indirectly encroach upon the rights of the States or tend to consolidate all political power in the General Government. But of equal and, indeed of incalculable, importance is the union of these States, and the **sacred** duty of all to contribute to its preservation by a liberal support of the General Government in the exercise of its just powers. You have been wisely **admonished** to "accustom yourselves to think and speak of the Union as of the **palladium** of your political safety and prosperity, watching for its preservation with Jealous anxiety, **discountenancing** whatever may suggest even a suspicion that it can in any event be abandoned, and **indignantly** frowning upon the first dawning of any attempt to alienate any portion of our country from the rest or to enfeeble the sacred ties which now link together the various parts." Without union our independence and liberty would never have been achieved; without union they never can be maintained. Divided into twenty-four, or even a smaller number, of separate communities, we shall see our internal trade burdened with numberless restraints and **exactions**; communication between distant points and sections obstructed or cut off; our sons made soldiers to **deluge** with blood the fields they now **till** in peace; the mass of our people borne down and **impoverished** by taxes to support armies and navies, and military leaders at the head of their victorious **legions** becoming our lawgivers and judges. The loss of liberty, of all good government, of peace, plenty, and happiness, must inevitably follow a dissolution of the Union. In supporting it, therefore, we support all that is dear to the freeman and the **philanthropist**.

The time at which I stand before you is full of **interest**. The eyes of all nations are fixed on our Republic. The event of the existing crisis will be decisive in the opinion of mankind of the practicability of our federal system of government. Great is the **stake** placed in our hands; great is the responsibility which must rest upon the people of the United States. Let us realize the importance of the attitude in which we stand before the world. Let us exercise **forbearance** and firmness. Let us **extricate** our country from the dangers which surround it and learn wisdom from the lessons they **inculcate**....

Constantly bearing in mind that in entering into society "individuals must give up a share of liberty to preserve the rest," it will be my desire so to discharge my duties as to foster with our brethren in all parts of the country a spirit of liberal **concession** and compromise, and, by reconciling our fellow-citizens to those partial sacrifices which they must unavoidably make for the preservation of a greater good, to recommend our invaluable Government and Union to the confidence and affections of the American people.

indignantly: angrily

exaction: enforced payment by authority
deluge: shed large amount of (blood)
till: plough
impoverish: become poor
legion: army (in marching)
philanthropist: people who love humankind

interest: opportunity and meaning

stake: share of interest; role

forbearance: endurance; patience
extricate: free; release
inculcate: teach repeatedly

concession: acknowledgement; admission

■ 重点述评与提示

1. The foreign policy adopted by our Government soon after the formation of our

present Constitution, and very generally pursued by successive Administrations, has been crowned with almost complete success, and has elevated our character among the nations of the earth.

此话没错。自立宪建国以来,各届政府都大致遵循华盛顿制定的外交中立和不结盟政策,避开欧洲的革命和战火。美国自从1814年在本土与英国打成平手之后,经过随后的领土扩张,人口和经济的增长,敢于抛出《门罗宣言》,基本立于世界大国之列。杰克逊此前四年任内疲于国内危机,处理外交事务并无亮点,这里一笔带过,赞誉前人也标榜了自己,收一石二鸟之功效。

2. In the domestic policy of this Government there are two objects ... which have been and will continue to be the subjects of my increasing solicitude. They are the preservation of the rights of the several States and the integrity of the Union.

的确,这是杰克逊第二届总统任期的主要问题,也是本演讲的主题。第一届任内,他因关税问题与南部州权主义者闹翻,曾扬言用武力维护联邦的统一,同时又否决美国中央银行延期,造成金融混乱和土地投机,仅此两桩就集中地反映了当时南部州权与联邦政府之间的矛盾和分裂的危机。

3. My experience in public concerns and the observation of a life somewhat advanced confirm the opinions long since imbibed by me, that the destruction of our State governments or the annihilation of their control over the local concerns of the people would lead directly to revolution and anarchy, and finally to despotism and military domination.

一般认为,杰克逊是个粗人,就职演讲稿由内阁高参集体完成。但以杰克逊强硬的性格和作风,往往在关键时刻会有个性张扬的表现。此句即为一例。杰克逊此时已70高龄,是那个时期美国总统最年长的一位。此处彰显老资格,但却也是语重心长。此句中所说的州权的破坏造成的后果虽然严重,但杰克逊在以下的语句中却也强势表示,保护州权的存在关键在于保障联邦政府的完整和权力(见以下第4句)。

4. But of equal and, indeed of incalculable, importance is the union of these States, and the sacred duty of all to contribute to its preservation by a liberal support of the General Government in the exercise of its just powers.

杰克逊在这里表达了依据宪法制止分裂,维护联邦完整统一和权力的决心,语气坚定,不容置疑。这也是他前4年一直在实施的政治行为。他前4年的行事作风独断专行,甚至以武力相威胁,以至于后来崛起的辉格党称之为"安德鲁国王"。此句以下他引用华盛顿当年告别演说中的名句来说明联邦统一的至关重要,似乎也意在修正自己的形象。

5. Without union our independence and liberty would never have been achieved; without union they never can be maintained.

  此句以及以下一连串的排比句应该是杰克逊内阁写手的杰作：句式整一，用词周正，具象煽情，是标准的政治演说腔。

6. The eyes of all nations are fixed on our Republic. The event of the existing crisis will be decisive in the opinion of mankind of the practicability of our federal system of government. Great is the stake placed in our hands; great is the responsibility which must rest upon the people of the United States.

  杰克逊在此义不容辞，表现出一种不计政治分歧和区域纷争的超然态度，让美国肩负起对于世界历史成败的责任感和使命感。这也是以后许多美国领导人反复展示的"替天行道"的意识形态基调。

■ 思考及讨论题

1. Why was Andrew Jackson enthusiastically cheered by American people in general?
2. What are the issues of taxes and "nullification" during Jackson's presidency?
3. Why was Jackson strongly against the recharter of the second Bank of the United States?
4. What did Jackson mainly do to remove Indians further to the west? Why did he do that?

■ 阅读书目

1. Howe, Daniel Walker. *What Hath God Wrought, The Transformation of America, 1815—1848*, Oxford University Press, 2007。
2. Remini, Robert V. *Andrew Jackson*, Palgrave Macmillan, 2008.
3. Syret, Harold C. *Andrew Jackson: His Contribution to the American Tradition*, Bobbs-Merrill, Indianapolis, 1953。
4. Ward, John William. *Andrew Jackson: Symbol for an Age.* London: Oxford University Press, 1962.

第五章 ‖ 西部领土扩张的时代

> We should do our duty towards both Mexico and Great Britain and firmly maintain our rights, and leave the rest to God and the country.
>
> —James K. Polk

> Ifanyone desires to know the leading and paramount object of my public life, the preservation of this Union will furnish him the key.)
>
> —John Clay

> Let him be just and deal kindly with my people, for the dead are not powerless.
>
> —Chief Seattle

Preview Questions

01/

What is generally the driving force to the westward expansion in the Antebellum America?

02/

How was the idea of "Manifest Destiny" formulated and how did it become the ideological weapon for the westward movement?

03/

How did the issue of slavery affect the expansion of western territories?

04/

How did American expansionists rationalize the removal of American Indians during the westward movement?

第十六讲

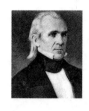

詹姆斯·K.波尔克(James K. Polk 1758—1831)

■ 政治历史评述

詹姆斯·波尔克:美国天定命运和西部领土扩张的强权者

"詹姆斯·波尔克是谁呀?"这是美国政治历史上的一句经典笑话。1844年,美国总统大选开张,民主党总统候选人难以产生,年轻的波尔克异军突起,成为美国政治历史上第一位"黑马"总统候选人。对此,实力雄厚的辉格党竞选班子当然不放在眼里。他们互相打趣地问道:"詹姆斯·波尔克是谁呀?"在他们眼里,波尔克不过是在家乡都当不了州长的无能之辈,不过是杰克逊战马的"马鬃上飘落下的一根枯毛"。辉格党总统候选人亨利·克莱甚至不无遗憾地说"(他们)怎么就找不到能配得上与我们过招的人呢。"在他看来,对付这么一个新手看来是稳超胜券了。此后的总统竞选过程中,"詹姆斯·波尔克是谁呀?"这一问句成了辉格党嘲笑民主党阵营人才捉襟见肘的噱头。

那么,波尔克是谁呢?

1795年11月2日,波尔克出生在北卡罗来纳州一个农场主家庭。他少年时健康不佳,干不了农活,极力说服父亲让他上学。村民们常常看到小波尔克每天光着脚丫,卷着裤腿,走几英里路去上学。18岁后,波尔克发愤用功,进入北卡罗来纳大学。大学期间,他除了学习规定的古典语言和哲学课程外,对数学有感兴趣,同时对演讲和辩论也情有独钟,学习成绩一直保持优秀,在毕业典礼上用拉丁语致欢迎词。毕业后,波尔克立志从政,到田纳西州的纳什维尔拜师学习法律,1820年成为开业律师。波尔克为人低调,是有名的工作狂。他对社交、艺术和游历一概没有兴趣。倒是对政治极为用心,处理政事必躬亲,细大不捐。波尔克长期担任国会议员和议长,但一直韬光养晦,不露声色,至多提出竞选副总统职务,而且屡试不中,甚至在自己的家乡田纳西州竞选连任州长也惨遭淘汰。然而,这次不同,"黑马"波尔克志在必得,他承诺坚持杰克逊的货币和关税政策,同时坚决主张西部扩张,吞并得克萨斯并向英国提出整个俄勒冈地区的领土要求。同时,为取悦南方民主党人,波尔克在奴隶制问题上小心翼翼地走出一条中间道路,一方面确保现有奴隶制的合法和完整,另一方面避开在新的西部领土实行奴隶制这个敏感问题。此外,他承诺不寻求连任,给民主党不少梦想总统宝座的人留下希望的空间。这些坚持己见,取悦两边,妥协中间,留有余地的策略不仅赢得了南部民主党的一致支持,还获得了北部民主党的欢心。就这样,波尔克后来居上,出乎意料地当选总统。

波尔克的成功也是顺应大势的必然结果。19世纪40年代,英国和西班牙在北美的殖民统治已经风雨飘摇。英国忙于欧洲事务,对俄勒冈领地已经鞭长莫及;西班牙在美洲的庞大殖民帝国也分崩离析,各殖民地相继宣告独立。墨西哥也于1824年宣告独立。相反,美国呈现出一个年轻的大国崛起的征象。杰克逊民主的平等主义运动在唤醒个人主义意识的同时也极大地刺激了人们的开拓精神和物质欲望。在北方,工业的发展和技术的进步相得益彰,运河的开凿,铁路的修建,特

别是电报的发明,使得资本主义的生产和消费急需扩展更广阔的市场。波尔克西部领土扩张政策使北方资本家们看到了新的机遇。这一时期也是移民人数增长迅猛的时期。截至1850年,大约400万移民涌入美国东海岸地区,其中爱尔兰移民居多,德国移民次之。这些移民怀揣着新大陆新生活的美梦,向往着西部廉价的土地,成了波尔克西部领土扩张的忠实选民。此外,加利福尼亚发现金矿,淘金热方兴未艾,俄勒冈太平洋沿岸肥沃的土地,无不在呈现出一幅富裕美好的生活憧憬。在南方,由于轧棉机的发明和使用,英国和欧洲市场对棉花的需求不断增长,使得棉花价格上扬,南方的种植园大范围扩大,增加了对奴隶的需求,带动了奴隶市场。南方奴隶主们早就看中了得克萨斯和墨西哥广阔的棉田。波尔克坚持的强权领土扩张政策正合了南方奴隶主的意。甚至有人提出美国应该兼并整个墨西哥,成就北美大一统的,以农业为主的美利坚帝国。

波尔克的强权政治也表现出对待奴隶制问题的策略性。波尔克拥有数十名奴隶和庞大的棉花种植园。西进领土扩张势必使奴隶制进一步蔓延,这是与波尔克本人的利益和南方民主党的根本利益一致的,也是北方辉格党和废奴主义者反对用武力扩张领土的根本原因。奴隶制问题已经急剧上升为国内主要政治和道德问题。波尔克为了缓和国内矛盾,取得西进领土扩张的政治共识,不得不表示不赞同奴隶制,认为那是不道德的,是"一个既成的罪恶,奴隶们也是有理性的人类"。但是在强权领土扩张的大趋势下,奴隶制问题应该搁置。他认为联邦政府首要任务是把握历史机遇,实施国家强权,为不断增长的人口和物质需求创造条件,而不应该介入南北双方关于奴隶制的争论。为此,他有十分美国式的理由:"奴隶制是我们的祖先遗留下来的问题,也受到宪法的保护,因此,联邦政府最好不要去碰它。"值得注意的是,对待奴隶制问题的这种权宜思维一直延续到20年以后的林肯时代,导致了美国南北战争的爆发,所不同的是,林肯把这个历史遗留问题的后果引向内部的武力解决,而不是波尔克的外部扩张战争。不过在19世纪40—50年代,有关奴隶制问题的争论尽管激烈,但在波尔克强权西进领土扩张主义的大局中,仍是可以通过南北利益妥协得以暂时解决的。这也充分显示了波尔克为了领土扩张不择手段的马基雅维利式的强权策略。

在此过程中,渐次兴起的新闻媒体鼓吹美国"天定命运"观,为这股民族主义和西进

扩张势力起到推波助澜的作用。所谓的美国"天定命运"观形成于19世纪40年代。这一观念鼓吹美国大国的兴起是上帝在人类实行的一次伟大试验,美国人将注定从地缘,政治体制和生活方式各个方面都全部占有北美大陆。当时,这一观念直接为波尔克政府的帝国扩张主义政策提供理论依据和社会舆论,为美国在此时期大规模的领土扩张和西进运动起到推波助澜的作用。

"天定命运观"是美国政治历史底蕴中的核心观念,在美国西进扩张的关键时刻明确表述出来并逐渐演化为美国政治生活中的主流意识形态。这里有必要对此观念做一简要的梳理。

在1845年8月,纽约有名的杂志主编奥沙利文(John L. O'Sullivan 1813—1895)在自己创办的《美国杂志和民主评论》7-8月刊上发表题为《兼并》的文章,针对英法两国暗中插手得克萨斯的企图,鼓吹美国国会应尽快批准兼并得克萨斯。奥沙利文在文中称,"为了我国每年以百万人计增长的人口,我们必须向外拓展,直至覆盖这片上帝赐予我们的大陆,这也是实现我们的天定命运。"《民主评论》是有名的杂志,是倡导美国本土文学的急先锋,曾刊登过美国著名作家爱默生、惠特曼、霍桑、梭罗等人的文章。可见其文化影响力。

稍后,奥沙利文为"天定命运"注入新的含义:在12月27日的《纽约早报》的评论文中,他再次宣称,美国对全部的俄勒冈领土拥有主权,这是"我们天定命运的权力,这项权力规定我们必须向外拓展,直至拥有整个北美大陆。因为这片大陆是上帝赐予我们,以促进一场人类自由和人民做主的联邦自治的伟大尝试。"这一强调美国政体优越的提法明显针对英国对俄勒冈的领土要求,也是对"旧欧洲"政体的一种嘲弄。自此,标榜美国政治体制的优越也就成了"天定命运"的内涵之一。此后奥沙利文再三使用"天定命运",营造美国大国扩张的意识形态。当时美国西部领土扩张已经逐渐为美国南北各政治势力认同,民主党和辉格党虽然在奴隶制问题上原则对立,但就美国利益和影响应遍及美洲大陆这一点是一致的。并且,波尔克政府力图避开奴隶制在西部蔓延这一敏感的问题,积极推行领土扩张政策并开始诉诸军事行动。在此情势下,"天定命运"这个言简意赅的词语也就自然被广泛用来为美国的西部领土扩张主张目,鼓动美国理直气壮地通过外交和军事手段占领北美大陆。

墨西哥战争后,美国的版图延伸到太平洋沿岸,同时与英国达成妥协,获得北纬49度以南的俄勒冈领地,实现了昆西·亚当斯当年宣称的,美国终将"无可争议地获得了两大洋之间,日出和日落之间广袤大陆的主权"的愿望。美国的"天定命运"观于是得以现实印证和强化。

以社会历史眼光审视这一颇有宗教神秘和浪漫色彩却又十分实用的观念,我们不难发现,"天定命运观"积淀着诸多的美国社会历史因素,其中既有清教圣徒"山巅之城"的余韵,独立革命时期孕育的爱国主义激情和对美国共和政体的自豪,杰斐逊农业立国的理想主义传统,也有门罗宣言的大国意识,还有杰克逊民主在西部培植的个人主义边疆开拓精神以及白人种族主义的优越感,甚至还有美国新兴的中产阶级对于技术进步的骄傲。这些因素都融入了19世纪社会进步的理想之中,也构成当时美国浪漫主义文化的主流意识,甚至经过政治权力话语的强化得以延绵至今,彰示着美国在世界范围内推行美国式"民主"和"自由"的现代使命和经济与文化霸权。

在这一建构美国优越身份的过程中,文化思想界的声音也十分地强烈。美国大诗人瓦特·惠特曼在1847年发表文章说"美国的国力和领土应该不断拓展,这是有利于全人类的事业……我们对那些土地提出领土要求……的法律依据是高于人间的协议和那些枯燥无味的外交规则的。"他在那篇充满激情的《草叶集序》(1855)中称美洲大陆的山川草木是美国不可分割的有机整体,号召美国诗人包容古今,置身人民,因为美国是一切种族中的优等种族,掌握着世界和时代的未来。

另一位同时代的大文豪,美国超验主义哲学家拉尔夫·沃尔多·爱默生在1844年发表的题为《年轻的美国人》的演讲中坚信,世界的每一个时代都有一个引领潮流的国家,这个国家非美国莫属。而美国年轻的一代正是这个时代的领导者。"有一种崇高和友善的命运在指引着人类前进的步伐。"而美国正是天定命运属于未来的国家。美国没有过去,只有面向未来的各种开端和宏伟的计划,载负着人类的希望。爱默生在演说中充满自信地说:"这富庶繁茂的大陆是我们的,各州相连,领土相接,一直通向太平洋的万顷波涛。"这番话与当时狂热鼓吹"天定命运"观的扩张主义者的话语如出一辙。

重要的是,这些代表"时代精神"的文化自我建构一旦被政治话语捕获,就上升成了政治利益集团的意志,可能付诸现实的国家行为。事实证明,波尔克不愧是杰克逊强权主义的继承者,领土扩张的强权者,也是急于推行帝国扩张主义的行动者。他上台以后不久,高扬"天定命运"的意识形态,出兵兼并了得克萨斯,进而觊觎墨西哥北方领土。在随后两年的墨西哥战争中,美军一直打到墨西哥城,迫使墨西哥政府签订条约,

割让新墨西哥领地和加利福尼亚近525万平方英里的土地。此前,波尔克向英国提出"北纬54度40分,否则就是战争"的强硬威胁,后达成妥协获得了北纬49度以南约280万平方英里的俄勒冈领土。这就是波尔克强权领土扩张的丰厚成果,这为美国在内战后的高速发展和今天的世界霸主地位提供了最有力的原始积累和基础。"天定命运"的意识形态在19世纪中叶美国领土扩张的大势中可谓力量无穷,所向披靡。

1845年3月4日是波尔克当选总统就职日,滂沱大雨之后的华盛顿,阴雨蒙蒙,国

会山前的宾夕法尼亚大街散落着被大雨淋坏的游行彩车,波尔克在国会山面对着被昆西·亚当斯戏称的"雨伞集会"做了他历时30分钟的就职演说,其中例行地表达了对美国政治体制的赞美,同时明确表示反对国家银行和维护低关税的政策,表现出对杰斐逊主义和杰克逊强权政策的承袭。对于奴隶制这个敏感的话题,波尔克避开"奴隶制"这一措辞,但是却十分明确地反对废奴,同时表示了坚定的维护这一"受到宪法组织和保护的国内体制"的决心。更为重要的是,波尔克借此机会用一种强势的语气,标榜美国政府对不断增加的西部人口提供政治和经济保障义务,表达了对西部领土扩张的决心和立场。波尔克的就职演说直截了当,许多地方措辞强硬,底气十足,甚至带有威胁的语气,反复表达了美国对俄勒冈"明确和不容置疑"的权利。

对于波尔克的演说能力,昆西·亚当斯同样予以全盘否定。这位以修辞学养著称的前总统认为波尔克的演说"毫无思想亮点","讲演时毫无风度","语言毫不高雅","毫无即兴的欢愉"。然而,亚当斯侧重典雅修辞,把玩语言文体的评价标准显然是用错了地方。19世纪中叶美国西进的步伐带出个逐渐讲求实际,注重实用的时代。人们在波尔克的演讲中读到的是明确的国家利益旨向和措施,也从中看到了个人的发展机遇。这就是为什么波尔克这篇就职演讲虽然冗长,但却受到包括部分波尔克的反对派在内的广大美国人普遍的欢迎的缘故。波尔克在他的总统就职演说中宣称:"我不会仅仅做部分人的总统,而是要做全体美国人民的总统。"这样突出主词,直截了当而又巧妙对偶的宣言言简意赅,显示了强权当仁不让的自信,因而更具有意识形态感召力,更能引起广大普通美国人的遐想和共鸣。个中道理也就不言自明了。

演讲文(节选)

First Presidential Inaugural Address

James K. Polk

Fellow citizens

...

It will be my first care to **administer** the Government in the true spirit of that instrument, the Constitution, and to assume no powers not expressly granted or clearly implied in its terms. The Government of the United States is one of **delegated** and limited powers, and it is by a strict **adherence** to the clearly granted powers and by **abstaining from** the exercise of doubtful or unauthorized implied powers that we have the only sure guaranty against the recurrence of those unfortunate **collisions** between the Federal and State authorities which

administer: operate

delegate: represent
adherence: insistence
abstain from: keep strictly away from
collision: conflict

have occasionally so much disturbed the harmony of our system and even threatened the **perpetuity** of our glorious Union.

"To the States, respectively, or to the people" have been reserved "the powers not delegated to the United States by the Constitution nor **prohibited** by it to the States." Each State is a complete sovereignty within the sphere of its reserved powers. The Government of the Union, acting within the sphere of its delegated authority, is also a complete sovereignty. While the General Government should abstain from the exercise of authority not clearly delegated to it, the States should be equally careful that in the maintenance of their rights they do not **overstep** the limits of powers reserved to them. One of the most distinguished of my **predecessors** attached deserved importance to "the support of the State governments in all their rights, as the most competent administration for our domestic concerns and the surest **bulwark** against antirepublican tendencies," and to the "preservation of the General Government in its whole constitutional vigor, as the **sheet anchor** of our peace at home and safety abroad."

To the Government of the United States has been entrusted the exclusive management of our foreign affairs. Beyond that it **wields** a few general **enumerated** powers. It does not force reform on the States. It leaves individuals, over whom it casts its protecting influence, entirely free to improve their own condition by the **legitimate** exercise of all their mental and physical powers. It is a common protector of each and all the States; of every man who lives upon our soil, whether of native or foreign birth; of every religious **sect**, in their worship of the Almighty according to the **dictates** of their own conscience; of every shade of opinion, and the most free inquiry; of every art, trade, and occupation consistent with the laws of the States. And we rejoice in the general happiness, prosperity, and advancement of our country, which have been the **offspring** of freedom, and not of power....

The Republic of Texas has made known her desire to come into our Union, to form a part of our Confederacy and enjoy with us the blessings of liberty secured and guaranteed by our Constitution. Texas was once a part of our country—was unwisely **ceded** away to a foreign power—is now independent, and possesses an undoubted right to **dispose of** a part or the whole of her territory and to merge her sovereignty as a separate and independent state in ours. I congratulate my country that by an act of the late Congress of the United States the **assent** of this Government has been given to the reunion, and it

perpetuity: everlasting eternity

prohibited: forbid; disallow

overstep: go beyond
predecessor: forerunner (here it refers to Thomas Jefferson)
bulwark: defense; protection
sheet anchor: strongest foundation
wield: exercise
enumerated: counted; listed

legitimate: lawful

sect: group, party
dictate: decision

offspring: children; generation

cede: give

dispose of: handle as one's own
assent: agreement

only remains for the two countries to agree upon the terms to **consummate** an object so important to both.

I regard the question of **annexation** as belonging exclusively to the United States and Texas. They are independent powers competent to **contract**, and foreign nations have no right to interfere with them or to take exceptions to their reunion. Foreign powers do not seem to appreciate the true character of our Government. Our Union is confederation of independent States, whose policy is peace with each other and all the world. To enlarge its limits is to extend the **dominions** of peace over additional territories and increasing millions. The world has nothing to fear from military ambition in our Government. While the **Chief Magistrate** and the popular branch of Congress are elected for short terms by the **suffrages** of those millions who must in their own persons bear all the burdens and miseries of war, our Government can not be otherwise than **pacific**. Foreign powers should therefore look on the annexation of Texas to the United States not as the conquest of a nation seeking to extend her dominions by arms and violence, but as the peaceful **acquisition** of a territory once her own, by adding another member to our confederation, with the consent of that member, thereby **diminishing** the chances of war and opening to them new and ever-increasing markets for their products.

To Texas the reunion is important, because the strong protecting arm of our Government would be extended over her, and the vast resources of her fertile soil and **genial** climate would be speedily developed, while the safety of New Orleans and of our whole southwestern frontier against hostile aggression, as well as the interests of the whole Union, would be promoted by it.

In the earlier stages of our national existence the opinion **prevailed** with some that our system of confederated States could not operate successfully over an extended territory, and serious objections have at different times been made to the enlargement of our boundaries. These objections were earnestly urged when we acquired Louisiana. Experience has shown that they were not well founded. The title of numerous Indian tribes to vast **tracts** of country has been **extinguished**; new States have been admitted into the Union; new Territories have been created and our **jurisdiction** and laws extended over them. As our population has expanded, the Union has been **cemented** and strengthened. As our boundaries have been enlarged and our agricultural population has been spread over a large surface, our

---

consummate: finalize, complete

annexation: taking as a part of a bigger country

contract: (v.) sign a contract

dominion: region, territory; country

Chief Magistrate: President of USA

suffrage: right to vote

pacific: mild; peaceful

acquisition: obtaining, gain

diminish: reduce

genial: warm and mild; comfortable

prevail: popular, overwhelm;

tract: large area of land

extinguish: disappear; wipe out

jurisdiction: areas covered by law

cement: consolidate; fix

federative system has acquired additional strength and security. It may well be doubted whether it would not be in greater danger of overthrow if our present population were **confined to** the comparatively narrow limits of the original thirteen States than it is now that they are **sparsely** settled over a more expanded territory. It is confidently believed that our system may be safely extended to the utmost bounds of our territorial limits, and that as it shall be extended the **bonds** of our Union, so far from being weakened, will become stronger....

Nor will it become in a less degree my duty to assert and maintain by all constitutional means the right of the United States to that portion of our territory which lies beyond the **Rocky Mountains**. Our title to the country of the Oregon is "clear and unquestionable," and already are our people preparing to perfect that title by occupying it with their wives and children. But eighty years ago our population was confined on the west by the **ridge** of the **Alleghanies**. Within that period—within the lifetime, I might say, of some of my hearers—our people, increasing to many millions, have filled the eastern valley of the Mississippi, adventurously ascended **the Missouri** to its **headsprings**, and are already engaged in establishing the blessings of self-government in valleys of which the rivers flow to the Pacific. The world **beholds** the peaceful triumphs of the **industry** of our emigrants. To us belongs the duty of protecting them adequately wherever they may be upon our soil. The jurisdiction of our laws and the benefits of our republican institutions should be extended over them in the distant regions which they have selected for their homes. The increasing facilities of **intercourse** will easily bring the States, of which the formation in that part of our territory can not be long delayed, within the sphere of our federative Union. In the meantime every obligation imposed by treaty or conventional **stipulations** should be sacredly respected.

confined to: limited to
sparsely: thinly; scant; not much

bond: territorial limits by contract
Rocky Mountains: the mountains west of the Midwest of USA
ridge: a serious of connected high peaks
Alleghenies: the mountain ridge east of Mississippi
the Missouri: Missouri River
headsprings: the source of a river

behold: watch; look on
industry: hardworking

intercourse: communication
stipulation: regulation; provision of law

■ 重点述评与提示

1. ...that we have the only sure guaranty against the recurrence of those unfortunate collisions between the Federal and State authorities which have occasionally so much disturbed the harmony of our system and even threatened the perpetuity of our glorious Union.

历届美国总统演说大都开篇标榜美国宪政体制的优越,这是总统施政的基础。波尔克此处不例外,但同时也透露出,随着西部扩张导致的南北分歧,此时不仅在此政体中注入不和谐之音,而且甚至威胁到联邦的完整统一和长治久安。波尔克紧接下文中引用杰斐逊,也表现出力图平衡州权和联邦权力的意愿,为其西部扩张做出政策铺垫。

2. It is a common protector of each and all the States; of every man who lives upon our soil, whether of native or foreign birth; of every religious sect, in their worship of the Almighty according to the dictates of their own conscience; of every shade of opinion, and the most free inquiry; of every art, trade, and occupation consistent with the laws of the States.

这里有意突出联邦政府在对外事务中的绝对权力,强调联邦政府是每个公民生存,信仰,言论自由和一切合法权利的保护者,直接为兼并得克萨斯,吞并新墨西哥和俄勒冈领地建立"合法的"强权依据。有关国家可以在此听出言外的威胁之音。

3. Foreign powers do not seem to appreciate the true character of our Government. Our Union is confederation of independent States, whose policy is peace with each other and all the world. To enlarge its limits is to extend the dominions of peace over additional territories and increasing millions. The world has nothing to fear from military ambition in our Government.

波尔克在此施放和平烟幕弹。其实在1844年的竞选过程中,国内舆论和两党在西部扩张问题上的立场基本一致,为领土扩张不惜与墨西哥和英国一战的舆论已经不绝于耳。此处最后一句表白美国概无军事野心,语义效果正好相反。

4. The title of numerous Indian tribes to vast tracts of country has been extinguished; new States have been admitted into the Union; new Territories have been created and our jurisdiction and laws extended over them. As our population has expanded, the Union has been cemented and strengthened.

1803年美国购买路易斯安那领地以来,逐渐形成的美国主宰北美大陆的"天定命运"观,约翰·昆西·亚当斯就曾宣布美国终将"无可争议地获得了两大洋之间,日出和日落之间广袤大陆的主权"。波尔克这里描述的正是"天定命运"的进程,其中表现出对印第安人命运的冷漠,对美国宪政的自信和强权的荣耀。

5. It is confidently believed that our system may be safely extended to the utmost bounds of our territorial limits, and that as it shall be extended the bonds of our Union, so far from being weakened, will become stronger....

事实上,随着西部扩张的日益深入,奴隶制问题益发彰显,南北分裂益发加剧。

波尔克这里表达的是自我合法化话语，也是权力的权益之智。

6. Our title to the country of the Oregon is "clear and unquestionable," and already are our people preparing to perfect that title by occupying it with their wives and children.

   波尔克政府在俄勒冈领地问题上虽力图避免战争，但对英国的强硬态度（clear and unquestionable）最终在谈判桌上占到了便宜：虽然没有取得全部的俄勒冈领地，却也获得了北纬49度以南的大片富庶领土。

7. To us belongs the duty of protecting them adequately wherever they may be upon our soil. The jurisdiction of our laws and the benefits of our republican institutions should be extended over them in the distant regions which they have selected for their homes.

   这是美国"天定命运时代精神"的政治话语表达，其中仿佛可以听到当今美国在世界上推行美国式"民主"和"自由"的现代使命和文化霸权的遥远回音。几个月前，美国哲学家爱默生在《年轻的美国人》的演讲中也充满自信地说："这富庶繁茂的大陆是我们的，各州相连，领土相接，一直通向太平洋的万顷波涛。"

■ 思考及讨论题

1. What were the central issues during the 1844 presidential election?
2. How did Mexico and the United States dispute over Texas?
3. When and how were part of the Oregon territory settled by Americans?
4. What were the consequences of the US-Mexico War of 1846—1848?

■ 阅读书目

1. Byrnes, Mark E. *James K. Polk: A Biographical Companion*. ABC-CLIO Inc., 2001.
2. Mountjoy, Shane. *Manifest Destiny: Westward Expansion*. New York: Chelsea House, 2009.
3. Howe, Daniel Walker. *What has God Wrought: Transformation of America 1815—1848*. Oxford University Press, 2007.
4. http://www.enotes.com/american-history-literature/manifest-destiny

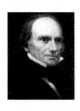

第十七讲
亨利·克莱(Henry Clay 1777—1845)

■ 政治历史评述

亨利·克莱： 求同存异的妥协家,政坛的无冕之王

在19世纪上半叶的美国政治历史舞台上,亨利·克莱无疑是最活跃的演员。他的名字与一系列"最"联系在一起。他参加政治活动年纪最轻,活跃在政治舞台时间最长:从1799年23岁在肯塔基州修宪起始,直到1852年76岁去世那年在纽约州议会辩论1850年妥协案实施问题,长达半个多世纪,他一直都是政坛的风云人物;他是19世纪美国最具魅力的政治活动家:不知疲倦地出入国会大小会议,彬彬有礼,气质尊贵,谈吐高雅;甚至连政敌都受到他性格魅力的感染;他是国会任职时间最长的众议院议长:自1811年到1824年,历届国会都一致选举他为众议院议长;他也是最想当美国总统但却最不走运的总统候选人,从1820年以来近30年的时间里,他曾先后5次作为辉格党总统提名人参与总统竞选角逐,却5次都遭到无情地淘汰,克莱虽对此耿耿于怀,曾以"与其当总统,不如总是正确的"的话加以自嘲。克莱还是最有影响力的政治演说家,他的演说率真而饱含激情,虽然少了些理性的深度和思维的缜密,却富有直觉感染力,直趋听众的心灵,让人立刻产生思想的共鸣;最后,他还是美国政治历史上被称为最伟大的"妥协家",在19世纪上半叶美国联邦和州权斗争,领土扩张和奴隶制问题等复杂的政治格局中禅思竭虑,斡旋各方,促成1821年密苏里妥协案、1833年关税妥协案、1850年的堪萨斯妥协案等一系列有关美国存亡的重大妥协。

都说一部美国政治史就是政治原则和现实妥协的历史。的确,美国人凡处理国内政治冲突,大都表面言之凿凿,暗中却调和妥协,化解矛盾。毕竟,关起门来一家人都好说。但对外就不一样了。国家贫弱时可以自我妥协,大唱中立政策和孤立主义调子,一旦国力开始强盛,天佑美国,天定命运的精神又大行其道,对外强权,领土扩张没得商量,及至今日,美国对外霸权十足,大有替天行道,民主舍我其谁的架势。当然,19世纪60年代的美国南北战争是唯一的重大例外,那是因为南北双方的政治和经济冲突伤筋动骨,直接危及联邦国家大厦之废立,不动武不流血不足以解决问题。这是后话。

说到美国历史上重大的政治妥协,例子比比皆是。众所周知,美国宪法本身就是各州利益冲突的妥协结果;批准宪法的政治体制原则大论战也以"权利法案"修正案的均衡作用而告终;杰斐逊民主的自由重农与汉弥尔顿的国家集权和工商主义虽然水火不容,但在历史现实的条件下实行起来却是你中有我,我中有你:既要大一统的国家权力以求富国强兵,又要保持地方州权乃至个人自由的种种权利。即便矛盾冲突不可调和,双方战场上刀兵相见,在血与火的废墟上还是必须妥协的:南北战争后,哪怕是最激进的北方共和党人在南方民主党复兴咄咄逼人的态势面前也顾不得广大黑人的权利,必须采取息事宁人的妥协态度,宣布战后重建草草收场。每四年一度的总统竞选堪称是这一妥协精神最好的政治象征:共和党和民主党驴象大战你死我活,尘埃落定后又是携手共进,利益均沾。

美国政治历史上,最显眼的原则妥协还是关于奴隶制存废的大妥协。1820年的密苏里妥协案和1850年妥协案都缓和了南北关于奴隶制的矛盾,避免了流血冲突,保全了联邦。其中我们都可以看到一个忙碌的身影,这就是被誉为"大妥协家"的亨利·克莱。

1819年2月13日,众议院讨论密苏里作为奴隶州申请加入联邦的议案。当时,北方主张废奴的自由州和南方蓄奴州的数量相等,都是十一州,人口也大致相当。因此,密苏里不论作为自由州或蓄奴州加入联邦都会打破这一政治均势。而且,北方的经济实力和人口都呈迅猛上升之势,对于南方各州,争取密苏里作为蓄奴州加入联邦可谓生死攸关。

于是,参众两院中,南北双方都抓住宪法对奴隶制语焉未详的弱点,分别站在联邦权威和州权的立场上,在密苏里州奴隶制存废问题上互不相让,甚至走到分裂联邦,走向内战的边缘。在此矛盾趋于激化的情势中,克莱显示出一个"大妥协家"的作用。一方面,他在国会不断发表演讲,既表示支持州权立法,各州自行决定是否实行奴隶制,又明确谴责奴隶制,主张逐步废除奴隶制。这种和稀泥的调和态度在面上起到了缓和作用。另一方面,克莱身为议长,在国会辩论中充分发挥主持和操盘手的作用,巧妙地过滤了双方一些激烈的言辞,规避了冲突。此外,克莱利用其性格魅力和政治影响,穿梭于参众两院,找双方的关键人物私下做工作。就这样,在克莱的努力下,国会终于通过了由妥协案:同意密苏里立宪组建蓄奴州加入联邦,而北方的缅因州则作为自由州加入联邦;同时规定北纬36°30′以北的领地禁止实行奴隶制度。

这就是美国历史上著名的"密苏里妥协案"。它延缓了南北各州在奴隶制问题上的尖锐矛盾冲突,框定了双方的政治意识和经济利益的对峙格局,但也为40年之后的南北战争留下了祸根。也许,那时的克莱没有弄明白,奴隶制问题牵涉政治体制、国家法律、经济利益、道德正义、种族平等、社会稳定等等至关重大原则立场问题。随着美国19世纪中叶领土大扩张和人口急剧膨胀,现实经济利益和意识形态的关系错综复杂,交互砥砺,这一原则问题的不可调和性将成为绝对的现实。因此,对待奴隶制问题的任何重大妥协虽然能够延迟直面的冲突,却不能阻止矛盾能量的集聚,即将到来的是矛盾冲突的升级,是血与火的对抗,直至这一问题得以彻底地解决。

1850年的联邦分裂危机充分说明了这一点。"密苏里妥协案"后30年间,美国领土扩张其势凶猛,强权总统波尔克通过兼并得克萨斯和对墨西哥的战争获得大片的领土。在新的领地上是建立蓄奴州还是自由州,这自然引发了南北势力的新一轮较量。1848年8月,来自宾夕法尼亚州的参议员戴维·威尔默(David Wilmot)向国会提交一份限制性条款,要求国会禁止在西部新领地实行奴隶制。随着加利福尼亚申请以自由州的身份加入联邦,"密苏里妥协案"维持的南北政治势力平衡的框架被突破,新墨西哥和犹他领地也很有可能成为自由州而加入联邦。况且,长期以来,北方各州漠视宪法有关条文,对于追缉逃奴百般阻挠,还不断煽动在哥伦比亚特区废除奴隶制,鼓动国会限制州际奴隶贸易。此时,在威尔默条款的刺激下,南部各州情绪激越。一时之间,分裂联邦,武力解决的威胁呼声在南方不绝于耳。在此关系到联邦存亡的关头,年逾古稀的克莱再次担当起"大妥协家"的历史责任。此时的他对奴隶制基本持否定态度;主张逐步废除。但在国将不国的危亡局势下,拯救统一的联邦国家成了他唯一的目的。克莱提出一整套妥协方案,经过在国会连续的演讲,辩论和劝说,终于使南北双方再次互相让步,接受妥协。克莱也再次展示了"大妥协家"的魅力。当然,好景不长。1850年的妥协在10多年后即被血腥的美国南北战争彻底撕碎。在对待奴隶制存废问题上,这也是历史的必然。

克莱还是美国政治历史上少有的大演说家。

克莱少年时代曾在律师事务所里当过文书抄写员,干活十分仔细认真,锻炼出来的对文字的敏锐分辨能力和基本思维能力。他的政治生涯始于在国会的演讲才能。他抓住偶然的机会补缺当上国会参议员,从此乐此不疲,逐渐活跃于参众两院的讲坛上。他能言善辩,乐于争锋,更喜欢众议院热烈辩论的气氛,而且几乎对当时的热点问题都能说会道,演说中充满热情和生机。据说克莱的演说能力超群,他一旦在众议院演讲,参议院就必须休会,因为参议员们都争先恐后地到众议院去听克莱演讲。在国会堪称一绝。

克莱在演说中喜用反问句吸引听众的注意,然后斩钉截铁地自答,把情绪推向高潮。例如,1812年,克莱在国会发表长篇演讲,鼓动国会向英国开战:"有人也许会问:战争将为我们赢得什么呢?我的回答是:和平会让我们失去什么呢?是失去商业繁荣,失去国格,失去一个国家最宝贵的荣誉!"又如,克莱发表演说,力主联邦政府出资建设国内交通设施,以利各州之交通和商业往来,其中大量运用排比设问,短促自答的修辞方式,调动听众情绪,不容置疑地烘托出主论。当时各届政府都否决国会议案,认为宪法没有授权国会动用联邦资金修建州际交通设施。克莱反问:"宪法授权国会建立邮局,修建邮政驿道了

吗？宪法授权国会统筹各州之间的商业往来了吗？宪法仅仅是为了这个国家的大西洋沿岸的利益而制定的吗？宪法仅仅是为了当时居住在这片大陆的几百万居民而制定的吗？不！"设问之中已经包含了否定，而最后的短促否定则是煽情的高潮。克莱还善用矛盾对偶形成警句，然后话锋一转，喊出鼓舞人心的口号："光荣的和平只能用胜利的战争赢得。但是，如果我们失败，那么就让我们忍受折磨，流尽勇敢的热血，在最后的共同斗争中一起光荣地死去，因为我们是为自由贸易和海员的权利而战！"当时的美国，独立、民主、权利等仍是民众心中的主要诉求，克莱如此的修辞力量足以让人们热血沸腾。

当然，激情演说家都有过犹不及的通病，口若悬河的语流往往消弭了理性的力量。克莱也概莫能外。在他的演讲中，过度概括，前后矛盾，以偏概全的例子不在偶然。他缺乏杰斐逊和麦迪逊等人的学问和才气，对论题的分析往往浅尝辄止，缺乏论据，激情过后难以令人信服。但这又怎么样呢？古往今来，杰出的政治家都是制造意识形态的高手。而在那个人民民主意识高涨，但参政议政尚不普遍的时代，政治家高亢的话语建构和意识形态召唤，不正是民主政治的基础得以巩固的有效途径吗？

■ 演讲文（节选）

Speech on the Compromise of 1850

Henry Clay

...

Mr. President, I am directly opposed to any purpose of **secession**, of separation. I am for staying within the Union, and **defying** any portion of this Union to expel or drive me out of the Union. I am for staying within the Union, and fighting for my rights—if necessary, with the sword—within the bounds and under the safeguard of the Union. I am for **vindicating** these rights; but not by being driven out of the Union **rashly** and unceremoniously by any portion of this confederacy. Here I am within it, and here I mean to stand and die; as far as my individual purposes or wishes can go—within it to protect myself and to defy all power upon earth to expel me or drive me from the situation in which I am placed. Will there not be more safety in fighting within the Union than without it?

...

It has been objected against this **measure** that it is a compromise. It has been said that it is a compromise of principle, or of a principle.

secession: claim of independence
defy: directly oppose

vindicate: prove not guilty
rashly: cruelly and hastily

measure: solution; action (here, the compromise proposal)

第十七讲 | Henry Clay

Mr. President, what is a compromise? It is a work of mutual **concession**—an agreement in which there are **reciprocal stipulations**—a work in which, for the sake of peace and concord, one party **abates** his extreme demands in consideration of an abatement of extreme demands by the other party: it is a measure of mutual concession—a measure of mutual sacrifice. Undoubtedly, Mr. President, in all such measures of compromise, one **party** would be very glad to get what he wants, and reject what he does not desire but which the other party wants. But when he comes to **reflect** that, from the nature of the government and its operations, and from those with whom he is dealing, it is necessary upon his part, in order to secure what he wants, to grant something to the other side, he should be **reconciled** to the concession which he has made in consequence of the concession which he is to receive, if there is no great principle involved, such as a **violation** of the Constitution of the United States. I admit that such a compromise as that ought never to be **sanctioned** or adopted. But I now call upon any senator in his place to point out from the beginning to the end, from California to New Mexico, a solitary **provision** in this **bill** which is violative of the Constitution of the United States.

The responsibility of this great measure passes from the hands of the committee, and from my hands. They know, and I know, that it is an **awful** and tremendous responsibility. I hope that you will meet it with a just conception and a true appreciation of its magnitude, and the magnitude of the consequences that may **ensue** from your decision one way or the other. The alternatives, I fear, which the measure presents, are concord and increased **discord**. . . I believe from the bottom of my soul that the measure is the reunion of this Union. I believe it is the **dove** of peace, which, taking its aerial flight from the dome of the Capitol, carries the glad **tidings** of assured peace and restored harmony to all the remotest extremities of this **distracted** land. I believe that it will be attended with all these beneficent effects. And now let us discard all **resentment**, all passions, all petty jealousies, all personal desires, all **love of place**, all **hankerings** after the gilded **crumbs** which fall from the table of power. Let us forget popular fears, from whatever quarter they may spring. Let us go to the **limpid** fountain of **unadulterated** patriotism, and, performing a solemn **lustration**, return **divested** of all selfish, sinister, and **sordid impurities**, and think alone of our God, our country, our consciences, and our glorious Union—that Union without which we shall be torn into hostile fragments, and sooner or later become the victims of military

---

concession: permission;
reciprocal: mutual
stipulation: articles; term
abate: reduce
party: side (in negotiation talk)

reflect: think of

reconcile: accept an agreement
violation: denial; disregard

sanction: prove; confirm
provision: term; article
bill: act; document

awful: extremely great; huge
ensue: happen as a result
discord: chaos
dove: pigeon, bird of peace

tiding: news; message
distracted: divided (in opinion)
resentment: anger
love of place: desire for power
hankering: longing
crumb: small pieces
limpid: transparent
unadulterated: pure
lustration: washing
divested of: free from; clear from
sordid: dirty
impurity: dirt; evil

despotism or foreign dominion.

...

Let us look to our country and our cause, elevate ourselves to the dignity of pure and disinterested patriots, and save our country from all **impending** dangers. What if, in the march of this nation to greatness and power, we should be buried beneath the wheels that propel it onwards.

I call upon all the South. Sir, we have had hard words, bitter words, bitter thoughts, unpleasant feelings toward each other in the progress of this great measure. Let us forget them. Let us sacrifice these feelings. Let us go to the **altar** of our country and swear, as the oath was taken **of old**, that we will stand by her; that we will support her; that we will uphold her Constitution; that we will preserve her union; and that we will pass this great, comprehensive, and healing system of measures, which will **hush** all the **jarring** elements and bring peace and tranquility to our home.

Let me, Mr. President, in conclusion, say that the most disastrous consequences would occur, in my opinion, were we to go home, doing nothing to satisfy and tranquillize the country upon these great questions. What will be the judgment of mankind, what the judgment of that portion of mankind who are looking upon the progress of this **scheme** of self-government as being that which holds the highest hopes and expectations of **ameliorating** the condition of mankind—what will their judgment be? Will not all the monarchs of the **Old World** pronounce our glorious republic a disgraceful! failure? Will you go home and leave all in disorder and confusion—all unsettled—all open? The contentions and agitations of the past will be increased and **augmented** by the agitations resulting from our neglect to decide them.

Sir, we shall stand **condemned** by all human judgment below, and of that above it is not for me to speak. We shall stand condemned in our own consciences, by our own **constituents**, and by our own country. The measure may be defeated. I have been aware that its **passage** for many days was not absolutely certain. ...But, if defeated, it will be a triumph of **altruism** and impracticability—a triumph of a most extraordinary conjunction of extremes; a victory won by abolitionism; a victory achieved by **freesoilism**; a victory of discord and agitation over peace and tranquility; and I pray to Almighty God that it may not, in consequence of the **inauspicious** result, lead to the most unhappy and disastrous consequences to our beloved country.

---

despotism: dictatorship

impending: approaching; upcoming

altar: place where to practice religious ceremony
of old: by the ancient
hush: silence
jarring: noisy; harsh (voice)

scheme: design; structure
ameliorate: improve
Old World: most European nations

augment: add
condemned: hopelessly damned; doomed
constituent: voter
passage: approval (by the Congress)
altruism: extremism;
freesoilism: beliefs of the Free-Soil Party that opposes slavery in new territories
inauspicious: potentially dangerous

■ 重点述评与提示

1. Here I am within it, and here I mean to stand and die; ... within it to protect myself and to defy all power upon earth to expel me or drive me from the situation in which I am placed. Will there not be more safety in fighting within the Union than without it?

   面对因奴隶制存废争论造成的可能的联邦分裂危机，克莱表达反对分裂，誓死捍卫联邦统一的基本的立场，这也是整篇演讲的主旨。这里用重复使用 within，并与 without 相对，简洁而又力。善用设问也是克莱修辞的一大特点。

2. But I now call upon any senator in his place to point out from the beginning to the end, from California to New Mexico, a solitary provision in this bill which is violative of the Constitution of the United States.

   如此直接质询的语句在克莱的演讲中比比皆是。美国宪法诠释可塑性较大，引起宽严之争。其实，克莱善变通宪法条文，达到现实的妥协。他说过如下一段实事求是的话："这部宪法永恒不变，永远这同一部宪法。但是，形势演进，世事恒变，永无止境。而且人非圣贤，对于执行宪法的人来说，他们在前一个时期也未必会预见到今天实施某项具体的建设性权力的可行性和必要性。"这是克莱善于妥协的思想根源。

3. I believe it is the dove of peace, which, taking its aerial flight from the dome of the Capitol, carries the glad tidings of assured peace and restored harmony to all the remotest extremities of this distracted land.

   为了促成国会通过此项妥协案，克莱对妥协带来的和谐社会极尽具象渲染，付诸听众的感官。这是大演说家的想象力和语言表达力。这样的重彩叠加，烘托气氛的连续暗喻手法在后世的演说家如马丁·路德·金的《我有一个梦想》尤为突出。

4. And now let us discard all resentment, all passions, all petty jealousies, all personal desires, all love of place, all hankerings after the gilded crumbs which fall from the table of power.

   简捷的祈使句，动词 discard 后连续跟进 6 个重复首次 all 的宾语，一气呵成，末了采用连环隐喻，隐射人类不同的情感和欲望的对象就是权欲，两相以对，相得益彰。

5. ...that we will stand by her; that we will support her; that we will uphold her Constitution; that we will preserve her union; and that we will pass this great, comprehensive, and healing system of measures, which will hush all the jarring elements and bring peace and tranquility to our home.

   演说家有时会忘乎所以，沉浸在某一修辞技巧中不可自拔。本句的语义重心是号召南部议员支持妥协案,还国家以安宁。这里紧接上文的重复祈使句,反复叠用 5 处 that we will...,表达了消弭分歧,一致爱国的誓言和决心,倒显得拖沓累赘,不如直接排比各个动词,还显得更为铿锵有力。

6. What will be the judgment of mankind, what the judgment of that portion of mankind who are looking upon the progress of this scheme of self-government as being that which holds the highest hopes and expectations of ameliorating the condition of mankind-what will their judgment be?

  克莱的政治重心在维护联邦完整,推行其振兴国家经济的"美国体系",但也不可避免地感染到美国"天定命运"的时代精神,把全人类的福祉系于美国的政体成败。如果妥协失败就意味着联邦的分裂,国家的失败,也就是全人类的失败。这里用反问长句,首尾包容,别具匠心。

7. But, if defeated, it will be a triumph of altruism and impracticability—a triumph of a most extraordinary conjunction of extremes; a victory won by abolitionism; a victory achieved by freesoilism; a victory of discord and agitation over peace and tranquility;

  又是新一轮的连续排比和重复。妥协案一旦失败,那是南部奴隶制极端主义的胜利,也是北方废奴主义和自由土地派的胜利,但却是联邦分裂,全国动乱的开端,是和平安定的失败。这是克莱半个世纪从政经验积累的政治洞见,危言,但却中听。

■ 思考及讨论题

1. How did Henry Clay contribute to the beginning of the War of 1812?
2. What did the "Missouri Compromise of 1820" settle and how did it affect the issue of slavery later?
3. What did the "Compromise of 1850" settle and what did it mean to both American North and South?
4. What are some schemes included in Henry Clay's American System?

■ 阅读书目

1. Brown, Thomas. *Politics and Statesmanship: Essays on the American Whig Party*. New York: Columbia University Press, 1985.

2. Churz, Carl. *Life of Henry Clay: American Statesmen*. Cambridge: Houghton Mifflin, 1899.
3. Forbes, Robert Pierce. *The Missouri Compromise and Its Aftermath: Slavery and the Meaning of America*. Chapel Hill, NC: University of North Carolina Press, 2007.
4. Stegmaier, Mark J. *Texas, New Mexico, and the Compromise of 1850: Boundary Dispute & Sectional Crisis*. Kent State University Press, 1996.

第十八讲
西雅图酋长(Chief Seattle 1788—1866)

■ 政治历史评述

西雅图酋长:印第安文明随风而去的悲鸣和惊叹

1492年10月11日,哥伦布的"圣玛利亚号"等3艘航船经过了两个多月在大西洋艰难的航行,终于到达巴哈马群岛。岸上丛林中的印第安人带着警惕和好奇的目光,注视着这些鼓着风帆的庞然大物的到来。他们看见船上有同类在招手,呼喊着什么。不久,土著人的疑虑烟消云散,他们奔向海滩,接纳着一种奇异陌生的文化以及随之而来的暴力和疾病,谁也没有意识到,这是美洲印第安人种族厄运的开始,是一个近千年的文明的失落的开端。

17世纪中叶欧洲向美洲大迁徙以来,西方殖民者纷至沓来。在北美大陆东部,英国殖民者建立了美利坚国家。种族优越感和对土地和财富的渴望,促使他们利用优势的国家机器和武器杀戮驱赶"劣势"的土著人。据保守统计,西方在北美的殖民掠夺和携带的瘟疫导致北美印第安人近千万人的死亡。随着殖民者西进边疆的拓展,幸存的印第安人的生存"边界"一直向西,他们踏着"血泪之路",被迫迁到边远西部的"印第安保留

地"。不久,殖民者在加利福尼亚发现金矿,梦想一夜暴富的人们蜂拥而至。于是,在太平洋沿岸生活的原住民也遭到同样的命运。

1854年1月22日,天空阴沉。在俄勒冈领地最西北角三角洲地区一个叫做艾略艾特角的地方,2,300余名当地的印第安人聚集在一起,见证了北美最西边一块印第安部落领地落入美国殖民统治的最后时刻。在这里,他们德高望重的西雅图酋长将屈从于新来的白人总督艾萨克·斯蒂芬,签署一项协定,割让印第安人世代赖以生存繁衍的大片土地,换取美国当局为他们划定的印第安居留地。当时,加利福尼亚淘金热正酣,美国殖民者通过俄勒冈小道翻越落基山脉到达俄勒冈地区居留的人数已达1万多人,波尔克总统通过武力威胁与英国签订北纬49度边界协定已经8年,美国在俄勒冈领地建州已成定局。面对屈辱和战死的选择,为了保存种族的延续,西雅图酋长选择了前者。据当时签订协议在场的翻译亨利·阿·史密斯博士1887年10月29日发表在《西雅图之星报》

上的日记回忆，西雅图酋长身材魁梧匀称，气度非凡。他的大眼睛目光如炬，充满智慧和友善，显示出一个心灵的宽宏和稳健。在此决定种族部落命运的特殊集会中，他的举手投足无不令人感到敬畏，连在场的白人都对他肃然起敬。酋长将在此发表演说，接受美国联邦政府的苛刻条件，承诺不发动战争，接受联邦政府"保护"。

　　这样的描写多了几分殖民者对归顺的印第安酋长进行悲剧人物式的话语建构，但从西雅图酋长的成长经历和思想构成来看，这也是时势造就的必然和无奈。大约 1788 年，西雅图酋长出生于离今西雅图市西南不远的"黑岛"，父亲是当地苏瓜米族首领，对白人定居者保持良好关系，提倡和平共处。西雅图尚年幼时，因父去世而子承父位，勇武无比，在普各特桑得地区（Puget Sound）各部落间表现出合众连横的领导才能，后来联合周边部落打败了其他印第安部落，成为当地 6 个印第安部落的酋长。1792 年，英国海军乔治·温哥华船长探险太平洋沿岸，抵达普各特桑得地区。西雅图酋长目睹欧洲人的船坚炮利，深感印第安人的劣势和抵抗的徒劳，加之幼年受到父亲的影响，对和平生活充满想象。此时，美国加快了对俄勒冈领地的殖民化进程，把印第安人赶到狭小的居留地，不少印第安部落群起反抗，遭到灭顶之灾。西雅图酋长眼见大势如此，为了避免本部族印第安人生灵涂炭，保全部族的延续，决定忍辱负重，号召本部族保持克

制，提倡与殖民者采取合作态度。他自己开始了解欧洲文化和宗教，甚至与 1838 年受洗为天主教徒，取名"诺亚"。他 1854 年带头搬迁到居留地，1866 年月 7 日因染疟疾卒于家中，后按天主教和并苏瓜米族印第安人习俗安葬于家族墓地。西雅图酋长生前对美国殖民政策的明智顺从和无奈选择使西方殖民者大悦，殖民地当局决定采纳来自俄亥俄州的冒险家，西雅图酋长的朋友大卫·麦纳德医生的提议，把当时的殖民定居点命名为西雅图，即现今的西雅图市。

　　按照史密斯博士发表在《西雅图之星报》上描述，西雅图酋长还是一个颇具感染力的演说家。1854 年 1 月 22 日阴冷的那一天，他用本族印第安语做了最后的演讲。"会上，酋长起身演发言，众目瞩望，但听到深沉雄浑的语句滚滚而出，犹如无尽的涌泉奔突，不息的瀑布倾泻。"据有关记载，史密斯博士颇具诗才，这样的描述当属诗意的夸张。此人当时来到俄勒冈地区仅一年，可能不通当地的印第安语，但却翻译了西雅图酋长的演讲，并做了记录。30 年之后，他发表了这篇演讲的英文全文，辞藻流畅，诗意盎然，其翻译和真伪都受到普遍的质疑。但是，长期以来，历史学家都以此作为唯一接近原作的文本而加以阐释，毕竟，史密斯是当时的翻译和目击者。上世纪 70 年代初，西雅图酋长又备受关注。电影剧作家泰德·佩里在这篇演讲中加入生态保护的内容，制作出影片《家园》。西雅图酋长于是又成了环境保护主义者的先驱。于是，一个顺应大势，放弃抵抗的印第安人酋长的演说成了西方话语建构他者的模板，赋予了互文的形式意义和非意识

形态的内容,遮蔽了历史上直面的文化冲突和北美印第安人几乎种族灭绝的悲惨命运。

其实,不论这篇演讲的真伪如何,也不论西方殖民者对其的诠释如何,我们在其中读到的是历史逻辑的真实。不论战争与和平,强夺与谈判,巧取还是豪夺,美国十九世纪中叶白人至上"天定命运"的意识形态和领土扩张的欲望在西方工业技术的推动下,必定荡平西进道路上的一切他者物质和文化存在。

美国历史上也曾涌现出不少奋起反抗英法和西班牙殖民者以及美国扩张主义者的印第安部落英雄豪杰:早期新英格兰有号称"菲利普国王"的梅塔科姆;在伊利诺伊地区有外号"黑鹰"的索克和福克斯酋长;中西部广大地区有特库姆塞酋长;在密西西比和迈阿密的丛林中有外号"小龟王"的勇武斗士;俄亥俄和五大湖地区有著名的"庞蒂亚克造反"等等,这些印第安酋长中不乏天然的演讲者,发出至死抵抗的铿锵之音。但是,在现代性大势下,他们都是古老的文化传达出来的遥远的尚武精神的绝响。

西雅图酋长的演讲尽管经过了西方殖民者的文本塑构,但是,在这篇演说中那些表达了人与自然和谐相处的理想中,在那些充满了哀怨和讽刺的话语中,我们分明听到了无奈的抉择压抑下的无语抗争,听到了一个古老文明随风而去的悲鸣。可以说,西雅图酋长的演说正是这个文明最后的句号和惊叹。

■ 演讲文(节选)

The Fall of a Civilization: Chief Seattle's 1854 Oration

Chief Seattle

Yonder sky that has wept tears of **compassion** upon my people for centuries untold, and which to us appears changeless and eternal, may change. Today is fair. Tomorrow it may be overcast with clouds. My words are like the stars that never change. Whatever Seattle says, the **great chief at Washington** can rely upon with as much certainty as he can upon the return of the sun or the seasons. The **white chief** says that Big Chief at Washington sends us greetings of friendship and goodwill. This is kind of him for we know he has little need of our friendship in return. His people are many. They are like the grass that covers vast **prairies**. My people are few. They resemble the scattering

yonder: over there
compassion: sympathy

great chief at Washington: US President
white chief: (here) the new governor from Washington
prairie: (North America) grassland

trees of a storm-swept plain. The great, and I presume—good, White Chief sends us word that he wishes to buy our land but is willing to allow us enough to live comfortably. This indeed appears just, even generous, for the **Red Man** no longer has rights that he need respect, and the offer may be wise, also, as we are no longer in need of an extensive country.

There was a time when our people covered the land as the waves of a **wind-ruffled** sea cover its shell-paved floor, but that time long since passed away with the greatness of tribes that are now but a mournful memory. I will not dwell on, nor mourn over, our untimely decay, nor **reproach** my **paleface** brothers with hastening it, as we too may have been somewhat to blame.

Youth is impulsive. When our young men grow angry at some real or imaginary wrong, and **disfigure** their faces with black paint, it denotes that their hearts are black, and that they are often cruel and **relentless**, and our old men and old women are unable to restrain them. Thus it has ever been. Thus it was when the white man began to push our forefathers ever westward. But let us hope that the **hostilities** between us may never return. We would have everything to lose and nothing to gain. Revenge by young men is considered gain, even at the cost of their own lives, but old men who stay at home in times of war, and mothers who have sons to lose, know better.

Our good father in Washington—for I presume he is now our father as well as yours, since **King George** has moved his boundaries further north—our great and good father, I say, sends us word that if we do as he desires he will protect us. His brave warriors will be to us a **bristling** wall of strength, and his wonderful ships of war will fill our harbors, so that our ancient enemies far to the northward—the **Haidas** and **Tsimshians**—will cease to frighten our women, children, and old men. Then in reality he will be our father and we his children. But can that ever be? Your God is not our God! Your God loves your people and hates mine! ...Our God, the **Great Spirit**, seems also to have forsaken us. Your God makes your people **wax** stronger every day. Soon they will fill all the land. Our people are **ebbing away** like a rapidly receding tide that will never return. The white man's God cannot love our people or He would protect them. They seem to be **orphans** who can look nowhere for help. How then can we be brothers? How can your God become our God and renew our prosperity and awaken in us dreams of returning greatness? ...No: we are two **distinct** races with separate origins and separate destinies. There is little in common between us.

To us the ashes of our ancestors are sacred and their resting place is **hallowed** ground. You wander far from the graves of your ancestors and seemingly without regret. Your religion was written upon **tablets of stone** by the iron finger of your God so that you could not forget. The Red Man could never comprehend or remember it. Our religion is the **traditions** of our ancestors—the dreams of our old men, given them in solemn hours of the night by the Great Spirit; and the visions of our **sachems**, and is written in the hearts of our people.

Your dead cease to love you and the land of their **nativity** as soon as they pass the **portals** of the tomb and wander away beyond the stars. They are soon forgotten and never return. Our dead never forget this beautiful world that gave them **being**. They still love its **verdant** valleys, its murmuring rivers, its magnificent mountains, **sequestered** vales and verdant lined lakes and bays, and ever yearn in tender fond affection over the lonely hearted living, and often return from the happy hunting ground to visit, guide, **console**, and comfort them.

Day and night cannot dwell together. The Red Man has ever fled the approach of the White Man, as the morning mist flees before the morning sun. However, your proposition seems fair and I think that my people will accept it and will retire to the **reservation** you offer them. Then we will dwell apart in peace, for the words of the Great White Chief seem to be the words of nature speaking to my people out of dense darkness.

It matters little where we pass the **remnant** of our days. They will not be many. The Indian's night promises to be dark. Not a single star of hope **hovers** above his horizon. Sad-voiced winds moan in the distance. Grim fate seems to be on the Red Man's **trail**, and wherever he will hear the approaching footsteps of his **fell** destroyer and prepare **stolidly** to meet his doom, as does the wounded **doe** that hears the approaching footsteps of the hunter.

When the buffalo are all slaughtered, the wild horses all tamed, the secret corners of the forest heavy with the scent of many men, and the view of the ripe hills **blotted** by **talking wires**, where is the thicket? Gone. Where is the eagle? Gone. ...What is man without the beasts? If all the beasts were gone, men would die from great loneliness of spirit, for whatever happens to the beasts also happens to man. All things are connected. Whatever **befalls** the earth befalls the children of the earth.

A few more moons, a few more winters, and not one of the

---

distinct: completely different

hallowed: holy; sanctified

traditions: stories and beliefs passed down by generations
sachem: chief; political leader
nativity: birth; origin
portal: entrance; entrance

being: existence; livelihood
verdant: (poetic) green
sequestered: remote and solitude
console: ease (the pain); cheer up

reservation: special area kept for Indian residence

remnant: rest, remaining part

hover: fly (in circle)
trail: rear, footstep
fell: cruel
stolid: unskillfully, clumsily
doe: female deer

blot: ruin; mark
talking wire: cable (for telephone)

befall: surely happen to

descendants of the **mighty hosts** that once moved over this broad land or lived in happy homes, protected by the Great Spirit, will remain to mourn over the graves of a people once more powerful and hopeful than yours. But why should I mourn at the **untimely** fate of my people? Tribe follows tribe, and nation follows nation, like the waves of the sea. It is the order of nature, and regret is useless. Your time of decay may be distant, but it will surely come, for even the White Man whose God walked and talked with him as friend to friend, cannot be **exempt from** the common destiny. We may be brothers after all. We will see.

We will **ponder** your proposition and when we decide we will let you know. But should we accept it, I here and now make this condition that we will not be denied the privilege without **molestation** of visiting at any time the tombs of our ancestors, friends, and children. Every part of this soil is sacred in the estimation of my people. Every hillside, every valley, every plain and **grove**, has been hallowed by some sad or happy event in days long vanished. Even the rocks, which seem to be dumb and dead as the **swelter** in the sun along the silent shore, thrill with memories of stirring events connected with the lives of my people,... Our **departed braves**, fond mothers, glad, happy hearted maidens, and even the little children who lived here and rejoiced here for a brief season, will love these **somber** solitudes and at **eventide** they greet shadowy returning spirits. And when the last Red Man shall have perished, and the memory of my tribe shall have become a myth among the White Men, these shores will **swarm with** the invisible dead of my tribe, and when your children's children think themselves alone in the field, the store, the shop, upon the highway, or in the silence of the pathless woods, they will not be alone. In all the earth there is no place dedicated to solitude. At night when the streets of your cities and villages are silent and you think them **deserted**, they will **throng with** the returning **hosts** that once filled them and still love this beautiful land. The White Man will never be alone.

Let him be just and deal kindly with my people, for the dead are not powerless. Dead, did I say? There is no death, only a change of worlds.

■ 重点述评与提示

1. My words are like the stars that never change. Whatever Seattle says, the great chief at Washington can rely upon with as much certainty as he can upon the return of the sun or the seasons.

   万物更替,世事恒变,但延续种族的决心不变。西雅图酋长开篇不卑不亢,言之既出,掷地有声,比喻中有天地之气,表现出一种"野蛮人"的高贵气质。以年迈的酋长当时的威望而论,此话似合乎情理。

2. This indeed appears just, even generous, for the Red Man no longer has rights that he need respect, and the offer may be wise, also, as we are no longer in need of an extensive country.

   美国政府"购买"印第安人世代赖以生存和繁衍的大片土地,并划定狭小的保留地"妥善安置"印第安人。而印第安人在武力的威逼下无权拒绝,今后也没有土地之需。这里话里带刺(indeed appears just, even generous 传达出来的讽刺意味尤其明显),西雅图酋长在大势面前的无奈心情也跃然纸上。

3. Thus it has ever been. Thus it was when the white man began to push our forefathers ever westward. But let us hope that the hostilities between us may never return. We would have everything to lose and nothing to gain. Revenge by young men is considered gain, even at the cost of their own lives, but old men who stay at home in times of war, and mothers who have sons to lose, know better.

   两个"Thus"连用,展示出美国向西驱赶印第安部落和年轻的印第安武士不屈的反抗的历史画面。紧接的转折道出了酋长久经风霜后的认识:年轻人誓死捍卫土地,但大局已定,一切皆为徒劳;委曲求全,结束仇恨,方能保证印第安种族的延绵。

4. Your religion was written upon tablets of stone by the iron finger of your God so that you could not forget. The Red Man could never comprehend or remember it. Our religion is the traditions of our ancestors—the dreams of our old men, given them in solemn hours of the night by the Great Spirit; and the visions of our sachems, and is written in the hearts of our people.

   和而不同,这是这篇演讲的主题之一。西方人的宗教是形而上的教条,是上帝刻在石板上的"戒律",而印第安的宗教是祖先崇拜,是世代相传生命信息,是万物之神留在人们心中的梦想。两相对照,格格不入。

5. Day and night cannot dwell together. The Red Man has ever fled the approach of the White Man, as the morning mist flees before the morning sun.

   这是明显的东方式比兴手法,却也带有西方式的诗意情趣,让人想起莎士比亚描写清晨的鬼魂在一片雾霭中匆匆逃离晨曦的诗句(《哈姆雷特》)。画家加斯特1872年题为"美国的进步"的著名油画几乎完全就是这句话的视觉注解。画中的自由女神背负着清晨的太阳,在一片雾霭中引领着白人殖民者,向西驱赶着惊恐万状,奔向黑暗的印第安人。

6. When the buffalo are all slaughtered, the wild horses all tamed, the secret corners of the forest heavy with the scent of many men, and the view of the ripe hills blotted by talking wires, where is the thicket? Gone. Where is the eagle? Gone. ...All things are connected. Whatever befalls the earth befalls the children of the earth.

   西雅图酋长一生从未离开俄勒冈海岸的普格特角,从未见过美洲野牛,也不知电报通讯为何物,何来此番天人合一,倡导生态环境保护的议论?这显然是后人的炒作添加。但以我们对印第安文化的了解,这里传达的是否也有历史文化逻辑的真实呢?

7. Tribe follows tribe, and nation follows nation, like the waves of the sea. It is the order of nature, and regret is useless. Your time of decay may be distant, but it will surely come, for even the White Man whose God walked and talked with him as friend to friend, cannot be exempt from the common destiny.

   在大自然造化和时间的长河中,一切事物都不可避免地归于虚无,美国扩张的未来帝国也不例外,也都将走向消亡,不在此刻,就在他时。把这话置于西雅图酋长之口,让人在叹息其怒而不争之余,平添了几分尊敬。这是智者抹平文化的哲思,犹如英哲培根之警言:"思想和知识之丰碑亘古耸立,而权力和人为之辉煌都已付与断壁残垣。"(how far the monuments of wit and learning are more durable than the monuments of power or of the hands.)

8. At night when the streets of your cities and villages are silent and you think them deserted, they will throng with the returning hosts that once filled them and still love this beautiful land. The White Man will never be alone.

   印第安人相信灵魂不灭之说,认为人死后,在灵魂飞离躯壳的刹那间,就各有安置,或安然享乐,或受苦受难。入夜,灵魂们就回到生前故土,与家人同乐。可以想象,白人殖民者强夺了印第安人土地和家园,他们在西雅图酋长如此的咒语面前,何以安然入睡?

■ 思考及讨论题

1. What was the relationship between Native Americans and the west colonists in the early period of European settlement?
2. How did the US government reach the agreement with the Great Britain about the Oregon territories?
3. What were some major battles fought by the Indian warriors against the American pioneers?
4. What do you know about the living condition of Native American in the United States today?

■ 阅读书目

1. Thatcher, B. B. *Indian Biography: Or, an Historical Account of Those Individuals Who Have Been Distinguished among the North American Natives as Orators, Warriors, Statesmen, and Other Remarkable Characters*. New York: A. L. Fowle, 1900.
2. Sayre, Gordon M. *The Indian Chief as Tragic Hero: Native Resistance and the Literatures of America, from Moctezuma to Tecumseh*. Chapel Hill: University of North Carolina Press, 2005.
3. Nichol, Roger L. *Indians in the United States and Canada: A Comparative History*, University of Nebraska Press, 1998.
4. http://www.ilhawaii.net/~stony/seattle.html

第六章 ‖ 奴隶制与美国内战

> But it is great error to suppose, as many do, that the right of a majority to govern is a natural and not a conventional right, and therefore absolute and unlimited.
>
> ——John C. Calhoun

> I, John Brown, am now quite certain that the crimes of this guilty land will never be purged away but with Blood.
>
> ——John Brown

> A house divided against itself cannot stand. I believe this government cannot endure, permanently, half slave and half free. I do not expect the Union to be dissolved —I do not expect the house to fall —but I do expect it will cease to be divided.
>
> ——Abraham Lincoln

Preview Questions

01/

Aside from slavery, what could be some other causes of American Civil War?

02/

How did the issue of slavery affect the expansion of the western territories?

03/

How did the American expansionists rationalize the removal of American Indians during the westward movement?

04/

To what extent was the Reconstruction a failure/success?

第十九讲
约翰·C.卡尔霍恩(John C. Calhoun 1782—1850)

■ 政治历史评述

约翰·C.卡尔霍恩：南方帝国主义的倡导者和理论家

耶鲁大学教授大卫·W.布莱特在耶鲁公开课《美国内战与重建》中不无揶揄地说道，美国总统老布什曾经宣称，为了让美国人民生活在一个没有奴隶制的美好国家，在美国内战中有60万的美国青年为了废除奴隶制而献出宝贵的生命。但是，老布什却忘记了一个事实：这60多万的牺牲者中至少有30万人拥护南部脱离联邦，他们为了捍卫奴隶制而走向战场，在血与火中献出了年轻的生命。

这话如果传到九泉之下，有一个灵魂一定会倍感欣慰和激动。这个人就是约翰·C.卡尔霍恩。在美国南北战争前的二十来年间，他一直为维护州主权地位和奴隶制的合法性而呐喊，形成自己的一套理论和实践，他的思想和行动直接促成了南部各州脱离联邦，走向内战。美国著名思想史家沃农·路易·帕灵顿在其《美国思想主流》中称卡尔霍恩是"南方帝国主义的倡导者和哲学家"。

卡尔霍恩1782年3月18日出生在南卡罗来纳州一个偏僻的农庄，父亲是来自苏格兰-爱尔兰的移民，性情彪悍，在边远的山区打拼，及至独立战争结束，终有了自己的家业并拥有30多个黑人奴隶。约翰从小在加尔文教严厉的训诫中长大，一生都信奉"生命就是对邪恶的战争"的训条。他承继了父亲沉郁而刚毅的性格，少年老成，沉思独处，常常独处数月无语，至多带上他的黑奴陪伴，游走山林，全不知外界之事。他的早期教育除了断断续续上过几个月的乡学外，几乎一片空白，13岁时才开始接触第一本书。但是，书籍却与卡尔霍恩有着不解之缘。14岁那年，姐夫瓦德尔把卡尔霍恩带到自己办的教会学校就学。一次，瓦德尔外出布道一个多月，及至回到家，惊见小约翰奄奄一息，身边翻开了一地的书籍，其中有不少历史和游记，甚至还有洛克的《论人类的理解力》。母亲见儿子如此聪明出众，又嗜书如命，于是决定送他到新英格兰大地方受点正规教育。谁知小约翰坚决不从，表示只愿陪伴母亲，做一辈子的农人。土地是卡尔霍恩脚踏实地的生活现实，也是魂归守舍的精神家园。从小在偏远山区培养出对土地的热爱，对农耕的信赖，这也是他一生政治思想的基础。两个哥哥见状，极力劝学，这才说服约翰。那年卡尔霍恩20岁，进入耶鲁学院学习。2年以后即以优异成绩完成了学业。这既得益于他的禀赋和自学能力，又得益于他律己专一的性格，还得益于他在教会学校短暂的几个月里每天背诵古文1000多行的苦功夫。

在耶鲁校园,卡尔霍恩是一个怪人。耶鲁人都知道这个瘦高个,表情严峻,眼窝深陷,留着一头黑发的年轻人,这个操着浓重南方口音,来自南卡罗来纳边远地区的优等生,他们经常看到他独自漫步校园中的榆树林下,仰望星空,没有人知道他心中在想什么。人们后来在他的政治生涯中有了答案:那时他想得最多的问题,就是南方是否应该保持自己独特的文化,是否应该从联邦分离出去。中心问题就是独立中的独立。那时的他对政治已经深感兴趣,他最大的担心就是:联邦拥有扩大权力的机制,可以借用人民的名义限制人民的自由。

卡尔霍恩不久就成为年轻一代的美国政治家。1810—1811年间,他曾在众议院狂热鼓吹向英国开战,被誉为"肩负着战争的年轻大力士"。他也曾认为,对于宪法应该作宽容解释,为的是在现实中更好地联合各州人民,组成和加强实际的联邦体系。为此,他还在1817年2月在国会提出建立美国第二中央银行,以集资为改善国内交通建设。这些主张与他后来的州权主义、分离主义和维护奴隶制的政治立场大相径庭。

但是,卡尔霍恩骨子里是一个极具政治抱负和实用精神的人,为了实现政治目的他可以出尔反尔,不断变幻政治立场。他先当了门罗的国防部长,后又担任昆西·亚当斯的副总统,屡屡对总统发难;1829年当了杰克逊的副总统,先恭后倨,在国家银行和行使州否决联邦之权问题上与杰克逊彻底闹翻;接着又当了泰勒总统的国务卿,力主领土扩张,吞并得克萨斯,不过又变幻立场,反对波尔克总统的俄勒冈领地扩张政策,反对美墨战争,不久又宣布支持波尔克,被任命驻英大使,结果再反,辞职了事。以此观之,作为政治家的卡尔霍恩像是长了"反骨"的多事者,但是,风云变幻的政治也造就出了坚定的州权主义和分离主义者卡尔霍恩。

由于卡尔霍恩在美国政治史上有着独特的理论贡献,有必要略展篇幅,对其理论做一简要介绍和评述。

简言之,卡尔霍恩坚持各州保留否决联邦有违各州利益的权力,他的州权理论基于"主权"这一政治学的基本观念。他坚持反对麦迪逊和汉弥尔顿等人有关联邦主权和州主权并行不悖的观点,认为联邦宪法正是各州约定的联盟,其合法性来自各州人民的认可,而并非来自一个整体观念的"人民"的观念。因此,主权在各州,不在联邦政府,判决权也不在联邦法院。各州有权判定联邦政府是否超越宪法权限,侵犯各州人民的利益。各州行使这一主权的手段就是通过阐释或修正联邦宪法,正如当初各州"审批"通过宪法那样。如果联邦国会执意通过各州认为违宪的法案(比如杰克逊签署的1832关税法案),那么各州人民就可以行使主权,宣布该联邦法案"无效"。如果某一州(比如当时的南卡罗来纳州)在"宣布无效"过程中属于少数,那么该州可以服从多数,也可以考虑退出联邦。而退出联邦体制这一行为是有先例的。当初十三州殖民地宣布脱离英联邦正是例子,而《独立宣言》中也明文写道:"任何形式的(联邦)政府,一旦破坏了这些权利(生命权、自由权和追求幸福的权利),人民有权改变,或罢免该政府,建立新的政府。"这也就是洛克理论中所说的人的"自然权利"。

另一方面,宣示州主权和分离主义与维护奴隶制是互为一体的。卡尔霍恩的思想具有极强的历史唯物倾向,他总是从经济利益的角度考虑国家体制,权力和个人自由的因素。他力图消解杰斐逊理想主义的神话,说道:"认为每个人都平等地享有自然权利,这是一个极大而又危险的错误。"这是因为,人类的存在不是以自然法则,是以其社会性为前提。人性的本质就是对社会和政府的祈求。个体的欲望与社会的规则构成永久的矛盾。为此,政府应运而生,担负起保证社会安全(即每个个体安全)的责任。这一认识有马克思"人是一切社会关系的总和"这一论断的痕迹,但由于他不能像马克思那样深入剖析在资本主义条件下资本、劳动和货币的实质及其在社会生产过程的作用,他也就未能发现剩余价值的秘密,从而也就无法理解生产力和生产关系之间的矛盾运动。而且,问题在于,卡尔霍恩把人类生而不平等这一认识延伸到对人类不同种族的理解,从而为奴隶制进行辩护。基于人类不平等是阶级社会的必然条件,卡尔霍恩坚持认为,奴隶制是一种"美好的,积极的德行",是白人和黑人这两种完全不同的种族共同生活的最佳方式。奴隶制既有利于奴隶主,也有利于奴隶本人。南方的黑奴们在白人种植园主的庇护下,过着安定祥和的生活,比起北方工厂作坊里在资本家的监视下持续劳动的白人工人的生活还要好得多。卡尔霍恩警告,废奴主义将会打乱种族不平等的规律,把社会引向种族对立和国家分裂。

用今天的眼光看,卡尔霍恩的思想死结在于,他坚定地站在资本主义财产不可剥夺的立场上,维护着州权以及作为州权的"财产"的奴隶制,同时,他也看到资本主义生产关系中的危机,即资本对于个人劳动价值的无情剥夺和无产阶级革命的可能,但这些都是为了反衬南方种植园生活方式的美好,凸显黑人奴隶在奴隶制度下的所谓安稳生活。他号召北方的资本家警惕无产阶级革命,保护自己的资本财产,但却反对资本主义进一步,也是不可抗拒的蔓延和发展。他的历史决定论注定止于他个人醉心的政治领域,成了狭隘的地方主义和维护奴隶制的辩护词。

卡尔霍恩的思想深处是典型的严格的二项式对立分析原则:南方/北方(地域);理想/现实;联邦权力/州主权;奴隶制/废奴主义等等,唯独缺乏对立统一的辩证原则。不错,在解释这些对立的观念过程中,卡尔霍恩有清醒的历史感,试图重建历史的过程和框架来支撑他的理论大厦。在人类从来就没有实现真正的平等这一前提下,他看到了阶级斗争,看到社会能量在人类欲望的驱使下互相运动,而实现渐变的进步。但由于他的目光多停留在美国南方崇尚的古代文明,和希腊式的古典生活方式,也就无视社会进步带来的意识形态变化,和随着经济发展带动下的生活方式的转变。也就是说,卡尔霍恩的历史眼光试图分辨出局部的清晰和准确，但却看不到历史总的趋势和进程。他对美国北方资本主义的发展和劳资之间的矛盾所将导致的社会革命感到忧心忡忡，但却不能意识到这是人类社会走向现代性不可避免的代价。一句话，他的历史感和现实感使他沉湎于过去的美好时光，而忘记了前行的道路。

总之，卡尔霍恩没有坚守他青年时代的农耕田园梦，也没有实现他的耶鲁导师蒂姆西·德赖特说他日后必定当上美国总统的预言，他前半生扮演的是美国政坛多面人的角色。但是，卡尔霍恩却是一个思想的大家，他以倡导州主权，鼓吹分离，捍卫奴隶制而立身，并提出与之相应的政治权利理论。在历史上，他的政治立场随着南北战争联邦的胜利而宣告破产，但他的政治权利理论却对今天的协商式民主和公民社会的建立有着积极的影响。

文如其人。卡尔霍恩长于理论思维，但对人文知识和语言艺术不感兴趣。他阅读了众多的理论家，特别是洛克、霍布斯、马基雅维利、亚当·斯密、亚里士多德和埃德蒙伯克的著作，但对文学作品却知之甚少。他的语言逻辑清晰，条理缜密，表达准确，但也缺乏那个时代政治家的宏大的视野和激情的感染力。除了早期鼓动战争的演说尚可与克莱和韦伯斯特等大演说家一比，后期的文字和演说多是冷峻的理性产物，是对"政治正确性"(political correctness)的追求。本讲中收录的"弗特山演说"①可资一例。

■ 演讲文（节选）

Fort Hill Address

John C. Calhoun

The question of the relation which the States and the General Government bear to each other is not one of recent origin. From the **commencement** of our system, it had divided public **sentiment**. Even in the convention, while the Constitution was struggling into existence, there two parties as to what this relationship should be, whose different sentiments **constituted** no small **impediment** in forming that **instrument**. After the General Government went into operation, experience soon proved that the question had not terminated with the labors of the Convention. The great struggle that preceded the

commencement: beginning
sentiment: opinion
constitute: form(v), establish;
impediment: obstacle; difficulty
instrument: (here) the Constitution

---

① 这是卡尔霍恩1831年7月在住所"弗特山庄"写下的长篇讲稿，后刊登在纽约"访谈者通讯报"。这篇讲稿虽没有在公众场合演说，但却是卡尔霍恩在"州权否决风波"的关键时刻，深思熟虑地向南北方人坦言的思想。就其内容，目的和文体而论，也算得上一篇杰出的演讲。

第十九讲 | John C. Calhoun

political revolution of 1801, which brought Mr. Jefferson into power, turned essentially on it, and **doctrines** and arguments on both sides were embodied and ably sustained—on the one, in Virginia, and Kentucky Resolutions, and the Report to the Virginia Legislature—and others, **in replies of** Legislature of Massachusetts and some other States. ...

The great and leading principle is, that the General Government **emanated from** the people of several States, forming distinct political communities, and acting in their separate sovereign capacity, and not from all the people forming one **aggregate** political community; that the Constitution of the United States is, in fact, a **compact** to which each State is a party, in the character already described; and that The several States, or parties, have a right to judge of its **infractions**; and in the case of deliberate, **palpable**, and dangerous exercise of power not delegated, they have the right, in the last resort, to use the language of the Virginia Resolutions, "to **interpose** for arresting the progress of evil, and for maintaining, within their respective limits, the authorities, rights and liberties **appertaining to** them." This right of interposition, thus solemnly asserted by the State of Virginia, be it called what it may—State-right, veto, **nullification**, or by any other name—I conceive to be the fundamental principle of our system, resting on facts historically as certain as our own revolution itself, and **deductions** as simple and demonstrative as that of any political or moral truth whatever; and I firmly believe that on its recognition depends the stability and safety of our political institutions.

I am not ignorant that those opposed to the doctrine have always, now and formally, regarded it in a very different light, as **anarchical** and revolutionary. Could I believe such, in fact, to be its tendency, to me it would be no recommendation. I yield to none, I trust in a deep and sincere attachment to our political institutions and union of the States. I never breathed an opposite sentiment; but, on the contrary, I have ever considered them the great instruments of preserving our liberty and promoting the happiness for ourselves and our **posterity**; and next to these I have held them most dear. Nearly half my life has passed in the service of the Union, and whatever public reputation I have acquired is indissolubly identified with it. To be too national has been considered by many, even of my friends, my greatest political fault.

With strong feelings of attachment, I have examined, with utmost care, the **bearing** of the doctrine in question; and so far (very

---

doctrine: *principle; belief*

in reply of: *in response to*

emanate: *produce; generate*

aggregate: *overall; sum total*

compact: *contract; agreement*

infraction: *violation of laws*

palpable: *obvious; observable*

interpose: *interrupt; check*

appertaining to: *concerning to*

nullification: *declaration of noneffectiveness (of law)*

deduction: *process of reasoning*

anarchical: *chaotic (without government)*

posterity: *next generation, children*

bearing: *basic meaning*

unlike these descriptions, I firmly believe otherwise) from anarchical or revolutionary, I **solemnly** believe it to be the only solid foundation of our system, and of the Union itself; and that opposite doctrine, which denies to the States the right of protecting their **reserved** and would **vest** in the General Government (it matters not through what department) the right of determining, exclusively and finally the powers delegated to it, is incompatible with the sovereignty of the States, and of the Constitution itself, considered as a basis of a Federal Union. As strong as this language is, it is not stronger than that used by the **Illustrious** Jefferson, who said, to give to the General Government, the final and exclusive right to judge of its powers, is to make "its **discretion**, and not the Constitution the measures of its powers; "and that" in all cases of compacts between parties having no common judge, each party has an equal right to judge for itself as well of infraction as of the mode and measure of **redress**." Language cannot be more explicit, nor can a higher authority be **adduced**.

...

It has been said by one of the most **sagacious** men of **antiquity**, that the object of a constitution is, to restrain the government, as that of laws is to restrain individuals. The remark is correct; nor is it less true where the government is vested in a majority, than where it is in a single or a few individuals—in a republic, than a monarchy or aristocracy. No one can have a higher respect for **maxim** that the majority ought to govern than I have, taken in its proper sense, subject to the restrictions **imposed** by the Constitution, and confined to objects in which every portion of the community have similar interests; but it is great error to suppose, as many do, that the right of a majority to govern is a natural and not a **conventional right**, and therefore absolute and unlimited. By nature, every individual has a right to govern himself; and governments, whether founded on majorities or minorities, must derive their right from **assent**, expressed or implied, of the governed, and be subject to such limitations as they may impose. Where the interest are the same, that is, where the laws that benefit one will benefit all, or the **reverse**, it is just and proper to place them under the control of the majority; but when they are dissimilar, so that the law that may benefit one portion may be **ruinous** to another, it would be contrary, unjust and absurd to subject them to its will; and such I **conceive** to be the theory on which our Constitutions rests.

That such dissimilarity of interest may exist, it is impossible to doubt. They are found to be in every community, in a great or less degree, however small or **homogeneous** and they constitute everywhere the greater difficulty of forming and preserving free institutions. To guard against unequal action of laws, when applied to dissimilar and opposing interests is, in fact, what mainly renders a constitution **indispensable**; to overlook which, in reasoning on our Constitution, would be to omit the principle element by which to determine its character. Were there no **contrariety** of interests, nothing would be more simple and easy than to form and preserve free institutions. The right of **suffrage** alone, would be a sufficient guarantee. It is the conflict of opposing interests which renders it the most difficult work of man.

...

Happily for us, we have no artificial and separate class of society. We have wisely **exploded** all such distinctions; but we are not, on account, exempt from distinctions; but we are not, on that account, exempt from all contrariety of interests, as the present **distracted** and dangerous condition of our country, unfortunately, but too clearly proves. With us they are almost exclusively geographical, resulting mainly from difference of climate, soil, situation, industry and production; but are not, therefore, less necessary to be protected by an adequate constitutional **provision**, then where is the distinct exist in separate classes. ...

So numerous and **diversified** are the interests of our country, that they could not be fairly represented in a single government, organized so as to give each great and leading interest a separate and distinct voice, as in governments to which I have referred. A plan was adopted better suited to our situation, but perfectly **novel** in its character. The powers of the government were divided, not, as **heretofore**, in reference to classes, but geographically. One General Government was formed for the whole, to which were delegated all powers supposed to be necessary to regulate the interests common to all the States, leaving others subject to the separate control of the States, being, from their local and peculiar character, such that they could not be subject to the will of a majority of the whole Union, without the certain **hazard** of injustice and oppression. It was thus that the interests of the whole were subjected, as they ought to be, to the will of the whole, while the peculiar and local interests were left under the control of the States separately, to whose **custody** only they could be safely **confided**. The distribution of power, settled solemnly by a

---

homogeneous: of the same kind

indispensable: absolutely necessary
contrariety: total difference; opposite
suffrage: the right to vote

explode: destroy; blow up
distracted: varied; decentralized

provision: written rules and regulation
diversified: varied

novel: new
heretofore: what have happened before

hazard: risk; danger

custody: protection
confide: trust

constitutional compact, to which all the States are parties, constitutes the peculiar character and excellence of our political system. It is truly and emphatically American, without example or **parallel**.

...

It is thus our Constitution, by authorizing **amendments**, and by prescribing the authority and the mode of making them, has by a simple **contrivance**, with its characteristic wisdom, provided a power which, in the last resort, **supersedes** effectually the necessity and even **pretext** of force; a power to which none can fairly object; with which the interests of all are safe; which can definitively close all controversies in the only effectual mode, by freeing the compact of every **defect** and uncertainty, by an amendment of the instrument itself. It is impossible for human wisdom in a system like ours, to devise another mode that shall be safe and effectual, and at the same time, **consistent with** what our relations and acknowledged powers of two great departments of our government. It gives beauty and security peculiar to our system, which if duly appreciated, will transmit its blessings to the remotest generations; but, if not, our splendid anticipations of the future will be proven an empty dream. ...

Stripped of all its covering, the naked question is, whether ours is a federal or a **consolidated** government; a constitutional or an absolute one; a government resting ultimately on the solid basis of the sovereignty of the States or on an unrestrained will of the majority; a form of government, as in all other unlimited ones, in which injustice, and violence and force must **prevail**. Let it never be forgotten, that where a majority rules without restriction, the minority is the subject; and that, if we should absurdly **attribute** to the former the exclusive right of **construing** the Constitution, there would be, in fact between sovereign and subject, under such a government, no Constitution, or at least nothing deserving the name or serving the **legitimate** object of so sacred an instrument.

parallel: anything comparable; equal part
amendment: additional acts as correction
contrivance: means; invention
supersede: replace
pretext: excuse

defect: mistake; shortcoming

consistent with: in line with; match

strip of: take everything away
consolidated: substantial; actually functioning

prevail: win; succeed, dominate
attribute: assign; offer
construe: explain; interpret
legitimate: lawful

■ 重点述评与提示

1. The question of the relation which the States and the General Government bear to each other is not one of recent origin. From the commencement of our system, it had divided public sentiment.

各州权力与联邦政府权力之间的矛盾一直贯穿着大部分的美国政治史,归根结底是体制的问题。历史分析是卡尔霍恩的逻辑起点,通过对这个问题历史性回顾,指出矛盾双方的政治立场和诉求,解答美国社会何以走向分裂。

2. The great and leading principle is, that the General Government emanated from the people of several States, forming distinct political communities, and acting in their separate sovereign capacity, and not from all the people forming one aggregate political community.

联邦政府的权力来自各州主权,是政治盟约产生的权力,并不是主权,因而也没有代表全体人民利益的性质。这是问题的症结所在,也是州权论的基石。在卡尔霍恩看来,民主政治的生命在于各州人民各自组成的社团,这也是他一直坚持的立场。

3. Nearly half my life has passed in the service of the Union, and whatever public reputation I have acquired is indissolubly identified with it. To be too national has been considered by many, even of my friends, my greatest political fault.

卡尔霍恩在这里申明,坚持各州主权,并不意味着反对联邦政体。他本人一直在联邦政府任职,官居副总统,也曾经高调支持联邦政府的国家内外政策,这是与反联邦党人的不同。但是,此后20余年,随着西部领土扩张,南北在高关税和奴隶制问题上的分歧加深,州权理论必然走向分离主义。

4. but it is great error to suppose, as many do, that the right of a majority to govern is a natural and not a conventional right, and therefore absolute and unlimited.

卡尔霍恩对多数人统治这一民主政治的原则有着基于社会现实的认识。这是对洛克自然法则的一种反叛。多数人的权力也是基于每个个体的人有着共同的利益和兴趣而约定形成的权力。

5. but when they are dissimilar, so that the law that may benefit one portion may be ruinous to another, it would be contrary, unjust and absurd to subject them to its will; and such I conceive to be the theory on which our Constitutions rests.

这是卡尔霍恩州权分离主义最直白的表述。像麦迪逊一样,他看到了人类社会中个体人欲望和利益的不同,但不同意用民主政治体制的权力来操纵或规约这些不同,而是选择高扬个体主体自由,倡导走向权力的反面。

6. So numerous and diversified are the interests of our country, that they could not be fairly represented in a single government, organized so as to give each great and leading interest a separate and distinct voice, as in governments to which I have referred.

这里的表面文章似乎不无道理:在幅员辽阔,利益分散的国度,中央联邦的制度难以维系有效的统筹，而各州分而治之，则可因地制宜，事半功倍。但是，潜在的问题却是生产关系和生产方式的区别。1831年在南北奴隶制问题冲突不断，卡尔霍恩有时被南方利益驱使，后来竟然想出南北各设一个总统的馊主意。这样的妥协实际上就是激化矛盾，使国家走向分裂和战争。这就是所谓一国三公，无所适从的道理。对于这点，还是后来的林肯一语中的："一座分裂的房子必定会坍塌的"。

7. Let it never be forgotten, that where a majority rules without restriction, the minority is the subject; and that, if we should absurdly attribute to the former the exclusive right of construing the Constitution, there would be...no Constitution, or at least nothing deserving the name or serving the legitimate object of so sacred an instrument.

在承认联邦宪法的基础上提出各州有分享宪法解释权的权利，认为这是宪法尊重全体公民的最好选择，这也是卡尔霍恩在考察了多数人民主和少数人权利之后提出的"协同式民主"（concordant democracy）原则的基础。

■ 思考及讨论题

1. What made John Calhoun determine to safeguard the state sovereignty and slavery?
2. How does John Calhoun define the term "nullification"?
3. Why does John Calhoun reject the doctrine that "All men are created equal"?
4. What can we learn from Calhoun to build a more efficient democratic society?

■ 阅读书目

1. Coit, Margaret L. *John C. Calhoun: American Portrait*. Boston：Houghton Mifflin. 1950.
2. Capers, Gerald M. *John C. Calhoun, Opportunist: A Reappraisal*. Gainesville: University of Florida Press. 1960.
3. Cheek, H. Lee, Jr. *Calhoun and Popular Rule: The political Theory of the disquisition and Discourse*. University of Columbia and London: Missouri Press, 2001.
4. Current, Richard M. *John C. Calhoun*. New York: Washington Square Press. 1963.

第二十讲
约翰·布朗(John Brown 1800—1859)

■ 政治历史评述

约翰·布朗:美国奴隶制的掘墓人

2008年5月3日,美国堪萨斯城,一出全新的大型歌剧《约翰·布朗》在音乐剧院首演。在大型合唱赞美诗的旋律和美国乡村音乐中,150年前在堪萨斯首举武力反奴大旗的约翰·布朗此时登上舞台。他的第一句台词回响着《圣经》马太福音的警世之言:"不要指望我的到来会给世界带来和平,我带来的不是和平,而是利剑。"这部剧的演出持续近3个小时,在弥漫着战争和流血氛围中,始终回旋布朗用暴力推翻奴隶制的主题旋律。剧中的布朗更像一位横空出世的摩西,秉承上帝的旨意,宣示暴力反抗邪恶是正义之举,号召用血与火的斗争把自己的人民从奴隶制的邪恶中解救出来。剧作家麦钦表示,此剧的创作历经近20年,他的目的就是通过此剧警示美国社会,让人们充分意识到种族和宗教压迫所导致的严重后果,用他的话说就是,"社会的不公正是灾难之母"。2008年美国反恐战争正酣,此剧传达出来的声音微妙而复杂。

其实,布朗的前半生并没有轰轰烈烈的传奇故事。他于1800年5月9日出生在康狄涅格州的一个小镇上,当时虔诚的清教徒父亲手捧着刚出生的男婴,嘴里喃喃自语:"但愿我们世界上所有人都能和平相处。"不想到,布朗从小绝不安分。他伴随着一本《圣经》长大,在加尔文教严峻的律条训诫下长大,但却没有受过像样的教育。他是个理想主义者,喜欢走南闯北,做过皮革匠,土地测量员、邮务员,经营过农牧场。奔波半生,做成的事不多,到头来还债台高筑。但他受过父亲的教育和感染,始终对南方的奴隶制怀有强烈的愤慨,怀着对上帝崇敬的信仰,以解救黑人奴隶为己任。及至50多岁,结交了不少的黑人领袖,成了坚定的废奴主义者,1850年代美国国会通过了逃奴追缉法后,布朗对奴隶制的憎恶到达了顶点,平时只要一提到奴隶制便情绪激动,不能自已。他坚决地主张抛弃废奴主义领袖威廉·罗伊德·加里森的和平斗争策略,号召黑奴拿起武器,通过武装起义解放自己。

时间到了1854年3月,美国国会通过了堪萨斯-内布拉斯加法案,宣布密苏里妥协案和 1850 年妥协案作废;堪萨斯-内布拉斯加领地建州是否实行奴隶制应由该领地居民投票公决。一时之间,南部的奴隶主,废奴主义者,自由土壤派等纷纷涌向该领地造势拉票,拥奴和废奴两派剑拔弩张,势不两立。拥奴狂热分子雇佣几千被称为"边界亡命徒"狂呼口号,挥舞着武器挑起事端,在劳伦斯镇制造了流血事件。废奴派一时陷入劣势。1855 年 5 月的一天,一直坚信只有武装斗争才能彻底废除奴隶制的约翰·布朗带着四个儿子和其他几个支持者,进入奴隶主据点奥萨瓦塔米,处决了 5 个狂热的奴隶制拥护者,声称这是代表上帝伸张了人间的正义。此举大振了废奴派的声势,武装废奴

的声浪愈高。此后,布朗暂时撤回北方,又在弗吉尼亚一个偏僻之地筹集经费,招募人员,购买武器,组建了他的废奴游击队。此时,布朗好像沉静下来,每天天不亮就起床,背诵《圣经》,默默祷告。他的队员常常看到他长久背着手踱步,陷入沉思之中。也许,他在心中已经开始实施他的暴动计划。

1859 年 10 月日,布朗认为时机已经成熟,只需他的枪声在弗吉尼亚一响,就可点燃南方大规模奴隶起义的熊熊大火。于是,他带着 21 人组成的小分队,攻占了联邦政府设在哈珀渡口的军火仓库。然而,此举并未得到周边地区的奴隶们的响应。布朗孤军无援,遭到了罗伯特·E.李上校(后来南北内战中南军最高统帅)率领的政府军的镇压。战斗中,布朗的 3 个儿子和其他 9 名队员阵亡,布朗受伤被俘。经过两个月的监禁和审讯,布朗被判绞刑。1859 年 12 月 2 日是布朗的死刑执行日。清晨,他照常端坐桌旁给友人写信。10 点半,日头高照,典狱长出现,告诉他准备上路。布朗说了声"谢谢",然后从容写下了最后的遗言:"我,约翰·布朗,此刻坚信,只有鲜血才能最终洗净这罪恶土地

上的种种罪行。"一语成谶。两年之后,美国南北战争爆发,近百万人的生命和鲜血流过,奴隶制的罪恶最终在美国大地上被洗刷干净。

1860 年前后,美国政治力量在奴隶制存废问题上不断分化重组,形成两极尖锐对立。在此关头,布朗的枪声无疑催化了南北分裂过程。南部种植园里的奴隶主无不为哈珀军火库事件感到震惊,他们害怕奴隶起义随时发生,对废奴运动更为仇视。他们咒骂布朗是盗马贼,精神分裂和恐怖主义杀手,种族的背叛者,是文明国家的敌人。当时,还是国会参议员的林肯在南方各州威胁退出联邦的压力下,出于政治策略的考虑,称布朗是"误入歧途的狂热分子"。与此相反,布朗的武装起义为北方非暴力废奴主义者注入了一剂强心针,他在绞架前表现出来的宗教信念和大义凛然也使北方的反奴情绪增加了道德的救世想象和正义的精神力量。文学家梭罗把布朗比作耶稣基督在世,思想家爱默生则这样评价狱中的布朗:"这位圣子,他的命运尚悬一线,但是他的烈士献身精神

如果终须完美,则他的绞架将与救世主的十字架同辉。"布朗的精神也鼓舞着新一代的年轻人。几年后,联邦军队的士兵们高唱着名为"约翰·布朗的遗体"的进行曲,奔赴战场,为废除奴隶制,捍卫联邦的统一流血牺牲。布朗起义的影响甚至超越了国界。布朗在狱中关押期间,法国作家雨果发表文章,要求当局停止审讯,赦免布朗。马克思1860年1月在给恩格斯的信中这样写道:"约翰·布朗的死引发的美国奴隶运动和俄国的农奴运动,这是当今世界上正在发生的两个最重大的事件。"可见,布朗起义虽然规模有限,以失败告终,但是在当时资本主义拓展市场,彻底打碎人类最后的人身奴役关系的关键时刻,这样的暴力革命却有石破天惊的现实意义和影响。

1859年11月2日,法庭宣布判处布朗绞刑。那一天,布朗在法庭上做了最后的陈述。这就是这篇著名的布朗法庭演讲。有目击者后来回忆,那天,布朗戴着镣铐,忍受着巨大的伤痛,神色安详地出现在法庭上,犹如"屹立的岩石"。宣读死刑判决前,审判长帕克法官问布朗还有什么要申辩的,布朗艰难地站立起来,两只手放在胸前的桌子上,面部庄严肃穆,向法庭和观众陈述了自己最后的立场。布朗在演说中否认自己有罪,申明自己的所做作为都是为了解放黑人奴隶和劳苦大众。他引用《圣经》中上帝之言:"记住那些被奴役的人们,就像是和他们同受奴役一样",雄辩地说明了自己行为的正义。布朗宣布,自己愿意把自己的生命和鲜血与百万的黑奴的鲜血融为一体,对此毫无遗憾。布朗的演讲用词平易,要言不烦,语气平和而

带有威严,整篇陈词大义凛然,立场坚定,爱憎分明,宽容大度。法庭大厅被一种上帝般的声音所感染,肃静而安详。正是这神圣和庄严,150余年来让这位一手握着《圣经》,一手举着利剑的约翰·布朗一直站在历史的舞台上。

■ 演讲文

To Mingle My Blood with the Blood of Millions of Black Slaves

John Brown

> I have, may it please the Court, a few words to say.
> In the first place, I deny everything but what I have all along admitted, the design on my part to free the slaves. I intended certainly

to have made a **clean thing** of that matter, as I did last winter, when I went into Missouri and there took slaves without the **snapping** of a gun on either side, moved them through the country, and finally left them in Canada. I designed to have done the same thing again, on a larger scale. That was all I intended. I never did intend murder, or treason, or the destruction of property, or to excite or **incite**. slaves to rebellion, or to make **insurrection.**

I have another objection; and that is, it is unjust that I should suffer such a **penalty**. Had I interfered in the manner which I admit, and which I admit has been fairly proved (for I admire the truthfulness and **candor** of the greater portion of the witnesses who have testified in this case), had I so interfered in behalf of the rich, the powerful, the intelligent, the so-called great, or in behalf of any of their friends, either father, mother, brother, sister, wife, or children, or any of that class, and suffered and sacrificed what I have in this interference, it would have been all right; and every man in this court would have **deemed** it an act worthy of reward rather than punishment.

This court acknowledges, as I suppose, the **validity** of the law of God. I see a book kissed here which I suppose to be the Bible, or at least the New Testament. That teaches me that all things whatsoever I would that men should do to me, I should do even so to them. It teaches me, further, to "remember them that are in bonds, as bound with them." I **endeavored** to act up to that instruction. I say, I am yet **too young** to understand that God is any respecter of persons. I believe that to have interfered as I have done as I have always freely admitted I have done in behalf of His despised poor, was not wrong, but right. Now, if it is deemed necessary that I should **forfeit** my life for the **furtherance** of the ends of justice, and mingle my blood further with the blood of my children and with the blood of millions in this slave country whose rights are disregarded by wicked, cruel, and unjust **enactments**, I submit; so let it be done!

Let me say one word further.

I feel entirely satisfied with the treatment I have received on my trial. Considering all the circumstances. it has been more generous than I expected. But I feel no consciousness of guilt. I have stated from the first what was my intention and what was not. I never had any design against the life of any person, nor any **disposition** to commit treason, or excite slaves to rebel, or make any general insurrection. I never encouraged any man to do so, but always discouraged any idea of that kind.

---

clean thing: (here) free the slaves without bloodshed
snapping: sudden sound (of a gun)

incite: encourage emotionally
insurrection: uprising
penalty: punishment
candor: honesty; sincerity; frankness

deem: consider; think

validity: truthfulness; lawfulness

endeavor: try hard
young: (here) less learned and less experienced in terms of the truth of God.

forfeit: lose; sacrifice
furtherance: promotion
enactment: action; proceeding

disposition: intention; desire

induce: persuade skillfully for special purpose
of his own accord: out of his own decision

Let me say, also, a word in regard to the statements made by some of those connected with me. I hear it has been stated by some of them that I have **induced** them to join me. But the contrary is true. I do not say this to injure them, but as regretting their weakness. There is not one of them but joined me **of his own accord**, and the greater part of them at their own expense. A number of them I never saw, and never had a word of conversation with, till the day they came to me; and that was for the purpose I have stated.

Now I have done.

■ 重点述评与提示

1. I intended certainly to have made a clean thing of that matter, as I did last winter, when I went into Missouri and there took slaves without the snapping of a gun on either side, moved them through the country, and finally left them in Canada.

   布朗一直通过"地下铁道"解救黑奴,这是废奴主义者从事的不流血的工作。但是他认为这样不能最终解决问题。流血冲突不可避免,他本人也曾在堪萨斯处决过5名狂热的拥奴分子,最后攻占哈珀军火库时也杀了奴隶主,这也是法庭指控布朗的主要"罪状"。具有讽刺意义的是:当年殖民地因反抗英国议会而抗税杀人,那是正义的行为,而今天布朗为解救奴隶而杀人却是不赦的死罪。

2. had I so interfered in behalf of the rich, the powerful, the intelligent, the so-called great, or in behalf of any of their friends, either father, mother, brother, sister, wife, or children, or any of that class, and suffered and sacrificed what I have in this interference, it would have been all right; and every man in this court would have deemed it an act worthy of reward rather than punishment.

   布朗此处的申辩涉及了法律的阶级性问题。在他满脑子的基督教人道主义理想和朴素的平等思想中,虽然表现出清醒的阶级意识,但没有对阶级和作为意识形态的法律有着清醒的认识,他不可能理解马克思关于"统治阶级的思想在每一时代都是占统治地位的思想"这一论断的深刻含义。

3. That teaches me that all things whatsoever I would that men should do to me, I should do even so to them. It teaches me, further, to "remember them that are in bonds, as bound with them." I endeavored to act up to that instruction.

   "记住那些被奴役的人们,就像是和他们同受奴役一样。"布朗熟读《圣经》,此处引用上帝之言可谓信手拈来,恰到好处,也为自己的申辩增添了神圣的气氛。《圣经》记载,以色列人首领摩西目睹奴隶被主人暴打,一怒之下,杀了奴隶主,解救了奴隶。

布朗的行为如同一辙。这也为布朗的形象增添了神秘的色彩。

4. Now, if it is deemed necessary that I should forfeit my life for the furtherance of the ends of justice, and mingle my blood further with the blood of my children and with the blood of millions in this slave country whose rights are disregarded by wicked, cruel, and unjust enactments, I submit; so let it be done!

  这是大义凛然，从容就义的豪言壮语，其中意象清晰（突出"热血"的意象），排比紧凑，爱憎分明，末尾的分句，短促有力，尽显整个句子重尾的修辞功能，具有较强的感染力。

5. I hear it has been stated by some of them that I have induced them to join me. But the contrary is true. I do not say this to injure them, but as regretting their weakness. There is not one of them but joined me of his own accord, and the greater part of them at their own expense.

  布朗在此申明，参加此次武装起义的人员都是自愿的，目的在于宣示这项事业的正义性。据说，在赴刑场之前，布朗逐一看望了难友，鼓励他们坚持自己的信念，告诫其中的人不可出卖同志。由此可见，在生与死的考验面前，舍生取义只有少数人才能做到。这也是后人尊崇布朗是"殉道者"（martyr）的原因了。

■ 思考及讨论题

1. How do you understand John Brown as a radical abolitionist and as a Christian martyr?
2. Why was Brown's attack on Harper Ferry not responded by a general slave uprising?
3. What could be the meaning of John Brown to the Civil War that followed so close?

■ 阅读书目

1. Oates, Stephen B. *Our Fiery Trial: Abraham Lincoln, John Brown, and the Civil War Era*. Amherst: University of Massachusetts, 1979.
2. Patterson, Margot. "'John Brown' Looks at the Cost of Freedom: A Truly American Opera about the Struggle to End Slavery" in *National Catholic Reporter* 30 May 2008.
3. Toledo, Gregory. *The Hanging of Old Brown: A Story of Slaves, Statesmen, and Redemption*. Westport, CT: Praeger, 2002.
4. Redpath, James. *The Public Life of Capt. John Brown*. Boston: Thayer and Eldridge, 1860.

第二十一讲
亚伯拉罕·林肯(Abraham Lincoln 1809—1865)(上)

■ 政治历史评述

亚伯拉罕·林肯:美国人心中的教父和政治之谜

　　林肯在现代美国人心中是一代伟人,是"人人生而平等"的实践者和实现者,是现代美国的奠基人,是最受人爱戴的美国总统。美国著名史学家梅里厄·皮特森有一句发人深省的名言:"美国人崇敬华盛顿,不忘杰斐逊,爱戴林肯。"的确,华盛顿是美国民族英雄的典范,杰斐逊是美国民主的奠基者,在那个民族意识觉醒,呼唤领袖的年代,他们自然是人们心中崇拜的偶像。而相比华盛顿和杰斐逊那高大的美国国父的经典形象,林肯纪念堂中那位端坐上方,用深邃而慈祥的目光注视着络绎不绝的游客的白玉塑像,更像一位美国人的教父,他教会美国人在磨难中坚韧前行,走向成熟,步入现代。他让人在当今动荡浮躁的年代能够平心静气地想到一个个难以忘怀的美国故事。

　　林肯同时也是一个解不开的谜:一个来自肯塔基边地木屋,只会成天劈削枕木的伐木工,一个几乎没有接受过正规教育的穷小子,一个喜欢讲故事,相貌丑陋,一脸苦相的瘦削年轻人,竟然能够满口的莎士比亚台词,满脑的上帝意识和《圣经》辞句,生活中诙谐幽默,风趣平易,政坛上机智权变,雄辩滔滔。正是这个毫无政治和经济背景,身无尺寸军功的平常人,竟然通过刻苦自学,在伊利诺伊州的斯普林菲尔德当上律师,以自嘲式的演讲崛起于政坛,弄潮于南北奴隶制存废的风口浪尖,游走于联邦州权,党派更替的风云政坛,舌战民主党领袖道格拉斯,最终在新崛起的共和党人和部分民主党人的拥戴下,成为美国第16届总统。林肯表面上平易近人,坚韧果断,但却时常情绪低落,郁郁寡欢,甚至痛不欲生。林肯被刺身亡也是一个难解的谜。这位经常沉浸于莎士比亚戏剧世界中的美国总统最终被一位著名的莎剧演员在一座著名的大剧院中开枪射杀。这是巧合,而人生如戏,无巧不成,这也正如林肯本人常常表现出来的人生无常的意识一样。这位名叫布斯的刺客行刺后跳上舞台,高呼"暴君已死!这是一切独裁者的下场"。他不久被判处死刑,临刑时留下遗言:"告诉母亲,儿已为国捐躯!"此种场景也为后世留下扑朔迷离的想象:当年约翰·布朗为了解放黑奴武装起义而被判绞刑,布斯作为刑场维持秩序的士兵,持枪站在队列中,目睹老布朗艰难地登上绞架,是否也想象到自己人生戏剧如此的终场?

　　然而,我认为,150多年来的林肯研究无论如何卷帙浩繁,观点各异,扑朔迷离,其实都最终归结于"解放者林肯"和"独裁者林肯"两大褒贬形象,折射出美国历史上那场南北对决,不可调和的意识形态斗争和血与火的炼狱。

一方面,林肯是美国联邦国家伟大捍卫者和黑人奴隶的解放者,是他受命于国家分离的危难之中,坚决维护联邦的统一,捍卫神圣的宪法,他是著名诗人惠特曼心中反复呼喊的"船长",带领着美国即将解体的航船在内战的惊涛骇浪中艰难前行,却倒在了国家安全靠岸后的港湾。他坚信"人人生而平等"的真谛,在维护联邦统一和废除奴隶制的政治悖论的艰难抉择中机智果敢,在内战的关键签署

了《解放宣言》,使400万美国黑人奴隶终于看到了"令人振奋的黎明曙光,结束了被奴役的漫漫长夜"(马丁·路德·金语)。这位目睹内战屠杀,生灵涂炭而感到负罪悲怆的美国总统凭借着坚强的意志竞选连任,不遗余力地促使美国国会通过了宪法第十三条修正案,以国家法律的形式在美国大地上永久废除了奴隶制,自美国建国以来终于认可了黑人种族作为人的存在,向种族平等自由权利的现代美国迈出了关键的一步。在美国内战硝烟渐散,人心悲怆的日子里,正是这位面容枯槁,即将走到生命尽头的美国总统表现出关乎宇宙,以人为本的胸怀,号召以宽容大度的基督精神重建满目疮痍的国家,让美国人民在经历了内战的血雨腥风后重新认识到人性的价值,看到一个统一的国家继续前行的希望。

林肯的这一正面形象在斯蒂芬·斯皮尔伯格导演的史诗电影《林肯》中再次闪烁出时代的光芒。电影的开头,林肯已经签署了《解放黑奴宣言》,大量的黑人士兵加入了联邦军队,为自己的自由而战;南北战争关键之战葛底斯堡战役以联邦军的胜利结束,林肯也在战场发表了他那旷世的"葛底斯堡演说"。丹尼尔·戴·路易斯扮演的林肯惟妙惟肖,出现在行军途中。他端坐营帐,慈眉善目,正在与两名黑人士兵亲切交谈。斯皮尔伯格可谓导演大家,他让两位白人士兵以坚定的语气,背诵了林肯在"葛底斯堡演说"中关于为国家的统一而捐躯的部分演说词,让一名黑人士兵铿锵有力地背诵出最后的警句:"这个国家,在上帝荫庇下,将迎来自由的新生;一个民有、民治、民享的政府将永立于世"。这是美国人家喻户晓,引以自豪的立国铭言,也是林肯传世的语言丰碑。在此精神的感召下,北军士兵高唱着"我们来了,亚伯拉罕父亲"的进行曲,别妻离子,源源不断奔赴战场,赢得最后的胜利,解放了黑奴,解救的联邦。这就是"解放者林肯"形象最典型的艺术再现。影片中,林肯为了使宪法第十三条修正案在国会获得通过,不遗余力争取议员选票,对着他的智囊团成员吼道:"我是美利坚合众国总统,拥有巨大的权力,你们必须去获得这些选票!"这显示了林肯的政治决断和为废除奴隶制的决心,同时也是他对战时总统权力的理解和自信。但是,这却也是"独裁者林肯"形象最典型的展现。

按照对"独裁者林肯"形象的诠释,林肯是美国有史以来最独断专权的总统。他当选后不久就置美国宪法不顾,采取了一系列完全违背宪法,超越总统权限的政策和措施。首先,林肯命令北军向位于查尔斯顿的塞姆特要塞增兵,直接引发了南部邦联军队于

1861年4月12日向塞姆特开炮，打响了南北战争的第一枪。事发第二天，他绕开国会直接宣布南部各蓄奴州为叛乱，命令集结7万5千联邦军队平叛，而这是宪法明文规定非国会不可动用的权力；第三天，他宣布国会两个月后方可举行会议，而在几天之内，他连续发布了一系列必须经过国会同意才能颁布实施的政令：4月19日宣布海军封锁南部海岸；4月21日，宣布海军新购5艘战舰；4月27日，宣布无限期终止宪法的根本权利条款"人身保护法"，关闭了300多家报社，未经起诉和审判把成百上千有支持南部分离嫌疑的议员、编辑和其他人士投入监狱，此后每天都有许多人因表示对林肯政府的不满而被投入监狱。而这些政府行为都是对宪法粗暴的践踏。此外，林肯还是一个坚定的白人至上主义者，对有色种族并无好感。这使他"黑人奴隶的解放者"的形象大打折扣。早在1858年，林肯在与道格拉斯的辩论中明确表示，他坚定地反对白人和黑人种族平等，反对给予黑人选举权，杜绝给予黑人在政府中任职。他坚持认为白种人远远优于黑人，不可能同居共处，因而主张把黑人统统迁移大陆以外的黑人居留地。非洲裔美国作家贝内特在《林肯的白人梦》中描述了林肯在许多演说和文件中，甚至在《解放黑奴宣言》的原始版本中都号召把黑人迁出美国，而且付诸实施，在签署了《解放黑奴宣言》之后3个月后，亲自督办，把450名黑人男女和儿童强行迁移到靠近海地的一个毒蛇出没的海岛。这个"首例林肯黑人殖民计划"最终失败，造成不少人死亡，幸存者也是奄奄一息，疾病缠身。而且，林肯也反复表示，《解放黑奴宣言》仅仅是战时权宜措施。在联邦军队战事屡遭败绩之后，林肯抓住一次安提艾姆战役胜利之机，签署了此项宣言，据此便可以大量地征用黑人入伍或参与军事行动。据统计，《解放黑奴宣言》之后，约有近19万黑人被征用入伍，其中约7万人死于各次战役。

当然，这些都可以用林肯有关维护联邦统一至上的政治立场来加以解释，其中最明确的表达就是："我在这场战争中最重大的目标是拯救联邦，不是拯救奴隶制，也不是废除奴隶制。"在1864年4月4日的一封信件中，林肯这样写道："我认为，任何措施，尽管是违反宪法的，但只要是有利于国家的统一，并以此而成为保全宪法必不可少的措施，那都是合法的。"这就是"解放者林肯"和"独裁者林肯"背后凸显出来的"政治智慧者林肯"的形象。作为联邦政府总统，他那律师的头脑和政治理性不会允许他置国家机器和政府权力于不顾，去实现社会正义和道义的责任。"皮之不存，毛将焉附"的道理，那些激进的共和党人和废奴主义者可以一知半解，但作为强权国家主义政治家，林肯对之可是深谙其义的。

说到林肯的演说口才，那也是一个令人执着的迷。他没有受过任何的语言和修辞训练，也没有博览群书的经历，但他却痴迷于《圣经》、《伊索寓言》、班扬的《天路历程》、莎士比亚戏剧、笛福的《鲁滨孙漂流记》等好书，反复阅读成诵，加之善于观察思考，乐于聆听模仿，久之却内化生成出一种谦卑中显自信，平易中见犀利，执着中现包容，说理透彻，动情入心的演说风格。他的二届总统就职演说堪称政治演说的精品，那篇3分钟的"葛底斯堡演说"更是庄重典雅，简洁点睛，诗意盎然，微言大义的经典名篇，被誉为"美国伟大的诗篇"。1861年5月林肯就职总统时，南部7个蓄奴州已经公开宣布退出，林肯已经做好战争部署，但在就职演说中力图挽回局面，劝说南部联盟回到联邦的轨道上来。演说中林肯突出主词"I"，显示了当今乱世"舍我其谁"的自信，他引用宪法条款等法律文件，既重申了自己保护奴隶主私有财产，反对废除奴隶制，支持追缉逃奴等原则立场，又通过论述联邦的永久合法性，明确把脱离联邦之举定性为必须予以坚决镇压的叛乱行为，不容置疑地表明了自己维护国家统一的决心。

这篇演说最后的段落直称南部各州为"同胞"，试图用诗化的语言和共同的建国历史感染听众，拉近与南部各州的距离，是至今美国人耳熟能详的文学名句，也显示了林肯与冷峻的政治理性保持距离，召唤人性良善的人文胸怀。

■ 演讲文（节选）

First Presidential Inaugural Address

Abraham Lincoln

Apprehension seems to exist among the people of the Southern States that by the **accession** of a Republican Administration their property and their peace and personal security are to be endangered. There has never been any reasonable cause for such apprehension. Indeed, the most **ample** evidence to the contrary has all the while existed and been open to their **inspection**. It is found in nearly all the published speeches of **him** who now addresses you. I do but quote from one of those speeches when I declare that—I have no purpose, directly or indirectly, to interfere with the **institution** of slavery in the States where it exists. I believe I have no lawful right to do so, and I have no inclination to do so.

Those who nominated and elected me did so with full knowledge that I had made this and many similar declarations and had never **recanted** them; and more than this, they placed in the platform for my acceptance, and as a law to themselves and to me, the clear and emphatic resolution which I now read:

apprehension: anxiety; worry
accession: taking office; come to power
ample: plenty of
inspection: examination
him: (here) Lincoln himself
institution: system

recant: withdraw; declare invalid

inviolate: not to be violated or invaded	

Resolved, That the maintenance **inviolate** of the rights of the States, and especially the right of each State to order and control its own domestic institutions according to its own judgment exclusively, is essential to that balance of power on which the perfection and endurance of our political **fabric** depend; and we **denounce** the lawless invasion by armed force of the soil of any State or Territory, no matter what **pretext**, as among the gravest of crimes.

fabric: system
denounce: accuse; condemn
pretext: excuse
reiterate: repeat for emphasis
press upon: make clear to
susceptible: sensitive
in any wise: in case cases

I now **reiterate** these sentiments, and in doing so I only **press upon** the public attention the most conclusive evidence of which the case is **susceptible** that the property, peace, and security of no section are to be **in any wise** endangered by the now incoming Administration. I add, too, that all the protection which, consistently with the Constitution and the laws, can be given will be cheerfully given to all the States when lawfully demanded, for whatever cause—as cheerfully to one section as to another.

fugitives: runaway (slaves)

provision: terms; written statement in law

discharge: release; declare free

There is much controversy about the delivering up of **fugitives** from service or labor. The clause I now read is as plainly written in the Constitution as any other of its **provisions**:

"No person held to service or labor in one State, under the laws thereof, escaping into another, shall in consequence of any law or regulation therein be **discharged** from such service or labor, but shall be delivered up on claim of the party to whom such service or labor may be due."

It is scarcely questioned that this provision was intended by those who made it for the reclaiming of what we call fugitive slaves; and the intention of the lawgiver is the law. All members of Congress swear their support to the whole Constitution—to this provision as much as to any other. To the **proposition**, then, that slaves whose cases come within the terms of this clause "shall be delivered up," their oaths are **unanimous**. Now, if they would make the effort in good temper, could they not with nearly equal unanimity frame and pass a law by means of which to keep good that unanimous oath? There is some difference of opinion whether this clause should be enforced by national or by State authority, but surely that difference is not a very **material** one. If the slave is to be **surrendered**, it can be of but little consequence to him or to others by which authority it is done. And should anyone in any case be content that his oath shall go unkept on a merely **unsubstantial** controversy as to how it shall be kept?

proposition: proposal; suggestion
unanimous: of one voice; agreed by everyone

material: realistic
surrender: hand over (as prisoner)
unsubstantial: having no significant meaning
humane: human sympathy and love
jurisprudence: system of law

Again: In any law upon this subject ought not all the safeguards of liberty known in civilized and **humane jurisprudence** to be introduced, so that a free man is not in any case surrendered as a slave? And might it not be well at the same time to provide by law for the **enforcement** of that clause in the Constitution which guarantees that "the citizens of each State shall be entitled to all privileges and **immunities** of citizens in the several states"?

I take the official oath today with no mental reservations and with no purpose to **construe** the Constitution or laws by any **hypercritical** rules; and while I do not choose now to specify particular acts of Congress as proper to be enforced, I do suggest that it will be much safer for all, both in official and private stations, to conform to and abide by all those acts which stand **unrepeated** than to violate any of them trusting to find impunity in having them held to be unconstitutional.

...

I hold that in contemplation of universal law and of the Constitution the Union of these States is **perpetual**. Perpetuity is implied, if not expressed, in the fundamental law of all national governments. It is safe to assert that no government **proper** ever had a provision in its organic law for its own termination. Continue to execute all the express provisions of our National Constitution, and the Union will endure forever, it being impossible to destroy it except by some action not provided for in the **instrument** itself.

Again: If the United States be not a government proper, but an association of States in the nature of contract merely, can it, as a contract, be peaceably **unmade** by less than all the parties who made it? One party to a contract may violate it—break it, so to speak—but does it not require all to lawfully **rescind** it?

Descending from these general principles, we find the proposition that in legal contemplation the Union is perpetual confirmed by the history of the Union itself. The Union is much older than the Constitution. It was formed, in fact, by the Articles of Association in 1774. It was matured and continued by the Declaration of Independence in 1776. It was further matured, and the faith of all the then thirteen States expressly **plighted** and engaged that it should be perpetual, by the Articles of Confederation in 1778. And finally, in 1787, one of the declared objects for **ordaining** and establishing the Constitution was "to form a more perfect Union."

But if destruction of the Union by one or by a part only of the States be lawfully possible, the Union is less perfect than before the Constitution, having lost the **vital** element of perpetuity.

---

enforcement: putting into effect
immunity: freedom from duty; right to be exempted
construe: interpret; understand
hypercritical: strict; hair-splitting
unrepeal: still valid and lawful

perpetual: ever-lasting

proper: normally established

instrument: (here) government legalized by its constitution
unmade: dissolved; dismiss; destroyed
rescind: declare invalid; withdraw (an act of law)

plight: agree in lawful contract

ordain: declare as law

vital: important (for survival)

第二十一讲 | Abraham Lincoln

resolve: *decision*
ordinance: *act of law*
void: *ineffective*
insurrectionary: *rebellious*
revolutionary: *of using violence to take power*
enjoin upon: *order; instruct*

requisite: *necessary*
menace: *threat; deterrence*

It follows from these views that no State upon its own mere motion can lawfully get out of the Union; that **resolves** and **ordinances** to that effect are legally **void**, and that acts of violence within any State or States against the authority of the United States are **insurrectionary** or **revolutionary**, according to circumstances.

I therefore consider that in view of the Constitution and the laws the Union is unbroken, and to the extent of my ability, I shall take care, as the Constitution itself expressly **enjoins upon** me, that the laws of the Union be faithfully executed in all the States. Doing this I deem to be only a simple duty on my part, and I shall perform it so far as practicable unless my rightful masters, the American people, shall withhold the **requisite** means or in some authoritative manner direct the contrary. I trust this will not be regarded as a **menace**, but only as the declared purpose of the Union that it will constitutionally defend and maintain itself.

...

assail: *attack*
strain: *pull away in tension (from each other)*

In your hands, my dissatisfied fellow-countrymen, and not in mine, is the momentous issue of civil war. The Government will not **assail** you close. We are not enemies, but friends. We must not be enemies. Though passion may have **strained** it. You can have no conflict without being yourselves the aggressors. You have no oath registered in heaven to destroy the Government, while I shall have the most solemn one to "preserve, protect, and defend it."

loath: *unwilling*
mystic: *mysterious; unknown*
hearthstone: *family*
swell: *increase the volume of voice*

I am **loath** to must not break our bonds of affection. The **mystic** chords of memory, stretching from every battlefield and patriot grave to every living heart and hearthstone all over this broad land, will yet **swell** the **chorus** of the Union, when again touched, as surely they will be, by the better angels of our nature.

■ 重点述评与提示

1. I have no purpose, directly or indirectly, to interfere with the institution of slavery in the States where it exists. I believe I have no lawful right to do so, and I have no inclination to do so.

    承认南部各州现存奴隶制的合法，但反对奴隶制在新领土上的蔓延，这是林肯坚守的政治立场。这里，林肯在简洁的陈述句中连用了 4 个主词"I"，显示了就职总统的权力和自信。此时，南部各蓄奴州已经相继宣布脱离联邦，组成南部邦联临时政府，临时总统杰斐逊·戴维斯也在一个月前宣誓就职。林肯明知形势不可逆转，但为争取舆论主动,在就职演说中仍取守势,表达了希望南部重回联邦的愿望。

2. It is scarcely questioned that this provision was intended by those who made it for the reclaiming of what we call fugitive slaves; and the intention of the lawgiver is the law.

美国宪法在涉及奴隶制的条款中语焉不详,造成了后世的麻烦。林肯在此明确指出,宪法的有关条款就是针对逃奴的,因此行文中毫不含糊:黑奴逃至自由州,不会因此而改变身份,而应予以拘捕,归还其主人,这是宪法的法律强制行为,也是1850年妥协案和1857年"司考特案"的基本精神。但是,奴隶在北方废奴主义者的协助下大量逃亡北方,林肯此时向南部蓄奴州的"法律示好"已经不能取得南部的信任了。

3. There is some difference of opinion whether this clause should be enforced by national or by State authority, but surely that difference is not a very material one.

对于南部蓄奴州,这是一个实质的问题,逃奴属于私人财产,应由各州政府追缉,押解归还其主人,而不是由联邦政府处理。林肯在这里用了律师的聪明,试图混同州权与联邦权,从而强化联邦政府的权威。

4. I hold that in contemplation of universal law and of the Constitution the Union of these States is perpetual. Perpetuity is implied, if not expressed, in the fundamental law of all national governments.

这是林肯这篇演讲的主要法理原则:任何政府制定的宪法都是具有永久性的国家大法,美国宪法当然也法定联邦政府存在的永久性,除非发生法律规定之外的事件。林肯是成功的律师,论述法律普适性问题可是言之凿凿,无懈可击。

5. Descending from these general principles, we find the proposition that in legal contemplation the Union is perpetual confirmed by the history of the Union itself. The Union is much older than the Constitution.

"联邦早于宪法",这是林肯通过美国法律发展历史回顾得出的逻辑结论,从而申明了"联邦至上"的原则。因此,解释宪法的权力在联邦,而不在州政府。这样,以"州法律早于宪法"为由来为脱离联邦做合法辩护就可不攻自破了。

6. It follows from these views that no State upon its own mere motion can lawfully get out of the Union; that resolves and ordinances to that effect are legally void, and that acts of violence within any State or States against the authority of the United States are insurrectionary or revolutionary, according to circumstances.

有了上述的法理论述,林肯即可为各蓄奴州脱离联邦的行为定性:各州宣布脱离联邦是违法的行为,是试图用暴力推翻政府的反叛行为,这就为联邦总统招募军队平叛提供了合法性依据。

7. In your hands, my dissatisfied fellow-countrymen, and not in mine, is the momentous issue of civil war. The Government will not assail you. You can have no conflict without being yourselves the aggressors.

   林肯在写着句话时三易其稿,思忖再三。以"同胞"(countrymen)相称淡化了意识形态分歧,拉近了文化心理距离;承诺联邦政府不会首先打响战争,也就把战争的责任推给对方,既是规劝,也带有威胁,拉拉打打,恩威并施,显示了林肯的良苦用心。

8. The mystic chords of memory, stretching from every battlefield and patriot grave to every living heart and hearthstone all over this broad land, will yet swell the chorus of the Union, when again touched, as surely they will be, by the betterangel of our nature.

   这个句子是全篇演说的警句,也是常被后世引用的名句。句中把南北共同的政治文化记忆比作割不断的琴弦,在天使的弹奏下,必将唱出统一国家优美的歌声。整个句式舒缓松散,意象清晰如画,让人看到美国南北共同建国的光荣历史,听到未来南北重归于好的和谐之音。

■ 思考及讨论题

1. What was the central issue of famous Lincoln-Douglas Debates?
2. Why didn't Lincoln sign "The Emancipation Proclamation" at the beginning of the American Civil War?
3. How do you understand Lincoln's belief in "white supremacy" and his vow that his ultimate goal in the war was to "save the Union", not to "free the slaves"?
4. What is your view of Lincoln as a "strong" American President who sometimes acted without constitutional legitimization?

■ 阅读书目

1. Raymond, Henry J. *The Life and Public Services of Abraham Lincoln*. New York: Derby and Miller, 1865.
2. Stephenson, Nathaniel Wright. Ed. *An Autobiography of Abraham Lincoln: Consisting of the Personal Portions of His Letters, Speeches, and Conversations*. Indianapolis:

Bobbs-Merrill, 1926.
3. Guelzo, Allen C. "The Prudence of Abraham Lincoln" in *First Things: A Monthly Journal of Religion and Public Life*. 159 : 2006.
4. Horn, Tom. "Behind the Legacy; the Persistence of Abraham Lincoln" in *Success*, August-September 2008.

第二十二讲
亚伯拉罕·林肯(Abraham Lincoln 1809—1865)(下)

■ 政治历史评述

亚伯拉罕·林肯:伟大的抑郁者,宿命论的现实平常人

林肯不论是"伟大的解放者",还是"坚定的独裁者",都是美国人心中的伟人。但是,伟人也是人,不是神,也不是半神。林肯是一个有着多重性格,尝尽了56年人生酸甜苦辣、喜怒哀乐的普通人,也是一个备受压抑、心理抑郁的特殊人。美国史学界长期以来对林肯圣徒式研究之后,也出现了新的转向,开始专注于林肯的家庭、心灵、思想构成和宗教信仰等的研究。于是,林肯走下圣堂,以普通人的身份平等地进入普通人的视野。

据2012年统计,研究林肯的出版著作已高达近2万部,各种论文和文章更是难以计数。近年来研究林肯的书越写越厚,文章越写越长。有些研究者十年如一日,细大不捐,爬罗剔抉,搜遍林肯演说文稿,书信文字,文案档书,加以详细考证分析,出书动辄2500页;林肯传记也不断翻新:传记作家柏林盖姆(Michael Burlingame)2008年出版的林肯传洋洋洒洒2024页,笔触深入到林肯的日常生活,婚姻心理活动层面和从政的心路历程。就连医学专家也加入了林肯研究的行列。著名心脏病学家约翰·G.斯欧特斯2008年出版了《林肯的生理》,(*The Physical Lincoln Complete*)全书820页,全面分析了林肯的健康状况,得出结论:林肯患有一种遗传性病理癌症。作者宣称,这一发现解释了林肯为什么长期处于临床性抑郁和焦虑型的身体疾病。

我们从这些研究中看到,步入政坛的林肯在谈笑风生,纵论天下的同时,也长期处于内心的挣扎之中,尤其是当选总统后,在内战责任的重负下,在死亡阴影的笼罩下,艰难地度过每一天的时光。我们禁不住感慨,这位心怀仁慈、内心抑郁的总统如何忍受着心灵的痛楚,坚强地熬过了艰难时世,直到1865年4月4日福特大剧院里刺客的枪声让他获得了最终的解脱。

研究者们发现,林肯家族有着挥之不去的抑郁病史。他的母亲经常被人谈论,称之为"情绪低落"的人;父亲虽然是个文盲,但时常表现出莫名的沉郁和绝望;他的叔伯们和表兄患有明显的抑郁症,其中不乏表现出狂躁和偏执,有一个表兄的女儿精神失常,被终生禁闭于伊利诺伊州疯人院。

林肯的少年在肯塔基边地的山林中度过，每天都干着伐木的苦活儿，没有机会上学，但却也暗中励志发奋，用木炭在枕木上写字学习，夜深人静之时，常常捧着《圣经》、《莎士比亚戏剧》、《华盛顿小传》和其他能够弄到的政治和军事书籍，一读就到深夜，遇到精彩的段落，即反复记诵。在那艰苦单调的生活中，他在书中找到了点人生的快乐和意义。有了书的激励和心中的偶像，小林肯也表现出胸怀大志的迹象：一次，几个小女孩嘲笑地问他以后能干点什么，小林肯竟然冲口而出："当美国总统。"可是，在闭塞的生活中积极进取的林肯成年后似乎也逃不过抑郁症的攻击。20多岁的林肯曾经两次陷入几乎崩溃的精神危机。一次发生在26岁那年，起因是他的女友死于伤寒，林肯伤心欲绝；6年以后，女友玛丽·托德（后来成为林肯夫人）提出分手，林肯又陷入绝望。这两次精神崩溃，都有自杀倾向，幸亏朋友通宵守夜，方保无事。所幸，林肯对自己的抑郁倾向有着自觉的意识。多少年以后，他曾对一个朋友承认，自己身上从不带锐器，以防情绪低落时伤了自己。

　　林肯一生似乎都被笼罩在突然死亡的阴影之中。还在孩提时代，他的母亲和姐姐不幸突然死去；及至成人，他又眼睁睁地看着幼小的儿子艾迪和威利相继夭亡；内战双方大规模的死亡人数更是压得他透不过气来。起初以为几个月便可结束的南北军事冲突结果演变成千军万马长期的对决；不论是在华盛顿和里士满之间的广袤荒地上，弗吉尼亚开阔的原野上，还是在密西西比河维克斯堡湾泥泞的洼地中，两军拉开阵势，几次冲锋和肉搏，动辄就是几万人的伤亡。1863年7月在宾夕法尼亚州葛底斯堡战役中，不到3天，双方伤亡5万1千多人，战场上遗尸成山。3个多月过后，林肯应邀前去演讲，战场尸体安葬不到一半，林肯目睹这残酷的屠杀场面，在仍散发着尸臭的公墓地发表感言，可想心理上承受着多么沉重的压力和悲怆！一次林肯对到访的友人说："我这个杀鸡都不会，见血就晕的人竟然被抛到一场四周血流成河的大战中，你不觉得有些怪异吗？"据白宫助手回忆，林肯有时站在离白宫不远的住所窗前，眼望路边成千上万的新坟，喟然长叹，这场战争在"慢慢吞噬着我的生命！"现实中，林肯本人不断受到死亡威胁。早在1860年底当选总统之时，南方激进奴隶主就杀声不断，林肯不得不化装潜行，深夜溜进华盛顿首府就职。林肯夫人玛丽不止一次梦见丈夫被暗杀；远在家乡的继母也梦见林肯突然死去；据林肯的贴身保镖回忆，一天傍晚，总统从白宫骑马回家，突然传来一声枪响，将他头上的圆沿高顶礼帽洞穿，击落在地，坐骑受到惊吓，突然狂飙，发疯似地载着林肯飞奔回到住所，上演了一场"爱驹救主"的好戏。1864年9月，一位自称"W. S. 丽兹"的神秘女人向林肯寄来一封警告信，声称有大批的反叛分子在内部策应了叛军的行动，而且反叛分子刺杀总统的阴谋已经进入倒计时。没过几天，刺杀林肯的刺客约翰·威利·布斯在打台球时对球友说道："林肯的任期快满了，不管他连任与否，他的大麻烦就来了。"此话说过不久，林肯即遇刺身亡。

这就是林肯的一生,既是轰轰烈烈的政治活剧,也是阴郁悲情的内心挣扎,当然也闪烁着伟人的人格光辉。在重压和逆境中,林肯也表现出临危不惧,力挽狂澜的勇气。1864 年 7 月,南军突袭守备空虚的首府华盛顿,林肯闻讯神情沮丧,但突然振奋精神,发布简短命令坚守城防:"保持戒备,沉着应对"。他竟然亲自策马到斯蒂芬高地要塞督战,在子弹的呼啸声中用望远镜看着敌方士兵潮水般地往上涌。据说当时一个军官没认出林肯,对他厉声喝道:"快趴下,你这蠢货!"

林肯的精神意识中也有一种通过诙谐自嘲和诗意叙事得以自我排遣,反弹振作的力量。1864 年的总统竞选是对林肯的政治韧力的严峻考验。他坚持《解放黑奴宣言》是战时措施,并发布新一轮的 50 万人征兵令,因此不仅受到反对党的大肆攻击,还受到共和党内部广泛的不信任,指责他权欲熏心,仇恨和平。曾有一时,林肯的竞选智囊甚至估计他至多只能赢得 3 个州的选票,建议他中途退选,或立刻与南部联盟停战议和,或许还有转机。林肯则坚持不能拿士兵的鲜血做政治交易:"如果国家没了,这总统职位就一文不名了。"他这样告诉他的选民:"也许有人会比我干得更好……不过,我已经在这了,那些更好的人还没有到呢。"在白宫的日子里,林肯时常失眠,于是干脆穿着睡衣上楼与年轻的助手聊天,或大段朗诵莎士比亚戏剧台词,或轮流讲笑话。此时的林肯快活得像个孩子,楼道里时常传来爽朗的笑声。

林肯曾这样总结自己的人生:"我一生都是一个宿命论者,该发生的一定会发生,或者可以这么说,我觉得我全部的生命就像哈姆雷特说的那样:'我们一切努力的结果早由冥冥上苍安排;鬼斧神工之间不由你我挑选。"(There's a divinity that shapes our ends,/ Rough-hew them how we will.)林肯的这一宿命观在第二届总统就职演说中表现得十分明显。

1865 年 11 月,林肯在总统竞选中扭转败局,意外获胜连任。此时谢尔曼将军已经攻占南部重镇亚特兰大,格兰特将军也在西线战场取得空前的胜利,联邦胜局已定。此时,淡化南北仇恨,弥合战争创伤,前瞻战后重建,成了林肯连任后的要务之一。在这篇演说中,林肯第一次明确表示,引起这场内战的主要原因是美国的奴隶制,南部联盟为了捍卫奴隶制不惜分裂联邦,而联邦政府也曾容忍奴隶制的现实存在。但追究战争责任或判定正义已经没有意义。因为"全能的上帝自有安排"。林肯引用《圣经》(马太福音 18:7)中耶稣的名言:"让灾难降临世界,因为人们有罪了;因为罪过是不可避免的;但是让灾难降临到那个唆使人们犯罪的人身上吧!"林肯把美国奴隶制比作人间罪恶,而这场空前浩劫的内战是上帝因此降临人间的灾难。上帝此时安排结束这场灾难;但是如果按照冥冥之中的意愿,

这场灾难必须继续下去,直至耗尽人类千百年积累的财富和能量,那么这也是上苍公正

的安排，人类对此又能说些什么，或改变什么呢？他们只能怀着对上帝的敬畏，按照上帝的旨意，以"不对任何人怀有恶意，对所有人都心存仁义"的人文博爱精神，抚恤心灵的伤痛，医治战争的创伤，建立公正的、永久的和平。在这篇演讲中，林肯的视野穿越历史和国界，为美国内战这场大灾难寻求到终极的渊源，为灾后重建树立了起码的信心。这里，宿命的思想在宗教人文精神的包容中，对饱受伤痛的心灵起到了安抚作用。这就是为什么有人把这篇演说与80多年前华盛顿的"告别演说"媲美，称之为"美国政治圣经的新约"。

这篇演讲也堪称英语文学的名篇。林肯喜爱诗人朗费罗的激情，醉心于莎士比亚的睿智和圣经文学的简洁，这些都融入了这篇演讲的主题思想和语言风格之中。与第一届就职演说不同，林肯避免使用主词"I"，避免使用"南部"或"北部"这样的字眼，代之以"所有人"，"二者都"这样的语汇，文中多用被动语态，象征着和解与统一，也表达了在大势面前人力的局限和徒劳，宣示了一种尽人事以听天命的宗教精神。整篇演说词中频繁迭出的叠句和排比，产生出一种政治演说意识渗透力和说服力；同时，文中的首字重复，谐音韵律和鲜明的意象和类比，又使听众获得韵律和谐，节奏明快的文学感染力。当时在场的联邦将军，后来的国会参议员卡尔·舒尔茨深受感染，称这是一首"神圣的诗篇"，"美国从来没有任何一位总统像林肯那样从内心深处发出这样的语句。"甚至林肯的宿敌，南部联盟总统杰斐逊·戴维斯也为林肯的演说感动。一个月以后，林肯遇刺身亡，戴维斯闻讯说道："除了南部联盟的覆灭，亚伯拉罕·林肯的死是南方人心中最为悲伤的一天。"

公元前4世纪，亚里士多德曾感慨：为什么在哲学、政治学、诗歌和艺术方面卓然出众的人物都是郁郁寡欢的人？两千年过去，亚伯拉罕·林肯再次向人们提出这个同样难解的问题。

■ 演讲文

Second Presidential Inaugural Address

Abraham Lincoln

Fellow-Countrymen:

At this second **appearing** to take the oath of the Presidential office there is less occasion for an extended address than there was at the first. Then a statement somewhat in detail of a course to be pursued seemed fitting and proper. Now, at the **expiration** of four years, during which public declarations have been constantly called

appearing: occasion to show up

expiration: the end of an specified term of period

engross: occupy; spend **arms**: military; army **venture**: put forward without much con-siderations	forth on every point and phase of the great contest which still absorbs the attention and **engrosses** the energies of the nation, little that is new could be presented. The progress of our **arms**, upon which all else chiefly depends, is as well known to the public as to myself, and it is, I trust, reasonably satisfactory and encouraging to all. With high hope for the future, no prediction in regard to it is **ventured**.
impending: upcoming **avert**: avoid **agent**: spy and representatives **deprecate**: oppose	On the occasion corresponding to this, four years ago all thoughts were anxiously directed to an **impending** civil war. All dreaded it all sought to **avert** it. While the inaugural address was being delivered from this place, devoted altogether to saving the Union without war, urgent **agents** were in the city seeking to destroy it without war— seeking to dissolve the Union and divide effects by negotiation. Both parties **deprecated** war, but one of them would make war rather than let the nation survive, and the other would accept war rather than let it perish, and the war came.
constitute: consist of; make (part of) **interest**: concern (social, political and economic) **perpetuate**: make it everlasting **insurgent**: rebel **magnitude**: large scale	One-eighth of the whole population were colored slaves, not distributed generally over the Union, but localized in the southern part of it. These slaves **constituted** a peculiar and powerful **interest**. All knew that this interest was somehow the cause of the war. To strengthen, **perpetuate**, and extend this interest was the object for which the **insurgents** would rend the Union even by war, while the Government claimed no right to do more than to restrict the territorial enlargement of it. Neither party expected for the war the **magnitude** or the duration which it has already attained. Neither anticipated that the cause of the conflict might cease with or even before the conflict itself should cease. Each looked for an easier
astounding: unimaginably surprising **invoke**: call for **wring**: take (grab) with force	triumph, and a result less fundamental and **astounding**. Both read the same Bible and pray to the same God, and each **invokes** His aid against the other. It may seem strange that any men should dare to ask a just God's assistance in **wringing** their bread from the sweat of other men's faces, but let us judge not, that we be not judged. The prayers of both could not be answered. That of neither has been answered fully. The Almighty has His own purposes. " **Woe** unto the world because of
woe: misery **cometh**: comes **providence**: divine power and will **discern**: see; make out **attribute**: character; feature	offenses; for it must needs be that offenses come, but woe to that man by whom the offense **cometh**." If we shall suppose that American slavery is one of those offenses which, in the **providence** of God, must needs come, but which, having continued through His appointed time, He now wills to remove, and that He gives to both North and South this terrible war as the woe due to those by whom the offense came, shall we **discern** therein any departure from those divine **attributes**

which the believers in a living God always ascribe to Him? **Fondly** do we hope, fervently do we pray, that this mighty **scourge** of war may speedily pass away. Yet, if God wills that it continue until all the wealth piled by the bondsman's two hundred and fifty years of **unrequited** toil shall be sunk, and until every drop of blood drawn with the lash shall be paid by another drawn with the sword, as was said three thousand years ago, so still it must be said "the judgments of the Lord are true and righteous altogether."

With **malice** toward none, with charity for all, with firmness in the right as God gives us to see the right, let us **strive** on to finish the work we are in, to bind up the nation's wounds, to care for him who shall have borne the battle and for his widow and his orphan, to do all which may achieve and cherish a just and lasting peace among ourselves and with all nations.

fondly: with good will
scourge: disaster; misery
unrequited: unpaid

malice: hatred; ill-purpose
strive: work hard

■ 重点述评与提示

1. At this second appearing to take the oath of the Presidential office there is less occasion for an extended address than there was at the first. Then a statement somewhat in detail of a course to be pursued seemed fitting and proper.

   林肯熬过漫长艰苦的战争,熬过了第二任期总统竞选的逆境,此时甘苦自知,不堪回首。眼看胜利在望,听众也自然更注意新一届政府对战争的评价和如何处理战后事宜。林肯开篇表示演讲从简,直奔主题,智也。这也让人想起莎剧中《哈姆莱特》中大臣波罗涅斯的名言:"简洁是智慧的灵魂"(Brevity is the soul of wit.)。这也是林肯常诵的莎翁名句。

2. Both parties deprecated war, but one of them would make war rather than let the nation survive, and the other would accept war rather than let it perish, and the war came.

   这里虽然避免使用战时的敌对称谓(北方联邦,南部邦联等),而用"两边都"(both)这一中性字眼,也避免对战争的正义对错做出直接评价,但是,林肯通过巧妙的对称排比结构,用 make 和 accept 的语义对比,转达出政府的基本立场:南部主动挑起战争,而北方的联邦政府是为了捍卫国家的统一而被动接受战争。于是,在听众的潜意识中,胜利者再胜一筹。

3. These slaves constituted a peculiar and powerful interest. All knew that this interest was somehow the cause of the war.

　　林肯在此第一次承认奴隶制是这场战争的根本原因,其间用了 somehow 一词,留有余地,以便使自己一直坚持的联邦至上的政策有个过渡,同时也使战时签署的《解放黑奴宣言》获得南北双方更多的支持。实际上,正如有的历史学家指出的那样,在社会和经济实际中,奴隶制在内战一开始便已经开始瓦解,《解放黑奴宣言》仅仅在此过程中起到促进的作用。

4. The Almighty has His own purposes. "Woe unto the world because of offenses; for it must needs be that offenses come, but woe to that man by whom the offense cometh."

　　林肯读到的第一本书是《圣经》,此后反复用心诵读,必是了然于胸,此处信手拈来(马太福音 18:7),为这场战争涂上浓重的宿命论色彩:奴隶制是人类必然犯下的罪恶,上帝降祸于犯下此罪的人,让他们互相残杀。而灾难是否已经过去,这取决于冥冥中上帝的安排。林肯此举既消解了南方北方的敌对关系,又减轻了个人责任的沉重心理包袱,还传达了双方共同的宗教精神,可谓一箭三雕。

5. Yet, if God wills that it continue until all the wealth piled by the bondsman's two hundred and fifty years of unrequited toil shall be sunk, and until every drop of blood drawn with the lash shall be paid by another drawn with the sword, as was said three thousand years ago, so still it must be said "the judgments of the Lord are true and righteous altogether."

　　演说到此突转,林肯在低沉的宿命观论述后,突然感情迸发,回望 250 年,表达了对黑人奴隶的同情和对奴隶制的憎恨。在经历了多年的政治斗争和 4 年内战的苦旅后,这应该是林肯心灵中人道主义的自然流露,也是对宿命论的一次无奈的抗争。

6. With malice toward none, with charity for all, with firmness in the right as God gives us to see the right, let us strive on to finish the work we are in, to bind up the nation's wounds, to care for him who shall have borne the battle and for his widow and his orphan, to do all which may achieve and cherish a just and lasting peace among ourselves and with all nations.

　　这是林肯传世的名句,用完美的对称排比语句带起,在宗教精神的感召下,发出政治和解,抚平战争创伤,重建国家的号召。这也是人们期待听到的新一届政府的总目标。演说至此,戛然而止,回味无穷。

■ 思考及讨论题

1. How do you view Lincoln as a determined self-made man? Do his endeavor and success represent part of the "American Dream"?
2. How did the signing of "The Emancipation Proclamation" benefit the Union in the war?
3. How did Lincoln cooperate with his generals to win the war?
4. How did Lincoln's assassination affect the post-war politics, the Reconstruction?

■ 阅读书目

1. Browne, Francis Fisher. *The Every-Day Life of Abraham Lincoln*. Lincoln: University of Nebraska Press. 1995.
2. Beschloss, Michael. *Presidential Courage: Brave Leaders and How They Changed America 1789—1989*. New York: Simon & Schuster Paperbacks, 2007.
3. Horn, Tom. "Behind the legacy: the Persistence of Abraham Lincoln". *Success*, September 2008.
4. Anonymous. "Lincoln, Depression, and Greatness" in *The Saturday Evening Post*, May/June, 2006.

第七章 ‖ 黑人为自由平等权利而斗争

Where justice is denied, where poverty is enforced, where ignorance prevails, and where any one in a class is made to feel that society is an organized conspiracy to oppress, rob and degrade them, neither person nor property will be safe.

—Frederick Douglass

Our greatest danger is that in the great leap from slavery to freedom we may overlook the fact that the masses of us are to live by the productions of our hands...

—Booker T. Washington

An American, a Negro... two souls, two thoughts, two unreconciled strivings; two warring ideals in one dark body, whose dogged strength alone keeps it from being torn asunder.

—W. E. B. Dubois

Preview Questions

01/

What were the political and economic condition of former slaves in post-bellum America?

02/

What changes have been brought to black population by the industrialization?

03/

What were some legislative improvements made to the blacks as a result of the Civil War and the Reconstruction?

04/

What were main differences in opinion of some major black leaders?

第二十三讲
弗雷德里克·道格拉斯
（Frederic Douglass 1718？—1895）

■ 政治历史评述

弗雷德里克·道格拉斯：为废除奴隶制，争取黑人自由平等的呐喊者

华盛顿市区，庄严的林肯纪念堂每年吸引着络绎不绝的游客，聆听着微风中传来的历史回声。但很少有人由此往东，沿着长长的倒影池，穿过二战纪念馆和国家公园草坪中央高耸的乔治·华盛顿纪念碑，行过不远处的美国国会大厦继续往东，来到一处林荫蔽日，幽静闲适的公园。这就是默默无闻的林肯公园。这里矗立着林肯被刺后黑人们自发捐款建造的"解放奴隶纪念雕像"。1876年4月的一天，华盛顿春光明媚，人们为这座雕像举行揭幕仪式，当时的格兰特总统，政府内阁成员和大法官全部到场，现场也挤满了获得解放的黑人。仪式开幕祷告后，由一位黑人嘉宾上台发表演讲。这位瘦削高个，留着一头蓬松白发和胡须的演讲人就是美国著名黑人领袖弗雷德里克·道格拉斯。

道格拉斯曾对林肯上任初期搁置奴隶制问题，联邦至上的政策不满，对林肯就职总统后的演说深感失望，公开谴责林肯在奴隶制问题上的"三心二意和优柔寡断"。但随着内战的进程和《解放黑奴宣言》的生效，他成了林肯的重要盟友，发表了题为"黑人武装起来"的宣言，充任联邦政府首席征兵官员，招募黑人青年加入联邦军队，组建了全部由黑人士兵组成的马萨诸塞第54军团，并以身作则，送两个儿子参军上前线，后来战死在南卡罗来纳州的瓦格纳要塞。

此时，在林肯公园的"解放奴隶纪念碑"前，道格拉斯代表广大获得自由的黑人奴隶纪念这位"解放者"，称之为"烈士总统"，表达了对林肯的感激之情："感谢他对我们，对我们这个种族，对我们这个国家，对全世界做出的崇高而博大的杰出贡献。"然而，值得注意的是，道格拉斯仍然采取一分为二的态度，回顾林肯的白人种族偏见和对奴隶制的容忍态度，称林肯是"全身心地致力于白人利益的，白人的杰出总统"，是一个"为了这个国家的白人的利益不惜否决、拖延或牺牲有色人种权利的总统"。这就是弗雷德里克·道格拉斯，一个彻头彻尾的废奴主义者，一个直言不讳，号召黑人奴隶自主自尊，通过不懈斗争，最终获得种族平等和自由解放的不知疲倦的呐喊者。

道格拉斯之所以对林肯内战初期的基本政策耿耿于怀，是因为他对他称之为"野蛮主义"的奴隶制刻骨的仇恨和黑人种族强烈的自尊感。道格拉斯生下来就是奴隶，不知其父为何人，只知道是一个白人奴隶主。他还是婴儿时就与母亲生离死别，祖母把他拉扯到7岁又被强行分离,被奴隶主互相转让于种植园之间。在他的自传《一个美国奴隶的生平叙事》中,道格拉斯记叙了残暴的奴隶主如何以鞭打奴隶为乐。一次在拂晓时分,他的一个姨母被剥光了上身,捆在木梁上遭到鞭打,撕心裂肺分惨叫声把他惊醒,看着姨母被鞭打得皮开肉绽,浑身是血;奴隶主狂笑着,惨叫声越大,皮鞭挥舞得越有力,哪儿血流如注,就往哪里狠命抽打,直打得可怜的姨母奄奄一息,奴隶主筋疲力尽。另一个名叫塞威尔的恶魔般的奴隶主,当着孩子的面鞭打一位母亲,在孩子们的哭喊和哀求声中发疯般地挥舞皮鞭,母亲的鲜血流淌了半个多小时。这些都在道格

拉斯幼小的心灵埋下了对奴隶制刻骨仇恨的种子。在这本早期的自传中,他也叙述了自己的苦难,饥饿难忍的寒冬,蜷曲在一条破麻袋里瑟瑟发抖,露在外面的双脚堆上了厚厚的霜,完全冻僵;道格拉斯还记叙了奴隶们外出劳作时从心底里发出的悲伤的歌声。多少年后,他回忆说:"奴隶们最悲伤时最能唱出心中的歌……每一个音符都是仇恨奴隶制的见证,都是祈求上帝解脱奴隶镣铐的祷告。每次听到这些原始的音符,我的都感到无比的沉重,心中涌起哽咽的悲伤;常常不觉之中已经泪流满面。"1838年9月,道格拉斯在友人的帮助下,化装成水手,成功逃到北方,到达纽约。他这样诉说当时的心情:"我感到终于从一群饥饿的狮子窝里逃了出来。"然而,奴隶制的阴影也笼罩着北方,无所不在的逃奴追缉者和告密者时刻都在威胁着道格拉斯,他不得不小心翼翼,远离白人,避免与任何人接触,陷入了孤独和绝望之中。此间,道格拉斯多亏获得了一位好心人鲁格斯先生的热心帮助。不久,协助他成功出逃的自由黑人女孩安娜也及时赶到纽约,二人在鲁格斯的安排下正式结婚。至此,道格拉斯才算勉强挣脱了奴隶制的枷锁,能够呼喊出自己心中对罪恶的奴隶制无尽的愤怒和批判。

道格拉斯是杰出的黑人演说家,从1841年受到著名废奴主义者威廉·L.加里森和他的杂志《解放者》的启蒙后的第一场演讲起,他历经了内战前的奴隶制危机,布朗起义,内战和战后重建等重要的历史事件。50多年以来,道格拉斯以杰出的演说活跃在国内外各种社会团体聚会和政府组织的正式场合,活跃在大学的讲台上,为废除奴隶制,解放奴隶,赋予黑人真正的平等和自由而呐喊。道格拉斯从未上过学,获得自由后竟能够成为演讲家,写出3本自传,在奴隶制存废的危机时代影响着几代人的人性道德选择,成为杰出的黑人领袖,甚至后来被推选为美国副总统候选人。这是一个奇迹。12岁那年,善良的女主人苏菲教他识字,受到奴隶主丈夫的责难:"如果你教会他读书,那以后就管不了他……他以后就不会当奴隶,就不会满足现状了。"此话深深触及了道格拉斯的灵魂,唤醒了他朦胧之

中的自由之梦,使他认识到,知识是"从奴隶到自由的必然之路"。于是,他又在田头地脚与一些年轻的奴隶组成识字班,偷偷认字学习,直至在逃亡之前竟然能够读懂报纸。然而,就凭着这点文化功底,在废奴和倡导种族平等和自由的讲台上,他何以能够克服了初期演讲的紧张和尴尬,口才滔滔,一泻千里?除了他本人可能有点语言天赋,勤奋阅读并创办废奴主义刊物而外,原因只有一个,那就是,这是一个历尽奴隶制给人类带来的罪恶和苦难的心灵,一个不屈服于命运,信仰人人自由平等的主体,他以呼唤平等自由为己任,敞开自我意识,任凭自己的心灵和意识自然流露,与听众的期待和思想产生共鸣。

在道格拉斯的大部分演讲中,都贯穿一切种族平等自由的朴素思想,字里行间都透出黑人作为平等的人的自尊和独立精神,表达出不对白人拯救黑人给予任何的希望。他在美国内战期间曾经大声疾呼:"如果黑人不能自己站立起来,就让他们毁灭吧。……让他们有一次站立起来的机会吧!别去管他们吧!"这样的执着的态度在他著名的"1852年美国独立日演讲"中展示的淋漓尽致。1852年7月4日,纽约州的罗彻斯特市举行盛大的庆祝国庆游行集会,特邀道格拉斯会上演讲。道格拉斯以一种局外人的语气回顾了美国建国的过程,称这是"你们的(白人的)国家独立的生日,是你们政治独立的开端。"此后,道格拉斯话锋突转,尖锐地发出一连串的质问:"为什么把我请到这里来讲话?我和我所代表的人于你们国家的独立又何相干?你们的《独立宣言》里蕴含的政治独立和自然法则正义原则惠及我们黑人了吗?……"此时的美国,联邦政府刚刚与南部蓄奴州达成妥协,通过了承认奴隶制在南部的合法存在,加大追缉逃奴的法案。达格拉斯认为这是联邦政府的出卖行为,此时他在演说中一针见血,话语之尖锐,语气之坚决,讽喻之明显,让听众愕然,震撼。道格拉斯接下来毫不掩饰:"7月4日是你们的国庆,不是我的,你们欢庆,我悲伤。"而且,"(你们)把一个带着枷锁的人拉进一座装点得金碧辉煌的自由圣殿,让他加入你们欢乐的国歌演唱,这是不人道的奚落,是亵渎神灵的讽刺。"在白人国庆彩车、礼炮和欢呼声中,道格拉斯听到了"几百万黑人奴隶的悲号声"。因此,他来到此种场合,不是为了国庆,而是为了谴责万恶的奴隶制。面对着白人听众,道格拉斯以三个有力的排比,直言不讳地发表了他的极端言论:"美国对过去虚伪,对现在虚伪,现在又道貌岸然地走向未来的虚伪。"这样激烈的言辞

不是书本的文化积累,不是刻意的语言修辞,而是遵循着自然心理律动,自然奔泻出来的心声。当然,随着《解放黑奴宣言》的签署生效和内战的进程,道格拉斯修正了自己对美国《独立宣言》和宪法的看法,但作为一名杰出的黑人领袖,他坚持黑人的平等自由的权力和独立自尊的身份,看到了黑人在美国意识形态中争取真正获得平等自由的艰苦性和长期性,这一点为后来战后重建黑人的遭遇乃

至20世纪的民权运动所证实。

至此,我们不难理解,近30年过去,道格拉斯为什么在林肯公园为"解放奴隶纪念雕像"揭幕的仪式上对林肯采取褒贬不一的折中态度。可想而知,看着这座雕像的造型,看着林肯手持《解放黑奴宣言》,另一只手抚慰着跪在身边感激涕零的前奴隶,道格拉斯的心情是多么的沉重!奴隶制虽然已废除,但要让一个受到践踏的种族站立起来,任重而道远。

■ 演讲文(节选)

What to the Slave Is the Fourth of July?
—Independence Day Speech at Rochester, 1852

Frederick Douglass

Mr. President, Friends and Fellow Citizens:

This, for the purpose of this celebration, is the 4th of July. It is the birthday of your National Independence, and of your political freedom. This, to you, is what the **Passover** was to the emancipated people of God. It carries your minds back to the day, and to the act of your great **deliverance**; and to the signs, and to the wonders, associated with that act, and that day. This celebration also marks the beginning of another year of your national life; and reminds you that the Republic of America is now 76 years old. ...

Friends and citizens, I need not enter further into the causes which led to this **anniversary**. Many of you understand them better than I do. You could instruct me in regard to them. That is a branch of knowledge in which you feel, perhaps, a much deeper interest than your speaker. The causes which led to the separation of the colonies from the British crown have never lacked for a **tongue**. They have all been taught in your common schools, narrated at your firesides, **unfolded** from your **pulpits**, and thundered from your legislative halls, and are as familiar to you as household words. They form the **staple** of your national poetry and eloquence....

Fellow citizens, pardon me, allow me to ask, why am I called upon to speak here today? What have I, or those I represent, to do with your national independence? Are the great principles of political freedom and of natural justice, **embodied** in that Declaration of

Passover: Jewish spring festival celebrating the liberation of Israelites from slavery
deliverance: liberation; freedom

anniversary: yearly celebration of a special day

tongue: speech by someone
unfolded: describe
pulpit: platform for a speech
staple: most important part

embody: expressed clearly

Independence, extended to us? And am I, therefore, called upon to bring our humble offering to the national **altar**, and to confess the benefits and express devout gratitude for the blessings resulting from your independence to us?

Would to God, both for your sakes and ours, that an affirmative answer could be truthfully returned to these questions! Then would my **task** be light, and my burden easy and delightful. For who is there so cold that a nation's sympathy could not warm him? Who so **obdurate** and dead to the claims of gratitude that would not thankfully acknowledge such priceless benefits? Who so **stolid** and selfish that would not give his voice to swell the **hallelujahs** of a nation's **jubilee**, when the chains of servitude had been torn from his limbs? I am not that man. In a case like that the dumb might eloquently speak and the "lame man leap as an **hart**."

But such is not the state of the case. I say it with a sad sense of the **disparity** between us. I am not included within the **pale** of this glorious anniversary! Your high independence only reveals the immeasurable distance between us. The blessings in which you, this day, rejoice are not enjoyed in common. The rich inheritance of justice, liberty, prosperity, and independence **bequeathed** by your fathers is shared by you, not by me. The sunlight that brought light and healing to you has brought **stripes** and death to me. This Fourth of July is yours, not mine. You may rejoice, I must mourn. To drag a man in **fetters** into the grand illuminated temple of liberty, and call upon him to join you in joyous anthems, were inhuman mockery and **sacrilegious** irony. Do you mean, citizens, to mock me by asking me to speak today? If so, there is a parallel to your conduct. And let me warn that it is dangerous to copy the example of nation whose crimes, towering up to heaven, were thrown down by the breath of the Almighty, burying that nation in **irrevocable** ruin! I can today take up the **plaintive** lament of a **peeled** and woe-smitten people.

"By the rivers of Babylon, there we sat down. Yea! We wept when we remembered **Zion**. We hanged our harps upon the willows in the midst thereof. For there, they that carried us away captive, required of us a song; and they who wasted us required of us mirth, saying, Sing us one of the songs of Zion. How can we sing the Lord's song in a strange land? If I forget thee, O Jerusalem, let my right hand forget her **cunning**. If do not remember thee, let my tongue **cleave to** the roof of my mouth."

Fellow citizens, above your national, **tumultuous** joy, I hear the mournful wail of millions! Whose chains, heavy and grievous yesterday, are, today, rendered more intolerable by the jubilee shouts that reach them. If I do forget, if I do not faithfully remember those bleeding children of sorry this day, "may my right hand cleave to the roof of my mouth"! To forget them, to pass lightly over their wrongs, and to **chime** in with the popular theme would be treason most scandalous and shocking, and would make me a **reproach** before God and the world. My subject, then, fellow citizens, is American slavery. I shall see this day and its popular characteristics from the slave's point of view. Standing there identified with the American bondman, making his **wrongs** mine. I do not hesitate to declare with all my soul that the character and conduct of this nation never looked blacker to me than on this Fourth of July! Whether we turn to the declarations of the past or to the professions of the present, the conduct of the nation seems equally **hideous** and revolting. America is false to the past, false to the present, and solemnly binds herself to be false to the future. Standing with God and **the crushed** and bleeding slave on this occasion, I will, in the name of humanity which is outraged, in the name of liberty which is fettered, in the name of the Constitution and the Bible which are disregarded and **trampled** upon, dare to call in question a curse; I will use the severest language I can command; and yet not one word shall escape me that any man, whose judgment is not blinded by prejudice, shall not confess to be right and just....

For the present, it is enough to affirm the equal manhood of the Negro race. Is it not as astonishing that, while we are plowing, planting, and reaping, using all kinds of mechanical tools, **erecting** houses, constructing bridges, building ships, working in metals of brass, iron, copper, and secretaries, having among us lawyers doctors, ministers, poets, authors, editors, orators, and teachers; and that, while we are engaged in all manner of enterprises common to other men, digging gold in California, capturing the whale in the Pacific, feeding sheep and cattle on the hillside, living, moving, acting, thinking, planning, living in families as husbands, wives, and children, and above all, **confessing** and worshiping the Christian's God, and looking hopefully for life and **immortality** beyond the grave, we are called upon to prove that we are men!...

What, am I to argue that it is wrong to make men brutes, to rob them of their liberty, to work them without wages, to keep them ignorant of their relations to their fellow men, to beat them with sticks, to **flay** their flesh with the lash, to load their limbs with irons,

chime: response; echo
reproach: shame

wrong: pains and sufferings of being wronged

hideous: very ugly and horrifying

the crushed: the oppressed people

strample: (here) violated cruelly

erect: put up

confess: to admit one's sins in church for God's forgiveness
immortality: everlasting names and honor
flay: to cut the skin from

sunder: separate by force

pollution: (here) corruption

swelling: growing rapidly
denunciation: accusation; cursing
brass-fronted impudence: ornamented cruelty
bombast: empty and exaggerating

to hunt them with dogs, to sell them at auction, to **sunder** their families, to knock out their teeth, to burn their flesh, to starve them into obedience and submission to their masters? Must I argue that a system thus marked with blood, and stained with **pollution**, is wrong? No! I will not. I have better employment for my time and strength than such arguments would imply....

What, to the American slave, is your Fourth of July? I answer: a day that reveals to him, more than all other days in the year, the gross injustice and cruelty to which he is the constant victim. To him, your celebration is a sham; your boasted liberty, an unholy license; your national greatness, **swelling** vanity; your sounds of rejoicing are empty and heartless; your **denunciation** of tyrants, **brass-fronted impudence**; your shouts of liberty and equality, hollow mockery; your prayers and hymns, your sermons and thanksgivings, with all your religious parade and solemnity, are, to Him, mere **bombast**, fraud, deception, impiety, and hypocrisy—a thin veil to cover up crimes which would disgrace a nation of savages. There is not a nation of savages. There is not a nation on the earth guilty of practices more shocking and bloody than are the people of the United States at this very hour.

■ 重点述评与提示

1. Fellow citizens, pardon me, allow me to ask, why am I called upon to speak here today? What have I, or those I represent, to do with your national independence? Are the great principles of political freedom and of natural justice, embodied in that Declaration of Independence, extended to us?

话锋突转，连续质问，烘托出全篇演讲的主题：只要奴隶制存在一天，美国独立日就是自欺欺人和自我嘲弄的节日。《独立宣言》中有名言："我们认为下述真理是不言而喻的：人人生而平等。"但在历史现实中，黑人并未包括其中，这是美国种族问题的起源，也是道格拉斯这篇演讲辛辣讽刺和猛烈抨击的对象。

2. For who is there so cold that a nation's sympathy could not warm him? Who so obdurate and dead to the claims of gratitude that would not thankfully acknowledge such priceless benefits? Who so stolid and selfish that would not give his voice to swell the hallelujahs of a nation's jubilee, when the chains of servitude had been torn from his limbs?

道格拉斯连续叠用诘问修辞句进一步凸显自己的演讲主题与独立日庆典的不和

谐。三个修辞问句由短至长,层层推进,每一句中形容词的前后搭配恰如其分;在句式上大有莎士比亚戏剧中布鲁托斯刺杀恺撒后对罗马暴民演讲中的气势:"Who is here so base that would be a bondman?...; Who is here so rude that would not be Roman?... Who is here so vile that will not love his country?"二者如此相近,不能不猜想道格拉斯也下过莎剧的功夫?

3. This Fourth of July is yours, not mine. You may rejoice, I must mourn. To drag a man in fetters into the grand illuminated temple of liberty, and call upon him to join you in joyous anthems, were inhuman mockery and sacrilegious irony.

　　长短句配合使用,一为警示,二为重描;整体呈松散结构,局部为重尾式强调,最后落在 inhuman mockery 和 sacrilegious irony,正是语义主旨。两句话中的"mourn"和"mockery"遥相呼应,尤为传神,而带辅音"m"和"n"的音节竟有 23 个之多,在整体音韵上也表达出一种沉闷和压抑的氛围。希望不是道格拉斯有意为之。

4. My subject, then, fellow citizens, is American slavery. ... I do not hesitate to declare with all my soul that the character and conduct of this nation never looked blacker to me than on this Fourth of July!

　　短促的陈述句正面阐明演说目的,句中的"black"一词的语义双关,与强势否定和比较级搭配,产生出强烈的讽刺意义。

5. Whether we turn to the declarations of the past or to the professions of the present, the conduct of the nation seems equally hideous and revolting. America is false to the past, false to the present, and solemnly binds herself to be false to the future.

　　在展示过去、现在、将来的排比句中重复关键词"false",语义明确,语气坚决,不留余地,以道格拉斯的身世和观点而论,可见言如其人。但是,演说家有时为了先声夺人,振聋发聩,往往把话说绝,产生过犹不及之感。

6. Is it not as astonishing that, while we are plowing, planting, ... living in families as husbands, wives, and children, and above all, confessing and worshiping the Christian's God, and looking hopefully for life and immortality beyond the grave, we are called upon to prove that we are men!

　　这里,道格拉斯刻意描绘黑人作为人的各种经济和社会文化生活图景,表明了黑人享有人的自由和权利。话语间透出了他对洛克思想的理解:人通过各种劳动创造了私有财产,应该享受自然法则规定的人的一切权利,而在此情形下还试图证明黑人是人,这是多么不可思议的事!

7. There is not a nation of savages. There is not a nation on the earth guilty of practices more shocking and bloody than are the people of the United States at this very hour.

　　反复堆砌,用词尖刻,强化句式,甚至扩大指责对象,把矛头指向全体美国白人,有些失控的感觉,如果不是最后用突降法,限定时间范围,则这近乎诅咒的话语将起到适得其反的效果。

■ 思考及讨论题

1. What was the so-called "Underground Railroad" and how did it help slave escape from slavery?
2. What was the "Fugitive Slave Law" and how was it implemented in the North?
3. What roles did former slaves play to enhance the victory of Union in the War?
4. Why was Douglass so critical of Lincoln's early policy of slavery?

■ 阅读书目

1. Douglass, Frederic. *Narrative of the Life of Frederic Douglass: An American Slave*. Cambridge: Harvard University Press, 1996.
2. Martin Waldo E. Jr. *The Mind of Frederick Douglass*. Chapel Hill: University of North Carolina Press. 1984.
3. Sturdevant, Katherine Scott. "Frederick Douglass and Abraham Lincoln on Black Equity in the Civil War: A Historical-Rhetorical Perspective" in *Black History Bulletin*, Fall, 2010.
4. Rocca, Al M. "Frederick Douglass: Freedom's Force" in *Social Studies Review*. Fall 2002.

第二十四讲
布克·T. 华盛顿
(Booker T. Washington 1857—1915)

■ 政治历史评述

布克·T. 华盛顿：争取种族平等的温和派、社会活动家和教育家

19世纪末，新千年的晨光熹微。此时，美国内战已成为远去的记忆，战后重建几经波折，以新一轮的南北妥协收场，美国步入了经济繁荣和道德沦丧共存的所谓"镀金时代"。

这一时期，黑人争取真正的平等的社会经济地位和政治权利的斗争仍步履维艰。内战和重建时期对黑人最大的成果就是通过了宪法第十三、十四、十五修正案，以国家根本法律的形式废除了奴隶制、给予黑人公民权和政治选举权。但实际上，大多数获得自由的奴隶在政治和经济的现实中仍然生活在赤贫，屈辱和严酷的种族歧视和私刑的恐怖之中。

在经济上，黑人没有自己的土地，沦为工资微薄的雇工和长年欠债的佃农。1866的南方《宅地法》虽然在5个州内划出4千多万顷土地，但仅有不到4,000个黑人农户获得少量的土地，而且，由于1873年起持续的经济衰退，棉花价格跌至50%，多数黑人无力购买农业设备和种子，生活陷于绝境。政治上，南方各州相继制定"黑人法典"，限制黑人的人身自由和政治权利；1866年，三K党在田纳西州成立，与"白山茶花骑士"和"红衫军"等其他种族主义恐怖组织一道，在南方城镇和乡村多以强奸为罪名对黑人处以私刑，甚至残酷地将死者被烧焦肢解的尸骸挂在商店门窗示众。在上述行为遭到联邦共和党政府的一定遏制后，1876年后的南方院邦联各州通过了《吉姆法案》，以"隔离中的平等"为由长期对黑人实行种族隔离，把有色人种实际降为二等公民。在政治权利方面，在格兰特总统的共和党联邦政府采取强制手段，1870年批准美国宪法第十五修正案赋予黑人以选举权，黑人在政坛上开始有了微弱的声音。1870年在联邦参议院出现了第一位黑人参议员，此后7年又有2名黑人参议员和15名众议员。各州议院也开始有了黑人的代表。但是，随着联邦军队从南方撤出，战后重建结束，黑人的政治权利在欺骗、恐吓和暴力的逼迫下又一落千丈。重新掌权的南方各州相继规定，黑人必须通过文化水平测试，或缴纳2美元的选举费用才能参与选举投票，后来又规定黑人必须证明其祖父参与选举，方能有投票资格。这样，大多数的黑人选民被排除在选举之外，例如，1896年，路易斯安那州有黑人登记选民130,344人，4年之后所剩不过5,320人；1900年，阿拉巴马州有黑人选民约 181,000 人,登记参选的人数只有不到 3,000 人,而到了 1900 年,联邦国会中任议员的黑人也只剩 1 人。

与此同时,废除奴隶制后使生产力得以一定程度的解放,资本主义得到发展,工业化和城市化的进程加快,贫富差距迅速加大。大批的黑人和移民涌向北方一些工业城市,财富迅速聚集到少数的工业大亨手中,卡耐基、洛克菲勒和摩根等大财团分别控制着全国主要的钢铁、石油和金融等经济命脉。

1895 年 2 月 20 日,著名黑人政治家道格拉斯在两场有关妇女权利的演讲的间歇中突然去世。数月之后,9 月 18 日,为期 100 天的"亚特兰大棉花州国际博览会"开幕,克利夫兰总统出席开幕式。著名黑人教育家和社会活动家布克·T.华盛顿应州长布多克的邀请,在开幕式上以黑人代表的身份发言。

华盛顿在他 10 多分钟的演讲中,号召黑人立足南方的家园,脚踏实地,培养生产技能,用自己勤劳的双手,加入工业和商业发展,实现与白人社会的种族合作,共同建设新南方。华盛顿还赞扬了黑人天性善良和对白人社会的善意和忠实,认为黑人和白人是一只手上不同的指头,可以分开而独立,也同属一个劳动的整体。整篇演讲一气呵成,即席应景,巧设比喻,堪称政治演说中的杰作。著名黑人历史学家和政治活动家雷福德·拉根后评论道:"这是美国历史上最有实际效果的一篇政治演说……从结构而论,这是谋篇布局,主题连贯一致,表述清晰简洁的典范之作。"

华盛顿的这篇演讲一反道格拉斯激进的种族立场,主张通过经济地位的自我改善,自下而上地争取黑人的平等政治权利,传达出反对暴力对抗,放弃政治斗争,倡导种族和解的信息,受到白人和相当一部分黑人的欢迎。演说一结束,立刻引起了巨大的轰动。一时之间,布克·T.华盛顿成了南方社会家喻户晓的人物。第二天,华盛顿在亚特兰大所到之处,都被白人和黑人民众所欢呼和簇拥,在他返回阿拉巴马州塔斯克基学院的沿途车站,都受到等待多时的欢迎人群。华盛顿成了继道格拉斯之后美国黑人社会的领袖。一年之间,竟有 335 名黑人婴儿起名为布克·T;以他命名的黑人店铺也不断开业,体现了他自强自立的精神。华盛顿的演说也立即受到北方舆论媒体的交口赞扬,称之为"划时代的启示录","黑人种族进步的一个转折点"。华盛顿也成了一些媒体和各种社团的香饽饽,杂志报纸的主编纷纷写信,高价邀请他撰写文章,一些演讲协会甚至开出 5 万美元的天价,邀请他加盟。克利夫兰总统也写信称道:"你的词句让所有祝福你们种族的人们都感到兴奋和备受鼓舞。"罗斯福总统后来甚至在白宫宴请华盛顿,美国历史上从未有过黑人领袖做客白宫,这是破天荒第一次。华盛顿也成了北方工业大佬和慈善家的座上客,酒席和谈吐之间为他的塔基斯克学院募到巨额的捐款,其中钢铁大亨卡耐基一次就捐赠了 60 万美元。在美国黑人的社会政治地位和经济状况还处于十分低下,种族迫害和种族隔离还十分严酷的年代,布克·T.华盛顿鲜明的种族融合共处和渐进主义思想能够引起如此强烈的社会共鸣,这在美国政治历史上还是罕见的。

当然,也有相当一部分黑人,特别是黑人领袖对华盛顿的温和妥协态度表示不满,他们称他的演讲是"亚特兰大妥协演讲"或"亚特兰大出卖演讲";许多黑人认为他受到白人的"招安",对种族隔离采取了默认态度,甘愿做美国社会的二等公民,是对"白人至上论"的投降。还有的黑人批评华盛顿对战后重建中黑人的政治诉求持否定态度,间接的承认黑人不宜在政府中任职,只适合参与职业技术培训等等。对华盛顿保守主义种族观的强力批评来自黑人知识分子领袖 W. E. B. 杜波依斯。在《黑人的心灵》这本书中,杜波依斯认为华盛顿宣扬放弃主义,误导黑人放弃政治斗争,放弃民权,放弃接受人文通识的高等教育的权利,结果只会导致黑人选举权的完全丧失,从而在政治法定对黑人是劣等种族,也就没有必要接受高等教育。这对于一个种族的生存是极其危险的。杜波依斯指责华盛顿扮演了一种操纵黑人意识的黑老大角色:建立"塔基斯克关系网",拉拢亲信,让他们宣誓效忠,雇用文人写手,利用金钱收买反对派黑人报纸和作者,这些行为与那个时代垄断资本家没有两样。

杜波依斯是第一位在哈佛大学获得博士学位的黑人精英知识分子,他的思想意识更具有理想主义的成分,同时也更具有尖锐的人文洞察力的政治批判力,对黑人争取平等权利似乎更具远见,这与华盛顿更为现实和实用的主张自然是大相径庭。

问题在于,我们必须看到,与第一代的黑人领袖道格拉斯一样,华盛顿也不可能超越他的生活经历和奋斗历程,前者在奴隶制的残暴中长大,获得自由后多有人资助而为废奴而激烈呐喊,而华盛顿虽同为奴隶,但却在西弗吉尼亚相对缓和的种族关系中长大,少年时就因内战结束而获得了解放,他的生命动力更多来源于对受教育的渴望,严于律己的新教道德精神和通过勤劳获得个人价值和社会认可的信念。凭着这股精神,他在 16 岁那年怀揣几个美元,只身投奔近一千公里之外的汉普顿黑人学院,一路忍饥挨饿,露宿野地,半夜到了里士满,身无分文,只能钻到人行道下的空隙间过夜,就像进了坟墓。第二天,饿得两眼昏花的他挣扎着爬出人行道,看到港口工人卸船,硬是凭着最后的力气卖力干活,挣回了自己的生命和继续赶路的希望。及至赶到汉普顿学院,他已筋疲力尽,又瘦又脏,像个少年流浪汉,但他又凭着自己对受教育的渴望和执着,把教室打扫得一尘不染,终于感动了教学主任,留下当了个看门人。此后他得到白人校长阿姆斯特朗的帮助,免了学费,留校当了教师,后来又受校长推荐,到了阿拉巴马州的塔基斯克白手起家,在荒地上创办了黑人职业学校。在

塔基斯克,他看到的是赤贫的黑人渴望认字和学习生产技术的期待,感到的是他在学校仅有的一间破旧窝棚里上课时下起了雨,学生起身为他撑起伞的那份温暖。硬是凭这教育图存图兴的信念和勤奋的工作精神,华盛顿把塔基斯克学校从一个只有 2 千元捐款,没有教师和校舍的黑人职业学校,创办成一所全美黑人职业教育的模范学院,学校

的捐款达到 150 多万美元,并与教育慈善家合作,投资 400 万美元,在塔基斯克学院大量毕业生的积极参与下,在南方创办了 5,000 所黑人地方社区职业学校和配套设施。这不

能不说是美国黑人教育史上的奇迹,也是当今发展中国家提倡走向广大农村,大力发展基层教育的榜样。

如是观之,华盛顿的温和种族融合和渐进主义思想,尽管在政治上显得低调而底气不足,但却不失为一种现实的策略,为黑人能够真正站立起来提供了现实的基础。布克·T. 华盛顿逝世后,经过了 110 年的渐进,竟然有一位黑人当上了美国总统,这不仅是美国民主体制和民权运动的影响使然,还应是非裔美国人教育为先、自强自立,不断在主导的白人社会意识形态中不断渗透,获取社会和政治地位的必然结果。无怪乎黑人总统奥巴马对布克·华盛顿的书喜爱有加。他们都在白人主流的政治文化中尝到了有色人种自强而成功的滋味。

美国著名的女诗人艾米莉·迪金森有诗曰:"一生都失败的人/最懂得成功的甜美;/只有经历生死的饥渴,/方能真正品味花蜜的甘美。"奥巴马总统二次胜选,对此应该深有体会。

■ 演讲文

Atlanta Exposition Address

Booker T. Washington

Mr. President and Gentlemen of the Board of Directors and Citizens:

One-third of the population of the South is of the Negro race. No **enterprise** seeking the material, civil, or moral welfare of this section can disregard this element of our population and reach the highest success. I but convey to you, Mr. President and Directors, the **sentiment** of the masses of my race when I say that in no way have the value and manhood of the American Negro been more fittingly and generously recognized than by the managers of this magnificent Exposition at every stage of its progress. It is a recognition that will do more to **cement** the friendship of the two races than any **occurrence** since the dawn of our freedom.

Not only this, but the opportunity here **afforded** will awaken among us a new era of industrial progress. Ignorant and inexperienced, it is not strange that in the first years of our new life we began at the

---

enterprise: endeavor to seek for great achievement
sentiment: opinion and feeling

cement: combine; unite; bind
occurrence: event
afford: offer itself

top instead of at the bottom; that a seat in Congress or the state legislature was more sought than real estate or industrial skill; that the political convention or **stump speaking** had more attractions than starting a **dairy** farm or truck garden.

A ship lost at sea for many days suddenly sighted a friendly **vessel**. From the mast of the unfortunate vessel was seen a signal, "Water, water; we die of thirst!" The answer from the friendly vessel at once came back, "Cast down your **bucket** where you are." A second time the signal, "Water, water; send us water!" ran up from the **distressed** vessel, and was answered, "Cast down your bucket where you are." And a third and fourth signal for water was answered, "Cast down your bucket where you are." The captain of the distressed vessel, at last **heeding** the **injunction**, cast down his bucket, and it came up full of fresh, sparkling water from the mouth of the Amazon River. To those of my race who depend on **bettering** their condition in a foreign land or who underestimate the importance of cultivating friendly relations with the Southern white man, who is their next-door neighbor, I would say: "Cast down your bucket where you are"—cast it down in making friends in every **manly** way of the people of all races by whom we are surrounded.

Cast it down in agriculture, mechanics, in commerce, in domestic service, and in the professions. And in this connection it is well to bear in mind that whatever other sins the South may **be called to bear**, when it comes to business, pure and simple, it is in the South that the Negro is given a man's chance in the commercial world, and in nothing is this Exposition more eloquent than in emphasizing this chance. Our greatest danger is that in the great leap from slavery to freedom we may **overlook** the fact that the masses of us are to live by the productions of our hands, and fail to keep in mind that we shall prosper in proportion as we learn to dignify and glorify common labor, and put brains and skill into the common occupations of life; shall prosper in proportion as we learn to draw the line between the **superficial** and the **substantial**, the ornamental **gewgaws** of life and the useful. No race can prosper till it learns that there is as much dignity in tilling a field as in writing a poem. It is at the bottom of life we must begin, and not at the top. Nor should we permit our grievances to overshadow our opportunities.

To those of the white race who look to the incoming of those of **foreign birth and strange tongue** and habits for the prosperity of the South, were I permitted I would repeat what I say to my own race,

stump speaking: political speech in public places
dairy: milk
vessel: ship; boat

bucket: container of water
distressed: troubled; desperate

heed: notice; realize
injunction: order; instruction
better: (v.) improve; do for the better

manly: dignified

be call to bear: be responsible

overlook: ignore

superficial: (here) political agitation
substantial: practical business of making a living
gewgaw: things beautiful but useless
foreign birth and strange tongue: immigrant

fidelity: loyalty	
fireside: family	
till: plough	
bowel: inside	
law-abiding: following laws	
unresentful: mild; moderate	
foreigner: (here) stranger; invader	
interlace: interrelate	
curtail: stop; arrest	
invest: put (money or resources) in business at a risk	
abreast: side by side; hand in hand	

"Cast down your bucket where you are." Cast it down among the eight millions of Negroes whose habits you know, whose **fidelity** and love you have tested in days when to have proved treacherous meant the ruin of your **firesides**. Cast down your bucket among these people who have, without strikes and labor wars, **tilled** your fields, cleared your forests, built your railroads and cities, and brought forth treasures from the **bowels** of the earth, and helped make possible this magnificent representation of the progress of the South. Casting down your bucket among my people, helping and encouraging them as you are doing on these grounds, and to education of head, hand, and heart, you will find that they will buy your surplus land, make blossom the waste places in your fields, and run your factories. While doing this, you can be sure in the future, as in the past, that you and your families will be surrounded by the most patient, faithful, **law-abiding**, and **unresentful** people that the world has seen. As we have proved our loyalty to you in the past, in nursing your children, watching by the sick-bed of your mothers and fathers, and often following them with tear-dimmed eyes to their graves, so in the future, in our humble way, we shall stand by you with a devotion that no **foreigner** can approach, ready to lay down our lives, if need be, in defense of yours, **interlacing** our industrial, commercial, civil, and religious life with yours in a way that shall make the interests of both races one. In all things that are purely social we can be as separate as the fingers, yet one as the hand in all things essential to mutual progress.

There is no defense or security for any of us except in the highest intelligence and development of all. If anywhere there are efforts tending to **curtail** the fullest growth of the Negro, let these efforts be turned into stimulating, encouraging, and making him the most useful and intelligent citizen. Effort or means so **invested** will pay a thousand per cent interest. These efforts will be twice blessed—blessing him that gives and him that takes. There is no escape through law of man or God from the inevitable:

The laws of changeless justice bind Oppressor with oppressed;
And close as sin and suffering joined We march to fate **abreast.**

Nearly sixteen millions of hands will aid you in pulling the load upward, or they will pull against you the load downward. We shall constitute one-third and more of the ignorance and crime of the South, or one-third of its intelligence and progress; we shall contribute one-third to the business and industrial prosperity of the South, or we shall prove a veritable body of death, **stagnating**, depressing, retarding every effort to advance the **body politic**.

Gentlemen of the Exposition, as we present to you our humble effort at an exhibition of our progress, you must not expect **overmuch**. Starting thirty years ago with ownership here and there in a few **quilts** and pumpkins and chickens (gathered from **miscellaneous** sources), remember the path that has led from these to the inventions and production of agricultural implements, **buggies**, steam-engines, newspapers, books, statuary, carving, paintings, the management of drug stores and banks, has not been trodden without contact with **thorns and thistles**. While we take pride in what we exhibit as a result of our independent efforts, we do not for a moment forget that our part in this exhibition would fall far short of your expectations but for the constant help that has come to our educational life, not only from the Southern states, but especially from Northern **philanthropists**, who have made their gifts a constant stream of blessing and encouragement.

The wisest among my race understand that the agitation of questions of social equality is theextremist folly, and that progress in the enjoyment of all the privileges that will come to us must be the result of **severe** and constant struggle rather than of artificial forcing. No race that has anything to contribute to the markets of the world is long in any degree **ostracized**. It is important and right that all privileges of the law be ours, but it is vastly more important that we be prepared for the exercise of these privileges. The opportunity to earn a dollar in a factory just now is worth infinitely more than the opportunity to spend a dollar in an **opera-house**.

In conclusion, may I repeat that nothing in thirty years has given us more hope and encouragement, and drawn us so near to you of the white race, as this opportunity offered by the Exposition; and here bending, as it were, over the **altar** that represents the results of the struggles of your race and mine, both starting practically empty-handed three decades ago, I pledge that in your effort to work out the great and **intricate** problem which God has laid at the doors of the South, you shall have at all times the patient, sympathetic help of my race; only let this be constantly in mind, that, while from **representations** in these buildings of the product of field, of forest, of mine, of factory, letters, and art, much good will come, yet far above and beyond material benefits will be that higher good, that, let us pray God, will come, in a **blotting out** of sectional differences and racial **animosities**

---

stagnating: slow and difficult in moving forward
body politics: political system as a whole
overmuch: more than it is possible
quilt: sheet on bed
miscellaneous: all kinds of
buggy: cart with two wheels

thorns and thistles: (here) difficulties and hardships

philanthropist: rich people who give money for the general welfare.

severe: serious and hard

ostracized: abandoned; banished

opera-house: (here) art that is beyond taste of an unprepared mind

altar: place for offering sacrifice; (here) platform of the speech
intricate: complicated

representation: (here) samples
blotting out: defective appearance
animosity: hostility

	and suspicions, in a determination to administer absolute justice, in a willing obedience among all classes to the **mandates** of law. This, coupled with our material prosperity, will bring into our beloved South a new heaven and a new earth.
mandate: order; authority	

■ 重点述评与提示

1. Ignorant and inexperienced, it is not strange that in the first years of our new life we began at the top instead of at the bottom; that a seat in Congress or the state legislature was more sought than real estate or industrial skill; that the political convention or stump speaking had more attractions than starting a dairy farm or truck garden.

   华盛顿认为，刚获得解放的黑人奴隶遇上了美国工业化的大变革，不去学习基本的生存技能，却汲汲于在社会上层谋求平等的权利和地位，这是不切合实际的做法，是愚昧和缺乏经验的表现。这是他提出的经济生活优先于政治权力的"渐进主义"策略的前提认识。这段话里把上层的高昂的政治活动和实际生活中的经济活动两厢对照，形象地烘托出黑人种族"自下而上"发展道路的现实可行性。

2. "Cast down your bucket where you are."

   这是本篇演讲反复出现的中心比喻，既适合于黑人，提倡黑人就地发展农业，提高工业技能的自助行动，也适合白人工业家，号召他们雇佣黑人劳动力，而不是去雇佣已经大量涌进美国劳动力市场的新移民。

3. Our greatest danger is that in the great leap from slavery to freedom we may overlook the fact that the masses of us are to live by the productions of our hands, and fail to keep in mind that we shall prosper in proportion as we learn to dignify and glorify common labor, and put brains and skill into the common occupations of life;

   这是华盛顿的现身说法。他年尚幼时，突然被宣布获得自由，接着到当地盐场工作，后来每逢困难，都是靠白手起家，用脚踏实地的劳动换来生活的改善，以至成就了他教育事业的成功。

4. It is at the bottom of life we must begin, and not at the top. Nor should we permit our grievances to overshadow our opportunities.

   再次强调主题：实际生活状况的改善优于上层政治权利的实现；黑人受到歧视，不平则鸣，却会在高喊政治口号的过程中错过了现实中的发展机遇。

5. While doing this, you can be sure in the future, as in the past, that you and your families will be surrounded by the most patient, faithful, law-abiding, and unresentful people that the world has seen. As we have proved our loyalty to you in the past, in nursing your children, watching by the sick-bed of your mothers and fathers, and often following them with tear-dimmed eyes to their graves, so in the future, in our humble way, we shall stand by you with a devotion that no foreigner can approach, ready to lay down our lives, if need be, in defense of yours,

华盛顿这段话描述了黑人忠厚驯服的天性,一直引起相当一部分黑人的反感,认为这是他讨好白人社会的败笔。但却很少人注意到,这是他对部分奴隶制中种族关系的真实写照。在那些地区,黑人奴隶和白人主人同居一处,黑人奴隶养育主人的孩子,为主人的老人送终;黑白小孩一起玩耍长大,白人青年在内战中战死,黑人奴隶悲哀恸哭,主动要求守夜祭奠亡灵;北方联邦军迫近时,黑人奴隶以命保护女主人安全,至死不出卖主人掩藏财物的地点,等等。这里,华盛顿的失误就在于,他用局部的经验现象,掩盖了整个种族受到奴役的事实。

6. In all things that are purely social we can be as separate as the fingers, yet one as the hand in all things essential to mutual progress.

这个比喻很生动,而且把这幅种族"和而不同"的景象限制在社会交往领域中。但是,华盛顿却以此默认了南方普遍实行的种族隔离政策,等于承认了南方"吉姆法"所谓"隔离中的平等"的意识形态,这对黑人争取平等的政治权力和社会公正是致命的。

7. The wisest among my race understand that the agitation of questions of social equality is theextremist folly, and that progress in the enjoyment of all the privileges that will come to us must be the result of severe and constant struggle rather than of artificial forcing.

华盛顿演说至此,直接攻击道格拉斯一派的黑人领袖,指责他们争取黑人在政治和社会生活中全面地平等权利是"大错特错",是"人为强制的结果",以此反衬自己提倡的种族合作和"渐进主义"的高明。

■ 思考及讨论题

1. What was the political status of the average African-Americans in the post-bellum America?
2. What improvement and progress have been made for the social condition of average black Americans?

3. What is the main idea of Booker T. Washington's "Atlanta Compromise Speech"?
4. Why did this speech appeal not only to the whites but to some black Americans as well?

■ 阅读书目

1. Hope, John. *Three Negro Classics*. A Discus Book, printed in Canada, 1965.
2. Stowe, Lyman Beecher. *Booker T. Washington, Builder of a Civilization*. Garden City: Doubleday, 1916.
3. Spiller, John. "African Americans after the Civil War: John Spiller Surveys Race Relations in the United States during Reconstruction and Constructs a Balance Sheet" in *History Review*. 2009:65.
4. Early, Gerald. "Booker T. Washington: A Man of His Times in St Louis Post-Dispatch" September 18, 1995.

第二十五讲
W. E. B. 杜波依斯（W. E. B. Dubois 1868—1963）

■ 政治历史评述

W. E. B. 杜波依斯：重建黑人身份，批判种族主义的黑人知识分子

W. E. B. 杜波依斯是一个为了重建黑人身份，批判种族主义，为争取黑人平等政治和社会权利不倦的书写者。他是历史学家、社会学家和政治活动家，是20世纪初非洲裔美国人的骄傲。1877年，美国西点军校产生了第一位黑人毕业生亨利·弗利皮尔，二十年后的1895年，哈佛大学向杜波依斯授予博士学位，使他成为美国历史上第一位获得哈佛大学博士学位的非白种人。如果说，弗利皮尔在西点军校毕业，更多地代表着美国政府对内战中大量黑人士兵的象征性奖励，那么杜波依斯在哈佛的博士学位却象征着战后重建时期美国黑人不畏艰险，追求受教育的权利，它标志着黑人身份的一大进步。

这位杰出的黑人知识分子于1868年2月23日生于马萨诸塞州巴林顿的自由黑人家庭。父母拥有自己的土地。杜波依斯从小性格内向，天资聪颖，勤奋敏学，求学之途可谓一帆风顺。他17岁进入田纳西州的费斯克黑人大学，3年后毕业，进入哈佛学院，深受大哲学家威廉·詹姆斯的学术影响，1890年获历史学学士学位，此后获奖学金转入哈佛研究生院，攻读社会学，2年以后获奖学金赴柏林大学学习，听过当时不少社会学大师的课，利用假期游历欧洲，最后回到哈佛完成学业，于1895年获哈佛社会学博士学位。

杜波依斯起初走的完全是学院派的道路。他辗转于大学任教，致力于野外调查，从社会学的角度研究美国黑人的心理和文化，很少涉及黑人的平等权利和选举权等政治问题。1897年7月，他受聘亚特兰大大学历史学和经济学教授，认真授课，也写出不少论文，甚至还获得美国政府资助，提供有关非洲裔美国人劳动力和文化的调查报告。

与此同时，黑人领袖布克·T.华盛顿因主张种族妥协和默认种族隔离而声名鹊起，杜波依斯对此大为反感，于是和其他一些黑人领袖一起，对华盛顿展开口诛笔伐。杜波依斯以一个历史学家的眼光，看到华盛顿思想的历史局限和政治脆弱性。他认为，华盛顿处于一个工业经济迅速发展，种族交往日益密切的时代，人们的生活追求发生了根本变化，但他仍然重弹地方农业经济和种族封闭隔绝的老调；内战时关于奴隶制的争论已经发展成对黑人的种族歧视和压迫，而华盛顿却还在拘泥于种族优劣的论调，默认黑人种族低人一等。这样做将必然导致黑人彻底丧失平等身份感，丧失政治选举权和民权等。在杜波依斯看来，更重要的是，如此下去，黑人将完全丧失受到高等人文教育的权利和机会，而那才是提高黑人思想素质，重建主体身份和意识，获得平等社会和经济地位的长久之计。

从此,杜波依斯走出学院派的局限,把批判和目光和思想锋芒投入反对种族歧视和争取黑人民权的现实斗争中。他是多产的思想者、文学家和社会批判家,一生写了约 2000 篇文章和 20 多部书,其中包括很大一部分针对具体种族问题的社会和社论文章。1903 年,在他最著名的《黑人的灵魂》一书中,他以一个学者的洞察力,预见到"20 世纪的问题是人种肤色的分界问题"。而黑人必须在这个问题意识中看到自己的种族历

史和现实的心理构成。他认为黑人种族在历史中被分化为个体的存在,黑人精神力量犹如一个个陨落的星辰,世界来不及看到他们的存在。在美国,由于长期的奴隶制压迫和摧残,黑人生而带有意识的屏障,没有了真正的自我意识,而只能通过白人世界鄙夷和同情的眼光看到自己的存在。这就是美国黑人的"双重意识"。杜波依斯对此有一段经典的描述:"(黑人)永远感到自己的双重性:既是一个美国人,又是一个黑人;两种灵魂,两种思想,两种不可调和的纠结;在同一黑色的肉体躯壳中包容着两种对抗的理想,只有坚韧的力量才能保证这躯壳不至于分崩离析。"这就是美国黑人的身份。从这一根本认识出发,杜波依斯提倡"有天赋的十分之一"的黑人教育精英主义,力图使黑人通过接受人文高等教育,建立自己的文化身份自觉,既不走向融合白人社会的道路,也不盲目寻求自我封闭隔离的道路,而是立足自我文化身份,在历史的视野中,深入黑人种族文化的内核,重铸黑人文化灵魂,在旗帜鲜明地反对种族歧视和压迫的过程中崛起,从而达到在全世界范围内振兴整个非洲裔有色人种之目的。

为此目的,杜波依斯积极投身于当时反对种族隔离,争取黑人民权的具体社会活动中。1905 年,他与其他黑人民权领袖一道,在加拿大的尼亚加拉发表共同声明,反对布克·T.华盛顿的种族妥协保守主义,由此发动了所谓"尼亚加拉运动",提出了鲜明的黑人民权要求:黑人立即全部地获得言论自由和新闻自由;不折不扣的选举权;废除一切基于种族和肤色的社会等级,实行人类一律平等的现实基本原则。黑人将"让美国人的耳中永远充斥着我们的抗议之声,直至全部实现这些目标"。杜波依斯任"尼亚加拉运动组织"的总干事,创办《月光周刊》和《地平线》等杂志。

"尼亚加拉运动"又在美国本土先后举行了 4 次会议。其中 1906 年第二次会议选址在布朗武装起义的地点哈珀渡口,象征着运动组织不妥协的激进主义态度。杜波依斯在会上发表了演讲,回顾了种族主义对黑人的歧视和迫害,介绍了"尼亚加拉运动"的立场和宗旨,鲜明地提出了实行黑人普遍的选举权,停止种族歧视,保障黑人行动和言论自由,平等法律诉讼权和黑人平等受教育权等五项要求,以及实现这些目标的具体行动。这篇演讲观点鲜明,要求明确,言辞激烈,号召全美黑人团结起来,在布朗起义的旗帜下,摒弃妥协和渐进主义思想,为黑人的彻底解放不解斗争。全篇演讲感召力激荡,柔

中带刚,气势如虹,直接启迪 60 年代民权运动领袖马丁·路德·金的演讲风格,堪称世纪初黑人民权的战斗檄文。

1910 年"尼亚加拉运动"创始人与白人民权运动领袖联手,创办了著名的"全美有色人种协进会"(NAACP),总部设在纽约。此协会大多由白人学者和民权领袖组成,其宗旨是通过非暴力行动,特别是法律和教育手段,在社会经济、政治法律、教育等领域为黑人(杜波依斯提议用"有色人种"取代之)争取到完全的平等权利。杜波依斯担任"宣传与研究部"主任,创办了有名的《危机》杂志并在每期杂志发表社论文章,内容涉及反种族主义方方面面,杂志也即时报道了全美种族歧视和冲突的事件,成了全美黑人的意识形态喉舌,其订阅量最高达到 10 万。杜波依斯的名字也几乎与《危机》杂志成了同义词,杂志的报道和文章也似乎都表达了杜波依斯个人的观点和评判。

1929 年,全球经济大萧条席卷美国,杜波依斯不满 NAACP 总干事瓦尔特·怀特的保守主义策略,认为 NAACP 未能对经济大萧条时期黑人的急剧下降的生活状况给予及时有效的关注和改善,因而与 1934 年辞去了《危机》杂志主编的职务,次年,又发表了一篇题为"一个国家内的黑人国家"的文章,阐述了他自己对经济危机和解决问题的看法,主张建立黑人自己独立运行的合作经济体系和消费模式。杜波依斯认为,资本主义的社会经济实验已经宣告失败,社会主义式的计划合作经济模式具有克服经济危机的优势。因此,在黑人种族内部建立社会合作机制应是克服经济大萧条的可选出路。当然,这种素朴的社会主义计划在罗斯福"新政"的总体格局中不可能得以实现,但是杜波依斯早在一战中访问苏联时就表现出来的社会主义倾向也由此昭然若揭。

不过,与社会主义国家意识形态所不同的是,杜波依斯的社会主义构想始终都是与他坚持黑人种族平等和民权的目的结合在一起的。认识到这一点对理解杜波依斯后期的思想倾向极为重要。二战期间,杜波依斯曾一度对德国的国家社会主义表示赞赏,批评美国政府在军中实行种族歧视,反对美国参战,后来受到麦卡锡主义的迫害;他在冷战期间两次访问中国,1959 年受到毛泽东主席的接见。2 年后,93 岁高龄的杜波依斯加入了美国共产党。在这一切政治态度和行为的背后,都可以看到一条清晰的黑人种族的界限划分,都可以看到杜波依斯为了捍卫非洲裔美国人的尊严,延续黑人种族,重建黑人身份,的努力。他的一生的文字和行为都没有离开这一理想,他在选择政治立场的纠结中显示了他的学术批判精神。1961 年,杜波依斯迁居非洲,执着于学术的领地,主持编纂《非洲大百科全书》,为实现他的泛非洲主义理想尽一个学术人最后的努力,直到 1963 年 95 岁高龄辞世。

1874 年的一天,新英格兰的一间小学教室中,学生们正在玩交

换卡片的游戏，一个深色皮肤的男孩满心欢喜，把自己的卡片递给一个新来的高个儿白人女孩。女孩拒绝了他，用鄙夷的眼光瞟了他一眼，转身离去。男孩感到"一片阴影掠过心头，突然意识到自己与其他孩子不一样，"他们之间隔着一层"巨大的屏障"。这个男孩从此不再试图"越过屏障"，而是暗暗努力学习，事事好强争先，一生都试图拆除这层隔障。88年后，这个男孩已耄耋之年，却选择了远离美国故土的非洲终老此生。这，就是杜波依斯。

■ 演讲文

Niagara Movement Address to the Nation

W. E. B. Dubois

toil: tiring and suffering

ten million: (here) black population
Negro-hater: racist; persecutor of black Americans
ballot: vote

brethren: brothers
thunder: accuse aloud
decency: least respect as man
one jot or little: one bit; a little

assail: attack

byword: meaningless catchword
hissing: meaningless sound
pretension: pretext; excuse
verbiage: beautiful words
subterfuge: tricks

The men of the Niagara Movement coming from the **toil** of the year's hard work and pausing a moment from the earning of their daily bread turn toward the nation and again ask in the name of **ten million** the privilege of a hearing. In the past year the work of the **Negro-hater** has flourished in the land. Step by step the defenders of the rights of American citizens have retreated. The work of stealing the black man's **ballot** has progressed and the fifty and more representatives of stolen votes still sit in the nation's capital. Discrimination in travel and public accommodation has so spread that some of our weaker **brethren** are actually afraid to **thunder** against color discrimination as such and are simply whispering for ordinary **decencies**.

Against this the Niagara Movement eternally protests. We will not be satisfied to take **one jot or little** less than our full manhood rights. We claim for ourselves every single right that belongs to a freeborn American, political, civil and social; and until we get these rights we will never cease to protest and **assail** the ears of America. The battle we wage is not for ourselves alone but for all true Americans. It is a fight for ideals, lest this, our common fatherland, false to its founding, become in truth the land of the thief and the home of the slave—a **byword** and a **hissing** among the nations for its sounding **pretensions** and pitiful accomplishment.

Never before in the modern age has a great and civilized folk threatened to adopt so cowardly a creed in the treatment of its fellow citizens born and bred on its soil. Stripped of **verbiage** and **subterfuge** and in its naked **nastiness**, the new American creed says: Fear to let the black men even try to rise lest they become the equals of the white. And this is the land that professes to follow Jesus Christ. The **blasphemy** of such a course is only matched by its cowardice.

Five demands in detail, our demands are clear and **unequivocal**. First, we would vote; with the right to vote goes everything: freedom, manhood, the honor of your wives, the chastity of your daughters, the right to work, and the chance to rise, and let no man listen to those who deny this.

We want full manhood **suffrage**, and we want it now, henceforth and forever.

Second. We want discrimination in public accommodation to cease. Separation in railway and street cars, based simply on race and **color**, is un-American, undemocratic, and silly. We protest against all such discrimination.

Third. We claim the right of freemen to walk, talk, and be with them that wish to be with us. No man has a right to choose another man's friends, and to attempt to do so is an **impudent** interference with the most fundamental human privilege.

Fourth. We want the law enforced against rich as well as poor; against capitalist as well as laborer; against white as well as black. We are not more lawless than the white race: we are more often arrested, **convicted and mobbed**. We want justice even for criminals and outlaws. We want the Constitution of the country enforced. We want Congress to take charge of Congressional elections. We want the Fourteenth Amendment carried out **to the letter** and every state **disfranchised** in Congress which attempts to disfranchise its rightful voters. We want the Fifteenth Amendment enforced and no state allowed to base its franchise simply on color.

The failure of the Republican Party in Congress at the session just closed to **redeem** its pledge of 1904 with reference to suffrage conditions at the South seems a plain, deliberate, and premeditated **breach** of promise, and **stamps** that party as guilty of obtaining votes under false pretense.

Fifth. We want our children educated. The school system in the country districts of the South is a **disgrace**, and in few towns and cities are the Negro schools what they ought to be. We want the national government to step in and wipe out illiteracy in the South. Either the United States will destroy ignorance or ignorance will destroy the United States.

And when we call for education we mean real education. We believe in work. We ourselves are workers, but work is not necessarily education. Education is the development of power and ideal. We want our children trained as intelligent human beings should be, and we will fight for all time against any proposal to educate black boys and girls simply as servants and **underlings**, or simply for the use of other people. They have a right to know, to think, to aspire.

Plan for action. These are some of the chief things we want. How shall we get them? By voting where we may vote, by persistent, unceasing **agitation**, by **hammering at** the truth, by sacrifice and work.

We do not believe in violence, neither in the despised violence of the raid nor the lauded violence of the soldier, nor the barbarous violence of the mob, but we do believe in John Brown, in that **incarnate** spirit of justice, that hatred of a lie, that willingness to sacrifice money, reputation, and life itself on the altar of right. And here on the scene of John Brown's martyrdom we **reconsecrate** ourselves, our honor, our property to the final emancipation of the race which John Brown died to make free.

Our enemies, triumphant for the present, are **fighting the stars** in their courses. Justice and humanity must prevail. We live to tell these **dark brothers** of ours—scattered in counsel, **wavering** and weak—that no bribe of money or **notoriety**, no promise of wealth or fame, is worth the surrender of a people's manhood or the loss of a man's self-respect. We refuse to surrender the leadership of this race to cowards and **trucklers**. On this rock we have planted our banners. We will never give up, though the **trump** of doom finds us still fighting.

And we shall win. The past promised it, the present foretells it. Thank God for John Brown! Thank God for Garrison and Douglass! Sumner and Phillips, Nat Turner and Robert Gould Shaw, and all the **hallowed** dead who died for freedom! Thank God for all those today, few though their voice be, who have not forgotten the divine brotherhood of all men; white and black, rich and poor, fortunate and unfortunate.

We appeal to the young men and women of this nation, to those whose nostrils are not yet **befouled** by greed and snobbery and racial narrowness: stand up for the right, prove yourselves worthy of your heritage and whether born North or South dare to treat men as men. Cannot the nation that has absorbed ten million foreigners into its political life without catastrophe absorb ten million Negro Americans into that same political life at less cost than their unjust and illegal

exclusion will involve?

    Courage, brothers! The battle for humanity is not lost or losing. All across the skies sit signs of promise. The Slav is rising in his might, the **yellow millions** are tasting liberty, the black Africans are **writhing** toward the light, and everywhere the laborer, with ballot in his hand, is voting open the gates of opportunity and peace. The morning breaks over blood-stained hills. We must not **falter**, we may not shrink. Above are the everlasting stars.

> **exclusion**: (here) declaration of ineffectiveness
>
> **yellow millions**: millions of Chinese and Asians
> **writhe**: moving forward in pain
> **falter**: hesitant

■ 重点述评与提示

1. Discrimination in travel and public accommodation has so spread that some of our weaker brethren are actually afraid to thunder against color discrimination as such and are simply whispering for ordinary decencies.

    可见布克·T. 华盛顿对黑人选举权和民权的负面影响有多么的深远。距1895年"亚特兰大博览会演讲"以来10多年过去，黑人民权运动衰退，种族歧视蔓延。演讲者开篇指明这一趋势，目的在于唤醒黑人民众，在"尼亚加拉运动组织"的鼓动下，兴起新一轮的黑人民权运动高潮。句中"thunder"一词和"whispering"对比强烈，巧妙地喻示这两种不同的立场和态度。

2. The battle we wage is not for ourselves alone but for all true Americans. It is a fight for ideals, lest this, our common fatherland, false to its founding, become in truth the land of the thief and the home of the slave—a byword and a hissing among the nations for its sounding pretensions and pitiful accomplishment.

    杜波依斯此时尚未提出他激进的"国中之黑人国"的构想，还必须高举国家的大旗来反对种族歧视和暴力迫害。显然这里提出为之奋斗的"理想"也喻指《独立宣言》"人人生而平等"的宣示。如果1000万美国黑人公民没有享受平等的政治和社会权利，美国的这条立国之本就成了空洞的口号和虚伪的矫饰，最终贻笑世界。

3. Five demandsin detail, our demands are clear and unequivocal.

    这篇演讲应是"尼亚加拉运动"成员们共同的宣言，这里以片言居要，简明而有力地提出五项具体的要求。"clear and unequivocal"，言辞坚决，不留余地，足见"尼亚加拉运动"的激进民权倾向。

4. The failure of the Republican Party in Congress at the session just closed to redeem its pledge of 1904 with reference to suffrage conditions at the South seems a plain,

deliberate, and premeditated breach of promise, and stamps that party as guilty of obtaining votes under false pretense.

  19 世纪 50 年代由西华德和林肯等人创立的美国共和党由于其限制奴隶制蔓延、废奴和人道的倾向,一直受到美国有色人种的支持。这个所谓"林肯的党"在内战后重建中也通过了"自由民局"等组织为南方各州的黑人社会做出了显著的支持和帮助,受到了黑人选民一致的拥护。但随着老一代共和党人(特别是激进共和党人)的逝去,新的共和党人为各自利益发生了进一步分裂,对南方民主党的咄咄逼人态势采取手势,对种族问题持保守态度。于是,共和党逐渐失去了黑人的绝对支持。杜波依斯在此指责共和党背信弃义,应是这一过程的开端。

5. We believe in work. We ourselves are workers, but work is not necessarily education. Education is the development of power and ideal. We want our children trained as intelligent human beings should be, and we will fight for all time against any proposal to educate black boys and girls simply as servants and underlings, or simply for the use of other people.

  这里表达的是杜波依斯在批驳布克·T. 华盛顿的塔斯基克职业教育模式的基础上提出对于黑人实行人文高等教育的主张,显示了一个学者对于教育的理解以及教育之于黑人民权斗争的重要性。相比之下,可见杜波依斯的教育理念更具政治化的长远意义。

6. We do not believe in violence, neither in the despised violence of the raid nor the lauded violence of the soldier, nor the barbarous violence of the mob, but we do believe in John Brown.

  黑人民权运动一直提倡非暴力斗争,约翰·布朗是一个例外。这里提及布朗,不用明说,也是一个警示。此后 60 年代的黑人民权运动领袖马丁·路德·金在其《我有一个梦想》的著名演说中,也同样发出如此的警示之音。这并非空穴来风,60 年代兴起了一些黑人组织如"黑豹党",枪不离身,都是暴力反抗种族主义的征兆。

7. We refuse to surrender the leadership of this race to cowards and trucklers.

  这话的锋芒直指布克·T. 华盛顿,如此激烈的言辞也见证着黑人民权运动新一代领袖的崛起。

8. Courage, brothers! The battle for humanity is not lost or losing. All across the skies sit signs of promise. The Slav is rising in his might, the yellow millions are tasting liberty, the black Africans are writhing toward the light, and everywhere the laborer, with ballot in his hand, is voting open the gates of opportunity and peace.

  杜波依斯这些口号式排比句,虽然略显空泛,但却也是这篇宣言式演讲的最好结尾。从内容上看，这也正好表达了演说者促进有色人种自由和平等的理想，其中亚洲黄种人的觉醒也是他后来十分关心的问题。开头的语句铿锵有力，不屈不挠，回响着弥尔顿《失乐园》中撒旦的反抗之声。

■ 思考及讨论题

1. What is the meaning of "separate but equal" and how did the idea affect the racial tension in the post-bellum south?
2. Under what circumstances was the Niagara Movement formed?
3. What was the mission of NAACP and how did the organization contribute to the African-American fight for political and social equality?
4. How shall we understand Dubois's proposition of Pan-Africanism and his inclination to socialism in his later years?

■ 阅读书目

1. Verney, Kevern. *Black Civil Rights in America*. London and New York: Rutledge, 2004.
2. Wright, W. D. *Black History and Black Identity: A Call for a New Historiography*. Westerport: Praeger Publisher, 2002.
3. Turner-Sadler, Joanne. *African American History: An Introduction*. Washington: Peter Lang Publishing, 2006.

第八章 ‖ 资本主义扩张中的改革和危机

Modern life is both complex and intense, and the tremendous changes wrought by the extraordinary industrial development of the last half century are felt in every fiber of our social and political being.

Speak softly and carry a big stick; you will go far.

—Theodore Roosevelt

We are provincials no longer. The tragic events of the thirty months of vital turmoil through which we have just passed have made us citizens of the world.

—Woodrow Wilson

Let me assert my firm belief that the only thing we have to fear is fear itself—nameless, unreasoning, unjustified terror which paralyzes needed efforts to convert retreat into advance.

—Franklin D. Roosevelt

Preview Questions

01/

What changes have been brought about by the turn of the 19th century to the 20th century?

02/

What is Progressivism? What were some important issues addressed by the Progressivist reformers?

03/

What could be the main causes of the WWI and WWII?

04/

What are the main causes of recurrent economic crises? What happened during the Great Depression of 1929?

第二十六讲
西奥多·罗斯福(Theodore Roosevelt 1858—1919)

■ 政治历史评述

西奥多·罗斯福:温言的政治改革家,手持大棒的泰迪毛毛熊

历史翻过新的一页,进入资本主义自由扩张和社会无序振荡的20世纪,美国迎来了新世纪第一位总统,也是历史上年纪最轻的总统:西奥多·罗斯福。这是一位性格另类,精力过人的美国总统,一位大胆而又精明的政治家和改革家。他提倡"有强度的人生"(strenuous life),喜好政治的喧嚣和功名,一生在政坛上演绎出传奇的经历和业绩,热衷于探险和自然环境保护,足迹遍布非洲草原和南美的丛林;他也是"尚武"的英雄,直至生命地最后的时光都反复向威尔逊总统递交申请,要求亲自率军奔赴欧洲战场杀敌报国。

但是,谁还能想到,这位23岁就入选纽约州议会,政坛叱咤风云近40年的政治家和美国牛仔式的硬汉,却还是美国儿童文学的作者和倡导者。他从小伴随着那本有名的儿童杂志《少年伙伴》长大,在母亲和婶婶的童话故事中向往着未来;他对大自然和小动物们有着特殊的感情,9岁就写出了他观察研究动物的文章;即便当了总统,他对儿童的心灵的关心也不亚于他对政治的兴趣:他和5个孩子都住在一起,白宫成了孩子的乐园,充满着孩子们的欢笑声,这位在政坛上和国际舞台上总喜欢挥舞大棒的政治家,在家里是慈祥的父亲,永远带着心底发出的微笑。他政务之余,总要给孩子们讲童话故事,外出巡视和演讲的空暇时间总用来给孩子们写信。从他大量的书信可以读到,他对儿童文学有着天生的偏爱,他一生都在读儿童文学作品,推广和普及儿童文学;他对天真和幼小的心灵总是充满了怜爱,有一次打猎,他看着瘢棘的幼熊而不忍开枪,此后,他的名字也就与那孩子们喜爱的泰迪毛毛熊永远地连在一起。

可以说,这是一个童心未泯,机智灵活,决而起行的美国总统。在他那充满活力,自由豪放并带有霸气的行为风格中,我们看到了一个现代美国人典型的性格。在这强悍尚武,视死如归的性格背后,我们可以看到一颗对自然界和人类社会永远充满好奇和探究的心灵,他的可爱和受人尊崇在相当程度上是因为他不墨守成规,敢于另辟蹊径,在处理国内外大事中处处表现出来机智,直率和天真。

西奥多·罗斯福1858年生于纽约市,父亲是成功的银行商业家。小西奥多从小体质羸弱,常常一犯哮喘,几至窒息。后来在父亲的引导下练习拳击和摔跤,逐渐增强了体质,在母亲和姨母的教导下,在家学习各种功课,对自然科学更是充满好奇和兴趣。经过14岁之前两次的欧洲和非洲游历,西奥多的各科知识得以整合,又经过勤奋的备考,于

18岁进入哈佛大学并以优等生的名次于1880年毕业。罗斯福在其自传中这样评价他在哈佛的学业:"……在哈佛的学习对我当然有益,不过那只是总体的好处,因为在哈佛学习的那些具体内容对我后来的人生几乎没有什么助益。"对于西奥多,教条总是苍白的,哈佛奉亚当·斯密的"放任主义"为政治经济学的金科玉律,解决起复杂的金融垄断和劳资纠纷,不如他当了总统后几次谈话来得实际。如此说来,马克·吐温笔下那个桀骜不驯,成天游荡山野寻宝的少年汤姆·索耶尔,应是西奥多阅读中的至交了。

西奥多在自己丰富多彩的公共政治生活中向世人证明,书本的知识不能造就生动的人生体验,学校的教条难以应对国际大势和国内工业化和城市化造成的复杂的社会变迁。

从1882年至1901年,西奥多随性而行,不断变幻活法,常常突然终止前途可观的事业,毅然投身于自己完全陌生的领域,甚至不计后果。而不论干什么,他一上手就会弄个风生水起,引起轰动。1881年,他被选为纽约州众议员,2年后就逃离政坛,到西部的牧场的荒野中体验牛仔的自由和猎手的兴奋;1886年,他又不甘寂寞,重返政坛,后在美国文官委员会任职,对民主党的政府职位"分赃制"大加挞伐,被称为"桀骜不驯,咄咄逼人,激情四射"之人。1895年,他目睹纽约市警察的无能和腐败,应聘做了市警署局长,整顿

警务,打黑扬善,赢得民众拥戴。他还对海军颇有研究,1897年谋得助理海军部长之职。从此,他的男子汉"尚武"精神有了用武之地。他上任后,警告美国公众要防止的不是"战争的威胁",而是"和平的威胁",他越俎代庖,指挥海军备战,一手促成了美国与西班牙的战争。但两国刚刚宣战,他又突然宣布辞职,不顾妻子和朋友的反对,到得克萨斯州招募志愿骑兵,直接奔赴古巴战场!1898年7月1日,身为骑兵团长的他在古巴战场身先士卒,带领着一群徒步的"莽骑兵"在圣胡安高地一战成名,成了全国家喻户晓的风云人物,不久就被选为纽约州州长。1900年2月,他发表声明,坚辞副总统提名,但不久变卦,作为共和党副总统候选人,5个月之内在全国各地共做了近700场竞选演说。1901年3月4日,时年才42岁的西奥多·罗斯福就任美国副总统。命运似乎特别偏爱这位精力充沛,骨子里喜欢人气和风头的年轻人。半年后,麦金利总统遇刺身亡,罗斯福就任美国总统。据说,当时年轻的总统曾抱怨说,共和党后台实力政客马克·汉纳把他当大男孩看,当面称呼他"泰迪"。这位权倾政坛的汉纳参议员还说了一句为新总统的性格定格的话:"那个该死的牛仔当了美国的总统。"

然而,正是这位大男孩牛仔总统,以他的大国视野和独特率性的行事风格,结束了林肯以后历届总统软弱,国会操纵大权的局面,建立了新世纪"强势总统"形象,对内积极干预解决经济问题,保护环境,对外帝国扩张,建立大国领袖地位,为现代美国的政治、经济、生态环境和世界大国领袖地位奠定了基础。

罗斯福说过,伟大的总统必须是甘冒"伟大风险"的总统,"总统就应该有魄力,总统

要有实权"。为此,必须首先树立"大政府"的权威,许多行政议案应该不受国会的约束而得以执行。在其 7 年的执政期间,总统直接批准的行政令达 1,000 多项,比其前任翻了近 10 倍,仅次于一战时的威尔逊和二战时的小罗斯福。罗斯福"大政府"直接干预经济也很有创意和效果。比如,他直接把工业劳资双方拉在一起,以政府接管煤矿为底线,解决宾夕法尼亚煤矿工人长期罢工问题,创造了政府有权审查大公司并干预劳资纠纷的所谓"公正解决"(Square Deal)的先例;在工业大公司日趋垄断经济,公平竞争失衡的状况下,他决定以反托拉斯法为依托进行有效的政府干预,巧妙地区分不同性质的托拉斯,起诉(最终解散)了铁路垄断巨头"北方证券公司",以儆效尤;在国家土地日益私有化和铁路征用,森林和矿产资源遭到严重破坏的状况下,他决定政

府干预,采取一系列政府政策和国会立法,由农业部收管大量土地,并建立了国家森林服务局,有效地遏制住了私有化进程,并新建水利灌溉工程,建立了 5 个国家公园,51 个野生动物保护地和 150 个国家森林区,这些都是美国历史上前所未有的创举。此外,面对工业化、城市化和科技日益发展而日益产生的经济和社会问题,罗斯福也提出他的"新国家主义"进步主义改革方案,决心进一步推动国家干预力度,以"扒粪者"的精神,揭露并改革资本主义无序竞争造成的种种弊端。

在国际外交方面,罗斯福总统有帝国扩张主义的气势。他推崇林肯的大气和坚毅,在白宫总统办公室的壁炉上方挂上林肯的画像,在办公室的墙壁上也贴有一张熊的照片和一首十四行诗,这首诗开头写道:"吾当为人类命运之主宰,/脚下是功名、爱和财富。"罗斯福总统正是以这样的帝国气势走向世界的。他以孩子般的创意语言,提出"好话不离口,大棒握在手"的"大棒"政策,以强大的海军为海外扩张,不惜充当世界警察的角色,把美国的势力向世界强行推展。他创造性地解释"门罗主义",提出有名的"罗斯福定理",为武装干涉南美国家提供霸权依据。首先,他以海军为支撑,颠覆哥伦比亚政府,扶持巴拿马政权,获取了巴拿马运河;其次,他武装干涉古巴内政,镇压古巴起义;同时,他也插手委内瑞拉、多米尼加和尼加拉瓜等国事务,为以后美国出兵海外,保护国民提供了先例;他还把手伸向亚洲,出面"调停"俄国和日本在中国东北的战争,为美国争取到在菲律宾和中国利益,为此还获得了 1905 年的诺贝尔和平奖。

1907 年,罗斯福组成一支 16 艘战舰的"白色舰队",环游了太平洋,历史 3 个月,一路耀武扬威,展现了美国海上霸主的风光。具有讽刺意义的是,历史往往会捉弄强者。当年"白色舰队"停靠日本港口,让日本军国主义分子看花了眼,发誓发展海军。结果,20 多年后,日本舰队突袭了美国在太平洋的珍珠港,重创了罗斯福"白色舰队"的继承人;另一方面,罗斯福热衷于挥舞大棒,建立世界霸权,出兵海外,干涉别国内政,使得美国人在世界范围内扬眉吐气。但是,多少年过后,历史又开始了它"否极泰来"的游戏,在 9.11

世贸大厦的灰烬烟尘和波士顿马拉松爆炸的鲜血中降下了恐怖主义的阴霾。当年,"雄狮"罗斯福也为他的"强度人生",战争荣誉和帝国之梦付出了个人生活的沉重代价:他的三个儿子战死欧洲战场,一个儿子重伤。一生最爱孩子,以养育孩子为人生最大幸福的罗斯福在暮年经历了常人难以想象的最大痛苦。

当然,西奥多·罗斯福古典主义式的荣誉感和生死观也显示了人类精神的力量。1912年10月14日,一名刺客悄然抵近,向正在前往竞选演说场地的罗斯福开枪射击,右胸中枪的罗斯福忍着剧痛,大声坚持"只要一息尚存",就要坚持既定演说。一小时后,演说结束,他才被送往医院。不到两星期,罗斯福又出现在讲台上,面对12000名备受感动的听众,慷慨激昂。

莎士比亚在《裘力斯·恺撒》一剧中,让罗马将军凯西斯说道:"懦夫在死前已经死过多次,英雄一生只死一次。"此西奥多·罗斯福之谓矣。

■ 演讲文

Second Presidential Inaugural Address

Theodore Roosevelt

My fellow citizens, no people on earth have more cause to be thankful than ours, and this is said **reverently**, in no spirit of boastfulness in our own strength, but with gratitude to the Giver of Good who has blessed us with the conditions which have enabled us to achieve so large a **measure** of well-being and of happiness. To us as a people it has been granted to lay the foundations of our national life in a new continent. We are the heir of the ages, and yet we have had to pay few of the **penalties** which in old countries are exacted by the dead hand of a **bygone** civilization. We have not been obliged to fight for our existence against any alien race; and yet our life has called for the vigor and effort without which the **manlier and hardier virtues** wither away. Under such conditions it would be our own fault if we failed; and the success which we have had in the past, the success which we confidently believe the future will bring, should cause in us no feeling of **vainglory**, but rather a deep and **abiding** realization of all which life has offered us; a full acknowledgment of the responsibility which is ours; and a fixed determination to show that under a free government a mighty people can thrive best, alike as regards the **things of the body**

---

reverently: with sincere respect and honor

measure: scale; magnitude

penalty: (here) cost; sacrifice
bygone: past

manlier and hardier virtues: merits of true man

vainglory: vain pride
abiding: lasting; enduring
things of body: material well-being

and the **things of the soul**.

Much has been given us, and much will rightfully be expected from us. We have duties to others and duties to ourselves; and we can **shirk** neither. We have become a great nation, forced by the fact of its greatness into relations with the other nations of the earth, and we must behave as **beseems** a people with such responsibilities. Toward all other nations, large and small, our attitude must be one of **cordial** and sincere friendship. We must show not only in our words, but in our deeds, that we are earnestly desirous of securing their good will by acting toward them in a spirit of just and generous recognition of all their rights. But justice and generosity in a nation, as in an individual, count most when shown not by the weak but by the strong. While ever careful to **refrain** from wrongdoing others, we must be no less insistent that we are not wronged ourselves. We wish peace, but we wish the peace of justice, the peace of **righteousness**. We wish it because we think it is right and not because we are afraid. No weak nation that acts manfully and justly should ever have cause to fear us, and no strong power should ever be able to **single us out** as a subject for **insolent** aggression.

Our relations with the other powers of the world are important; but still more important are our relations among ourselves. Such growth in wealth, in population, and in power as this nation has seen during the century and a quarter of its national life is inevitably accompanied by a like growth in the problems which are ever before every nation that rises to greatness. Power invariably means both responsibility and danger. Our forefathers faced certain **perils** which we have outgrown. We now face other perils, the very existence of which it was impossible that they should foresee. Modern life is both complex and intense, and the tremendous changes **wrought** by the extraordinary industrial development of the last half century are felt in every fiber of our social and political being. Never before have men tried so vast and **formidable** an experiment as that of administering the affairs of a continent under the forms of a Democratic republic. The conditions which have told for our marvelous material well-being, which have developed to a very high degree our energy, self-reliance, and individual **initiative**, have also brought the care and anxiety inseparable from the accumulation of great wealth in industrial centers. Upon the success of our experiment much depends, not only as regards our own welfare, but as regards the welfare of mankind. If we fail, the cause of free self-government throughout the world will

---

things of the soul: spiritualfulfillment
shirk: avoid
beseem: befit; appropriate
cordial: loving

refrain: hold back

righteousness: fair, just and respected

single us out: choose us; pick us out
insolent: bully; arrogant

peril: great danger

wrought: (old use)= worked

formidable: extremely powerful; overwhelming

initiative: originality and creativity

rock to its foundations, and therefore our responsibility is heavy, to ourselves, to the world as it is today, and to the generations yet unborn. There is no good reason why we should fear the future, but there is every reason why we should face it seriously, neither hiding from ourselves the **gravity** of the problems before us nor fearing to approach these problems with the unbending, **unflinching** purpose to solve them aright.

  Yet, after all, though the problems are new, though the tasks set before us differ from the tasks set before our fathers who founded and preserved this Republic, the spirit in which these tasks must be undertaken and these problems faced, if our duty is to be well done, remains essentially unchanged. We know that self-government is difficult. We know that no people needs such high **traits** of character as that people which seeks to govern its affairs aright through the freely expressed will of the freemen who compose it. But we have faith that we shall not prove false to the memories of the men of the mighty past. They did their work, they left us the splendid **heritage** we now enjoy. We in our turn have an assured confidence that we shall be able to leave this heritage unwasted and enlarged to our children and our children's children. To do so we must show, not merely in great crises, but in the everyday affairs of life, the qualities of practical intelligence, of courage, of hardihood, and endurance, and above all the power of devotion to a lofty ideal, which made great the men who founded this Republic in the days of Washington, which made great the men who preserved this Republic in the days of Abraham Lincoln.

rock: shake

gravity: bigness seriousness; magnitude
unflinching: persistent; never-giving-up

trait: feature; nature

heritage: legacy not only of political, but of environmental value

■ 重点述评与提示

1. We have not been obliged to fight for our existence against any alien race; and yet our life has called for the vigor and effort without which the manlier and hardier virtues wither away.
  罗斯福在例行赞美上帝对美国的偏爱和保佑的同时，重申他提出的"有强度的人生"（strenuous life）的硬汉精神。这是贯穿这篇演讲的主旋律。后来的小罗斯福在经济大萧条的危机中也反复强调了这一精神。

2. We have become a great nation, forced by the fact of its greatness into relations with the other nations of the earth, and we must behave as beseems a people with such

responsibilities.

　　此时美国的综合国力已经超越英国等欧洲国家,成为后来居上的世界强国。最近美国对西班牙战争的胜利,振奋了美国海外扩张的势头,加上罗斯福本人实力恃强的领导风格,直接肇始了20世纪美国充当"世界警察"的传统。

3. Such growth in wealth, in population, and in power as this nation has seen during the century and a quarter of its national life is inevitably accompanied by a like growth in the problems which are ever before every nation that rises to greatness.

　　19世纪末,美国资本主义迅速扩张,新技术和科学管理加快了工业化和城市化的进程,并吸引海外大批的移民的到来,美国迅速崛起成为世界强国。同时,作为20世纪开局第一位美国总统,罗斯福也面临着资本垄断、劳资紧张、种族矛盾和道德沦丧所带来的一系列社会问题。他在继任总统的3年多内,已经积累了处理这些问题的经验,此时重申这一问题意识,为新的任内中实施的进步主义改革定下了调子。

4. Upon the success of our experiment much depends, not only as regards our own welfare, but as regards the welfare of mankind. If we fail, the cause of free self-government throughout the world will rock to its foundations, and therefore our responsibility is heavy, to ourselves, to the world as it is today, and to the generations yet unborn.

　　这是一个现代性的命题。面对着工业化带来的经济繁荣,资本主义市场的无序拓展,社会改革必然到来。这是人类从未有过的社会实验,命运选择了美国充当其实验者。此外,这里也可以看出,美国充当世界老大的霸权意识应该追溯到罗斯福,他的"大棒政策"和"罗斯福定理"开始越过美国孤立主义的既定传统,把美国的意识形态和价值观念推向世界。

5. We in our turn have an assured confidence that we shall be able to leave this heritage unwasted and enlarged to our children and our children's children.

　　罗斯福是美国历史上第一个有生态保护意识的总统。这里所谓的遗产除了指美国的民主政治体制外,还应是自然环境的遗产。"unwasted"是演讲者自行合成的词,在此也明显地暗示了合理利用,保护自然生态环境之意。句中连用三个"children",强调为子孙后代造福,也成了后代美国总统就职演说中常用的典型修辞语。

6. ...great the men who founded this Republic in the days of Washington, which made great the men who preserved this Republic in the days of Abraham Lincoln.

　　华盛顿是开国元勋,独立战争中百折不挠,自然是罗斯福心中遥远的英雄。而林肯则是罗斯福自幼崇拜的偶像。6岁那年,他把下巴支在窗沿上,在自家窗口俯瞰林肯灵柩通过纽约的街道,自强的冲动在幼小的心灵油然而生。及至当了总统,对林肯强势的总统风格更有效仿，曾说道：每逢做出大的决策，"我抬头看着那幅画像（白宫办公室的林肯画像），我坚信林肯也会这么做的。"这里，罗斯福以这两位里程碑人物作为演说的结尾，把他们比作智慧、勇气、坚毅和耐心的化身，既起到铿锵有力之修辞效果，又为自己未来四年的执政风格定下基调。

■ 思考及讨论题

1. How did T. Roosevelt's early political and military experiences contribute to his later success as the President of USA?
2. What was TR's view of big corporate monopoly and how did he deal with that?
3. What was unique in TR's foreign policy and how did he succeed in Asia?
4. Relate some important measures by TR for the natural conservation.

■ 阅读书目

1. Roosevelt, Theodore. *Theodore Roosevelt: An Autobiography*. New York: Macmillan, 1913.
2. Foner, Eric. *The New American History*. Philadelphia: Temple University Press, 1997.
3. Gable, John Allen. "The Many Faces of Theodore Roosevelt" *in USA Today*, 2009.
4. Powell, Jim. "Theodore Roosevelt, Big-Government Man" *in Freeman*, 2010.

第二十七讲
伍德罗·威尔逊(Woodrow Wilson 1856—1919)

■ 政治历史评述

伍德罗·威尔逊:新自由主义的改革者,学者型的理想主义政治家

1866年12月的一天,美国佐治亚州,奥古斯塔镇边,一对父子抬头看着棉织厂的斩棉锯在阳光中上下翻飞。

儿子大约10岁,偏着头对站在一旁的父亲说:"你知道吗,爸,我觉得这世界上最好的职业就是美国总统。"

父亲觉得儿子的话十分有趣,问道:"你真的这么想吗?想试试吗?"

"嗯,"小男孩红着脸说道:"要不我还是当个参议员吧。"

这是美国女作家露丝·克莱斯顿1945年出版的《伍德罗·威尔逊的故事》的开篇描写。这个小男孩的父母都受过良好的宗教和人文教育,在他们的培养下,他17岁起就学于新泽西学院和弗吉尼亚大学法学院,虽然中途几次病退,但最终凭着自学优异的成绩进入约翰·霍普金斯大学,30岁而立之年获得了该校授予的政治学博士学位,成为一位非常受学生欢迎的教授,短短5年之后,他当选普林斯顿大学校长。此后被民主党党魁相中,在政界一路领跑,53岁当选新泽西州州长,2年后乘西奥多·罗斯福另立山头,分化共和党之机,一举登上美国总统宝座,成就了少年时的梦想。

伍德罗·威尔逊是美国历史上唯一拥有政治学博士学位的总统,也是自林肯以来第二位民主党的当选总统。更重要的是,这是一位教育家,一位学者型的理想主义政治家。他在政治学和法律学方面的学问造诣,使他的世界观念和施政多了一层理想主义的书卷气,另一方面,有了法制和政治理论的指引,他提出的"新自由主义"治国方略又在实践中切合了当时进步主义改革的潮流,使他成为继西奥多·罗斯福之后又一位新世纪复杂的国内外局势中成功的改革者。美国史家对威尔逊的评论总是各执一词,或判定他的内外政策受到他个人理想主义的深刻影响,或认为他具有现实的世界眼光,身体力行地进行了一系列务实的社会改革。其实,在这样一个教育家兼学者型的政治家身上,知识的负荷使其理性呈现出多重的指向;作为一个大国的领导人,20世纪初不断变化的现实不容单向的思维和选择,这使得威尔逊的政治判断和选择呈现出理想和现实的悖论。在国际和国内政治的大舞台上,威尔逊总统扮演的是理想与现实冲突中有实际作为的悲剧性人物。还是威尔逊同时代的报业主编、专栏作家和进步主义运动活动家威廉·艾伦·怀特的评论来得公允:"他肩负着艰难的使命,工作中面临着可怕的意外事件,许多内心的挣扎。他业绩斐然,也留下诸多的遗憾。但是他的执着和诚恳,他对现实中的工作的无私奉献赢得了世人一致的赞誉。"

威尔逊对知识和理论有着无比的热情与执着,对学生有着超乎寻常的现实平等意识。1910年从政之前的30多年都在大学里学习和教授政治经济学和法律,撰写了9本有关政治学和历史学的专著和大量的论文。在教学中,他与学生打成一片,循循善诱,是普林斯顿大学最受欢迎的教授,每次都有400多名学生争先恐后来听威尔逊教授讲课。课后许多学生到他家里做客聊天。每年全校投票选出最佳教授,威尔逊总是名列第一。威尔逊教授具有教育者强烈的人文精神和社会责任感。他在普林斯顿大学150周年纪念会上发表演说,坚持大学教育的方向不仅是培养个人的才能,而应服务于国家和社会的需求;他同时号召师生研究历史和政治,研究古往今来优秀的人文传统,以防止过分强调科学的工具理性所可能造成的社会弊端。1902年,威尔逊教授当选普林斯顿大学校长。

威尔逊校长治校具有远见,他引进了一流的师资,成功地进行了教育体制和课程的改革,打破德国式传统的讲授为主的教学模式,提倡启发式的学生辅导课教学。他本人身体力行,在课堂中使用提纲式启发教学,讲政治经济理论是结合现实人物和实例,用生动的语言把枯燥的理论转变成学生思维和行为的实际能力,全校教学一时蔚然成风。他提出建立全校性的学生食堂,以利于全校学生融合交流;大力推动研究生院的计划,以利于专门学科高深学问的研究。这些改革措施虽然遭到保守派的极力反对而半途而废,但客观上起到了推动新型教育理念和实践的作用,普林斯顿大学一跃成为全美远近闻名的著名大学。

光阴荏苒,威尔逊校长完全可能在学术圈子走完自己人生的道路。可是命运却要他走向政坛,去实现少年时代偶尔闪现的美国总统梦。1913年3月,年过半百的威尔逊宣誓就职美国第28任总统,走向问题重重的国内政坛,走向战争风云密布的国际舞台。

此时的美国,1911年3月25日在纽约三角衬衣厂火灾烧死141人的惨剧还历历在目。资本主义工业化、城市化和技术的迅猛发展带来了物质的丰腴,同时也暴露了一系列亟待解决的社会问题:妇女平等选举权、移民涌入造成的失业,童工问题,改善劳动条件,减少劳动强度,增加工人工资,工业寡头垄断,权力交易,贫富阶级分化,贫困导致的社会道德沦丧,市政管理的弊端等等。目睹这一切"社会达尔文主义"造成的自由资本主义无序竞争的弊端,中产阶级和知识文化各界有识之士自发地行动起来,开始了一场自下而上的社会改革运动。他们自愿组成民间组织,开展调查,发现并分析社会问题,寻求最佳的解决办法。这就是始于世纪初,一直延续到二战的进步主义运动。

正如西奥多·罗斯福总统那样,威尔逊总统响应了社会的改革呼声和行动,只不过他的进步主义改革更多是政府立法和行政职能的改革。理论上,他首先要论证是宪法分权制衡的造成联邦行政权力虚弱。从1885年以来,这位学者型政治家写了大量的文章阐述了立法权超越行政权的弊病，主张效仿欧洲议会模式，立法和行政联合执政，总统内阁成员必须有国会领袖的参与。目的在于从根本上扩大总统的权力。他认为，宪法修正案"是建立有效政府的先决条件。"重要的是，威尔逊把理论付诸实际。他提出的"新自由主义"强调，联邦政府的权力应该用来扫除社会和经济和政治特权，重建自由竞争，大企业垄断不仅应加以规约，而且应该彻底拆除。他抨击罗斯福的"新国家主义"是变相的专制，认为那会耗尽个体企业的能量，不受干涉的自由企业才是美国自由经济体制的基石。他亲自到国会发表咨文，与国会和政党紧密联系，最终制定并批准了一系列的宪法修正案和其他法案，成立了一些重要的联邦行政权力的委员会，从决策层面有力地推动了进步主义的改革运动。威尔逊执政期间通过的重大立法有：联邦储备委员会(1913)；铁路工人8小时工作制(1916)；联邦农业借贷法(1916)；建立联邦贸易委员会(1914)，以监管大公司垄断竞争；克莱顿反托拉斯法(1914)；直接普选国会参议员的宪法第17条修正案；禁酒的宪法第18条修正案；实现妇女选举权的宪法第19条修正案。

在国际政治舞台上，学者型的威尔逊总统具有理想主义的远见，却在现实中遭受了无情的幻灭。他对墨西哥和南美一些国家的武装干涉目的在于保持和巩固美国"后院"的稳定，从而更有底气的坚持不卷入欧洲冲突的中立原则。1914年9月，第一次世界大战爆发，威尔逊采用了观望政策，同时充当好人，调停交战各方。无奈德国潜艇不断击沉美国商船，国内参战呼声高涨，威尔逊只能暂时屏蔽孤立主义政策，于1917年4月2日在国会发表了充满理想主义的战争咨文，其中宣称，美国参战是为了永久的和平，"为了世界的民主，美国必须维护世界和平。"威尔逊这种以和平和民主为目的的战争思维注定在残酷的现实中被粉碎。美国参战时间很短，总共不过1年，伤亡人数却高达近6万人。德国的马克沁重机枪横扫英国骑兵的冲锋，天上的飞机和地上的毒气让成片的士兵瞬间死亡；西线堑壕中的泥泞中的尸臭和鼠患让活着的人精神崩溃。现代战争机

器初现大规模杀伤的威力，不断冲击着威尔逊的神经。他忧心忡忡的预测到人类战争的将来：这场战争"虽然使用了各种可怕的武器，但却无法与我们未来面临的战争相提并论。与德国人下次战争中将会使用的武器相比，他们在此次战争中使用的不过是小小的玩具而已。"由此，威尔逊的和平理想主义再次激发，他满怀热情地投入战后建设世界永久和平的理想之中。1918年12月至1919年7月间，威尔逊总统不顾国会的异议，多次往返长住巴黎，俨然一副救世主的姿态，打着"正义"、"自由"、"博爱"和"人道"的旗帜在巴黎和会上极力鼓吹他提出的"十四点"和平建议，力图说服各国建立"国际联盟"，一劳永逸地建立世界永久的和平。

威尔逊几近执拗地追求人类和平的理想，却看不到人类战争的必然。他获得了1919年度的诺贝尔和平奖，但却在那年的现实中遭受了一生最大的失败。《巴黎凡尔赛条约》并未全盘接受威尔逊的"十四点"建议，对战败国德国强加于领土割让，军事限制，

战争赔款等苛刻条件,为直接第二次世界大战埋下了伏笔;美国参议院也拒绝美国加入"国际联盟"。威尔逊感到深受打击,心灰意冷,健康每况愈下。但是他很快又聚集了生命最后的能量,巡游全国发表演讲,力图说服美国人民接受"国际联盟"。3周的时间之内,威尔逊总统行程万里,足迹遍布29个城市,做了40场大型的激情演讲。那时的威尔逊,犹如新世纪的先知救世主弥赛亚,看到人类面临自毁于自相残杀的劫难,大声呼号奔走于愚昧的人群之间,带领他们走出末日的危难。1919年9月,威尔逊回到华盛顿,精力耗尽,突然中风,颓然倒下。

由于威尔逊在政坛上多有学术名士的派头,固执己见,也得罪了包括民主党在内的不少人,因此,美国国会最终也没有批准巴黎和约,威尔逊病中闻之,心力交瘁,悲凉地对医生说道,如果他不是基督徒,宁愿就此结束自己的生命。他的以"国际联盟"维持世界永久和平的梦想也随着他的最后日子在经济大萧条和第二次世界大战的炮火中烟消云散。

可想而知,对于这样一位学者型的政治领导人,语言修辞演说的能力是何等地出色。威尔逊在大学期间就对语言修辞有着浓厚的兴趣,参加了演讲辩论俱乐部,悉心研习当代英国政治家的议会演讲。他担任过《普林斯顿人》杂志主编,参加了演讲辩论,后来还成为了著名的"杰斐逊演讲辩论协会"的主席。在从政的生涯中,他把语言修辞的能力广泛运用于公众演讲之中,在罗斯福的个人魅力式的演说的基础上,开创了所谓20世纪"演说总统"的先例。在此之前,总统更多的是发表仪式性的演说,而到了威尔逊,国家领导人的语言修辞能力成了赢得公众舆论,争取选票的有效手段。不过,威尔逊发挥他杰出的修辞和语言才能,却有些过犹未及,他过于依赖公众舆论,疏远甚至敌视台上的两党(特别是共和党)政客。大众的支持终敌不过两党政客的运作,他的语言魅力表现出他渊博的学问,也只能成为历史学家们笔下的记忆。

■ 演讲文(节选)

Second Presidential Inaugural Address

Woodrow Wilson

My Fellow citizens: The four years which have **elapsed** since last I stood in this place have been crowded with **counsel** and action of the most vital interest and consequence. Perhaps no equal period in our history has been so fruitful of important reforms in our economic and

elapse: pass

counsel: ideas; suggestion

	industrial life or so full of significant changes in the spirit and purpose of our political action. We have sought very thoughtfully to set our house in order, correct the **grosser** errors and **abuses** of our industrial life, liberate and quicken the processes of our national genius and energy, and lift our politics to a broader view of the people's essential interests.
gross: careless, obvious **abuse**: misuse	
distinction: area of attention	It is a record of singular variety and singular **distinction**. But I shall not attempt to review it. It speaks for itself and will be of increasing influence as the years go by. This is not the time for **retrospect**. It is time rather to speak our thoughts and purposes concerning the present and the immediate future.
retrospect: look back; review; recall	
legislation: law-making	Although we have centered counsel and action with such unusual concentration and success upon the great problems of domestic **legislation** to which we addressed ourselves four years ago, other matters have more and more forced themselves upon our attention—matters lying outside our own life as a nation and over which we had no control, but which, despite our wish to keep **free of them**, have drawn us more and more irresistibly into their own current and influence.
free of them: free from them	
apprehension: worry; anxiety **composite**: mixture **cosmopolitan**: global **indifferent**: careless; apathetic	It has been impossible to avoid them. They have affected the life of the whole world. They have shaken men everywhere with a passion and an **apprehension** they never knew before. It has been hard to preserve calm counsel while the thought of our own people **swayed** this way and that under their influence. We are a **composite** and **cosmopolitan** people. We are of the blood of all the nations that are at war. The currents of our thoughts as well as the currents of our trade run quick at all seasons back and forth between us and them. The war inevitably set its mark from the first alike upon our minds, our industries, our commerce, our politics and our social action. To be indifferent to it, or independent of it, was out of the question.
division: difference; faction	And yet all the while we have been conscious that we were not part of it. In that consciousness, despite many **divisions**, we have drawn closer together. We have been deeply wronged upon the seas, but we have not wished to wrong or injure in return; have retained throughout the consciousness of standing in some sort apart, intent upon an interest that **transcended** the immediate issues of the war itself.
transcend: surpass; go beyond **fair dealing**: equality in all forms of communication	As some of the injuries done us have become intolerable we have still been clear that we wished nothing for ourselves that we were not ready to demand for all mankind—**fair dealing**, justice, the freedom to

live and to be at ease against organized wrong.

It is in this spirit and with this thought that we have grown more and more aware, more and more certain that the part we wished to play was the part of those who mean to **vindicate** and fortify peace. We have been obliged to arm ourselves to make good our claim to a certain minimum of right and of freedom of action. We stand firm in armed neutrality since it seems that in no other way we can demonstrate what it is we insist upon and cannot forget. We may even be **drawn on**, by circumstances, not by our own purpose or desire, to a more active **assertion** of our rights as we see them and a more immediate association with the **great struggle** itself. But nothing will alter our thought or our purpose. They are too clear to be obscured. They are too deeply rooted in the principles of our national life to be altered. We desire neither conquest nor advantage. We wish nothing that can be **had** only at the cost of another people. We always **professed** unselfish purpose and we **covet** the opportunity to prove our professions are sincere.

There are many things still to be done at home, to clarify our own politics and add new **vitality** to the industrial processes of our own life, and we shall do them as time and opportunity serve, but we realize that the greatest things that remain to be done must be done with the whole world for stage and in cooperation with the wide and universal forces of mankind, and we are making our spirits ready for those things.

We are **provincials** no longer. The tragic events of the thirty months of vital **turmoil** through which we have just passed have made us citizens of the world. There can be no turning back. Our own fortunes as a nation are involved whether we would have it so or not.

And yet we are not the less Americans **on that account**. We shall be the more American if we but remain true to the principles in which we have been **bred**. They are not the principles of a province or of a single continent. We have known and boasted all along that they were the principles of a liberated mankind. These, therefore, are the things we shall stand for, whether in war or in peace:

That all nations are equally interested in the peace of the world and in the political stability of free peoples, and equally responsible for their maintenance; that the essential principle of peace is the actual equality of nations in all matters of right or privilege; that peace cannot securely or justly rest upon an armed balance of power; that governments derive all their just powers from the consent of the

vindicate: keep; safeguard; justify

drawn on: get involved in
assertion: firm claim
great struggle: (here) the war in Europe

had: obtained
profess: declare
covet: strongly desire

vitality: energy; living force

provincial: local
turmoil: noisy chaos; confusion

on that account: because of that
bred: brought up; raised

accessible: available; reachable

henceforth: from now on
see to it: oversee; take care of it
sternly: strictly

governed and that no other powers should be supported by the common thought, purpose or power of the family of nations; that the seas should be equally free and safe for the use of all peoples, under rules set up by common agreement and consent, and that, so far as practicable, they should be **accessible** to all upon equal terms; that national armaments shall be limited to the necessities of national order and domestic safety; that the community of interest and of power upon which peace must **henceforth** depend imposes upon each nation the duty of **seeing to it** that all influences proceeding from its own citizens meant to encourage or assist revolution in other states should be **sternly** and effectually suppressed and prevented.

...

We are to beware of all men who would turn the tasks and the necessities of the nation to their own private profit or use them for the building up of private power.

United alike in the conception of our duty and in the high resolve to perform it in the face of all men, let us dedicate ourselves to the great task to which we must now set our hand. For myself I beg your tolerance, your **countenance** and your united aid.

countenance: encouragement

The shadows that now lie dark upon our path will soon be dispelled, and we shall walk with the light all about us if we be but true to ourselves—to ourselves as we have wished to be known in the counsels of the world and in the thought of all those who love liberty and justice and the right **exalted.**

exalted: noble; elevated

■ 重点述评与提示

1. Perhaps no equal period in our history has been so fruitful of important reforms in our economic and industrial life or so full of significant changes in the spirit and purpose of our political action.

在西奥多·罗斯福进步主义的改革措施的基础上,威尔逊第一届总统任期在"新自由主义"的旗号下,实质上也继续了改革路线,通过多项立法进一步调整了资本主义生产关系的矛盾,加强了国家干预的力度。其中联邦储备委员会、联邦贸易委员会、克莱顿反托拉斯法,以及实现妇女选举权的宪法第19条修正案都是具有长远历史意义的成就。在此借第二任总统就职演说之机,将政绩昭示全国,也是美国总统第二任期演说常用的开场。

2. ...other matters have more and more forced themselves upon our attention—matters lying outside our own life as a nation and over which we had no control, but which, despite our wish to keep free of them, have drawn us more and more irresistibly into their own current and influence.

  此时第一次世界大战已经打了2年半,德国潜艇不断击沉美国商船。威尔逊虽然在竞选中许诺争取和平,美国不卷入战争,但他已经意识到,美国严守中立可能只是一厢情愿。事实上,此后不到一个月,威尔逊就向国会发表了战争咨文。由此可见,他说这番话的无奈。

3. We are a composite and cosmopolitan people. We are of the blood of all the nations that are at war.

  第一句话有两层意思:其一,美国人口构成的是世界性的;其二,美国人应该积极加入国际事务。第二句话暗示美国人可能被卷入战争,告诫人民做好思想准备。

4. It is in this spirit and with this thought that we have grown more and more aware, more and more certain that the part we wished to play was the part of those who mean to vindicate and fortify peace.

  这里体现了威尔逊一直坚持的国际和平理想主义精神,也是一个学者型领袖坚持用和平结束战争的理想。下文说道,即使不得不参战,也不是为了胜利,而是为了和平。这为威尔逊战后的和平努力埋下了伏笔。

5. ...but we realize that the greatest things that remain to be done must be done with the whole world for stage and in cooperation with the wide and universal forces of mankind, and we are making our spirits ready for those things.

  重申人类大家庭意识。不论参战与否,这是威尔逊心中的信念。他在战后提出并极力为之奔走的"国际联盟"正是建立在这一理念上的。这里,可见,美国孤立主义意识形态已经开始动摇。

6. We are provincials no longer. The tragic events of the thirty months of vital turmoil through which we have just passed have made us citizens of the world.

  世界大战使美国人眼界打开,成为世界公民!这是对战争的积极评价,实际上是在挖美国中立政策和孤立主义的墙角,为几个星期之后宣布参战做好舆论铺垫。

7. They are not the principles of a province or of a single continent. We have known and boasted all along that they were the principles of a liberated mankind.

  威尔逊在宣布美国参战时曾宣布:"为了世界的民主,必须首先让世界安全。"(The world must be made safe for democracy)战后,他又宣称,他的十四点建议将使世界实现永久的和平,因为那是建立在人类民主自由的原则上的。本句中所谓的"原则"也是十四点建议原则基础,其实质就是,各国不论大小都共享世界资源,也有责任捍卫世界和平,因此也有必要建立一个世界性的联盟以保证各国的政治独立和领土完整。

8. We are to beware of all men who would turn the tasks and the necessities of the nation to their own private profit or use them for the building up of private power.

　　此句话在反对独裁的老调中宣扬了美国政治体制的优越,但是这一理想很快就被希特勒和墨索里尼等大独裁者的崛起击破。这也是各协约国在巴黎和会上各取其利造成的直接后果。

■ 思考及讨论题

1. What are some important issues during the 1912 presidential campaign?
2. What are some fundamental prepositions of Wilson's "New Freedom"?
3. How was Wilson's idealism most obviously expressed during his second term as the president?
4. Why the US Senate rejected Wilson's "Fourteen Points" and why "The League of Nations" was not ratified by the US Congress?

■ 阅读书目

1. Cranston, Ruth. *The Story of Woodrow Wilson: Twenty-Eighth President of the United States, Pioneer of World Democracy.* New York: Simon & Schuster, 1945.
2. Tumulty, Joseph P. *Woodrow Wilson as I Know Him.* New York: Doubleday, 1921.
3. Clements, Kendrick A. "Woodrow Wilson and Administrative Reform" in *Presidential Studies Quarterly*, Spring 1998.
4. Wasniewski, Mathew A. "The Presidents As Statesmen: Woodrow Wilson and the Constitution" *The Virginia Magazine of History and Biography* in Autumn 1998.

第二十八讲
富兰克林·德拉诺·罗斯福
(Franklin Daleno Roosevelt 1882—1945)

■ 政治历史评述

富兰克林·德拉诺·罗斯福：
挽救现代资本主义的新政领袖，轮椅上运筹帷幄的战胜者

在美国历史上，富兰克林·罗斯福与亚伯拉罕·林肯一样，都是在艰难时世中力挽狂澜于既倒的伟人，但他却也不是横空出世的弥赛亚救世主。他的教育经历和仕途奋斗历程与他的远房表叔西奥多·罗斯福多有相似，两人都似乎循着一条罗斯福家族从政的既定道路一路奋斗，走进白宫。与西奥多一样，1882年1月30日出生在纽约的富兰克林也是生来体弱，从小在海德公园受到父母悉心的家庭教育，14岁离家到马萨诸塞州北边的格罗顿学院上学，后来顺利进入哈佛大学，在大学期间成绩平平，却十分热衷于学生社团活动，担任过校报主编。与西奥多一样，富兰克林也在20多岁进入纽约州议会，也因为总统助选有功而被委任海军助理部长职位，此后也当选纽约州州长。在此基础上，西奥多43岁继任总统，47岁成为当选总统，富兰克林50岁胜选成为美国第32届总统。两人都成为了纽约的罗斯福家族的光荣和骄傲。西奥多享年仅61岁，富兰克林也只活了63岁。然而，两人在许多方面却也截然不同：西奥多善于写书，政治上喜欢出点风头，不计后果，而富兰克林则一门心思从政，在政界踏实苦干，着眼未来；在政见上，西奥多是铁杆共和党人，而富兰克林则是坚定的民主党人；两人都对身体疾病做过乐观而顽强的抗争，所不同的是，西奥多战胜疾病，探险的足迹遍布世界各大洲，而富兰克林在1921年人近中年却罕见地患上灰质脊髓炎，从此在轮椅上坚强地历经了自己忙碌而充实的政治生涯。此外，西奥多竞选总统许诺只任一届，而富兰克林则在轮椅上努力掌权，连任四届，在美国历史上空前绝后。

20世纪上半叶，两位罗斯福总统个性鲜明，政绩出众，各领风骚，这一时期的美国几乎可以标榜为罗斯福时代。但两人最大的，也是最有意义的不同就是：老罗斯福执政于美国资本主义自由竞争经济上升和繁荣的年代，他的进步主义改革措施有效地调整了资本主义的生产关系，在一个相对和平的世界格局中提升了美国的世界地位；小罗斯福则不同，他上台时，正值全球经济大萧条，美国经济濒临崩溃，他临危受命，大权独揽，推行新政，挽救了美国的资本主义；在他的任内，第二次世界大战的风云冲破了美国长期的孤立主义，他领导美国卷入战争，走向胜利，战后使美国真正的现代的世界霸主。

1932年,富兰克林·罗斯福以选举人团472票对59票的绝对优势,击败了一蹶不振的在任总统赫伯特·胡佛,入主白宫。此时,始于1929年的经济大萧条席卷全美。至1932年,工业产值大跌50%,企业投资锐减90%,农产品价格一落千丈;全美5500多家银行纷纷倒闭,华尔街股市停业,成千上万的家庭辛辛苦苦积攒的存款一夜之间化为乌有,幸免于难的家庭把贬值的钞票藏在床垫下;失业率从1929年的3%攀升至1932的50%,贫病和饥饿威胁着1600万失业人口;无家可归的人们成群夜宿公园,桥洞,甚至寻觅山洞住宿;在华盛顿州,找工作找得发疯的人们甚至纵火烧山,为的是盼望有消防部门前来雇用他们去灭火。在城市,到处可见饥饿的孩子们在垃圾桶中翻翻捡捡,却找不到任何东西可以充饥。

人们开始绝望,1930年至1932年,美国的自杀率竟猛增25%。与此同时,社会危机日愈加重:银行外排队等候的人群愤怒地号召人们暴力兑现;纽约和芝加哥爆发了反饥饿游行,失业工人骚乱事件频频发生,骚乱的人群冲击商业区;在内布拉斯加州,4千饥民冲击并占领了州府大楼,在西雅图,5千饥民冲进政府,在芝加哥,一年没领到工资的教师上街示威,遭到了警察大棒驱赶;1932大选之年,2万多名一战老兵饥肠辘辘,衣衫褴褛,走上首府华盛顿街头,要求兑现退伍补贴,却遭到荷枪实弹的军队开着坦克将他们冲散。鉴于此,各政府部门如临大敌,加强警戒。罗斯福就职仪式一周前,华盛顿市"就像一座战时遭受围攻的城池",国会山联邦大楼各出入口都有军警把守,屋顶上架设了机枪。各大城市的军警接到命令,对于那些敢于持枪冲击政府大楼的乱民,杀无赦。

这就是1933年3月4日富兰克林·罗斯福总统宣誓就职时面对的美国。他需要的是自信和勇气,需要采取强硬的,甚至是独裁式的政府措施和行动。在就职演说中,这位被政敌轻视为"残疾人"的总统宣布:"我们唯一必须恐惧的就是恐惧本身",他要求国会按"国家遭受外敌入侵"的紧急状况,赋予总统"最大的行政权力"来实施"新政",以战胜这场空前的危机。

罗斯福的"新政"全面扩张总统行政职权,按照3R计划,即复兴(Recover)、救济(Relief)、改革(Reform)三个步骤展开,持续8年,在金融货币政策和银行整顿、工农业复兴、以工代赈开辟国有公园、修建政府基础工程、改善劳工关系、建立住房和医疗社会保障体系等各个方面全面实施政府对经济的干预。"新政"期间,罗斯福在其"智囊团"的协同下颁布了大量的法案,其中第一个"百日新政"期间就颁布实施了15条主要的法案。这些强制性的政府措施对恢复金融秩序,刺激工农业生产,创造就业机会等方面起到了重要作用,整体上重新建立了公众信心,为二战后的经济全面复兴奠定了基础。2年后即1935年夏,二次新政开始,罗斯福强化总统权力,凌驾国会之上,提高企业税收,动用联邦巨额资金,面向大众实施全面地救济和社会保障计划,其中包括就业保障、保障工资、失业保险、医疗保险和生活救济等各个方面,使几千万中下层人民直接受益,同时在爱国主义的旗号下鼓励了大规模的国家基础设施建设,是为"新政"之高潮。

罗斯福"新政"的三板斧几乎砍掉了资本主义市场自由竞争的古训，颠覆了社会达尔文主义"适者生存"的信条，获得了广大人民群众的支持，也树立了自己林肯式"强硬总统"和"人道主义者"的形象。同时，他也深知"得民心者得天下"的道理，借助无线电广播技术，以"炉边谈话"的亲民方式，用通俗易懂的语言，经常向公众讲述时局形势和政府的方针和政策，拉近与民众的距离，因而赢得了人民广泛的支持。在他们心目中，罗斯福是"真正关心劳动阶级的唯一的总统"，"前所未有的圣人"，甚至一贯支持共和党的黑人都把大部分的选票投给了罗斯福。

当然，"新政"独揽朝纲，连续立法，带有"劫富济贫"意味的政策也受最高法院、国会保守派议员和企业界一些高收入人群的激烈反对。他们控诉"新政"的一些法案违宪，是独裁者的"苛政"，是打击成功者，鼓励懒汉的国家社会主义，是变相的法西斯主义。

在反对罗斯福"新政"的保守派中，罗斯福同时代的约翰·弗莱因可谓急先锋。这位著名记者和作家在1948年出版了一本长达450页的书《罗斯福神话》。这本书一直是研究"新政"和罗斯福其人的另类权威之作。书中用切身的经历和辛辣的笔触，把罗斯福描述成一个毫无原则立场，满口俏皮话的政治流氓，是迎合大众求变心理的机会主义者。在弗莱因的笔下，"新政"不过是墨索里尼法西斯主义启示下的强权闹剧，罗斯福的"智囊团"成员也是一些不懂经济，自以为是的卑琐之人。书中内容丰富，史实真切，论述不乏精到之处。读之不由产生"兼听则明"之感。

不过，弗莱因对罗斯福形象的负面刻画，也可以让读者悟到罗斯福及其"新政"至今仍然广受赞誉的奥秘：罗斯福不是一个教条主义者，而是一个与时俱进的实用主义者。在社会和经济陷于空前危机的时刻，任何的主义都不是解决问题的灵丹妙药，任何既定的原则都是苍白无力的。相反，只有解放思想，研究实际问题，敢于采取行动，敢于在错误中摸索前行的勇气，方可有望解决大多数人的大多数问题，从而在实践的基础上构建新的可操作平台。这种"摸着石头过河"的精神也在不同政治制度下纷繁的社会和经济实践中证明是十分有效的。在这个意义上，美国著名喜剧演员克劳契奥·马克斯(Groucho Marx)那句俏皮话："这些就是我的原则，如果你不喜欢，我还有别的"却也正好道出了富兰克林·罗斯福处理危机的高明。

富兰克林·罗斯福"摸着石头过河"的高明还表现在随后的世界危局之中，他克服了强大的孤立主义一贯政策，最终领导美国在反法西斯战争中取得胜利。1939年始，罗斯福对纳粹德国在欧洲咄咄逼人的态势感到忧心忡忡，也十分关注日本帝国在亚洲发动的侵华战争。从长远看，法西斯称霸世界的企图终将威胁到美国的安全。但是，美国从华盛顿开始的中立和孤立主义外交政策一以贯之，一战短期参战欧洲的无奈还在反省之中。罗斯福早在1937年就试图改变美国公众冷眼向洋看世界的心理，表示一旦欧洲开战，美国将严守中立，但应给予民主国家尽可能的支援。1939年，希特勒进攻占领波兰,英法对德宣战。罗斯福发表"炉边谈话",表示美国严守中立,但同时也不忘告诫美国人民没有世界的和平就没有美国的和平,号召美国人民对事态的恶化做好充分的精神准备,同时采取行动,加紧战备。不久法国沦陷,英法联军在敦刻尔克几乎全军覆没,英国危在旦夕。面对英国首相丘吉尔的告急和求援,罗斯福开始触摸中立政策和孤立主义的底线,从外交偏袒英国走向实际的物资援助并表示将在大西洋上为物资商船护航。这样做实则向战争迈出了关键的一步。为了避免与孤立主义发生正面冲突,他巧妙地提出向盟国"租借"战争物资,此举属"非战争行为"。另一方面,他提出,美国应成为民主国家的巨大军火库,实则创造大量就业,开足美国军工生产。同时,他又采取行动,对日本实行石油禁运,以遏制其在太平洋的扩张。1941年6月,希特勒发动闪电战,全面入侵苏联。罗斯福利用"租借"的名义,同样向斯大林提供了军援。此时,美国的中立法已经名存实亡,孤立主义也在严酷的现实面前也行将瓦解。在整个过程中,罗斯福

心里明白战争已经迫近,这是不可抗拒的趋势。现在看来,1941年12月7日日本对珍珠港的偷袭也只是加速了美国参战的进程,而不是其参战的终极原因。也可以说,没有罗斯福执着而又巧妙的尝试和周旋,美国也许不可能最终以战胜国的姿态出现在1945年2月的雅尔塔会议,美国也许还在孤立主义的阴影之中偏安一隅,在狭小的民主视野中持续着新教伦理的传统。

总之,不论神化还是魔化罗斯福,在资本主义体制框架内的这场"新政"改革和美国在二战中对孤立主义的终结,成就卓然于历史,昭彰于现实。罗斯福后的美国,资本主义生成了自身的调节机制,呈现出福利国家的景象。政府行政体制完善,权力扩大,面对冷战和纷扰的世界,展现了大国吞吐的宏大气象,在20世纪下半叶的核时代中稳坐世界霸主的地位。

罗斯福从政时间长,总统又连任四届,政治演讲口才自然得到良好的锻炼。他学生时期成绩不佳,在哈佛对各门功课也没有狠下工夫,在学生社团中活跃异常,自然也对修辞演讲和公共辩论尤其感兴趣,常凝神细听哈佛文学教授大声背诵文学名篇。1923年当选纽约州长后,他开始认真训练演讲口才技能。但除了频繁即兴的竞选演说,正式演讲更多还是依靠他的演讲写作班子。

罗斯福第一届总统就职演说一直被认为是佳作,堪比林肯的第二届总统就职演说和肯尼迪的总统就职演说。这篇演说由写作班子集体完成,但罗斯福对草稿做了大幅度的修改和补充,基本表达了他的思想。演说的逻辑结构十分清晰,是十分务实的解决问题的结构,语言平实有力,修辞格多用首词重复、尾词重复和排比句,以鼓舞士气,强调行动。文中多次使用战争比喻,加重危机意识,以达到总统权力集中,凌驾国会之目的。这篇演讲通过无线电向全国广播。演讲后几个星期之内,大约50万封信从全国各地雪片般飞来,其中一封信这样说道:"你在演说中表达了对全国民众的人性关怀,太棒了!"

演讲文（节选）

First Presidential Inaugural Address

Franklin Delano Roosevelt

I am certain that my fellow Americans expect that on my **induction** into the Presidency I will address them with a **candor** and a decision which the present situation of our Nation impels. This is preeminently the time to speak the truth, the whole truth, frankly and boldly. Nor need we shrink from honestly facing conditions in our country today. This great Nation will endure as it has endured, will revive and will prosper. So, first of all, let me assert my firm belief that the only thing we have to fear is fear itself—**nameless**, unreasoning, unjustified terror which **paralyzes** needed efforts to convert retreat into advance. In every dark hour of our national life a leadership of frankness and vigor has met with that understanding and support of the people themselves which is essential to victory. I am convinced that you will again give that support to leadership in these **critical** days.

In such a spirit on my part and on yours we face our common difficulties. They concern, thank God, only **material things**. Values have shrunken to fantastic levels; taxes have risen; our ability to pay has fallen; government of all kinds is faced by serious **curtailment** of income; the means of exchange are frozen in the currents of trade; the withered leaves of industrial enterprise lie on every side; farmers find no markets for their produce; the savings of many years in thousands of families are gone.

More important, a host of unemployed citizens face the **grim** problem of existence, and an equally great number **toil** with little return. Only a foolish optimist can deny the dark realities of the moment.

Yet our **distress** comes from no failure of **substance**. We are stricken by no plague of locusts. Compared with the perils which our forefathers conquered because they believed and were not afraid, we have still much to be thankful for. Nature still offers her bounty and human efforts have multiplied it. Plenty is at our doorstep, but a generous use of it **languishes** in the very sight of the supply. Primarily this is because the rulers of the exchange of mankind's goods have failed, through their own stubbornness and their own incompetence,

---

induction: inauguration; beginning office
candor: honesty; straightforwardness

nameless: obscure; unspeakable
paralyze: made inactive

critical: life-or-death
material things: economy, not political
curtailment: decrease; reduction

grim: very serious
toil: work hard

distress: disaster; danger; anxiety
substance: (here) real economic production

languish: fail; becoming depressed

abdicate: give up (the leadership) **unscrupulous**: greedy **indicted**: accused of **outworn**: old; unworkable	have admitted their failure, and **abdicated**. Practices of the **unscrupulous** money changers stand **indicted** in the court of public opinion, rejected by the hearts and minds of men.

have admitted their failure, and **abdicated**. Practices of the **unscrupulous** money changers stand **indicted** in the court of public opinion, rejected by the hearts and minds of men.

True they have tried, but their efforts have been cast in the pattern of an **outworn** tradition. Faced by failure of credit they have proposed only the lending of more money. Stripped of the lure of profit by which to induce our people to follow their false leadership, they have resorted to **exhortations**, pleading tearfully for restored confidence. They know only the rules of a generation of self-seekers. They have no vision, and when there is no vision the people perish.

exhortation: persuasion

The money changers have fled from their **high seats** in the temple of our civilization. We may now restore that temple to the ancient truths. The measure of the restoration lies in the extent to which we apply social values more noble than mere monetary profit.

high seat: (here) false nobleness

Happiness lies not in the mere possession of money; it lies in the joy of achievement, in the **thrill** of creative effort. The joy and moral stimulation of work no longer must be forgotten in the mad chase of **evanescent** profits. These dark days will be worth all they cost us if they teach us that our true destiny is not to be **ministered** unto but to minister to ourselves and to our fellow men.

thrill: intensive concentration

evanescent: short-lived; quickly disappearing

ministered unto: to be handled by

Recognition of the falsity of material wealth as the standard of success goes hand in hand with the abandonment of the false belief that public office and high political position are to be valued only by the standards of **pride of place** and personal profit; and there must be an end to a conduct in banking and in business which too often has given to a sacred trust the likeness of **callous** and selfish wrongdoing. Small wonder that confidence languishes, for it thrives only on honesty, on honor, on the sacredness of obligations, on faithful protection, on unselfish performance; without them it cannot live.

pride of place: social status by official position

callous: cold; carelessness; heartless; insensitive

Restoration calls, however, not for changes in **ethics** alone. This Nation asks for action, and action now.

ethics: (here) moral justification

Our greatest primary task is to put people to work. This is no unsolvable problem if we face it wisely and courageously. It can be accomplished in part by direct **recruiting** by the Government itself, treating the task as we would treat the emergency of a war, but at the same time, through this employment, accomplishing greatly needed projects to stimulate and reorganize the use of our natural resources.

recruiting: official use; employment

Hand in hand with this we must frankly recognize the overbalance of population in our industrial centers and, by engaging on a national scale in a redistribution, **endeavor** to provide a better use of the land for those best fitted for the land. The task can be helped

endeavor: try hard

by definite efforts to raise the values of agricultural products and with this the power to purchase the **output** of our cities. It can be helped by preventing realistically the tragedy of the growing loss through **foreclosure** of our small homes and our farms. It can be helped by insistence that the Federal, State, and local governments act **forthwith** on the demand that their cost be drastically reduced. It can be helped by the unifying of relief activities which today are often scattered, uneconomical, and unequal. It can be helped by national planning for and supervision of all forms of transportation and of communications and other **utilities** which have a definitely public character. There are many ways in which it can be helped, but it can never be helped merely by talking about it. We must act and act quickly. ...

With this **pledge** taken, I assume unhesitatingly the leadership of this great army of our people dedicated to a disciplined attack upon our common problems.

Action in this image and to this end is **feasible** under the form of government which we have inherited from our ancestors. Our Constitution is so simple and practical that it is possible always to meet extraordinary needs by changes in emphasis and arrangement without loss of essential form. That is why our constitutional system has proved itself the most **superbly** enduring political **mechanism** the modern world has produced. It has met every stress of vast expansion of territory, of foreign wars, of bitter internal **strife**, of world relations.

It is to be hoped that the normal balance of executive and legislative authority may be wholly adequate to meet the **unprecedented** task before us. But it may be that an unprecedented demand and need for undelayed action may call for temporary departure from that normal balance of public procedure.

I am prepared under my constitutional duty to recommend the measures that a **stricken** nation in the midst of a stricken world may require. These measures, or such other measures as the Congress may build out of its experience and wisdom, I shall seek, within my constitutional authority, to bring to speedy **adoption**.

But in the event that the Congress shall fail to take one of these two courses, and in the event that the national emergency is still critical, I shall not **evade** the clear course of duty that will then confront me. I shall ask the Congress for the one remaining instrument to meet the crisis—broad Executive power to wage a war against the emergency, as great as the power that would be given to me if we were in fact invaded by a foreign **foe**.

...

---

output: (here) industrial and commercial products
foreclosure: taking possession of the property because of the failure to pay the mortgage
forthwith: right away; quickly
utility: facility

pledge: oath; determination

feasible: workable; appropriate

superbly: perfectly; most excellent
mechanism: workable system
strife: conflict; clash

unprecedented: never happened before; with no example

stricken: beaten; suffering

adoption: acceptance for action

evade: avoid; shun from

foe: hated enemy

第二十八讲 | Franklin Daleno Roosevelt

■ 重点述评与提示

1. I am certain that my fellow Americans expect that on my induction into the Presidency I will address them with a candor and a decision which the present situation of our Nation impels. This is preeminently the time to speak the truth, the whole truth, frankly and boldly.

　　开场申明敢于面对经济大萧条的真实,要求人民重建对政府的信心,也表示了本届政府的务实精神。此话的矛头也直指前任胡佛总统,指责他不敢面对不断恶化的经济,反而躲在白宫通过媒体不断宣布经济已经开始复苏。

2. So, first of all, let me assert my firm belief that the only thing we have to fear is fear itself—nameless, unreasoning, unjustified terror which paralyzes needed efforts to convert retreat into advance.

　　"我们唯一必须恐惧的就是恐惧本身。"这是美国人耳熟能详的罗斯福名句。重尾句式的应用加重了对"恐惧"的否定,起到了良好的鼓动作用,同时,后续的同位语用战场进退的喻像,增添了鼓舞士气,赢得胜利的决心。

3. Primarily this is because the rulers of the exchange of mankind's goods have failed, through their own stubbornness and their own incompetence, have admitted their failure, and abdicated. Practices of the unscrupulous money changers stand indicted in the court of public opinion, rejected by the hearts and minds of men.

　　在一般人眼里,经济大萧条始于股市和银行倒闭,其原因就是银行家和股市投机者的贪婪,他们蒙蔽股民,吸引资金不断投入,制造出大量的金融泡沫。大众却不懂得资本主义自由竞争和无序化生产导致经济危机这个道理。罗斯福在此一下子就找到了大众千夫所指的"替罪羊",即贪婪的银行家和股票投机家。

4. They know only the rules of a generation of self-seekers. They have no vision, and when there is no vision the people perish.

　　这是罗斯福意图建立领袖权威的绝好表述:资本主义自由经济鼓励资本家唯利是图,使他们看不见宏观的经济体制和大局,只有远见卓识的领袖,方能维护国家和人民的长远利益。

5. The money changers have fled from their high seats in the temple of our civilization. We may now restore that temple to the ancient truths. The measure of the restoration lies in the extent to which we apply social values more noble than mere monetary

profit.

　　罗斯福在此处用了《圣经》典故：耶稣基督来到耶路撒冷，进入了上帝圣殿，驱逐了放高利贷者。借此，罗斯福表示，银行家和金融投机家已经遁出文明之殿，新的政府将重建社会价值观，将社会的利益置于个人利益至上。这样的具有人道主义和社会主义意识的宣教当然受到人民的普遍欢迎。

6. Recognition of the falsity of material wealth as the standard of success goes hand in hand with the abandonment of the false belief that public office and high political position are to be valued only by the standards of pride of place and personal profit;

　　见证了经济大萧条的巨大破坏力后，这应该是美国进步主义改革以来对资本主义价值观和政治观念最深刻的反思：物质财富并不是成功的标志，一个人的政治地位也并不能用社会地位和物质利益来衡量。句子松散，长于思量，末尾的连续头韵给人与语重心长之感。

7. Restoration calls, however, not for changes in ethics alone. This Nation asks for action, and action now.

　　发现问题，分析问题，解决问题，这是这篇演讲结构的三个层次。至此，经过前两个步骤，已经找到问题的症结，应该提出解决问题的办法。罗斯福对此的答案是：见于行动。通过对 action 一词在省略句式中的重复，简洁有力地突出了演说的行动指向。

8. With this pledge taken, I assume unhesitatingly the leadership of this great army of our people dedicated to a disciplined attack upon our common problems.

　　罗斯福再次用战争意象，突出了总统在紧急状况下集中行使权力的紧迫性，为下文向国会要求扩大总统职权做好了铺垫。

9. Our Constitution is so simple and practical that it is possible always to meet extraordinary needs by changes in emphasis and arrangement without loss of essential form.

　　70 年前，林肯根据实际需要，对美国宪法条款做灵活的解释和运用，强固并扩大总统职权，从而能够领导美国在危难时刻转危为安。此时，罗斯福面临的危难可比国家分裂，对宪法采取这样的态度是与时俱进的务实态度。句中用"simple"和"practical"，事实证明，这也是美国宪法具有持久的生命力的特点。

10. I shall ask the Congress for the one remaining instrument to meet the crisis—broad Executive power to wage a war against the emergency, as great as the power that

would be given to me if we were in fact invaded by a foreign foe.

经过上文的再三铺垫,罗斯福此处明确提出,将不得不以国家受到外敌入侵的紧急状态为由,扩大总统行政职权,不经国会立法而采取必要的措施,解救国家于危难之中。罗斯福"新政"富有成效的事实证明,对社会经济实施强有力的国家行政干预对经济的复苏是至关重要的。罗斯福此处有言在先,国会也予以了积极的配合。当然,他后来为此也遭受了国会宪法保守派和最高法院的攻击,这是后话。

■ 思考及讨论题

1. What could be the main cause of "the Great Depression" and how did it start?
2. Why were the relief measures taken by President Herbert Hoover not effective?
3. How did "The New Deal" get started? And what were some of its important measures during the first hundred days?
4. Do you agree that FDR has led a socialist reform on capitalistic ill? Explain your reasons.

■ 阅读书目

1. Heale, M. J. *Franklin D. Roosevelt: The New Deal and War*. London and New York: Routledge, 1999.
2. Flynn, John T. *The Roosevelt Myth*. New York: Devin-Adair, 1948.
3. Ryan, Halford. *U.S. Presidents as Orators: A Bio-Critical Sourcebook*. Westport, CT: Greenwood Press, 1995.
4. Higgs, Robert. "The Mythology of Roosevelt and the New Deal" in *Freeman*. September, 1998.

第九章 ‖ 冷战与民权运动

For man holds in his mortal hands the power to abolish all forms of human poverty and all forms of human life.... Ask not what your country can do for you—ask what you can do for your country.

—John F. Kennedy

We know through painful experience that freedom is never voluntarily given by the oppressor; it must be demanded by the oppressed.

—Martin Luther King, Jr.

It'll be the ballot or the bullet. It'll be liberty or it'll be death.

—Malcolm X

Preview Questions

01/

How was the so-called "the Cold War" shaped up by the end of the World War II?

02/

What were some dangerous crises as a result of the Cold War?

03/

What were the major goals of the Civil Rights Movement?

04/

Why the Civil Rights Movement was known as the "Second Reconstruction"?

第二十九讲
约翰·F. 肯尼迪(John F. Kennedy 1917—1963)

■ 政治历史评述

约翰·F. 肯尼迪：与命运抗争的年轻总统，"新边疆"的开拓者

　　1943年8月1日，南太平洋所罗门群岛以外的海域，黑夜的浓雾之中，日本海军驱逐舰"天雾"号把正在执行巡逻任务的美国P—109号美国鱼雷艇撞成两截，艇上13名美国官兵两人当即死亡，其余大多受伤，纷纷跳海逃命。艇长约翰·肯尼迪落水后沉着冷静，忍着背部的伤痛带领幸存士兵乘着夜色，借着艇上的漂浮物，向附近的小岛游去。肯尼迪用牙齿咬住绳索，拖着一个受重伤的战友奋力挣扎，在冰冷的海水中浸泡了15多个小时，游程近5公里，终于抵达附近一个荒芜的小岛，他们靠海贝和雨水维持着生命，5天之后终于在另一荒岛上找到一个土著人，肯尼迪在一个椰子壳上刻下一条信息："土著人知道位置，11人幸存，需要小船，肯尼迪"。此后，这个好心的当地人找到附近的美军，奄奄一息的肯尼迪和他的士兵们终于获救。后来，肯尼迪成为了美国总统，这个救命椰子壳被一直陈放在白宫椭圆形办公室的桌子上，后被肯尼迪图书馆收藏。

　　战后，肯尼迪二战中的英雄事迹被四处传扬，人们把他看成了坚毅和勇气的化身。不过，他本人对此倒也十分地淡定。一次记者问他如何成为临危不惧，坚韧果敢的英雄，他的回答是："当英雄容易，因为他们撞沉了我的船。"这是肯尼迪一贯的低调风格。其实，当他跻身政坛，一步步逼近美国总统宝座时，他的欢呼者和支持者又何尝知道，电视屏幕上肯尼迪平和帅气的面庞后，隐藏了了多少常人无法忍受病痛和精神打击。20世纪前半叶，美国一连几任总统都顽强战胜了自身的身体病痛，锲而不舍地在政治上出人头地，因而受到美国人民的尊敬。西奥多·罗斯福常常哮喘窒息，却坚持训练"强度人生"，终成"硬汉"；威尔逊身体多病，反复休学或退学，终靠顽强写作，拿到博士学位；富兰克林·罗斯福更是令人惊叹，生来体弱，人近中年却下肢瘫痪，却硬是身残志坚，领导美国度过大萧条的危机和二战的烽烟。而肯尼迪的艰难却是长期的身心折磨，在一次次痛苦的抉择中反复经历了生与死的考验。

　　约翰·肯尼迪1917年5月29日诞生在离波士顿市区10公里的布鲁克莱恩小镇上，父亲约瑟夫·肯尼迪是天主教徒，多年的打拼和金融投机积累了大量的财富，后来担任了罗斯福政府的驻英大使。这位执着的父亲反复教导几个儿子，凡事都要争第一，取得第二名就是失败。他的用心就是培养儿子成为美国总统。约翰生下来先天性脊椎缺损，2岁染上了猩红热并过敏症，不得不在波士顿市医院隔离治疗，孤寂中没有了童年的欢乐。而这才是他短暂的一生中长期的病痛折磨的开端。此后,他相继患上了百日咳、阑尾炎、疟疾、黄疸、结肠炎、十二指肠溃疡、贫血症,肝炎,后来竟然又染上阿狄森病,即慢性肾上腺皮质功能减退症,每天疼痛不堪,必须注射可的松来缓解。1954年10月21日,37岁的参议员肯尼迪在曼哈顿医院秘密接受了脊椎双拼接手术,在背部安装金属托架,但却引起了大面积炎症,生命危在旦夕,天主教堂执事为他举行了最后的安魂仪式。但是,肯尼迪又奇迹般地活过来,而且,他在恢复期间写成了《勇敢者纪事》一书畅销全国,获得普利策奖。除了长年的病魔,肯尼迪的精神也遭受了一连串的打击。一方面,自幼被隔离治疗,孤寂压抑,后来也是因为身体病弱,在校学习成绩表现中下,申请哈佛被拒,转而普林斯顿大学。虽然因父亲关系,勉强进入哈佛就学,但学习断断续续,导师评价不佳,心理一直受到压抑;另一方面,家庭连遭悲剧:27岁那年,他的哥哥小约瑟夫驾驶的飞机在英国上空爆炸,肯尼迪家族最有希望当上总统的男丁长空殒命;不到一个月,妹夫在法国阵亡,噩耗传来,妹妹凯瑟琳痛不欲生,两年之后她乘坐的飞机在法国失事,追寻亡夫之魂。据密友回忆,肯尼迪此后私下常表现消沉,把每一天都当做生命的最后一天,情绪低落,可见一斑。

但是,父亲约瑟夫必须继续实现他肯尼迪家族的"总统梦",为此他的儿子们必须前仆后继。他对杰克说:"我们必须继续。"一如既往地要儿子参加竞选,争当第一。于是,肯尼迪抖擞精神,投入竞选,从不在公众面前流露丝毫的宿命情绪;他在1960的大选中面对千百万的电视观众,展示出一个精力充沛,思维敏捷的年轻领袖的形象,一举战胜共和党老牌政治家理查德·尼克松,当选美国总统,实现了父亲多年为之奋斗的夙愿。可惜,肯尼迪身心磨炼,艰苦玉成,却在成功的巅峰终于没有躲过命运的子弹。1963年11月22日,肯尼迪总统的头颅在得克萨斯州达拉斯市被刺客的两颗子弹打穿,不治身亡。

作为"新一代美国人"的总统,肯尼迪的施政纲领很鲜明:美国人不能满足于所谓"富裕社会"而止步不前,在60年代要开拓新的边疆,那就是寻找新的科技机遇,走向太空,同时也面对新的和平和战争的挑战,扫除愚昧和无知,克服新的种族偏见和贫困现象,建立社会的公正。这一生机勃勃的"新边疆"精神得到广大选民的支持,使这位美国史上最年轻的总统能够在短短的一千天中,在与倾向保守的国会的谨慎博弈中,发挥了有效的政治策略,在国内改革和国际冷战中都取得了显著的政绩。

在国内改革事务中,他灵活运用行政权力,推动实行了一系列改革措施,维护了社会平等,消除新的贫困。这些措施中主要包括:废除雇员性别歧视,实行男女同工同酬;提出社会医疗制度,联邦财政支持老年人和残疾人医疗服务;提高最低工资水平;通过立法推动了城市住房建设和就业培训;提出改变传统移民法中的国家移民人口指标政策,树立美国自由平等和更人性化的形象。同时,面对当时迅猛发展的民权运动,肯尼迪迫于南方种族隔离势力在国会的压力,谨慎地表示道义上的支持。除此之外,他也尽可能地行使行政权力给予响应,比如派遣国民警卫队保护黑人入学;保护"自由乘车行抗议者"不少种族隔离分子的暴力袭扰等。他还提出立法禁止在联邦政府机构范围内实现种族隔离;尽可能把一些黑人聘用到联邦政府重要位置。肯尼迪曾邀请民权运动的领袖马丁·路德·金到白宫,但对其提出的签署一项《第二解放宣言》,彻底废除种族隔离政策的请求不置可否,一再推延,导致非暴力民权运动进一步升级。1963年4月,亚拉巴马州的伯明翰爆发了大规模的抗议活动,民权运动示威者与前来暴力镇压的警察发生冲突,肯尼迪发表电视演讲,公开申明种族隔离是一个"我们主要面临着一个道德问题,……这个问题的实质就是,每一个美国人是否都能够被赋予平等的权利和机会。"他宣布,将尽快向国会提交一份重要的《民权法案》。4个月以后,全美20万人举行了"自由长征",聚集华盛顿市的林肯纪念堂前集会,马丁·路德·金在会上发表了《我有一个梦想》的著名演说,民权运动达到了新的高潮。可以说,民权运动逐渐扩大了肯尼迪"新边疆"的视野,逐渐坚定了他推动社会正义和谐的决心。《民权法案》在1964年由国会通过,约翰逊总统签署实行。可惜,肯尼迪没有能够活着看到这一天。

在国际冷战格局中,肯尼迪强硬面对苏联在古巴的核威胁,表现出冷战斗士的勇武,以反制手段迫使赫鲁晓夫让步,和平解决了古巴核导弹危机。此后,他继续了杜鲁门和艾森豪威尔两届政府遏制共产主义的政策,提出美国应该军事介入世界热点地区。因此,他扩充核军备,强化东西柏林对峙,增派美军顾问15000人支持南越政权,加剧了南亚紧张局势。同时,鉴于苏联成功的太空计划,肯尼迪也迎头赶上,拨付巨资,启动了阿波罗登月计划,宣称:"要想成为引领世界的国家,就不能在探索太空的竞赛中落后。"上述这些措施和计划的实施都进一步强化了20世纪美苏超级大国争霸的冷战格局。另一方面,肯尼迪也显出了和平使者的形象。他力图在全球增强美国的经济和政治影响力,号召美国年轻的一代承担世界和平的责任,建立"和平军"和"进步联盟",先后向全球63个发展中国家和地区派出成千上万的美国青年,服务于当地的社会教育和就业培训事业。同时,古巴导弹危机后,肯尼迪力图缓和与苏联的对立。他在美国大学的一次演讲中告诉听众:"我们都呼吸着同样的空气,都珍惜我们的子孙的未来,我们都是人类。"他要求美国公众从人类共同的命运感出发,对苏联有更为理性的理解。他首开两国热线谈判,并下令解禁,向苏联和一些东欧国家出售小麦。经过这些努力,两国终于达成一致,于1963年10月7日与英国一起共同签署了"禁止在大气层核试验的协议",有效地减缓了世界的核军备竞赛。

肯尼迪被公认为是杰出的演说家,但不是老练的演说家。他虽然勉强进入哈佛念书,专攻政治学,但由于多病,动辄休学,因为成绩不如中等。他也没有受过专门的演说修辞训练,只是后来从政,急用先学,请过人专门辅导修辞和发声技巧。从肯尼迪大学期间和此后写的书来看,他偏爱简洁直白的陈述句,避免使用陈旧的套语和俚语;他也喜欢使用对称和重复的句式,不时加以比喻,增添机趣。此外,他还汲取以往演讲语速过快,使得听众茫然无趣的经验教训,注意放慢语速和有意义的停顿,以此引起听众对一些观点的注意和深思。这些语言技巧和演说风格在他那篇脍炙人口的总统就职演说中得到了充分的体现。

在这篇不到2千字就职演说中,肯尼迪多以宣示的语体,表述了美国内外政策的基本立场,其中平行对偶句竟占54%,其中不乏日后被人广为传诵的佳句。整篇演说的语体特点正好对应上世纪60年代冷战核威胁,美苏两极平衡,战和分成的状况,也表达出肯尼迪政府强势中争取和平,传播美国民主价值观念的"新边疆"理念。听众在肯尼迪言简意赅,一顿一挫的演说中分明听到了美国年轻的一代力图以开放的心态,走出冷战模式,在人类互相的理解和谈判中走向未来的努力。肯尼迪在演说前投入了近两个月的时间和精力,不断练习,征求意见,不断修改润色,其对这篇演说看重可见一斑。演说过程中,肯尼迪对原稿的措辞做了23处即时的修改,避免使用过于强势的用词或指喻冷战的词汇,这也表明了美国愿意寻求缓和,发展国际合作的诚意。这篇就职演说对当时年轻一代的美国人影响巨大。有些佳句几代相传,其理念成为美国意识形态向年轻人宣教的重点,例如,"不要求国家为你做什么,问一问自己能为国家做什么";"一个自由的社会如果不能帮助贫困的大多数,也就不能拯救富裕的极少数。"

可惜肯尼迪本人及其家族的好运未能持久,新一轮的冷战把美国年轻的一代卷入越战的漩涡。60年代末和70年代初的思想反叛和反战运动让肯尼迪描绘的意识形态理想趋于幻灭,美国民主价值的大一统世界仍然是一个遥远的梦。

■ 演讲文(节选)

Presidential Inaugural Address

John Fitzgerald Kennedy

Vice President Johnson, Mr. Speaker, Mr. Chief Justice, President Eisenhower, Vice President Nixon, President Truman, reverend clergy, fellow citizens,

We **observe** today not a victory of party, but a celebration of freedom—symbolizing an end, as well as a beginning—signifying

observe: mark the occasion; celebrate

renewal, as well as change. For I have sworn before you and Almighty God the same solemn oath our **forebears** prescribed nearly a century and three quarters ago.

The world is very different now. For man holds in his **mortal** hands the power to abolish all forms of human poverty and all forms of human life. And yet the same revolutionary beliefs for which our forebears fought are still **at issue** around the globe—the belief that the rights of man come not from the generosity of the state, but from the hand of God.

We dare not forget today that we are the heirs of that first revolution. Let the word go forth from this time and place, to friend and **foe** alike, that the torch has been passed to a new generation of Americans—born in this century, **tempered** by war, disciplined by a hard and bitter peace, proud of our ancient heritage—and unwilling to witness or permit the slow **undoing** of those human rights to which this Nation has always been committed, and to which we are committed today at home and around the world.

Let every nation know, whether it wishes us well or ill, that we shall pay any price, bear any burden, meet any hardship, support any friend, oppose any foe, in order to assure the survival and the success of liberty.

This much we **pledge**—and more.

To those **old allies** whose cultural and spiritual origins we share, we pledge the loyalty of faithful friends. United, there is little we cannot do in a host of cooperative **ventures**. Divided, there is little we can do—for we dare not meet a powerful challenge **at odds** and split **asunder**.

To those **new States** whom we welcome to the ranks of the free, we pledge our word that one form of colonial control shall not have passed away merely to be replaced by a far more iron tyranny. We shall not always expect to find them supporting our view. But we shall always hope to find them strongly supporting their own freedom—and to remember that, in the past, those who foolishly sought power by riding the back of the tiger ended up inside.

To those peoples in the **huts** and villages across the globe struggling to break the bonds of mass misery, we pledge our best efforts to help them help themselves, for whatever period is required—not because the Communists may be doing it, not because we seek their votes, but because it is right. If a free society cannot

---

forebear: father; ancestor; elder

mortal: worldly; earthly

at issue: unsolved; being discussed

foe: enemy

tempered: made experienced (by hardship)

undoing: destruction

pledge: swear

old allies: NATO countries

venture: project

at odds: without hope to win because of weaker strength

asunder: apart

new States: newly independent countries from colonial control

hut: very simple shelter; shabby little room

help the many who are poor, it cannot save the few who are rich.

To our **sister republics** south of our border, we offer a special pledge—to convert our good words into good deeds—in a new alliance for progress—to assist free men and free governments in casting off the chains of poverty. But this peaceful revolution of hope cannot become the **prey** of hostile powers. Let all our neighbors know that we shall join with them to oppose aggression or **subversion** anywhere in the Americas. And let every other power know that this Hemisphere intends to remain the master of its own house.

To that world **assembly** of sovereign states, the United Nations, our last best hope in an age where the instruments of war have far outpaced the instruments of peace, we renew our pledge of support—to prevent it from becoming merely a forum for **invective**—to strengthen its shield of the new and the weak—and to enlarge the area in which its **writ** may **run**.

Finally, to those nations who would make themselves our **adversary**, we offer not a pledge but a request: that both sides begin anew the quest for peace, before the dark powers of destruction **unleashed** by science **engulf** all humanity in planned or accidental self-destruction.

We dare not tempt them with weakness. For only when our **arms** are sufficient beyond doubt can we be certain beyond doubt that they will never be employed.

But neither can two great and powerful groups of nations take comfort from our present course—both sides overburdened by the cost of modern weapons, both rightly alarmed by the steady spread of the deadly atom, yet both racing to alter that uncertain balance of terror that **stays** the hand of mankind's final war.

So let us begin anew—remembering on both sides that **civility** is not a sign of weakness, and sincerity is always subject to proof. Let us never negotiate out of fear. But let us never fear to negotiate.

Let both sides explore what problems unite us instead of **belaboring** those problems which divide us.

Let both sides, for the first time, formulate serious and precise proposals for the inspection and control of arms—and bring the absolute power to destroy other nations under the absolute control of all nations.

Let both sides seek to **invoke** the wonders of science instead of its terrors. Together let us explore the stars, conquer the deserts,

---

sister republic: South American countries

prey: victim
subversion: overthrow

assembly: organization

invective: bitter quarrel; scolding
writ: doctrine; document; act
run: put in effect
adversary: sworn enemy
unleashed: let loose
engulf: swallow
arms: weapons of mass destruction; military

stay: delay by control; hold back
civility: politeness

belabor: (archaic) work hard on especially for a long period of time

invoke: make it alive; induce

eradicate disease, **tap** the ocean depths, and encourage the arts and commerce.

Let both sides unite to heed in all corners of the earth the command of **Isaiah**—to "undo the heavy burdens ... and to let the oppressed go free."

And if a **beachhead** of cooperation may push back the jungle of suspicion, let both sides join in creating a new endeavor, not a new balance of power, but a new world of law, where the strong are just and the weak secure and the peace preserved.

All this will not be finished in the first 100 days. Nor will it be finished in the first 1,000 days, nor in the life of this Administration, nor even perhaps in our lifetime on this planet. But let us begin.

In your hands, my fellow citizens, more than in mine, will rest the final success or failure of our course. Since this country was founded, each generation of Americans has been summoned to give **testimony** to its national loyalty. The graves of young Americans who answered the call to service surround the globe.

Now the **trumpet** summons us again—not as a call to bear arms, though arms we need; not as a call to battle, though embattled we are—but a call to bear the burden of a long twilight struggle, year in and year out, "rejoicing in hope, patient in **tribulation**"—a struggle against the common enemies of man: tyranny, poverty, disease, and war itself.

Can we **forge** against these enemies a grand and global alliance, North and South, East and West, that can assure a more fruitful life for all mankind? Will you join in that historic effort?

In the long history of the world, only a few generations have been granted the role of defending freedom in its hour of **maximum** danger. I do not shrink from this responsibility—I welcome it. I do not believe that any of us would exchange places with any other people or any other generation. The energy, the faith, the devotion which we bring to this endeavor will light our country and all who serve it—and the glow from **that fire** can truly light the world.

And so, my fellow Americans: ask not what your country can do for you—ask what you can do for your country.

My fellow citizens of the world: ask not what America will do for you, but what together we can do for the freedom of man.

Finally, whether you are citizens of America or citizens of the world, ask of us the same high standards of strength and sacrifice

---

tap: explore by knocking the floor or ground

Isaiah: Hebrew prophet of 7—8 BC

beachhead: foothold on the beach; initial success

testimony: proof

trumpet: bugle; horn (used by military to pass signals

tribulation: suffering; hardship

forge: shape up with strength; form; organize

maximum: extreme; worst

that fire: (here) freedom and democracy

> which we ask of you. With a good conscience our only sure reward, with history the final judge of our deeds, let us go forth to lead the land we love, asking His blessing and His help, but knowing that here on earth God's work must truly be our own.

■ 重点述评与提示

1. The world is very different now. For man holds in his mortal hands the power to abolish all forms of human poverty and all forms of human life.

   二战后意识形态的对立,两大军事集团的对峙和军备竞赛,把世界带入了核时代。人类手中同时掌握生存繁荣或自我毁灭的科技工具。这是这篇演讲的认识出发点。肯尼迪在此认识基础上发出"缓和"的信号,以显示了谈判的诚意。

2. ...the torch has been passed to a new generation of Americans—born in this century, tempered by war, disciplined by a hard and bitter peace, proud of our ancient heritage—and unwilling to witness or permit the slow undoing of those human rights to which this Nation has always been committed, and to which we are committed today at home and around the world.

   肯尼迪是第一位生在20世纪,最年轻的美国总统。他在此宣布,美国之火炬已经传给了年轻一代的美国人,有点自喻之意。句中四个并列的修饰成分分别强调了年轻、战争的洗礼、冷战的历练和爱国的情怀等特征,这既是肯尼迪对年轻一代美国人的夸耀,也表明了自己绝好的政治资本,有了如此的渲染,句末的意识形态宣教也就自然而然了。

3. But we shall always hope to find them strongly supporting their own freedom—and to remember that, in the past, those who foolishly sought power by riding the back of the tiger ended up inside.

   这是对那些刚摆脱了殖民统治,获得独立的国家的呼吁。这里用了"骑虎背炫耀却终葬身虎腹"的比喻,说明不可借助外来势力解决国家内政问题的道理,提醒这些国家不可狐假虎威,引狼入室。当时美国和苏联严重对峙,肯尼迪此话可能有所指:4年前,匈牙利发生要求摆脱苏联模式,政治独立和经济改革的大规模游行,政府要求苏联出兵干涉。苏联坦克两次开进布达佩斯,最终造成严重流血事件,纳吉政府被苏军驱逐。匈牙利主权丧失。

4. But this peaceful revolution of hope cannot become the prey of hostile powers. Let all our neighbors know that we shall join with them to oppose aggression or

subversion anywhere in the Americas. And let every other power know that this Hemisphere intends to remain the master of its own house.

  肯尼迪再次重申了《门罗宣言》的精神：美洲是美洲的人的美洲，不容外来势力的干涉，同时也强调了老罗斯福宣示的"大棒"霸权原则：美国可以以"保护"的名义随时派兵干涉美洲任何国家的事务。

5. Finally, to those nations who would make themselves our adversary, we offer not a pledge but a request: that both sides begin anew the quest for peace, before the dark powers of destruction unleashed by science engulf all humanity in planned or accidental self-destruction.

  这是肯尼迪对一苏联为首的《华沙条约》集团发出的明显的"缓和"信号。演说者提及敌对状态时用了虚拟语气，同时力图找到双方的共识：核时代中军事抗衡没有赢家，科技的破坏力量很可能意外地毁灭整个人类。这也是冷战期间两大超级大国限制战略性核武器谈判的基础，即使冷战过去的今天，核武军备仍是高悬于人类头上的"达摩克勒斯之剑"。

6. Let us never negotiate out of fear. But let us never fear to negotiate.

  在平行对偶句中采用了典型的"多重词修辞法"（polyptoton），同一个词在对偶中以不同的词性或排列反复出现。句中重复了 never, negotiate 和 fear，其中 fear 取不同词性，突出 fear 的词义，表达了美国一贯以实力为后盾的外交政策。

7. Let both sides seek to invoke the wonders of science instead of its terrors. Together let us explore the stars, conquer the deserts, eradicate disease, tap the ocean depths, and encourage the arts and commerce.

  科学技术对于人类是双刃剑。肯尼迪在此演说中再次说出了当今的后现代意识，呼吁苏联共同携手，科技服务于人类的福祉。句中连续的 5 个并列成分表达了新一届美国政府开拓"新边疆"的视野。半个世纪过去，冷战结束，多极共生的今天，各国仍然面临着这些科技发展和社会建设的任务。

8. In your hands, my fellow citizens, more than in mine, will rest the final success or failure of our course. Since this country was founded, each generation of Americans has been summoned to give testimony to its national loyalty. The graves of young Americans who answered the call to service surround the globe.

  这句话明显借用林肯第一届就职演说中的名句，借以高扬国家政治意识形态，以国家传统意识凝聚人心。不过，最后的"surround the globe"有意表明，时代变迁，美国已经今非昔比，其视野早也超出了林肯的时代。对比林肯的语句，可相得益彰：In your hands, my dissatisfied fellow-countrymen, and not in mine, is the momentous issue of civil war... The mystic chords of memory, stretching from every battlefield and patriot grave to every living heart and hearthstone all over this broad land, ...

■ 思考及讨论题

1. In what way JFK was said to be the embodiment of a new generation of Americans?
2. What are some main projects as promoted by JFK's "New Frontiers"?
3. What made JFK decide to pursue a détente with the Soviet Union?
4. How did JFK change his measure of support to the Civil Rights Movement?

■ 阅读书目

1. Kennedy, Charles. *John F. Kennedy: The Presidential Portfolio : History as Told through the Collection of the John F. Kennedy Library and Museum.* New York, 2000.
2. Barnes, John A. *John F. Kennedy on Leadership: The Lessons and Legacy of a President.* New York, 2005.
3. Manweller, Mathew. Ed. *Chronology of US Presidency.* California: ABC-CLIO, 2012.
4. Branch, Taylor. "A Second Emancipation: One Hundred Years after Lincoln Signed the Proclamation, Martin Luther King Jr. Tried Unsuccessfully to Get President John F. Kennedy to Issue a Second One. That Failure Changed the Course of History." in *The Washington Monthly.* January-February 2013.

第三十讲

马丁·路德·金(Martin Luther King, Jr. 1929—1968)

■ 政治历史评述

马丁·路德·金：美国民权运动的领袖，非暴力抵抗运动的烈士

1964年，美国国会通过《1964年民权法案》，在主要公共场合废除种族隔离。这是美国民权运动的巨大成果之一。4年过去，民权运动高潮已过，但种族歧视和种族隔离势力仍十分强大，黑人平等的公民权在很多情况下仍得不到保障。1968年2月12日，田纳西州的孟菲斯市环卫工人举行罢工，反对种族歧视，争取合法平等权益。孟菲斯当局宣布罢工非法，派出警察弹压，与举着"我是人"标语牌的示威者发生冲突。于是，街头示威迅速发展成民权运动非暴力行动，这引起了民权领袖马丁·路德·金的注意与亲临支持。

1968年4月3日，金搭乘美国航空公司班机飞往孟菲斯。飞机遭到炸弹恐吓，航班晚点，机场盘查甚严。美国联邦调查局FBI至今已经侦查到不下50个暗杀阴谋，白人极端组织悬赏10万美元取金的项上人头。金对此类恐吓已经习以为常。自从投身民权运动，他10次入狱，住所多次遭到炸弹袭击，10年前在书店还被人捅过一刀。5年前肯尼迪总统遭到暗杀，金就已经视死如归了，当时他对妻子说道："我也将遭此同样命运，我反复对你这么说，因为这是一个病入膏肓的社会。"

金当日到达孟菲斯，住在常驻的洛林汽车旅店306房间。同一天，一个名叫詹姆斯·厄尔·雷伊的中年人也驾车从亚特兰大到达了孟菲斯，他随身带着一支带有高倍瞄准器的狙击步枪。雷伊听着电台有关金行踪的广播报道，找到洛林旅店，在对面的廉价旅店开了一间破旧的房间，房间唯一的窗口正对着金入住房间出门的过道。

金到达当日，与当地民权组织领导人会面。当晚，在淅淅沥沥的雨中，金在麦森大教堂里面对着2千多黑人听众做了题为"我曾到过高山之巅"。这是金一生中最后一次演讲，也是一篇充满了宿命和死亡预兆的演讲。金对满怀期待的听众这样说道："和其他人一样，我也希望活得更长，长寿是人生之愿。但是，现在我已不在乎了。我只想听从上帝的旨意。上帝让我登山高山之巅，俯视大地。我看见了恩惠之地。我也许不能与你们同往，但是，今晚，我想告诉你们，我们作为一个种族将到达这片上帝恩惠之福地。因此，今晚我很高兴。我已经无牵无挂了，我也不怕任何人，我的眼睛已经看到上帝向我走来的光环。"金在演说中情绪伤感，不时仰望虚空，引来听众一片的抽泣声。此时，教堂外雷声隆隆，金的同事们面面相觑。这时的金似乎被一种冥冥中的力量牵引，与5年前在林肯纪念堂发表"我有一个梦想"时的慷慨激昂完全判若两人。

第二天,金出现在洛林旅店306房间门口的过道上,楼下停着一辆白色的凯迪拉克。说来又是凶兆,这部车属于孟菲斯市殡仪馆,金也偏偏向馆长借来此车代步用。下午5时左右,金有些心神不宁,不知不觉下楼与他的胞弟一同给家里的母亲打了电话,似做最后的诀别。晚上7时左右,他准备出发,乘殡仪馆的车前往友人家

做客,去吃传统的非洲"灵餐"(soul food)。此时,金正欲下楼,枪声突然响起,金应声倒地,子弹击中金的下颚,撕开颈动脉和脊椎韧带,溅出满腔的鲜血。这是致命的一击,金的生命被无情地定格在39岁。凶手雷伊逃出旅店,跳上车,逃之夭夭。联邦调查局此后展开跨国缉凶,两个月后在英国伦敦希思罗机场抓获凶手,经法庭审理,以谋杀罪判处雷伊99年监禁。雷伊后来越狱未遂,被加刑至100年监禁,1998年死于狱中。

金的死震动了世界。各国媒体纷纷指责美国是个种族歧视,暴力动乱的国家。各非暴力组织强烈谴责这起"毫无人性的残杀"。人们把金的死与甘地和肯尼迪遇刺事件联系起来,,对美国未来的种族问题表示深深地忧虑。印度议会以及其他一些欧洲国家的议会也为金默哀。在美国国内,震惊之余的约翰逊总统下令,4月7日为马丁·路德·金全国哀悼日,并于一周后签署了《1968年民权法案》,废除住房方面的种族歧视。纽约和波士顿等一些大城市的市长纷纷出动,到黑人聚集得地区安抚人心,肯尼迪总统得弟弟罗伯特也立即发表演说,深切悼念金。但是,在全国范围内,这些抚慰式的政府措施在短期内于事无补。金的死让民权人士和广大黑人感到深深地悲痛和失望,也激起他们无比的愤怒。4月4日起一个月内,在华盛顿、巴尔的摩、芝加哥、路易斯城和堪萨斯城等大城市都先后爆发了示威游行,继而演变成打砸商店和流血骚乱。这场动乱造成巨大的生命和财产损失,其影响波及全美100多个城市,是美国历史上最大规模的暴力动乱。

马丁·路德·金在其短暂的一生都在倡导非暴力主义抵抗运动,并以此获得了1963年诺贝尔和平奖,但他却死于暴力,暴力又引发了新的暴力,这是历史的嘲弄?莎士比亚名言有曰:"人们生前的劣行在其死后长存,而善举却随着尸骨被永久埋葬。"身陷种族主义政治漩涡中的金也不例外。金死后,有人指出他有剽窃嫌疑和众多的绯闻,也有保守派指认金有共产主义倾向,但是,人非圣贤,瑕不掩瑜,金也不应该是意识形态斗争的替罪羊。

我们看到的是,金以非暴力抵抗的原则领导了美国民权运动,为了种族平等和社会进步所做的不懈的奋斗和努力,消除了美国根深蒂固的白人至上意识,促使联邦政府废除了长期的种族隔离政策,提高了美国黑人的平等社会身份感和尊严感,大大改善了黑人在美国社会各个领域的社会地位,从而推动美国社会步入一个自由和民主的新时期,

向不论肤色种族而一律平等的当代公民社会迈进了关键的一步。金也在短短的13年的领导民权运动的过程中,赢得了广大黑人,包括大多数白人的尊敬和爱戴,在美国社会历史中留下不可磨灭的印记。1983年8月至10月,美国国会两院先后通过决议,决定把每年1月第3个周一定为国家法定的"马丁·路德·金纪念日"。2011年8月28日,由中国艺术家雕塑的马丁·路德·金的纪念雕像在华盛顿国家广场揭幕,马丁·路德·金作为黑人领袖,沉思立于林肯和杰斐逊的雕像之间,与其他美国国父和伟人平起平坐,这也是在美国历史上绝无仅有的。现在的美国,以金的名字命名的大道和建筑比比皆是,许多大学

教室和办公室都挂着金的肖像,每逢金的诞辰纪念日,全美各地的人们举行宴会,发表演讲,组织游行等纪念活动。可以说,金以其短暂的生命在美国人心目中赢得了长久不衰的生命,他的政治生命力绝不亚于华盛顿和林肯这样的美国文化偶像。

同时,我们也应该注意到,上世纪50—60年代的民权运动是自美国内战以来,美国黑人为了争取社会平等地位和权利而进行长期抗争的继续,是一次由包括部分白人在内的多种社会阶层和社会组织参与,采取了多种斗争策略的大规模的群众运动。马丁·路德·金所代表的非暴力直接行动只是美国民权运动的一个主要组成部分。非暴力抵抗民权运动的原则早在1942年就由当时成立的"种族平等大会"提出,而金只是在

1955年蒙哥马利市黑人抵制乘公共车运动中被推选到"蒙哥马利权利促进会"(MIA)和后来的"南方基督徒领袖大会"(SCLC)的领导地位。他后来访问印度受到甘地非暴力抗议思想的启发,在伯明翰被监禁期间写了著名的《来自伯明翰的书信》,系统阐释了美国民权运动非暴力抗议的原因,原则和方法而声名鹊起。1963年20万人声势浩大的"向华盛顿进军"这样的大规模的群众非暴力行动也不是金的创意和组织,而是著名美国黑人民权领袖A.菲力普·伦道尔夫自从二战以来就屡试不爽的非暴力抗议行动。而且,金在民权运动中表现出来的优柔寡断、妥协求全和斗争的不彻底性等也受到其他组织和运动的质疑;他在民权运动后期开始厌倦了大规模群众集会、游行和连续的演讲,对美国白人群众的民权参与意识也表现出失望,对民权运动的前途也表现出信心不足,他似乎看不到新的历史条件下民权运动对美国社会的民主平等意识和社会公正所能产生的长远的积极意义。此外,金后期转向对资本主义的批判,积极反对越战,与约翰逊政府对立。但这决不应该是联邦调查局把他定为"自认的马克思主义分子"的借口。正如著名美国民权运动史家亚当斯·费尔克劳夫指出的那样,马丁·路德·金是典型的"黑人资产阶级"的产物,"一个来自中产阶级,追求中产阶级目标的中产阶级的布道

者"。他是一个布克·T. 华盛顿式的美国自由主义传统的黑人民权领袖。

当然，我们还必须看到，马丁·路德·金是20世纪美国少有的杰出演说家之一。他澎湃的激情和驾驭语言，巧用修辞的能力10多年间在各种大规模群众集会的强大心理场中被发挥到淋漓尽致的地步。1963年8月28日，金在林肯纪念堂台阶上，面对着20多万集会人群，发表了那篇世界著名的《我有一个梦想》的演说。这篇演说以充满激情的语言，述说了自林肯签署《解放宣言》以来美国黑人100多年所经历的种族歧视，隔离和迫害，展示了他们为争取真正自由和平等权利的斗争和经受的

痛苦和挫折，其描述具有极强的历史画面效果，令听者有触景生情之感。金在演说中也郑重警告美国政府和社会，黑人民权的实现与美国未来的强大息息相关，任何漠然态度，侥幸心理或渐进主义式的拖延都将导致国家内乱的危险。当然，金也不忘告诫黑人群众，必须用合法的手段，与其他白人兄弟一道，用非暴力的方式来争取自己合法的权利。金说到尽情处，脱离讲稿，即兴发挥，表达了内心深处"深深根植于美国之梦的我的梦想"，那就是，美国总有一天真正实现其"人人生而平等"的立国原则，各种肤色种族的人们及其子孙后代沐浴在上帝的荣光之中，享受着真正的平等、自由、和谐和幸福。全篇演讲主题鲜明，比喻生动，句式重叠，层层推进，动情处声情并茂，说理处语重心长，既有宗教布道的庄严，又有政治宣教的犀利，更有发自内心的渴望和激情。演说结尾处，金想起了少年时崇拜的著名黑人女低音歌唱家玛丽奥·安德森1939年在林肯纪念堂台阶上演唱的名歌"美国：我的祖国"，不禁动情地背诵了这首歌的第一节，并用其中的一句"让自由之声响起"做引子，加入典型地名，以爵士音乐般的渐强调子，重复这一句子，让自由之声在美国南北大地，东西平原上响起，由此把整篇如诗如画的演讲推向情感和音乐的高潮。

这是美国政治演说中的绝唱。演说的第二天，《纽约时报》著名记者詹姆斯·雷斯顿撰文写道："金博士的演讲囊括民权运动所有的主题，比任何人的论述都好。演说中充满了林肯和甘地式的比喻，回响着《圣经》的节奏；他既不屈抗争又显得悲伤，他让人们感到不虚此行，各自返回家乡。"美国国家电台此后全向全国播放了金的演讲，他的名字与"我有一个梦想"紧紧联系在一起，成为美国民权运动的重要标志。可惜，金未能坚持自己的梦想，他在1966年以后常常对人说起的一句话是："1963年我在华盛顿的梦想现在往往变成了一个噩梦。"大约半个世纪后的2008年，美国出了第一位黑人总统。不过，马丁·路德·金的梦想是否已经完全实现，只能让未来的历史评说了。

演讲文

I Have a Dream

Martin Luther King, Jr.

I am happy to join with you today in what will **go down** in history as the greatest demonstration for freedom in the history of our nation.

Five **score** years ago, a great American, in whose symbolic shadow we stand today, signed the Emancipation Proclamation. This **momentous** decree came as a great beacon light of hope to millions of Negro slaves who had been **seared** in the flames of withering injustice. It came as a joyous daybreak to end the long night of their **captivity**.

But one hundred years later, the Negro still is not free. One hundred years later, the life of the Negro is still sadly crippled by the **manacles** of **segregation** and the chains of **discrimination**. One hundred years later, the Negro lives on a lonely island of poverty in the midst of a vast ocean of material prosperity. One hundred years later, the Negro is still **languished** in the corners of American society and finds himself an **exile** in his own land. And so we've come here today to dramatize a shameful condition.

In a sense we've come to our nation's capital to cash a check. When the architects of our republic wrote the magnificent words of the Constitution and the Declaration of Independence, they were signing a **promissory note** to which every American was to fall heir. This note was a promise that all men, yes, black men as well as white men, would be guaranteed the "unalienable Rights" of "Life, Liberty and the pursuit of Happiness." It is obvious today that America has **defaulted** on this promissory note, insofar as her citizens of color are concerned. Instead of **honoring** this sacred obligation, America has given the Negro people a bad check, a check which has **come back** marked "insufficient funds."

But we refuse to believe that the bank of justice is bankrupt. We refuse to believe that there are insufficient funds in the great **vaults** of opportunity of this nation. And so, we've come to cash this check, a check that will give us **upon demand** the riches of freedom and the security of justice.

We have also come to this **hallowed** spot to remind America of the fierce urgency of Now. This is no time to engage in the luxury of

---

go down: pass on

score: twenty

momentous: influential; powerful
sear: made suffer (by fire)
captivity: imprisonment
manacles: handcuffs
segregation: racial separation
discrimination: racial prejudice
languish: suffer bitterly
exile: person driven out of his/her own country

promissory note: payable bank check
default: delay the payment (by the bank)
honor: (here) to acknowledge with credit
come back: (here) returned and rejected by the bank
vault: (here) vast space
upon demand: at request
hallowed: holy, sanctified

gradualism: the belief that things will be improved gradually **quicksand**: stream of sliding sand	cooling off or to take the tranquilizing drug of **gradualism**. Now is the time to make real the promises of democracy. Now is the time to rise from the dark and desolate valley of segregation to the sunlit path of racial justice. Now is the time to lift our nation from the **quicksands** of racial injustice to the solid rock of brotherhood. Now is the time to make justice a reality for all of God's children.

It would be fatal for the nation to overlook the urgency of the moment. This **sweltering** summer of the Negro's legitimate discontent will not pass until there is an **invigorating** autumn of freedom and equality. Nineteen sixty-three is not an end, but a beginning. And those who hope that the Negro needed to **blow off steam** and will now be content will have a rude awakening if the nation **returns to business as usual**. And there will be neither rest nor tranquility in America until the Negro is granted his citizenship rights. The whirlwinds of revolt will continue to shake the foundations of our nation until the bright day of justice emerges.

sweltering: very hot and stuffy
invigorating: lively with fresh and cool sensation
blow off steam: relieve by loudly expressing one's anger
return to business: do things as usual as if nothing has happened

But there is something that I must say to my people, who stand on the warm threshold which leads into the palace of justice: In the process of gaining our rightful place, we must not be guilty of wrongful deeds. Let us not seek to satisfy our thirst for freedom by drinking from the cup of bitterness and hatred. We must forever **conduct** our struggle on the high plane of **dignity** and discipline. We must not allow our creative protest to **degenerate** into physical violence. Again and again, we must rise to the **majestic** heights of meeting physical force with soul force.

conduct: perform
dignity: self-esteem
degenerate: fall morally
majestic: noble and elevated
militancy: the tendency to armed resistance
engulf: draw and engage forcefully
inextricably: inevitably; unavoidably
pledge: oath; solemn promise

The marvelous new **militancy** which has **engulfed** the Negro community must not lead us to a distrust of all white people, for many of our white brothers, as evidenced by their presence here today, have come to realize that their destiny is tied up with our destiny. And they have come to realize that their freedom is **inextricably** bound to our freedom.

We cannot walk alone.

And as we walk, we must make the **pledge** that we shall always march ahead.

We cannot turn back.

devotee: activist

There are those who are asking the **devotees** of civil rights, "When will you be satisfied?" We can never be satisfied as long as the Negro is the victim of the unspeakable horrors of police brutality. We can never be satisfied as long as our bodies, heavy with the **fatigue** of travel, cannot gain lodging in the motels of the highways and the

fatigue: tiredness; physical exhaustion

hotels of the cities. We cannot be satisfied as long as the negro's basic **mobility** is from a smaller **ghetto** to a larger one. We can never be satisfied as long as our children are stripped of their self-hood and robbed of their dignity by a sign stating: "For Whites Only." We cannot be satisfied as long as a Negro in Mississippi cannot vote and a Negro in New York believes he has nothing for which to vote. No, no, we are not satisfied, and we will not be satisfied until "justice rolls down like waters, and righteousness like a mighty stream."

I am not unmindful that some of you have come here out of great trials and **tribulations**. Some of you have come fresh from narrow jail cells. And some of you have come from areas where your quest—quest for freedom left you **battered** by the storms of persecution and **staggered** by the winds of police brutality. You have been the veterans of creative suffering. Continue to work with the faith that unearned suffering is **redemptive**. Go back to Mississippi, go back to Alabama, go back to South Carolina, go back to Georgia, go back to Louisiana, go back to the slums and ghettos of our northern cities, knowing that somehow this situation can and will be changed.

Let us not **wallow** in the valley of despair, I say to you today, my friends.

And so even though we face the difficulties of today and tomorrow, I still have a dream. It is a dream deeply rooted in the American dream.

I have a dream that one day this nation will rise up and **live out** the true meaning of its **creed**: "We hold these truths to be self-evident, that all men are created equal."

I have a dream that one day on the red hills of Georgia, the sons of former slaves and the sons of former slave owners will be able to sit down together at the table of brotherhood.

I have a dream that one day even the state of Mississippi, a state sweltering with the heat of injustice, sweltering with the heat of oppression, will be transformed into an **oasis** of freedom and justice.

I have a dream that my four little children will one day live in a nation where they will not be judged by the color of their skin but by the content of their character.

I have a dream today!

I have a dream that one day, down in Alabama, with its **vicious** racists, with its governor having his lips **dripping with** the words of "**interposition**" and "**nullification**"—one day right there in Alabama little black boys and black girls will be able to join hands with little

---

mobility: scope of moving around
ghetto: (here) small, shabby room for shelter

tribulation: suffering
batter: hit repeated and violently
stagger: stumble; not able to stand (in strong wind)
redemptive: to be repaid and awarded

wallow: indulge

live out: realize
creed: holy principle and belief

oasis: vegetated land in desert
vicious: evil
dripping with (here) uttering continuously
interposition: interference
nullification: declaration that something is invalid

white boys and white girls as sisters and brothers.

I have a dream today!

I have a dream that one day every valley shall be **exalted**, and every hill and mountain shall be made low, the rough places will be made plain, and the **crooked** places will be made straight; "and the glory of the Lord shall be revealed and all flesh shall see it together."

This is our hope, and this is the faith that I go back to the South with.

With this faith, we will be able to **hew** out of the mountain of despair a stone of hope. With this faith, we will be able to transform the **jangling** discords of our nation into a beautiful symphony of brotherhood. With this faith, we will be able to work together, to pray together, to struggle together, to go to jail together, to **stand up for** freedom together, knowing that we will be free one day.

And this will be the day—this will be the day when all of God's children will be able to sing with new meaning:

My country tis of **thee**, sweet land of liberty, of thee I sing.

Land where my fathers died, land of the Pilgrim's pride,

From every mountainside, let freedom ring!

And if America is to be a great nation, this must become true.

And so let freedom ring from the **prodigious** hilltops of New Hampshire.

Let freedom ring from the mighty mountains of New York.

Let freedom ring from the heightening **Alleghenies** of Pennsylvania.

Let freedom ring from the snow-capped Rockies of Colorado.

Let freedom ring from the **curvaceous** slopes of California.

But not only that:

Let freedom ring from Stone Mountain of Georgia.

Let freedom ring from Lookout Mountain of Tennessee.

Let freedom ring from every hill and **molehill** of Mississippi.

From every mountainside, let freedom ring.

And when this happens, when we allow freedom ring, when we let it ring from every village and every **hamlet**, from every state and every city, we will be able to speed up that day when all of God's children, black men and white men, Jews and **Gentiles**, Protestants and Catholics, will be able to join hands and sing in the words of the old Negro **spiritual**:

Free at last! Free at last!

Thank God Almighty, we are free at last!

---

exalt: raise; elevate
crooked: distorted; uneven

hew: cut

jangling: shrieking noises

stand up for: accept in honor

thee: you

prodigious: huge; magnificent

Alleghenies: part of the Appalachian mountain range located in the eastern USA
curvaceous: gracefully curving

molehill: small pile of earth made by small animals like moles
hamlet: small village
Gentiles: none-believers of Jewish faith; persons who are not Jewish
spiritual: typical African song

第三十讲 | Martin Luther King, Jr

■ 重点述评与提示

1. Five score years ago, a great American, in whose symbolic shadow we stand today, signed the Emancipation Proclamation.

　　金演讲当天是林肯签署《解放宣言》100周年纪念日。金此刻也站在纪念堂巨大的林肯坐像下演讲。这样的安排具有十分的象征意义，足见集会组织者的用意。此外，金的演讲以"Five score years ago"开篇，与林肯著名的葛底斯堡演讲的开篇"Four score and seven years ago"遥相呼应，接着点明，自《解放宣言》签署至今，100年过去，黑人要获得平等自由权利，仍遥遥无期。这是一个巨大的语言和行动的象征。民权人士可谓匠心独运。

2. And so we've come here today to dramatize a shameful condition.

　　"戏剧般地展示"（dramatize），这是美国民权运动非暴力抵抗主义的一个关键词语。金在其《来自伯明翰的书信》为此进行了阐述，其主旨就是，受压迫者通过抵制、静坐和集会游行等非暴力直接行动，展示自己所受到的肉体和精神的伤害，以此争取消除种族隔离和歧视，获得平等的权利。

3. We have also come to this hallowed spot to remind America of the fierce urgency of now. This is no time to engage in the luxury of cooling off or to take the tranquilizing drug of gradualism.

　　民权运动首起于1955年蒙哥马利市的黑人抵制乘坐公共车的运动，至此已经8年，期间也爆发了伯明翰市大规模的示威和"乘车自由行"等抗议活动，当局也使用警犬和消防水龙进行了镇压，种族主义份子在当局的纵容下甚至烧毁了黑人乘坐的汽车。在此期间，肯尼迪虽然同情民权运动，使用行政权力对民权人士多有保护，并采取了一定措施改善黑人的生活、医疗和就业培训等，但对立法废除种族隔离采取了观望和渐进主义的态度。国会中南方民主党人更是采取了阻挠和拖延的策略。金曾经再三促请肯尼迪签署一个"第二次解放宣言"即《民权法案》未果。这里，他明显表达了一种失望和不满，同时对国会中的种族主义势力也表示了较为强硬的态度。

4. The whirlwinds of revolt will continue to shake the foundations of our nation until the bright day of justice emerges.

　　这里的口气强硬，有警示之意。种族主义势力抓住此意，指责金有号召暴力抗争倾向。但在金的语汇里，"revolt"离"暴力反抗"还相距甚远。下文中告诫黑人同胞坚持合法的斗争，非暴力的反抗，即表现出金的谨慎。

5. We can never be satisfied as long as our bodies, heavy with the fatigue of travel, cannot gain lodging in the motels of the highways and the hotels of the cities. ...No, no, we are not satisfied, and we will not be satisfied until "justice rolls down like waters, and righteousness like a mighty stream."

  在包括本句话的段落里，金涉及民权运动的具体诉求：废除公共服务领域里的种族歧视，改善黑人的居住条件，尊重黑人的政治选举权。段落末套用《圣经》话语："让正义像河水奔流向前，让公正像永不枯竭的清泉流淌。"(Let justice rolls on like waters, and righteousness like ever-flowing stream)其中改动了两个词，改变了意象的视觉冲击力，增强了语气："让正义像河流奔涌而下，让公正像巨大的激流倾泻。"

6. And so even though we face the difficulties of today and tomorrow, I still have a dream. It is a dream deeply rooted in the American dream.

  在此之前，金在著名的"来自伯明翰的书信中"认为在咖啡馆里静坐示威的黑人学生用实际行动表达了对"美国之梦"的渴望。与白人寻求机会均等，通过个人奋斗而成就事业和财富的"美国之梦"不同，黑人的"美国之梦"深深植根于"人人生而平等"的立国原则。1964年2月5日，金又在新泽西州的德雷大学做了一场题为"美国之梦"的演讲，再次强调"人人生而平等"的普世价值。可以说，金在此处表达的梦想即是"黑人渴求平等的梦想"。

7. I have a dream that one day every valley shall be exalted, and every hill and mountain shall be made low, the rough places will be made plain, and the crooked places will be made straight; "and the glory of the Lord shall be revealed and all flesh shall see it together."

  金出生于黑人浸礼会牧师家庭。传记记载，他还没学会走路前就喜欢听祖母一遍遍地讲圣经故事，5岁就能背诵许多圣经段落，演唱许多圣经中的赞歌，后来子承父业，做了牧师，对《圣经》可谓烂熟于心。此处从"以赛亚书"中信手拈来一段，正好描述世界平等大同，与其表述的"梦想"可谓恰如其分。

8. And so let freedom ring from the prodigious hilltops of New Hampshire.

  此句以降，演说达到高潮。金以一种救世的祈使语气，连续8次叠用"Let freedom ring..."的句式，让自由之声响彻美国南北西部各州的高山峻岭。这些重复叠句一气呵成，令人荡气回肠；同时，激越渐强的节奏，似有爵士音乐的乐感，在政治演说中别具一格。

9. But not only that: Let freedom ring from Stone Mountain of Georgia. Let freedom ring from Lookout Mountain of Tennessee. Let freedom ring from every hill and molehill of Mississippi. From every mountainside, let freedom ring.

　　这些列举的南部州是种族隔离和歧视最严重的地区。金在稍加停顿的过渡语句之后,以最强的语气呼吁,让自由之声在这些州回响,起到突出强调和警示的效果。

■ 思考及讨论题

1. How did the Civil Rights Movement get started in 1955?
2. What was the role of Dr. Martin Luther King, Jr. in the Civil Rights Movement?
3. What are some main arguments of Dr. King's nonviolent resistance?
4. What legislature improvements did the Civil Rights Movement achieve up to the end of the 60s?

■ 阅读书目

1. Kirk, John A. *Martin Luther King, Jr. and the Civil Rights Movement: Controversies and Debates*. New York: Palgrave Macmillan, 2007.
2. Ling, Peter J. *Martin Luther King, Jr.* London and New York: Routledge, 2007.
3. Adams, Russell L. "The Legacy of Dr. Martin Luther King, Jr. Three Decades Later: How Fares the Dream" in *Diversity Employer*. February 2001.
4. Murphey, Dwight D. "Understanding America: The Martin Luther King Myth" in *The Journal of Social, Political, and Economic Studies*. Fall 2003.

第三十一讲

马尔科姆·X（Malcolm X 1925—1965）

■ 政治历史评述

马尔科姆·X：美国民权运动中的侠客，黑人人权和民族主义的呐喊者

纵观美国杰出的黑人领袖和政治家，无论是早期的废奴主义者，或提倡自救和种族融合的妥协者，还是非暴力抵抗的民权领袖，或是登上国家权力顶峰的成功者，都具有杰出的语言才能和演讲口才。所不同的是，道格拉斯话语锋芒毕露，反倒容易被人遗忘；布克·华盛顿外柔内刚，温和自励的话语一时遮蔽不了种族的矛盾；马丁·路德·金纠结于非暴力和强力抗争之间，高亢的呼吁和美好的梦想敌不过暗算的枪弹；奥巴马颓丧中崛起，跻身政治竞选，他口若悬河的国家主流政治话语为其圆了总统之梦；而这位桀骜不驯的马尔科姆·X在民权运动中特立独行，是黑人下层人群的杰出代言人。他对白人种族主义尖刻犀利的谴责话语和变幻的宗教立场终究引来杀身之祸。1965年2月21日，在一次演讲现场，马尔科姆身中3个恐怖主义份子射出的15颗子弹，惨烈地结束了他39岁的生命，他的种族分离主义的极端主张也随着他生命的终结而逐渐烟消云散。

马尔科姆·X是美国民权运动中的一位侠客式的人物。在60年代的美国民权运动中，他似乎是单打独斗的演说者。作为地位仅次于马丁·路德·金的黑人领袖，他从未组织过任何形式的群众罢工，抵制或游行，而是另辟蹊径，游走四方，到处演说。他在宗教信仰和种族立场各方面都保持着自己独特的，甚至是令人琢磨不透的看法，他的身世也曾有放荡不羁的荒唐，买卖毒品的堕落和犯罪的记录，也有不平则鸣，不达则变的冲动。同时，他用典型的黑人话语，高扬黑人的历史和文化，为自己的种族仗义执言，让后世的黑人年轻的一代的文化寻根和艺术创造找到了灵感。

首先，在民权运动的目标和策略上，马尔科姆与民权运动的最高目标保持一致，都是为了黑人种族的最终自由和幸福，但是，他与民权运动的主流意识和其他派别的都保持着距离，在宗教信仰上也与主流格格不入。他力图超越黑人民权，从世界黑人人权的角度来探讨种族问题。他不同意马丁·路德·金等民权领袖在白人种族社会内为废除种族隔离，争取黑人平等权利的宗旨，认为这种以融入美国社会为目的做法实际上就是对白人社会的妥协，是对黑人历史和文化的放弃。他猛烈抨击白人社会是"罪恶的，腐败的"的国度，基督教是白人奴隶主强加给黑人的罪恶的宗教，而白人种族的灭亡时历史的必然。与此相反，马尔科姆鼓吹黑人种族论，认为黑人种族有着灿烂的历史和文化，理应重建文化的自尊，而伊斯兰教包容了黑人文化的优秀成分，是黑人种族自己的宗教。

为此,马尔科姆加入了"伊斯兰民族教派"(Nation of Islam)并成为其高层领袖之一。在

斗争策略上,马尔科姆·X反对马丁·路德·金倡导的非暴力抵抗直接行动。他认为,如果政府不愿意或没有能力保护黑人的生命和财产,那么黑人必须用"一切必要的手段"来捍卫自己的尊严和自由。这两位美国民权运动最杰出的领袖于1964年3月26日在华盛顿有过一次不到一分钟的短暂会面,两人各执己见,心照不宣。事后马丁·路德·金回忆说:"我常希望他少谈暴力,因为暴力解决不了问题。……我觉得马尔科姆帮了自己的倒忙,也帮了我们的人民一个大大的倒忙。他在黑人贫民窟那些火药味十足的煽动性演讲,号召黑人武装起来,做好暴力对抗的准备。这些演讲所能收获的只会是悲伤。"马尔科姆则在《自传》中反问:"在今天这个国家的种族氛围里,任何人都可以拭目以待,看看这两种解决黑人问题'极端'的方式到底哪一种首先让个人遇到致命的灾难——是金博士的'非暴力',还是我的所谓'暴力'?"可惜历史上谁都猜不到:他们两人先后都在39岁那年遇到暴力而身亡。另一方面,马尔科姆1963年到过伊斯兰圣地麦加朝觐,眼界大开,他看到美国民权运动只是黑人在一国之内争取民权的运动,而黑人的平等权利和彻底的自由解放是全球,特别是广大第三世界国家黑人的共同事业。因此,他提出不仅要争取黑人在一国的民权,更应为争取世界黑人的人权。在这方面,马尔科姆也许更有远见,但他寄希望于联合国主持公道,匡扶正义,却又显得思想不成熟。

其次,马尔科姆·X屡经磨难,身世凄凉,是草根黑人在社会下层苦苦挣扎的典型。这也在他的性格中注入了桀骜不驯,愤世嫉俗的政治侠客之气。马尔科姆1925年5月于内布拉斯加州,取名马尔科姆·利头(Little)。父亲曾经是黑人领袖马库斯·加维倡导的所谓"回归非洲"运动的追随者。在他8岁那年,父亲遭到白人种族分子制造的车祸身亡,他的叔叔死于三K党的私刑,家园也遭种族主义分子付之一炬。母亲遭受精神打击,在经济大萧条时期还要独立养活6个孩子,不堪重负而精神失常。马尔科姆从小得不到家庭温暖,在学校成绩出众却受到歧视,想当律师的志向遭受打击。怨恨和复仇的心理促使他选择辍学,甘心流落街头当个小混混,混迹于夜店和舞厅,后来竟然买卖毒品,最后发展到入室抢劫的地步,被波士顿警方逮捕,判刑10年。那年他20岁。眼看这个自甘沉沦的黑人青年在犯罪的道路上已经无可救药,这是却出现了奇迹般的逆转。狱中的马尔科姆努力读书,有了救赎思想和敬畏意识,皈依伊斯兰教,参加了黑人伊斯兰民族会,改名马尔科姆·X,以示对未知的非洲祖先的追溯之意。从此,浪子回头,马尔科姆·X走上了唤醒下层黑

人民众,独立自主地探索黑人自由独立的道路。

马尔科姆·X的政治气质多变,浪迹天涯,语出惊人,自立门户,在此过程中积累政治体验,不断修正自己的观点和立场。1962年,洛杉矶警方防卫过度,射杀黑人伊斯兰民族教派成员罗纳德·斯多克斯。这个组织的教主,马尔科姆的恩师艾力佳·穆罕默德和其他领导成员却对此十分漠然,马尔科姆路见不平,在一系列的演讲中大力宣讲斯多克斯事件的政治意义。此时新闻媒体又报道了教主穆罕默德的系列绯闻,马尔科姆开始对教派的主要教义和策略产生怀疑。1963年11月,肯尼迪总统被刺,马尔科姆在回答记者提问时一语惊人,说这是"鸡仔回鸡窝",意思是说肯尼迪"自作自受"。一时舆论大哗,马尔科姆遭到教主9个月的封口。他随即愤而与"黑人伊斯兰民族教派"决裂。不久,他离开美国数月之久,周游非洲多国,一路演讲。在此过程中,他的观点和立场发生变化,在种族和政治问题上开始有包容之心,并公开指责"黑人伊斯兰民族教派"的基本教义。回到美国后,马尔科姆竖起自己的大旗,与一些志同道合者一起,成立了"穆斯林清真寺组织"和"非洲裔美国人联合会",总部设在纽约市哈莱区。此时的马尔科姆·X已是大义凛然,面对着数次的死亡威胁,他依旧不平则鸣,我行我素,视死如归。

最后,正是马尔科姆·X这些传奇般的游侠气质吸引了年轻的一代,构成了美国文化中一道独特的风景。上世纪80末以来,马尔科姆成了新一代的历史明星。他的《自传》被评为"改变美国的20本书"之一,是中学乃至大学课程的必读书目;他的生平被拍成了好莱坞大片;互联网上出现了成百上千的马尔科姆·X网站;标有大写"X"的广告牌挂在大街小巷;他的头像也出现在邮票上出入于美国千家万户。马尔科姆·X也成了新的黑人艺术的文化驱动力,他对黑人下层生活的贴近,他众多的演讲中表现出来的那种黑人优越感和典型的非裔美国人语言风格等等,合力直接启发了黑人说唱乐、街舞和涂鸦艺术等摇滚文化形式。最为重要的,还是马尔科姆生前表现出来的强烈的现实批判精神和种族叛逆思想,它对美国年轻一代,特别是大学生群体,产生了契合于时代文化心理和审美变迁的暗示,形成了与商业和消费社会同步的艺术表现。正如著名黑人神学家詹姆斯·H.科恩教授在《马丁、马尔科姆和美国》一书中指出的,"马尔科姆表达了对美国白人社会和黑人运动领导阶层的愤怒。这就是为什么他在深受黑人说唱艺术家和福音教派街头布道者欢迎的缘故,也是为什么他的头像和名言成为了纽扣、帽子和T恤上的时髦。"也许,这也是一个在白人主流社会中具有不合作精神的非正统的黑人领袖的魅力,它再次证明了:个性永远是艺术创造的源泉。

1964年4月3日,马尔科姆·X在俄亥俄州的科里教堂发表了题为"选票,还是子弹"的演说。1999年,137名美国公共演讲的学者评选出100篇20世纪最佳演讲,马尔科姆这篇演讲名列第7,第1名是马丁·路德·金的"我有一个梦想"。在这篇演讲中,马尔科姆展示了典型的黑人话语风格,用词简洁,句式短促而有力,重复而紧凑,反复推进。高潮迭出。在将近2个小时的演讲中,马尔科姆号召各黑人团体不分宗教和派别联手团结,形成合力,共同反对白人社会对黑人种族的压迫,剥削和歧视。马尔科姆提出黑人在美国社会的身份问题,树立黑人的独立身份,用辛辣的语言,谴责白人社会无偿压榨黑人的劳动 300 多年,欠下了黑人的血泪账。而美国政府则直接参与了对黑人的压剥削和歧视:"山姆大叔手上沾满了黑人的鲜血,沾满了这个国家的黑人的鲜血。山姆大叔是地球上头号伪善者"他告诉观众,种族隔离实际上就是美国政府的阴谋,而黑人应该用世界的视角看到自己举足轻重的政治力量,冷静地利用手中的选票,不仅在美国社会内部争取民权,还更应该在世界范围内争取黑人的人权。马尔科姆嘲笑马丁·路德·金的"深深根植于美国之梦的梦想",说他本人是美国虚伪的民主的牺牲品,他所看到的不是什么美国梦,而是美国噩梦。马尔科姆同时警告美国政府,新一代的黑人已经成长起来,他们不满足于非暴力的斗争,他们有权拥有自卫的武器,在遇到暴力压迫时武装保卫自己:"不是选票就是子弹,不是自由就是死亡。"在演说的后半部分,马尔科姆阐述了"黑人民族主义"在政治、经济和社会各方面的表现,号召黑人种族构建自己的政治和经济体系,自我提升黑人的教育和社会道德。为此,马尔科姆寄希望于召开"黑人民族主义全国大会",在广泛的交流和合作中达成共识,并在恰当的时候组建"黑人民族主义党",进而创建"黑人民族主义军"。演说中这种咄咄逼人的态势在反复出现的"不是选票就是子弹,不是自由就是死亡"的呼声中更加显得火药味十足,尽管马尔科姆不忘提醒人们要在法律的框架下追求自己的种族独立和自由平等。

　　这是一个侠骨傲然,正在成长的黑人政治家,是黑人下层人民心中的"黑王子"。但是,上世纪 60 年代的美国政治气氛容不得一个身世卑微,命运多舛的黑人怪才成功登上政治舞台的中心。40 多年以后,另一位与他有着许多相似经历的"黑王子"崛起,登上美国总统宝座,成就了美国有色人种世纪的梦想。不知马尔科姆九泉之下作何感想。

■ 演讲文(节选)

The Ballot or the Bullet

Malcolm X

Mr. **Moderator**, Brother Lomax, brothers and sisters, friends and enemies: I just can't believe everyone in here is a friend, and I don't want to leave anybody out. The question tonight, as I understand it, is "The Negro Revolt, and Where Do We Go From Here?" or "What Next?" In my little **humble** way of understanding it, it points toward either the ballot or the bullet. ...

moderator: chairman

humble: low; insignificant (it is used here for modesty)

If we don't do something real soon, I think you'll have to agree that we're going to be forced either to use the ballot or the bullet. It's one or the other in 1964. It isn't that time is running out—time has run out! ...

I'm not a politician, not even a student of politics; in fact, I'm not a student of much of anything. I'm not a Democrat. I'm not a Republican, and I don't even consider myself an American. If you and I were Americans, there'd be no problem. Those **Honkies** that just got off the boat, they're already Americans; Polacks are already Americans; the Italian refugees are already Americans. Everything that came out of Europe, every blue-eyed thing, is already an American. And as long as you and I have been over here, we aren't Americans yet.

Well, I am one who doesn't believe in **deluding** myself. I'm not going to sit at your table and watch you eat, with nothing on my plate, and call myself a **diner**. Sitting at the table doesn't make you a diner, unless you eat some of what's on that plate. Being here in America doesn't make you an American. Being born here in America doesn't make you an American. Why, if birth made you American, you wouldn't need any legislation; you wouldn't need any amendments to the Constitution; you wouldn't be faced with civil-rights **filibustering** in Washington, D.C., right now. They don't have to pass civil-rights legislation to make a Polack an American.

No, I'm not an American. I'm one of the 22 million black people who are the victims of Americanism. One of the 22 million black people who are the victims of democracy, nothing but disguised hypocrisy. So, I'm not standing here speaking to you as an American, or a patriot, or a **flag-saluter**, or a **flag-waver**—no, not I. I'm speaking as a victim of this American system. And I see America through the eyes of the victim. I don't see any American dream; I see an American nightmare.

These 22 million victims are waking up. Their eyes are coming open. They're beginning to see what they used to only look at. They're becoming politically mature. They are realizing that there are new political trends from coast to coast. As they see these new political trends, it's possible for them to see that every time there's an election the **races** are so close that they have to have a **recount**. ... Well, what does this mean? It means that when white people are evenly divided, and black people have a **bloc** of votes of their own, it is left up to them to determine who's going to sit in the White House and who's going to be in the dog house.

It was the black man's vote that put the present administration

---

honkie: (slang) white man

delude: cheat; deceive

diner: eater

filibuster: politician who make long speech to stop the passing of legislation

flag-saluter: patriot saluting the national flag

flag-waver: patriot waving the national flag

race: competition
recount: recount the ballots to decide who wins
bloc: large group of people with same political aims

in Washington, D.C. Your vote, your **dumb** vote, your ignorant vote, your wasted vote put in an administration in Washington, D.C., that has seen fit to pass every kind of legislation imaginable, saving you until last, then filibustering on top of that. And your and my leaders have the **audacity** to run around clapping their hands and talk about how much progress we're making. ...

So, what I'm trying to impress upon you, in **essence**, is this: You and I in America are faced not with a segregationist conspiracy, we're faced with a government conspiracy. Everyone who's filibustering is a senator—that's the government. Everyone who's **finagling** in Washington, D.C., is a congressman—that's the government. You don't have anybody putting blocks in your path but people who are a part of the government. The same government that you go abroad to fight for and die for is the government that is in a conspiracy to deprive you of your voting rights, deprive you of your economic opportunities, deprive you of **decent** housing, deprive you of decent education. You don't need to go to the employer alone, it is the government itself, the government of America, that is responsible for the oppression and **exploitation** and **degradation** of black people in this country. And you should drop it in their lap. This government has failed the Negro. This so-called democracy has failed the Negro. And all these white **liberals** have definitely failed the Negro.

So, where do we go from here? First, we need some friends. We need some new allies. The entire civil-rights struggle needs a new interpretation, a broader interpretation. We need to look at this civil-rights thing from another angle—from the inside as well as from the outside. To those of us whose philosophy is black nationalism, the only way you can get involved in the civil-rights struggle is give it a new interpretation. That old interpretation excluded us. It kept us out. So, we're giving a new interpretation to the civil-rights struggle, an interpretation that will enable us to come into it, take part in it. And these **handkerchief-heads** who have been **dillydallying** and **pussy footing** and compromising—we don't intend to let them pussyfoot and dillydally and compromise any longer....

And now you're facing a situation where the young Negro's coming up. They don't want to hear that "**turn the-other-cheek**" stuff, no. In Jacksonville, those were teenagers, they were throwing **Molotov cocktails**. Negroes have never done that before. But it shows you there's a new deal coming in. There's new thinking coming in. There's

---

dumb: silent; voiceless

audacity: shamelessly bold

essence: most basic sense

finagle: obtain by cheating and tricks

decent: good and morally acceptable

exploitation: excessive use to make profit
degradation: the act of making one worthless
liberal: promoter of free market capitalism
handkerchief-head: (slang) womanish man
dillydallying: (slang) hesitating; wavering
pussy footing: afraid of making tough decisions
turn the-other-cheek stuff: biblical stories about tolerance and non-violence
Molotov cocktail: self-made fire bomb used by street protesters

new strategy coming in. It'll be Molotov cocktails this month, hand grenades next month, and something else next month. It'll be ballots, or it'll be bullets. It'll be liberty, or it will be death. ...

Our mothers and fathers invested sweat and blood. Three hundred and ten years we worked in this country without a **dime** in return—I mean without a dime in return. You let the white man walk around here talking about how rich this country is, but you never stop to think how it got rich so quick. It got rich because you made it rich....

If you don't take this kind of **stand**, your little children will grow up and look at you and think "shame." If you don't take an uncompromising stand, I don't mean go out and get violent; but at the same time you should never be nonviolent unless you run into some nonviolence. I'm nonviolent with those who are nonviolent with me. But when you drop that violence on me, then you've made me go **insane**, and I'm not responsible for what I do. And that's the way every Negro should get. Any time you know you're within the law, within your legal rights, within your moral rights, in accord with justice, then die for what you believe in. But don't die alone. Let your dying be **reciprocal**. This is what is meant by equality. What's good for the goose is good for the **gander**.

When we begin to get in this area, we need new friends, we need new allies. We need to expand the civil-rights struggle to a higher level—to the level of human rights. Whenever you are in a civil-rights struggle, whether you know it or not, you are **confining** yourself to the **jurisdiction** of Uncle Sam. No one from the outside world can speak out in your behalf as long as your struggle is a civil-rights struggle. Civil rights comes within the domestic affairs of this country. All of our African brothers and our Asian brothers and our Latin-American brothers cannot open their mouths and **interfere** in the domestic affairs of the United States. And as long as it's civil rights, this comes under the jurisdiction of Uncle Sam ...

Uncle Sam's hands are dripping with blood, dripping with the blood of the black man in this country. He's the earth's number-one **hypocrite**. He has the audacity—yes, he has—imagine him posing as the leader of the free world. The free world! And you over here singing "**We Shall Overcome**." Expand the civil-rights struggle to the level of human rights. Take it into the United Nations, where our African brothers can **throw their weight on** our side, where our Asian

---

dime: a coin; a penny (referring to worthless amount of money)

stand: position; attitude

insane: mad; crazy

reciprocal: mutual; returned
gander: male goose

confine: limit
jurisdiction: authority; sovereignty
Uncle Sam: USA

interfere: interrupt; come in between

hypocrite: a person who pretends to be kind; deceiver; double-dealer
We Shall Overcome: a protest song popular in the Civil Rights Movement

brothers can throw their weight on our side, where our Latin-American brothers can throw their weight on our side, and where 800 million Chinamen are sitting there waiting to throw their weight on our side....

The political philosophy of black nationalism means that the black man should control the politics and the politicians in his own **community**; no more. The black man in the black community has to be re-educated into the science of politics so he will know what politics is supposed to bring him in return. Don't be throwing out any ballots. A ballot is like a bullet. You don't throw your ballots until you see a target, and if that target is not within your reach, keep your ballot in your pocket.

The political philosophy of black nationalism is being taught in the Christian church. It's being taught in the **NAACP**. It's being taught in **CORE** meetings. It's being taught in **SNCC** Student Nonviolent Coordinating Committee meetings. It's being taught in Muslim meetings. It's being taught where nothing but **atheists** and **agnostics** come together. It's being taught everywhere. Black people are fed up with the dillydallying, pussyfooting, compromising approach that we've been using toward getting our freedom. We want freedom now, but we're not going to get it saying "We Shall Overcome." We've got to fight until we overcome.

The economic philosophy of black nationalism is pure and simple. It only means that we should control the economy of our community. ... Our people have to be made to see that any time you take your dollar out of your community and spend it in a community where you don't live, the community where you live will get poorer and poorer, and the community where you spend your money will get richer and richer....

So the economic philosophy of black nationalism means in every church, in every civic organization, in every **fraternal order**, it's time now for our people to become conscious of the importance of controlling the economy of our community. If we own the stores, if we operate the businesses, if we try and establish some industry in our own community, then we're developing to the position where we are creating employment for our own **kind**. Once you gain control of the economy of your own community, then you don't have to **picket** and **boycott** and beg some **cracker** downtown for a job in his business.

The social philosophy of black nationalism only means that we have to get together and remove the evils, the vices, **alcoholism**, drug

---

community: society for people with same race, religion and interests

NAACP: National Association for the Advancement of Colored People
CORE: Congress of Racial Equality
SNCC: Student Non-violent Coordinating Committee
atheist: nonbeliever of God
agnostic: person who believe that people cannot know if there is a God

fraternal order: brotherly association
kind: (here) race
picket: protest outside a shop or government building
boycott: refuse to buy, use something as part of protest activity
cracker: corrupt politician
alcoholism: habit of abusive drink of alcohol

fiber: (here) component
knock one's way into: to be accepted unwillingly by
gospel: bless

addiction, and other evils that are destroying the moral **fiber** of our community. We ourselves have to lift the level of our community, the standard of our community to a higher level, make our own society beautiful so that we will be satisfied in our own social circles and won't be running around here trying to **knock our way into** a social circle where we're not wanted. So I say, in spreading a **gospel** such as black nationalism, it is not designed to make the black man re-evaluate the white man—you know him already—but to make the black man re-evaluate himself. Don't change the white man's mind—you can't change his mind, and that whole thing about **appealing to** the moral conscience of America—America's conscience is bankrupt. She lost all conscience a long time ago. Uncle Sam has no conscience....

appealing to: wishing to meet

We want to hear new ideas and new solutions and new answers. And at that time, if we see fit then to form a black nationalist party, we'll form a black nationalist party. If it's necessary to form a black nationalist army, we'll form a black nationalist army. It'll be the ballot or the bullet. It'll be liberty or it'll be death.

...

■ 重点述评与提示

1. I'm not a politician, not even a student of politics; in fact, I'm not a student of much of anything. I'm not a Democrat. I'm not a Republican, and I don't even consider myself an American.

    在一系列的重复句式中始终突出主语"I"的身份，重心最后落在句末。与美国划清界限的目的在于追溯黑人文化，重铸黑人人格，这也是马尔科姆否定美国白人主流价值，反对民权运动种族融合倾向，提倡种族分离，黑人自治的思想逻辑起点。

2. These 22 million victims are waking up. Their eyes are coming open. They're beginning to see what they used to only look at. They're becoming politically mature. They are realizing that there are new political trends from coast to coast.

    马尔科姆对于黑人身份感的追溯由个人延伸到整个种族，他试图唤醒广大黑人，让他们看到黑人种族自身的政治力量，看到新的时代需要新的思维。这话为此后提倡突破民权诉求，争取全球黑人人权的思想做了铺垫。句子中的"see"和"look at"两个词语的对比绝妙地解构了黑人政治旁观者的身份，建构了种族自信自觉的认知基础。

3. It was the black man's vote that put the present administration in Washington, D.C. Your vote, your dumb vote, your ignorant vote, your wasted vote put in an administration in Washington, D.C., that has seen fit to pass every kind of legislation imaginable, saving you until last, then filibustering on top of that.

   这里强调了黑人手中选票在美国大选中的重要作用,句子开头用短促的节奏,重复"vote",逐渐推向高潮。这是马尔科姆演讲语言风格的表现,本篇演讲中俯拾即是。三个形容词表面贬义:黑人选票无声无息,貌似无知,而且往往被视为无效选票,但是,这些选票关键时却可左右大势。相比之下,靠黑人选票胜选的政府出尔反尔,设置种种立法障碍的行为在这里显得十分地尴尬。

4. The entire civil-rights struggle needs a new interpretation, a broader interpretation.

   注意,这是马尔科姆从麦加朝圣归来后形成的新思路:超越美国民权,走向种族人权。句中的"interpretation"重复2次,言其新与广,而且在本段话紧接的下文中,此词重复出现多达4次,在整个段落中遥相呼应,构成共鸣,既表达了演讲者改弦易辙的决心,又突出关键词,起到震耳发聩之功效。

5. And these handkerchief-heads who have been dillydallying and pussy footing and compromising—we don't intend to let them pussyfoot and dillydally and compromise any longer....

   这话显然是针对以马丁·路德·金为首的"南方基督教领袖大会"的黑人民权领导集团。改领导集团倡导非暴力抵抗,对肯尼迪政府的民权政策抱有幻想,关键时候犹豫不决,去妥协态度。马尔科姆此处叠用俚语,对这些主要黑人领袖极尽挖苦之能事。

6. I don't mean go out and get violent; but at the same time you should never be nonviolent unless you run into some nonviolence. I'm nonviolent with those who are nonviolent with me.

   注意,这是整篇演说中唯一一处提到不采取暴力行动。但是,在上下文强硬号召以牙还牙,暴力自卫的呼吁中,这一句劝诫人们非暴力的插入语显得多么的勉强,多么的微弱!而且,在这短短的句子中,马尔科姆在否定的语境中一口气连续重复4次"nonviolence",犹如一段绕口令,其讽刺戏谑意义昭然若揭。

7. When we begin to get in this area, we need new friends, we need new allies. We need to expand the civil-rights struggle to a higher level—to the level of human rights.

   这是马尔科姆的创见:突破美国民权斗争的局限,争取世界范围内的黑人人权。这也是黑人逐渐觉醒,文化自觉,增强政治力量的必然结果。用这样一个宣示性的句子正面陈述出来,有昭示天下的意蕴。

8. A ballot is like a bullet. You don't throw your ballots until you see a target, and if that target is not within your reach, keep your ballot in your pocket.

选票用好了,犹如射出子弹。在这里,子弹的意象得到了延伸,不仅仅是暴力自卫之意。也就是说,黑人应提高自己的教育水平,提高政治能力,从而借助宪法修正案赋予的选举权,以自己的方式参与美国政治,形成黑人种族自己的政治影响力。

9. Our people have to be made to see that any time you take your dollar out of your community and spend it in a community where you don't live, the community where you live will get poorer and poorer, and the community where you spend your money will get richer and richer....

看来,马尔科姆的经济思想还停留在表象层面。号召黑人不在白人社区消费,创办自己的企业和商业,从而把握黑人社会自己的经济命脉,这在表面上是提高黑人种族经济地位和社会地位的直接途径。但是,马尔科姆可能没有意识到,20世纪下半世纪后,经过战后的繁荣和"富裕社会",美国经济已经进入经济发展快车道,社会化生产和商品经济市场化趋势已经不以人的意志为转移。在此过程中,决定的因素不是种族,也不是消费的领域,而是资本、技术和管理。

■ 思考及讨论题

1. What roles does Malcolm X play while he was with The Nation of Islam?
2. What are some major differences between Matin Luther King and Malcolm X?
3. How did Malcolm define his identity (and that of all the African-Americans) in American society?
4. What could be the difference between "the black Civil Rights" and "the black human right"?

■ 阅读书目

1. Terrill, Rober E. ed. *The Cambridge Companion to Malcolm.* New York: Cambridge University Press, 2010.
2. Jackson, Eric R. "A Review Essay of Malcolm X: A Life Reinvention by Mannning Marable" in *The Journal of Pan African Studies* (online), June 2012.
3. Whitaker, Charles, Ebony. "Who Was Malcolm X" in *Ebony*, February 1992.
4. Roedmeier, Chad. "Rethinking Malcolm" in *Black Issues in Higher Education*, October, 1999.

第十章 ‖ 全球新秩序中的经济危机和反恐战争

If an individual wants to be a leader and isn't controversial, that means he never stood for anything.

——Richard Milhous Nixon

Government is not asolution to our problem, government is the problem.

——Ronald Reagan

Terrorist attacks can shake the foundations of our biggest buildings, but they cannot touch the foundation of America. These acts shatter steel, but they cannot dent the steel of American resolve.

——George W. Bush

Preview Questions

01/

What does the Vietnam War mean to Americans in the 1960s and 1970s?

02/

How did the Cold War come to its end? And how does this event affect the world politics in general?

03/

How did terrorism grow and how does it become America's major enemy?

04/

What was the American economic situation when President Bush took office?

第三十二讲

理查德·M. 尼克松（Richard M. Nixon 1914—1994）

■ 政治历史评述

理查德·尼克松：
一个复杂时代中领导一个复杂国家的个性复杂的实用主义政治家

上世纪70年代，中美两国不相往来，已经隔绝20多年，但是，理查德·尼克松的大名在中国可是家喻户晓。1972年2月21日，尼克松偕夫人飞抵北京机场，开始了他的"破冰之旅"。在北京深冬微微的寒风中，尼克松走下舷梯，抢先一步与前来迎接的周恩来总理紧紧握手。尼克松访华期间签署了《中美上海联合公报》，中美两国从此延续了传统友谊，改善和发展了两国关系，开始了新的大国关系，奠定了世界新的秩序与格局。4年之后，毛泽东主席再次邀请尼克松访华。当时尼克松已经因为"水门事件"而在美国成了千夫指，几乎遭到弹劾审判，最后被迫辞职，他在美国政治舞台上已经名誉扫地。但是，毛泽东却说："西方政治，那是假的"，"水门事件""不就是几卷录音带，有什么了不起！"尼克松再度访问中国期间发自内心地说："毛主席是充满思想活力的伟人。"

尼克松自40年代轰动一时的"希斯间谍案"以来，一直是坚定地反共份子，常常指控政敌是共产主义份子，扮演着一个"麦卡锡主义"和"非美调查委员会"推波助澜者的角色。当选美国总统后，他敢于否定自己，审时度势，放弃两极意识形态思维，重新估计中美苏三国利益关系，打破坚冰，实现中国之行并衷心仰慕占世界人口四分之一的社会主义大国的领袖，这是需要政治家的勇气和胆略的。同时，尼克松在美国60—70年代动荡时代中展示出来的实用求变和复杂的个性特征，也使他成了美国政治历史界30多年来最受争议的政治家。

尼克松的拥护者认为他是一个不知疲倦地为营造世界新的和平和秩序而努力的美国总统，也是美国历史上最后一位自由主义的政治家和改革家。在国际事务中，1969年7月24日，尼克松在关岛迎接从太空归来的宇航员时发表了"尼克松宣言"，宣布美国增加对亚洲盟友的经济和军事援助，同时逐步消减在亚洲的驻军，这实际上标志着美国在世界范围内收缩干预势力，缓解冷战对立的外交政策的开始。几个月以后，他将此全球战略付诸实施，宣布

"越南化"政策,增加美国对南越西贡政权的经济和军事援助,同时逐步撤出美国地面部队,更多地由南越军队作战;在战场上放弃伤亡惨重的"搜索和摧毁"战术,采用"清除和固守"的守势,加强空中打击,力图切断北越军队的通讯和补给线。同时,他派出和谈代表与北越谈判,经过3年的谈谈打打,终于在1973年1月在巴黎签署和约,结束了美国人长达16年的噩梦般的越南战争。这应该是尼克松主义新思维的重要成果之一。另一

方面,尼克松于1969年11月24日与前苏联签署了《不扩散核武器条约》,《关于限制反弹道导弹系统条约》、和《关于限制进攻性战略武器的临时协定》等一系列双边协定,并建立了美苏新一轮缓和的谈判机制,这些措施导致90年代的冷战结束。尼克松对此可以说是功不可没。此外,尼克松访华之前中美关系松动,开始重新建立了中美两个大国的双边联系,也直接促成了中国重返联合国。另一方面,尼克松的历史功绩还表现在他的国内事务和改革政策中。政治改革方面,他在任内结束了南方各州学校的种族隔离,动用联邦资金支持企业中的"平权法案"项目;废止了教育领域中性别歧视;扩大了公民选举权;大幅增加了"美国教育学会"和"全国人文科学捐赠基金会"的经费;在公共事务方面,他延续了罗斯福"新政"以来的自由主义传统,签署了众多的环境保护法案;建立美国"职业安全与卫生条例",缓解了空气污染;通过了美国铁路客运服务法案,创建了美国国铁;实行新的社会福利改革措施;引入新的国家医疗保障计划等等。这些施政实绩足以说明为什么尼克松在1972年6月遭受"水门事件"影响后半年之内仍高票连任美国总统。

当然,尼克松的内外政策,特别是他在"水门事件"后的表现,也引来了美国国内众多的非议和谴责。反对者们认为,尼克松外交政策的变化表明他是一个缺乏立场和果敢决断精神的人。他的中国之行对美国的全球安全战略固然有利,但在随后的10多年并未给美国带来更多的实际利益,反而使冷战格局更为复杂化;而且,由于尼克松讨好中国,致使美国在1971年的印巴战争中"偏袒"中国的盟友巴基斯坦政府,在联合国中谴责了印度,令美国民主自由主义者和保守主义政客们蒙羞;此外,他对苏联的各项限制核武器条约不久就被新一届的美国政府所背弃,没有真正得以实行。在处理越战方面,虽然尼克松迫于国内反战呼声,终于体面地结束了越南战争,但为时已晚,在他任内在越南投入的数百万吨炸弹和一纸和约都没有能够阻挡北越军队的进攻,美国最终付出了失去南越的代价。

尼克松的经济政策也是盲目的:在美元流通量大大超过美联储黄金储备量的时候沉不住气,为了减少赤字,保持物价稳定,宣布放弃金本位制,瓦解了布莱顿森林体系,结果适得其反,造成失业率增高和一直持续到80年代里根时代的通货膨胀;他在任内与国会关系紧张,被指责屡次见不得人的手段施政立法,因此被一些国会议员送与"狡猾的狄克"的雅号。此外,不喜欢尼克松的人还把他描绘为言行和表里都不一致的人,比如他在公众场合口口声声节俭朴素,对物质奢华毫无兴趣,却在白宫排场铺张,为警卫和工

作人员添置豪华制服,而他自己也筹划着置办美国最豪华的游艇等等。

公众对尼克松政治诚信的怀疑在1972年6月"水门事件"曝光以后达到了不可逆转的地步。尼克松先是声称自己毫不知情,后又拒不交出在白宫监听有关谈话和电话记录的秘密录音带,结果欲盖弥彰,越抹越黑,终于几乎完全失去国会的支持和公众的信任,白宫高官相继辞职,尼克松也被持续升级的司法调查弄得焦头烂额,政治声誉又经受了大起大落。据1974年盖洛普民意测验统计,97％的美国人都知道"水门丑闻",尼克松的支持率从越战结束时的68％,几个月之间跌至24％。65％的美国人表示,总统应该遭到国会弹劾和司法审判。情急中的尼克松也曾竭力四处活动,在电视上发表演讲,力图改善自己的政治形象,但收效甚微。万般无奈之下,他只好选择辞职,成立美国历史上唯一辞职的总统。这还不算,幸灾乐祸的政敌们落井下石,传闻辞职后的尼克松一蹶不振,精神狂想,想死的念头都有。残酷的政治角逐和盲目的政治意识在尼克松身上又扮演了一出典型的活剧。

近40年过去,斯人已逝。美国史学界对尼克松近30年的政治沉浮,是非功过也自有了更为客观公正的说法。

2004年,即尼克松辞去总统职务30年之际,美国一些顶级的历史学家聚集位于加州橘县的尼克松图书馆,重新评估这位辞职总统对于20世纪美国政治独特的贡献和历史意义。宾州大学历史学教授,普利策奖获得者瓦尔特·麦克道伽尔在主旨发言中定下基调:"尼克松是一个复杂时代中领导一个复杂国家的个性复杂的人。"1969年的美国,无休止的越战严重分化了社会,反战派和学生运动此起彼伏,大学校园都成了意识形态冲突乃至暴力对抗的场所。国际上,冷战的阴霾催生区域意识形态冲突,世界局势动荡不安。在此形势下,尼克松肩负重任,以实用主义的精神调整美国内外政策,在国内外事务中都取得了有利于美国和世界安全的重大成就。这是一个"水门事件"抹杀不掉历史贡献。用麦克道伽尔的话来说:"尼克松愿意在1969年担任总统职务,仅此一点,就值得我们长久的尊重。"以此观之,尼克松5年半的执政就获得了新的历史意义。在这些历史学家看来,尼克松标志着美国政治历史上新的分水岭,他的内外政策框定了当今美国两党政治斗争新一轮的格局。在他的任内,民主党占多数的国会和司法机构不甘心长期臣服小罗斯福以来渐渐做大的总统权力,开始向总统行政权力发难,反抗历史学家施莱辛格所谓的"专横的总统权"。某种程度上说,就连"水门事件"都可以被视为国会和司法反抗总统权的一场戏剧性表演。麦克道伽尔甚至认为,"水门事件"时的美国在尼克松的领导下已经摆脱了内外危机,而正是他昭显的政绩导致了他的辞职,因为"水门事件"是国会和总统之间必须制造出来的危机,借以在没有危机和不安全因素的社会环境中保持公众对政治的关注度。在这次高端学术会议上,尼克松当年的演说稿主要写作者雷蒙·普莱斯也见证了这位实用主义政治家的灵活思辨和实际成效:尼克松在决策中往往靠一种精准的政治直觉,在变化中的把握决策的方向。普莱斯这样评价尼克松:"这是一个实用主义的共和党人。他对决不把任何事物看成教条。"正是这种以现实世界的多样性和多变性为政策依据的政治智慧把美国从60年代的困境中解脱出来,进入一个相对安全和平稳的世界政治环境之中。

在我看来，尼克松更是一个政治生涯大起大落而矢志不渝的杰出政治家。

这个从加州边远城镇走出来的年轻人性格内向，喜欢独处，却能言善辩。他18岁进入威提尔学院，勤工俭学一路走来，1937年以优秀的成绩毕业于杜克大学法学院。此后他前途并不看好，是个穿梭于公司之间的小律师，混到34岁时仍一事无成。1946年，时来运转，尼克松竞选国会议员，一上来就采取凌厉的攻势击败资深的竞选对手。此后他一帆风顺，先是以反共急先锋的形象吸引了公众眼球，当上参议员，紧接着1952年成为艾森豪威尔的副总统。他借艾森豪威尔无为而治的政策，乘机扩大了副总统的权限，代表总统主持会议，签署法案，访问拉丁美洲后院各国，在莫斯科美国博览会的厨房样板间舌战赫鲁晓夫。那时的尼克松可谓出尽风头，前途无限。然而，泰极否来，在1960年的总统竞选中，志在必得的老牌政治家尼克松竟败在政坛新秀肯尼迪手下，不得已回到老家加州竞选州长，却又是一败涂地，颜面尽失。至此，尼克松的政治生涯跌至最低谷。新闻媒体报道不失时机地宣布了尼克松从此与政治无缘，就连20多年前被尼克松整垮的艾格尔·希斯都被美国广播公司请出来大谈特谈尼克松政治生命的终结。

然而，正如尼克松后来写的那样："失败不能击垮一个男人，自己退出，那才是真正的完蛋"，尼克松没有退出，反而不遗余力，甘愿充当各级共和党候选人的马前卒。仅1966年，他就为86名共和党候选人摇旗助选，其中58人胜出。结果，前副总统尼克松的犬马之劳没有白费，他再次成为共和党的香饽饽，东山再起，于1968年当选美国总统并在1972年以绝对优势连任。尼克松再次回到政治和权力的峰巅。此后便是"水门事件"调查和弹劾听证，尼克松再次遭遇政治滑铁卢，黯然辞职，算是"自己退出"。但是，他并没有完蛋。

在随后的日子里，尼克松又振作精神，活跃在公众视野里。他在继任总统福特访问中国之后几乎喧宾夺主，再度来到北京见到毛泽东主席；他为后任总统里根和老布什出谋划策。在随后不甘寂寞的日子里，他又是写回忆录，又是出书，忙得不亦乐乎；他还到处发表演说，仅1985年一年的时间，72岁的他就收到414个演说或访谈邀请，让新闻媒体惊呼老尼再度出山。尼克松80岁高龄仍凭记忆发表公共演讲，1994年4月18日中风，抢救无效逝世，享年81岁。

在他的回忆录里，尼克松曾不无感慨地这样回忆毛泽东："谁也不能否认他已战斗到最后一息了。"也许，正是感染到伟人生命不息，战斗不止的精神风貌，尼克松的一生也活跃在喧嚣的政治舞台上，几经沉浮，"战斗"到生命的最后一息了。

演讲文

Presidential Resignation Address
Richard M. Nixon

Good evening.

This is the 37th time I have spoken to you from **this office**, where so many decisions have been made that shaped the history of this Nation. Each time I have done so to discuss with you some matter that I believe affected the national interest.

In all the decisions I have made in my public life, I have always tried to do what was best for the Nation. Throughout the long and difficult period of **Watergate**, I have felt it was my duty to **persevere**, to make every possible effort to complete the term of office to which you elected me.

In the past few days, however, it has become evident to me that I no longer have a strong enough political base in the Congress to justify continuing that effort. As long as there was such a base, I felt strongly that it was necessary to see the **constitutional process** through to its conclusion, that to do otherwise would be unfaithful to the spirit of that deliberately difficult process and a dangerously destabilizing **precedent** for the future.

But with the disappearance of that base, I now believe that the constitutional purpose has been served, and there is no longer a need for the process to be **prolonged**.

I would have preferred to carry through to the finish whatever the personal **agony** it would have involved, and my family **unanimously** urged me to do so. But the interest of the Nation must always come before any personal considerations.

From the discussions I have had with Congressional and other leaders, I have concluded that because of the Watergate matter I might not have the support of the Congress that I would consider necessary to back the very difficult decisions and carry out the duties of this **office** in the way the interests of the Nation would require.

I have never been a **quitter**. To leave office before my term is completed is **abhorrent** to every instinct in my body. But as President, I must put the interest of America first. America needs a full-time President and a full-time Congress, particularly at this time with problems we face at home and abroad.

To continue to fight through the months ahead for my personal

---

resignation: official declaration of leaving office

this office: the Oval office in the White House

Watergate: the Watergate scandal
persevere: carry on; continue regardless of difficulty

constitutional process: (here) the 4-year presidential term designated by the constitution
precedent: example
prolong: delay; postpone
agony: great pain
unanimously: with complete agreement by everyone

office: (here) the presidential duty
quitter: someone who leave office out of his own decision
abhorrent: extremely unpleasant

vindication: defense to prove not guilty
inflation: (economics) devaluation of money

high hopes: great expectation

turning over: handing over; passing over
nominate: recommend

assume: take up
heal: recover from pain

desperately: urgently

stand with: support; side with

eternally: forever
bitterness: hatred
final analysis: essential objective
however: even though
affirm: make sure again

vindication would almost totally absorb the time and attention of both the President and the Congress in a period when our entire focus should be on the great issues of peace abroad and prosperity without **inflation** at home.

Therefore, I shall resign the Presidency effective at noon tomorrow. Vice President Ford will be sworn in as President at that hour in this office.

As I recall the **high hopes** for America with which we began this second term, I feel a great sadness that I will not be here in this office working on your behalf to achieve those hopes in the next 2 1/2 years. But in **turning over** direction of the Government to Vice President Ford, I know, as I told the Nation when I **nominated** him for that office 10 months ago, that the leadership of America will be in good hands.

In passing this office to the Vice President, I also do so with the profound sense of the weight of responsibility that will fall on his shoulders tomorrow and, therefore, of the understanding, the patience, the cooperation he will need from all Americans.

As he **assumes** that responsibility, he will deserve the help and the support of all of us. As we look to the future, the first essential is to begin **healing** the wounds of this Nation, to put the bitterness and divisions of the recent past behind us, and to rediscover those shared ideals that lie at the heart of our strength and unity as a great and as a free people.

By taking this action, I hope that I will have hastened the start of that process of healing which is so **desperately** needed in America.

I regret deeply any injuries that may have been done in the course of the events that led to this decision. I would say only that if some of my judgments were wrong, and some were wrong, they were made in what I believed at the time to be the best interest of the Nation.

To those who have **stood with** me during these past difficult months, to my family, my friends, to many others who joined in supporting my cause because they believed it was right, I will be **eternally** grateful for your support.

And to those who have not felt able to give me your support, let me say I leave with no **bitterness** toward those who have opposed me, because all of us, in the **final analysis**, have been concerned with the good of the country, **however** our judgments might differ.

So, let us all now join together in **affirming** that common commitment and in helping our new President succeed for the benefit of all Americans.

I shall leave this office with regret at not completing my term, but with gratitude for the privilege of serving as your President for the past 5 1/2 years. These years have been a **momentous** time in the history of our Nation and the world. They have been a time of achievement in which we can all be proud, achievements that represent the shared efforts of the Administration, the Congress, and the people.

But the challenges ahead are equally great, and they, too, will require the support and the efforts of the Congress and the people working in cooperation with the new Administration.

We have ended America's **longest war**, but in the work of securing a lasting peace in the world, the goals ahead are even more far-reaching and more difficult. We must complete a **structure** of peace so that it will be said of this generation, our generation of Americans, by the people of all nations, not only that we ended one war but that we prevented future wars.

We have **unlocked the doors** that for a quarter of a century stood between the United States and the People's Republic of China.

We must now ensure that the one quarter of the world's people who live in the People's Republic of China will be and remain not our enemies but our friends.

In the Middle East, 100 million people in the Arab countries, many of whom have considered us their enemy for nearly 20 years, now **look on** us as their friends. We must continue to build on that friendship so that peace can settle at last over the Middle East and so that the cradle of civilization will not become its grave.

Together with the Soviet Union we have made the **crucial** breakthroughs that have begun the process of limiting nuclear arms. But we must set as our goal not just limiting but reducing and finally destroying these terrible weapons so that they cannot destroy civilization and so that the threat of nuclear war will no longer hang over the world and the people.

We have opened the new relation with the Soviet Union. We must continue to develop and expand that new relationship so that the two strongest nations of the world will live together in cooperation rather than **confrontation**.

Around the world, in Asia, in Africa, in Latin America, in the Middle East, there are millions of people who live in terrible poverty, even **starvation**. We must keep as our goal turning away from production for war and expanding production for peace so that people

---

momentous: full of great events: significant

longest war: the Vietnam war that lasted almost 20 years

structure: (here) ways of relations between the powers of the world

unlock the door: reestablish the communication

look on: regard

crucial: very important

confrontation: political and military opposition

starvation: death caused by lack of food

decent: honored and cultured
means: resources, material as well as spiritual
full and good: with enough food and good respect
strive: work hard

turbulent: full of troubles and crisis

take heart: be encouraged
in the arena: in the middle of a fight surrounded by cheering audience
marred: stained
come short: make a wrong move

daring: fighting bravely; challenging
that spirit: (here) the spirit of fighting on despite repeated failures

sacred: holy; elevated; godly
consecrate: devote; dedicate (to a cause)
office: term as the President

legacy: meaningful and valuable things left to later generations

everywhere on this earth can at last look forward in their children's time, if not in our own time, to having the necessities for a **decent** life.

Here in America, we are fortunate that most of our people have not only the blessings of liberty but also the **means** to live **full and good** and, by the world's standards, even abundant lives. We must press on, however, toward a goal of not only more and better jobs but of full opportunity for every American and of what we are **striving** so hard right now to achieve, prosperity without inflation.

For more than a quarter of a century in public life I have shared in the **turbulent** history of this era. I have fought for what I believed in. I have tried to the best of my ability to discharge those duties and meet those responsibilities that were entrusted to me.

Sometimes I have succeeded and sometimes I have failed, but always I have **taken heart** from what Theodore Roosevelt once said about the man **in the arena**, "whose face is **marred** by dust and sweat and blood, who strives valiantly, who errs and **comes short** again and again because there is not effort without error and shortcoming, but who does actually strive to do the deed, who knows the great enthusiasms, the great devotions, who spends himself in a worthy cause, who at the best knows in the end the triumphs of high achievements and who at the worst, if he fails, at least fails while **daring** greatly."

I pledge to you tonight that as long as I have a breath of life in my body, I shall continue in **that spirit**. I shall continue to work for the great causes to which I have been dedicated throughout my years as a Congressman, a Senator, a Vice President, and President, the cause of peace not just for America but among all nations, prosperity, justice, and opportunity for all of our people.

There is one cause above all to which I have been devoted and to which I shall always be devoted for as long as I live.

When I first took the oath of office as President 5 1/2 years ago, I made this **sacred** commitment, to "**consecrate** my **office**, my energies, and all the wisdom I can summon to the cause of peace among nations."

I have done my very best in all the days since to be true to that pledge. As a result of these efforts, I am confident that the world is a safer place today, not only for the people of America but for the people of all nations, and that all of our children have a better chance than before of living in peace rather than dying in war.

This, more than anything, is what I hoped to achieve when I sought the Presidency. This, more than anything, is what I hope will be my **legacy** to you, to our country, as I leave the Presidency.

To have served in this office is to have felt a very personal sense of **kinship** with each and every American. In leaving it, I do so with this prayer: May God's grace be with you in all the days ahead.

| kinship: loving family relationship |

■ 重点述评与提示

1. This is the 37th time I have spoken to you from this office, where so many decisions have been made that shaped the history of this Nation.

   说来也巧,尼克松是美国第37届总统,辞职演说正好是他担任总统5年半中第37次在白宫椭圆形办公室的电视演讲。可惜随着这第37次的演讲,他的第37届总统职务也走到了尽头。尼克松虽然不善即兴演讲,却是对书面演讲词十分认真的人,每次演讲之前都做长时间的准备,仔细揣摩字句的意义。他认真研究过华盛顿以来所有的总统就职演说,有时为了准备演讲可以把自己关进戴维营的房间伏案14个小时。尼克松对这次辞职演讲自然非常重视,说道:"这一次,我要说出心里话,这是我真正的演讲。"早晨11时琢磨出37数字这个象征意义,指示白宫秘书仔细查对这个数字后。下午,演讲稿即准备就绪,尼克松将在晚上9点向1100万电视观众宣读这篇演讲。

2. In the past few days, however, it has become evident to me that I no longer have a strong enough political base in the Congress to justify continuing that effort.

   水门事件调查开始后,尼克松曾努力开脱,试图重铸形象。但是,随着监听录音带问题持续发酵,媒体开始一致呼吁弹劾尼克松;2天前,共和党少数派领袖罗德宣布,除非尼克松辞职,他将投票支持弹劾总统。此时,尼克松也意识到,他在参众两院的支持者总共不到30人。1天前,国会两党领袖取得一致,正式告诫尼克松,他不再获得国会大多数的支持。至此,尼克松才终于决定避开弹劾,主动辞职。可以说,在尼克松看来,总统辞职的原因不是水门事件,而是国会和司法针对总统权力的政治反弹。

3. I have never been a quitter. To leave office before my term is completed is abhorrent to every instinct in my body. But as President, I must put the interest of America first.

   这是尼克松在演讲草稿中刻意写下的字句。也是他对自己近30年政治生涯和个性的总结。他的政治生命中多有大起大落,但他从未主动放弃,这是他的个性。后一句是典型的政治意识形态宣教,也是尼克松辞职的体面辞藻,却不是辞职的原因。

4. I regret deeply any injuries that may have been done in the course of the events that led to this decision. I would say only that if some of my judgments were wrong, and some were wrong, they were made in what I believed at the time to be the best interest of the Nation.

尼克松决定辞职时就召集幕僚,为这篇演讲定下基调:"这不是一篇沉痛悔过的演讲,其中不应承认没有犯过的过错。相反,这是一篇治疗国家创伤的演讲,一篇号召人民团结在继任者周围的演讲。"因此,这里出现的唯一一处表达道歉的话语也仅持续24秒,而且不是直接就水门事件向公众道歉,而是用"这些事件过程"一笔带过,虽然承认自己判断有所失误,那都是为国家的利益而犯下的过错。不了解尼克松个性的人当然要说:这篇演讲是敷衍之作。

5. These years have been a momentous time in the history of our Nation and the world. They have been a time of achievement in which we can all be proud, achievements that represent the shared efforts of the Administration, the Congress, and the people.

尼克松在这里强调,自己的总统任期处于国家危机四伏,世界动荡不安的年代,为的是突出自己的政绩。表面上是说,这些政绩是行政、立法和全体人民共同团结努力的结果,但是,在总统权力一直扩大的年代里,这些当然是尼克松自我标榜的最好话语,为以下列举总统政绩做好总体的铺垫。

6. But we must set as our goal not just limiting but reducing and finally destroying these terrible weapons so that they cannot destroy civilization and so that the threat of nuclear war will no longer hang over the world and the people.

除了结束越战和重开中美关系,尼克松任内的得意之作也许就是与苏联实现进一步实质性的缓和。这里用"多连词并列"的修辞方法把"限制"、"减少"和"销毁"三个动词珠联一起,明确地表示了双方核武谈判的阶段过程。后面的两个"so that"关系从句一虚一实,取得令人印象深刻的修辞效果。

7. I pledge to you tonight that as long as I have a breath of life in my body, I shall continue in that spirit. I shall continue to work for the great causes to which I have been dedicated throughout my years as a Congressman, a Senator, a Vice President, and President, ...

西奥多·罗斯福是美国历史上有名的"硬汉"总统。尼克松在此时刻借彼扬己,弘扬这种"一息尚存,永不言败"的精神,为自己不得已而辞职的决定挣回了点面子,同时不失时机地铺陈自己近30年一步步的政治轨迹,乘机重塑久经沙场的老牌政治家的形象,可谓一箭双雕,难怪他的一些政敌称他是政坛上"狡猾的狄克"。

8. As a result of these efforts, I am confident that the world is a safer place today, not only for the people of America but for the people of all nations, and that all of our children have a better chance than before of living in peace rather than dying in war.

尼克松曾告诫他的演说写稿人普莱斯,这篇演讲稿要让人们着眼未来,言下之意即让人们看到他5年半的任期的最大贡献就是结束战争,重建世界和平与安全的新秩序。下一段中反复重申,这就是他毕生的政治关怀,也是留给子孙后代的主要遗产。尼克松在念到这一段的时候,语速放慢,一字一顿,表现出极大诚意、信心和自豪。

■ 思考及讨论题

1. Why do we say that Nixon's visit to China in 1972 is an epoch-making event?
2. How did Nixon bring the protracted Vietnam War to an end?
3. Why Nixon was regarded as the last "Liberal President"?
4. Why some historians say that Nixon has a controversial character?

■ 阅读书目

1. Brodie, Fawn M. *Richard Nixon: The Shaping of His Character*. New York: W. W. Norton, 1981.
2. Genovese, Michael A. *The Nixon Presidency: Power and Politics in Turbulent Times*. Westport: Greenwood Press, 1990.
3. Anonymous. "A Reevaluation of Richard Nixon" in *The World and I*. September 2004.
4. Bochin, Hal W. "The Watergate and Resignation Speeches: Rhetoric Versus Fact" in *Rhetorical Strategist*. New York: Greenwood Press, 1990.

第三十三讲

罗纳德·W.里根(Ronald W. Reagan 1911—2004)

■ 政治历史评述

罗纳德·里根:戏剧人生的政治家,经济复苏和结束冷战的大国领袖

美国人其实也需要个人崇拜。200多年前的华盛顿就享受过英雄式的大众崇拜,到了2004年,罗纳德·里根总统逝世,如此的领袖崇拜也到了登峰造极的地步。

长达一周的缅怀活动:成千上万瞻仰遗容的人流,鲜花,追思会,盛大的国葬;电视24小时播放里根的好莱坞电影;米西谷山坡上肃穆的里根图书馆;"里根遗产工程"的杰作:华盛顿里根国家机场,里根联邦大楼;计划中在50个州建立的里根纪念碑;3,054个区县中以里根的名字命名的学校,公路,街道,公园和建筑;美国青年基金会的里根农场遗产工程;40个州宣布2月6日里根诞辰为"罗纳德·里根日"。

这些都是里根永存的纪念标志,纪念着这位美国年龄最大、最长寿、最受欢迎的总统。

说来这也并不奇怪,不论是表演家还是政治家,影星还是总统,罗纳德·里根生前也都是持续受到公众追捧的幸运人物。

他天生长得一副出镜的相貌:近1米9的高大身材,英俊帅气的容貌,运动员的体格,雄浑的嗓音带有磁性,展示出简洁而又风趣的口才。

里根在大学学的是经济学,成绩平平,酷爱运动,却不乏语言修辞和表演艺术的天赋。他在1932年大学毕业后不久就当上了广播体育评论员,靠嘴皮子吃饭,由此进入了公众视线。这在当时失业率为25%的经济大萧条时期是不多见的成功例子。这个意气风发的年轻人在当时竞争十分激烈的职场上妙语连珠,可谓一帆风顺,名气很大,几年来连续在广播荧屏上吸引着全美公众的眼球。

1937年,里根进军好莱坞,一心做个当红影星。不久,幸运的他就在华纳兄弟影业公司试镜成功,圆了自己多年的演员梦,每周薪水200美元。此后,里根迅速入戏,在一系列影片中扮演重要角色,而且短短3年后主演了几部大片,受到影迷的追捧,跻身好莱坞一流演员之列,每周薪水3500美元。从此步入富人阶层,购地置产,侍奉父母,娶妻生子,出入一副名流的派头。

那时的里根,沉迷于聚光灯下,哪有政治家的影子!

不过,里根可是一个骨子里涌动着戏剧(多半是喜剧)因子的人,不会甘于在一种生活模式中刻板地度过一生。生活的多彩是他内在的渴望,公众的心理场是他外在的追求。

巧的是,现实也为他提供了戏剧般的场合。1941年底,日本偷袭珍珠港,美日宣战。里根应召入伍,影星成了士兵,本想上前线拼杀,但体检时被发现高度近视,戏剧性地又被打回老家服役,在后方发挥影星的优势,专门负责拍摄军事训练的纪录片。

战争结束,里根退伍,受雇通用电气公司,做电视节目主持人,又回到公众的视野中。此时的他,在影像中目睹过战争的残酷,体验过政治的无处不在。因此,他对公众意识的期待又增添了新的内容。他开始在节目主持和公司产品宣传员的机会到全国各地演讲,越来越多地表达自己的政治见解,抨击高高在上的官僚主义,指责政府滥用权力和高税收。里根本来就长于在大众面前口若悬河,现在有了政治意识的推动,他的演讲口才更上一层,在政治话语的反复循环中逐渐走向了政治舞台的中心。

于是,里根的演艺天赋和演说才能与政治接轨,他戏剧性地宣布脱离民主党,加入共和党,投入到政治竞选场上。在滔滔不绝的演讲和选民的欢呼声中,里根似乎全然忘记老之将至,他56岁竞选成功,担任加州州长,一干2届就是8年。及至1980年总统大选击败在任总统吉米·卡特,登上美国总统宝座,这位永葆青春的影星政治家已至古稀之年。而此时,他的政治人生的大戏也才刚刚开始。

里根总统上任2个月零20天,一个名叫欣克列的年轻人在希尔顿饭店外,举枪向总统连开6枪。里根左胸中弹,生命垂危。但乐天知命的他仍不忘人生舞台的意识,吃力地对前来为他做手术的大夫说:"告诉我,你们都是共和党人。"惊恐的夫人南希赶到医院,里根苏醒过来见到南希的第一句话是:"亲爱的,我忘了猫腰躲闪了。"这是拳击手在台上的一句幽默名言。

里根大难不死,"生命始于70岁",在政治舞台上又红了一把。台下民众欢呼,支持率节节攀升。

里根不久痊愈,抖擞精神投入总统工作,在通货膨胀,失业率飙升和经济衰退的困境中干得有声有色,4年之后以绝对优势获得连任。1989年两任总统届满离任,里根的民众支持率达到破纪录的63%,这位曾经的电影明星又在政治舞台上赚足了人气,成为世界瞩目的政治明星,获得了"伟大的交流者","超级演说家","最伟大的美国人"等美名。

1989年1月11日,里根面对全国的电视观众,发表了"告别演说"。这位表演意识强烈的美国总统即将告别舞台,免不了表达了心中的惆怅。"离别是如此甜蜜的悲伤",里根在演说中告诉千千万万的粉丝和观众。这句莎士比亚名剧《罗密欧与朱丽叶》中有名的台词倒也恰如其分地表达了里根内心不舍的情感,是虚拟戏剧语言传统与现实政治意识完美的结合。

里根卸任后没有离开公众视线。他擅长台上发表演讲,有时幽默俏皮,有时笑话连篇,继续走着自己戏剧人生的道路,直到患上老年痴呆症,开始失去记忆。此时的里根,仍然不忘心中的美国观众。在一封公开信中,里根说道:"此时,我开始了人生的落日之旅,但我知道,美国人民将永远面对着黎明的光辉。"这是多么动人的诗化语言,其中既表达了一种戏剧人生的达观态度,也表述了一个政治家宏阔的政治意识,犹如一句精彩的经典电影台词。

里根的电影演艺经历曾是他的政治对手攻击他的主要话题。殊不知,这正是里根作为杰出政治家的长处。虚拟的电影世界,现实的政治舞台,并无本质的区别。以乐观的心态面对人生,以阳光的笑容面对观众,以幽默的语言和政治修辞表达一种坚信的政治信念,这应该就是一个成熟的政治领袖的智慧。在他之前,约翰逊、福特、卡特几届总统都是起早贪黑,没日没夜地工作,公众面前强推微笑,但却没有赢得公众的好评,被认为是尼克松之后弱势的几届总统。相比之下,里根的总统工作显得像演电影那样地生活化而又轻松:他每天保证8小时睡眠,早晨9点半才开始工作,下午5时结束工作,坚持健身1个半小时,每周三下午停止工作,晚上看电视节目,写日记,10点准时睡觉。不

仅如此,他每月都要举行盛大的宴会,款待各方朋友,周末则偕夫人南希到戴维营度假,忘却工作,彻底放松。然而,该干的活儿没有耽误,反而政绩卓越。里根总统两任后,国内经济形势大为好转,苏联也即将被美国的冷战政策拖垮,美国在世界愈发强势。"里根经济学"、"里根革命"等新鲜名词的流行也标志着里根在公众心目中神秘而又强大的地位。里根说,他1984年访问中国后学会了"治大国如烹小鲜"这样的老子智慧,正好印证了他"政府不是解决问题的办法,政府本身就是问题"的治国之道。里根这样的政治理念的形成,除了深受杰斐逊民主自由主义思想的影响之外,恐怕与他一生乐观幽默,戏剧人生,自然而法的心态分不开的。纵观美国历史,像里根这样,虚实之际,谈笑之间玩转政治的人也是少见的。

上世纪80年代的美国被称为"里根时代",足见里根作为大国领袖的政绩斐然。

里根就职时正值美国经济停滞,通货膨胀的滞胀时期。持续多年的两位数高通货膨胀率和银行利率难以保持经济增长,失业率也高居不下,工人平均工资下降。同时,国家财政赤字攀升,致使个人所得税率平均高达67%,由此循环,国债亦高达1万亿美元。

面临如此经济危机,里根奉行了供应学派和货币学派的经济学理论,提出全面的经济复兴计划,其内容综合了上述学派的经济理论观点,被称为"里根经济学"。里根在大学主修经济学,但成绩平平,后来也学非所用,无力创建独立的经济学派,但是根据现实经济状况移花接木,用通俗和感性的语言综合两大经济学派的经济理论观点,由此获得大众接受和支持,这也是擅长演讲,平易近人的里根的长处。里根的经济复兴计划主要包括:

大规模减税,以刺激商业投资,制造就业机会,促进经济增长;

削减财政开支,特别是社会福利开支,减少财政赤字,3年之内实现预算收支平衡;

鼓励市场自由竞争,减少国家对企业和金融商业的干预和监管;

严格控制货币供应量的增长,实行稳定的货币政策以抑制通货膨胀;

扩大国债和外债规模,减少国家财政赤字等。

这个经济复兴计划实施有效地遏制了通货膨胀,创造了大量的结业机会,增加了全社会从业人员的工资收入,使美国走出了经济低谷,带来了美国80年代后期经济的持续繁荣,在一定程度上恢复了美国人对未来的信心。

国外,持续的冷战开始出现相对平衡的缓和局面,但"越战综合症"还在持续,造成美国社会的分裂倾向。勃列日涅夫后的苏联仍咄咄逼人,限制核武器谈判仍在继续。另外,中东和南美一些地区的反美情绪高涨,恐怖主义的阴云开始聚集,同时,持续的两伊战争也给美国在中东的经济利益提出了诸多不确定因素的挑战。

对此,里根一反杜鲁门以来美国"遏制"和"缓和"的政策,主动出击,采取强硬对策,对抗苏联的核威胁。里根大规模投入国防预算,实行扩军计划,提出了所谓"星际大战"主动战略防御计划,在外层空间部署具有进攻性的导弹防御网,同时遏制苏联的高科技输入和苏联产品在世界市场上的经济竞争力。此外,里根大力支持阿富汗反苏游击队和波兰团结工会,呼吁推到柏林墙。这些政策和措施借助了80年代苏共"新思维"改革意见分歧和经济倒退的机会,促成了1991年苏联的解体和冷战的结束。

另一方面,里根执着于冷战意识,在中东和南美扩大反恐范围。他不惜美国海军陆战队的伤亡,强行军事介入中东热战地区,把反美的黎巴嫩真主党和部分巴勒斯坦游击队视作恐怖分子加以打击,同时也把尼加拉瓜,洪都拉斯和南非的反政府武装纳入共产恐怖分子之列;他称苏联为"邪恶帝国",把古巴、尼加拉瓜、朝鲜、伊朗和利比亚等国家一律划为邪恶恐怖主义国家之列。1983年,里根得知加勒比岛国格林纳达发生政变,古巴的卡斯特罗将从中获取利益,便立即派出1700名海军陆战队登陆作战,推翻政府,扶持亲美政权上台。

当然，史学界对美国"里根时代"的内外政策的得失也有争议，比如"里根经济学"对后世美国经济的负面影响，里根高调反共反恐政策导致21世纪恐怖主义威胁上升等等。但是，里根乐天的性格，引人注目的公众形象和大国领袖地位已经在美国人心目中扎根，这位历史上最长寿的美国总统的人气甚至高于华盛顿和林肯，2011年被选为"最受欢迎的美国总统"。

里根有着杰出的语言天赋，被誉为"超级演说家"。他有一个酒神精神作用下善讲故事的父亲和虔诚善良，循循善诱的母亲；他的一生都伴随着语言修辞和演说的成功，伴随着他忠实的听众。还在大学期间，他代表学生会的第一次演讲就获得意外的成功，随后的播音和演艺生涯更是与语言艺术结下了不解之缘。但是，只有政治，才能让他的演说才能达到辉煌的顶峰。1964年10月27日，里根第一次在电视上演说，为共和党候选人助选。这场演说获得巨大的成功，2次在国家电视台播放，上百次在当地电视台重播。不久，共和党上下一致推举里根竞选美国总统。里根后来回忆说："那场演讲改变了我的一生。"此后，里根幽默风趣，平易而又犀利的演讲风格在政治的舞台上所向披靡，一直到82岁高龄还以生动风趣的演讲活跃在公众的视野中。那个信息传播技术勃兴的年代和政治的喧嚣共同造就了里根这个"伟大的沟通者"。

里根政治演说成功的秘笈首先在于他的思想观念在演说中得以一以贯之的表述。听众在里根众多的演说中总能听到里根对自己思想的自信和诚恳，在他那动态双向的演说中把握住一个中心的思想和原则。这是政治演说的要务。其次，里根善于用口语化的表述在演说中拉近与听众的心理距离。他的演说总是充满了现实的画面感，无论趣闻轶事，场景描述，个人经历还是论点表述和论证，都能让听众如临其境，如述其意。有时，他还会以听众中的某人为例，直接与之对话，由此大大增加了与听众的亲和感。此外，里根善于发挥优势，在演说中直接使用或化用大众耳熟能详的影剧台词，让有时乏味的政治演讲产生出戏剧化的效果。在语言风格方面，里根崇尚电视节目制作的信条：说得少，意味多。他提倡清晰、直接和简明的口头语风格，特别注重语言的听觉效果。他对白宫写稿人员说："要使用简单的语言。永远记住，人们坐在那儿听讲，你必须让他们听懂你在讲什么。"演讲中，里根喜欢不时插入"well,"这样的语气词，让听众有一种促膝谈心的感觉。

总之，里根的演说风格具有平民化和大众化意识，展现了里根平易近人，戏剧化现实的个性特点，给人以一种在倾谈之中恍然大悟之感。这是罗纳德·里根的风格，也是信息化网络化世界人际沟通的特点。在政治舞台上，如此的风格表述出来的政治，是戏剧化的政治，是生活化的政治，也是为大众易于接受的政治。这也正如里根告别演说里结尾的一句话："说来说去，还不错，一点儿错不了。"(All in all, not bad, not bad at all.)

演讲文(节选)

Presidential Farewell Address

Ronald W. Reagan

My fellow Americans:

...

One of the things about the presidency is that you're always somewhat apart. You spend a lot of time going by too fast in a car someone else is driving, and seeing the people through **tinted** glass-the parents holding up a child, and the **wave** you saw too late and couldn't return. And so many times I wanted to stop and reach out from behind the glass, and connect. Well, maybe I can do a little of that tonight.

People ask how I feel about leaving. And the fact is, "parting is such **sweet sorrow**." The sweet part is California, and the **ranch** and freedom. The sorrow-the good-byes, of course, and leaving this beautiful place.

...

The fact is, from Grenada to the Washington and Moscow **summits**, from the **recession** of '81 to '82, to the expansion that began in late '82 and continues to this day, we've made a difference. The way I see it, there were two great triumphs, two things that I'm proudest of. One is the economic recovery, in which the people of America created-and filled-19 million new jobs. The other is the recovery of our **morale**. America is respected again in the world and looked to for leadership.

...

Well, back in 1980, when I was running for president, it was all so different. Some **pundits** said our programs would result in **catastrophe**. Our views on foreign affairs would cause war. Our plans for the economy would cause inflation to soar and bring about economic collapse. I even remember one highly respected economist saying, back in 1982, that "the engines of economic growth have **shut down** here, and they're likely to stay that way for years to come." Well, he and the other opinion leaders were wrong. The fact is, what they called "**radical**" was really "right." What they called "dangerous" was just "desperately needed."

And in all of that time I won a nickname, "The Great

---

tinted: colored
wave: (here) the waving of hand in greeting

sweet sorrow: ambivalent feeling of happiness and sadness
ranch: big pasture or farmland
Grenada: an island country in the Caribbean
summit: meeting of top leaders
morale: courage; confidence

pundit: well-learned man
catastrophe: large-scale destruction; disaster

shut down: stop working
radical: aggressively forward

Communicator." But I never thought it was my style or the words I used that made a difference: It was the content. I wasn't a great communicator, but I communicated great things, and they didn't spring **full bloom** from my **brow**, they came from the heart of a great nation-from our experience, our wisdom, and our belief in the principles that have guided us for two centuries. They called it the Reagan revolution. Well, I'll accept that, but for me it always seemed more like the great rediscovery, a rediscover of our values and our common sense.

Common sense told us that when you put a big **tax** on something, the people will produce less of it. So, we cut the people's tax rates, and the people produced more than ever before. The economy **bloomed** like a plant that had been cut back and could not grow quicker and stronger. Our economic program brought about the longest peacetime expansion in our history: real family income up, the poverty rate down, **entrepreneurship** booming, and an explosion in research and new technology. We're exporting more than ever because American industry became more competitive and at the same time, we **summoned** the national will to knock down protectionist walls abroad instead of **erecting** them at home. Common sense also told us that to preserve the peace, we'd have to become strong again after years of weakness and confusion. So, we rebuilt our defenses, and this New Year we **toasted** the new peacefulness around the globe. Not only have the superpowers actually begun to reduce their **stockpiles** of nuclear weapons-and hope for even more progress is bright-but the regional conflicts that **rack** the globe are also beginning to cease. The Persian Gulf is no longer a war zone. The Soviets are leaving Afghanistan. The Vietnamese are preparing to pull out of Cambodia, and an American-**mediated accord** will soon send 50,000 Cuban troops home to Angola.

The lesson of all this was, of course, that because we're a great nation, our challenges seem complex. It will always be this way. But as long as we remember our first principles and believe in ourselves, the future will always be ours. And something else we learned: Once you begin a great movement, there's no **telling** where it will end. We meant to change a nation, and instead, we changed a world.

Countries across the globe are turning to free markets and free speech and turning away from the ideologies of the past. For them, the great rediscovery of the 1980s has been that, **lo and behold**, the moral way of government is the **practical** way of government: Democracy, the profoundly good, is also profoundly productive.

---

full bloom: complete
brow: (here) mind

tax: money collected by government
bloom: grow into prosperity

entrepreneurship: private business
boom: grow rapidly
summon: call; mobilize
erect: set up
toast: make a good wish for
stockpile: large stock of goods for emergency use
rack: trouble constantly with pain
mediate: help to bring two rivals to negotiate
accord: treaty

telling: prediction; foretelling

lo and behold: look and see
practical: what works in reality

When you've got to the point when you can celebrate the anniversaries of your thirty-ninth birthday, you can sit back sometimes, review your life, and see it flowing before you. For me there was a **fork** in the river, and it was right in the middle of my life. I never meant to go into politics. It wasn't my intention when I was young. But I was raised to believe you had to pay your way for the blessings **bestowed on** you. I was happy with my career in the entertainment world, but I ultimately went into politics because I wanted to protect something precious.

Ours was the **first revolution** in the history of mankind that truly **reversed** the course of government, and with three little words: "We the people." "We the people" tell the government what to do, it doesn't tell us. "We the people" are the driver, the government is the car. And we decide where it should go, and by what route, and how fast. Almost all the world's constitutions are documents in which governments tell the people what their **privileges** are. Our Constitution is a document in which "We the people" tell the government what it is allowed to do. "We the people" are free. This belief has been the underlying basis for everything I've tried to do these past eight years.

But back in the 1960s, when I began, it seemed to me that we'd begun reversing the order of things—that through more and more rules and regulations and **confiscatory** taxes, the government was taking more of our money, more of our options, and more of our freedom. I went into politics in part to put up my hand and say, " Stop." I was a citizen politician, and it seemed the right thing for a citizen to do.

I think we have stopped a lot of what needed stopping. And I hope we have once again reminded the people that man is not free unless government is limited. There's a clear cause and effect here that is as neat and predictable as a law of physics: As government expands, liberty **contracts**.

Nothing is less free than pure communism, and yet we have, the past few years, **forged** a satisfying new closeness with the Soviet Union. I've been asked if this isn't a gamble, and my answer is no because we're basing our actions not on words but deeds. The **détente** of the 1970s was based not on actions but promises. They'd promise to treat their own people and the people of the world better. But the **gulag** was still the gulag, and the state was still expansionist, and they still waged **proxy** wars in Africa, Asia, and Latin America.

---

fork: *the point where the river divides into two directions;* (here) *a big choice in life*
bestow on: *kindly given to*
revolution: (here) *American Independence and the making of the US Constitution*
reverse: *change to the opposite*

privilege: *special rights and advantages*

confiscatory: *enforced for the benefit of authority*

contract: *become smaller; shrink*
forge: *mold; shape; cast; made permanent*
détente: *the eased tension between countries*
gulag: (here) *Soviet authority repressive of the innocent people in concentration camps*
proxy: *deputy*

Well, this time, so far, it's different. President Gorbachev has brought about some internal democratic reforms and begun the withdrawal from Afghanistan. He has also freed prisoners whose names I've given him every time we've met.

...

I've been asked if I have any regrets. Well, I do. The **deficit** is one. I've been talking a great deal about that lately, but tonight isn't for arguments. And I'm going to hold my tongue. But an observation: I've had my share of victories in the Congress, but what few people noticed is that I never won anything you didn't win for me. They never saw my troops, they never saw Reagan's **regiments**, the American people. You won every battle with every call you made and letter you wrote demanding action. Well, action is still needed. If we're to finish the job, Reagan's regiments will have to become the Bush **brigades**. Soon he'll be the **chief**, and he'll need you every bit as much as I did.

Finally, there is a great tradition of warnings in presidential farewells, and I've got one that's been on my mind for some time. But oddly enough it starts with one of the things I'm proudest of in the past eight years: the **resurgence** of national pride that I called the new patriotism. This national feeling is good, but it won't count for much, and it won't last unless it's grounded in thoughtfulness and knowledge.

An **informed** patriotism is what we want. And are we doing a good enough job teaching our children what America is and what she represents in the long history of the world? Those of us who are over thirty-five or so years of age grew up in a different America. We were taught, very directly, what it means to be an American. And we absorbed, almost in the air, a love of country and an appreciation of its **institutions**. If you didn't get these things from your family, you got them from the neighborhood, from the father down the street who fought in Korea or the family who lost someone at **Anzio**. Or you could get a sense of patriotism from school. And if all else failed, you could get a sense of patriotism from the popular culture. The movies celebrated democratic values and implicitly reinforced the idea that America was special. TV was like that, too, through the midsixties.

But now, we're about to enter the nineties, and some things have changed. Younger parents aren't sure that an **unambivalent** appreciation of America is the right thing to teach modern children. And as for those who create the popular culture, well-grounded patriotism is no longer the style. Our spirit is back, but we haven't **reinstitutionalized** it. We've got to do a better job of getting across

---

deficit: shortage of money in the government when the expenses exceeds income

regiment: disciplined corps of troops

brigade: large groups of soldiers
chief: commander

resurgence: recovery that quickly effects

informed: rational on the basis of thoughtfulness and knowledge

institution: political and social system
Anzio: Italian city famous for the site of the Allies landing during the WWII

unambivalent: precise; exact
reinstitutionalize: systematize again with renewed information; update

fragile: weak; easily broken	that America is freedom-freedom of speech, freedom of religion, freedom of enterprise. And freedom is special and rare. It's **fragile**; it need protection.

...

And that's about all I have to say tonight. Except for one thing. The past few days when I've been at that window upstairs, I've thought a bit of the "shining city upon a hill." The phrase comes from **John Winthrop**, who wrote it to describe the America he imagined. What he imagined was important because he was an early **Pilgrim**, an early freedom man. He journeyed here on what today we'd call a little wooden boat; and like the other Pilgrims, he was looking for a home that would be free.

John Winthrop: governor of Massachusetts Bay colony in 1640s
Pilgrim: people who come from afar to worship God

I've spoken of the shining city all my political life, but I don't know if I ever quite communicated what I saw when I said it. But in my mind it was a tall proud city built on rocks stronger than oceans, wind-swept, God-blessed, and **teeming with** people of all kinds living in harmony and peace, a city with free ports that **hummed with** commerce and creativity, and if there had to be city walls, the walls had doors and the doors were open to anyone with the will and the heart to get here. That's how I saw it, and see it still.

teem with: full of; multiply by
hummed with: be busy with

And how stand the city on this winter night? More prosperous, more secure, and happier than it was eight years ago. But more than that; after two hundred years, two centuries, she still stands strong and true on the **granite ridge**, and her glow has held steady no matter what storm. And she's still a beacon, still a magnet for all who must have freedom, for all the pilgrims from all the lost places who are **hurtling** through the darkness, toward home.

granite: a type of very hard stone
ridge: narrow top of mountain or hill
hurtle: move very quickly and restlessly

We've done our part. And as I walk off into the city streets, a final word to the men and women of the Reagan revolution, the men and women across America who for eight years did the work that brought America back. My friends: We did it. We weren't just marking time. We made a difference. We made the **city** stronger. We made the city freer, and we left her in good hands. All in all, not bad, not bad at all.

city: (here) the United States, the city on the hill

And so, good-bye, God bless you, and God bless the United States of America.

■ 重点学习点评和提示

1. People ask how I feel about leaving. And the fact is, "parting is such sweet sorrow." The sweet part is California, and the ranch and freedom. The sorrow-the good-byes, of course, and

leaving this beautiful place.

里根不愧是演员出身。这里用莎士比亚名剧《罗密欧与朱丽叶》中有名的矛盾修饰法戏词，表达了自己告老还乡的心情。诗意盎然而又十分贴切。白宫的一些工作人员，闻此失声痛哭，依依不舍。不过，加州的阳光和宽广的牧场让他沐浴在自由之中，但他却是闲不住的人。事实上，里根退休后没有闲着，他到大学发表演讲，发表文章，访问了日本、英国、法国和加拿大，直到1994年被诊断出阿尔兹莫尔症，他才完全消失在公众视野中。

2. One is the economic recovery, in which the people of America created—and filled—19 million new jobs. The other is the recovery of our morale. America is respected again in the world and looked to for leadership.

这正是里根两届总统政绩的高度概括。对内成功地克服了经济滞胀和衰退，自1984年开始，就业率大幅度提高，经济持续增长；对外，由于大幅增加军费，出兵中东和南美地区，钳制伊朗，拉拢中国，在经济和科技上打压苏联，重新取得冷战中的优势，也导致冷战的结束。美国的大国领袖地位愈显，为后来的美国单边霸权意识奠定了基础。

3. Common sense told us that when you put a big tax on something, the people will produce less of it. So, we cut the people's tax rates, and the people produced more than ever before. The economy bloomed like a plant that had been cut back and could not grow quicker and stronger.

美国"供应学派"主张利用政府调节税收来刺激供应，创造就业，增加生产和工人的实际收入。与此同时，政府应该削减社会福利开支，降低财政赤字，抑制通货膨胀。这是里根遵循的经济政策。这里，里根把经济理论"常识化"，用妇孺皆知的语言描述了政府税收于社会生产力的关系，可谓通俗易懂，恰到好处。里根还用修剪植物使之生长茂盛的道理来说明减税反而会增加经济总量的道理，这也是对"里根经济学"最好的形象说明。

4. Common sense also told us that to preserve the peace, we'd have to become strong again after years of weakness and confusion. So, we rebuilt our defenses, and this New Year we toasted the new peacefulness around the globe.

里根再次用"常识化"的手法来说明大幅度增加军费，实施主动战略防御的政策。保持强大军力以维护世界的和平，这也是从亚当斯以来许多美国总统的遗训，尤其是西奥多·罗斯福的"大棒"政策给人予深刻的印象。这一原则后来被小布什总统在9.11后发挥为"先发制人"的单边霸权主义政策。这里，里根在自誉外交政策的同时，也间接批评了尼克松主义以"缓和"为目的的"遏制"政策。

5. It wasn't my intention when I was young. But I was raised to believe you had to pay your way for the blessings bestowed on you. I was happy with my career in the entertainment world, but I ultimately went into politics because I wanted to protect something precious.

　　里根在这里表现得十分真实和诚恳,讲述自己的成长经历和感受,展示了自己在政治语境中平易而又轻松的风格。少年里根受到母亲内尔的教育和影响,他虔诚而又自强,认定必须通过自身的努力而获得机会和幸福。他在40左右选择疏远电影业,涉足政治,参加共和党,在演说中抨击政府是贫困的根源,是民主自由的钳制力量。这里,里根表示,他从政多年想要维护的,不是政府的权威,而是人民真正当家做主的地位。

6. And I hope we have once again reminded the people that man is not free unless government is limited. There's a clear cause and effect here that is as neat and predictable as a law of physics: As government expands, liberty contracts.

　　里根把自己定位为"平民政治家",笃信杰斐逊主义的自由民主理念,提出"政府不是解决问题的办法,政府本身就是问题"的口号。这里,他以绝对的口气,提出政府与自由的水火不容关系,目的就是为他的"减税"政策张目,以摆脱经济滞胀,迎来经济增长。但是,经济问题绝不是物理公式那样简单绝对。2006年的美国次贷危机爆发,若不是政府加强监管,救市干预,后果将不堪设想。这么说来,凯恩斯主义那只"有形的手"绝对可以拨动政府和自由的两极关系,从而显示,新自由主义也不是治百病的灵丹妙药。

7. I've had my share of victories in the Congress, but what few people noticed is that I never won anything you didn't win for me.

　　里根卸任时的财政赤字已上升至GDP的2.9%,国债也翻了近3番至3.5万亿美元,这是减税和扩大军备开支的代价。里根对此无能为力,只能一方面肯定自己与国会保持的良好关系,委婉地证明自己对此无大错,另一方则以人民的名义把这个赤字包袱抛给即将上任的老布什政府。

8. I've spoken of the shining city all my political life, but I don't know if I ever quite communicated what I saw when I said it.

　　事实上,里根早在11岁时就在耶稣门徒教会就深受神父克里弗的影响,对约翰·温斯罗普的"山巅之城"深信不疑。经过长达近40年的从政生涯,里根对这个美国例外论的古老故事自有新的认识,这里表达的一番溢美描写,以及下文基于意识形态的美化,也就不足为奇的了。

■ 思考及讨论题

1. How did Reagan get involved in politics and what were his political concerns at the time?
2. What were the major causes of 1981 stagflation and economic recession?
3. What is meant by the term "Reagan Revolution" and how did it affect American economy, and of the world?
4. How did Reagan's foreign policies contribute to the end of the cold war?

■ 阅读书目

1. Reeves, Richard. *President Reagan: the Triumph of Imagination*. New York: Simon & Schuster Paperbacks, 2005.
2. Carnes, Mark C. *Ronald Reagan and the Triumph of American Conservatism*. New York: Pearson Longman, 2006.
3. Ryan, Halford. *U.S. Presidents as Orators: A Bio-Critical Sourcebook*. Westport: Greenwood Press, 1995.
4. Heclo, Hugh, "The Mixed Legacies of Ronald Reagan" in *Presidential Studies Quarterly*. December 2008.

第三十四讲

乔治·W.布什(George W. Bush 1946—)

■ 政治历史评述

乔治·W.布什:浪子回头的州长,时运不济的反恐总统

美国历史上有两例"子承父业"当上总统的例子。一是1824年当选总统的约翰·昆西·亚当斯;再就是2000年有争议地当选总统的乔治·W.布什。

两人各自的父亲都只当了一届总统就被政治对手赶下台,两人胜选总统时都年纪相当,昆西·亚当斯56岁,小布什54岁。

不同的是,亚当斯好学慎思,成绩优秀,博览群书,10岁就跟随父亲遍游欧洲,见多识广,他虔诚自律,生活作风严谨,日记一记就是70多年不间断,政治法律,人文历史无不通晓,被聘为哈佛大学讲席教授;他从政后从基层做起,当个外交官,先后出任驻英国,普鲁士和俄国大使,干过总统谈判特使,做过国务卿,兢兢业业20多年后,众望所归,一步步登上总统宝座。

反观小布什,少年张狂,多恶作剧,靠拼爹进了耶鲁学历史后,无心念书,却出没夜店,酗酒泡妞,纵情声色,甚至因酒驾和偷窃被警察拘留;进入哈佛商学院读MBA后,这位反叛青年变本加厉,仍旧我行我素,喝着烈酒追逐女生,不问政治,读书不求甚解;毕业后,小布什回到得克萨斯州,自立门户,靠布什家族多年经营的关系网干起了石油生意,生活中得过且过,牛仔做派,及至遇到淑女劳拉,结婚生子,小布什的生活才有了些转变,在经营棒球队之余开始关心政治,以私人代表的身份为老父亲出力助选。1992年,父亲老布什竞选总统连任失败,小布什方才顿悟,自己有责任延续布什家族的政治薪火,于是戒酒自律,志存高远。就这么一个浪子,回头开始涉政不过四五年,竟然于1994年竞选得克萨斯州州长一举成功,1998年连任州长,任期内一鼓作气,直奔白宫,于2000年大选意外击败人气冲天的副总统戈尔,拿下了美国总统大任。

从亚当斯到小布什,170多年过去,美国的共和代议体制,民主选举的形式基本照旧,但社会的政治观念和意识不可能一成不变。经过了南北战争的洗礼,20世纪初进步主义、实用主义的熏陶和两次世界大战后的迷惘,特别是60年代以来的民权运动,文化反叛,摇滚的兴起和性解放文化的冲击,美国大众政治意识中那种以个人的"德行"和"品行"评判 政治能力的标准已被淡化,代之而起的是一种不避家族史,更为平等的,以解决实际问题的能力并且具有鲜明个性的形象为衡量标准的政治评价意识。远的不说,艾森豪威尔的微笑和干练,肯尼迪的年轻和自信,尼克松的多变和实用,里根的乐观和简洁,都为自己的领袖形象加分,这些人都没有出众的教育背景,也不是古典"品行皆优"的大众榜样。

小布什前半生放荡的生活和书本知识的贫乏,没有影响他的政治崛起,倒是他那堂吉诃德式的牛仔作风,迎合大众口味的俏皮,反而唤起美国精神文化中崇尚个性表现和开拓意识,让人想起西奥多·罗斯福的牛仔"硬汉"精神和里根乐天知命的平民作风。况且,布什在得克萨斯州州长任内发扬实干精神,大力提倡教育改革和社会责任,提高社会福利,维护社会治安,改革司法诉讼体制,干得还是相当不错,赢得了"富有同情心的保守主义者"这样的好评。更何况,美国成熟过头的政党政治联手各种利益集团,共和党上下一致鼓噪,在选战中极大地影响操纵了选民意向,加之媒体的推波助澜,使得小布什能够以保守亲民的姿态,在支持率落后的情况下追平才华横溢的副总统戈尔,继而布什家族倾巢出动,争取黑人和妇女选票,终于在比戈尔少53万普选票的情况下,多获得了4票选举人团票而侥幸当选美利坚第43任总统。

可是,小布什上台后国内外运气极为不佳。他还未就职就遭遇成千上万抗议者的示威,谴责他用卑鄙手段"窃取"了总统职位。美国社会在政治上产生了严重对立的局面;克林顿政府治下国内经济各项指标的强劲增长,此时出现下行的迹象;国外第一次

伊拉克战争的后遗症还在延续,曾是盟友的伊拉克总统萨达姆开始强硬反美;更为雪上加霜的是,小布什入住白宫几个月后,发生了震惊世界的9.11恐怖袭击,美国本土第一次遭到大规模的袭击,象征自由贸易的纽约双子星世贸大楼轰然倒塌,几千美国人的生命顷刻之间灰飞烟灭,恐怖主义的幽灵笼罩着进入新世纪的美国;这些变局和突发事件都敲打着小布什的神经;他的第二任期也充满了挑战,2007年美国次贷危机引发的全球金融风暴比2005年卡特琳娜飓风灾害更有破坏力,着实让在反恐战争、国内经济和社会福利之间疲于奔命的小布什力不从心,应接不暇。

面对充满危机和变数的国内经济形势,小布什首先效法里根的做法,实行大规模减税,上任第一年就通过了35万亿的庞大减税计划,试图刺激经济增长,增加就业机会。同时,他大打"有同情心的保守主义"牌,以"教育总统"的姿态,增拨联邦补贴,实施"一个孩子不拉下"的改革计划;同时,他大力实行社会保障改革,提倡医疗保险私有化,力图改善财政预算赤字;另一方面,为了反恐,国土安全和国内劳动市场的需要,提倡了更为宽松的移民政策,宣布保留近1200万非法移民工的长期"客工"待遇,改善美墨关系。

国外政策方面,小布什受到9.11的刺激,发誓要把恐怖分子绳之以法,呼吁全世界各国与美国站在一起,制定出咄咄逼人的霸权主义战略:他以非此即彼的简单逻辑宣布:"反恐斗争中,不是美国的朋友,就是美国的敌人",同时也宣布了单边霸权主义的"布什宣言":窝藏恐怖分子与恐怖分子同罪;美国先发制人攻击海外恐怖分子;消灭任何威胁于萌芽之中。与此同时,小布什采取战略进攻姿态,追求美国国家利益,想全世界推行

美国自由民主价值观念,主动干预国际事务,维护美国的"世界领导地位",支持北约东扩,把中国定为"战略竞争对手",加强在亚太地区的军事同盟体系以求遏制中国。

可惜,小布什不懂得"过犹不及"的道理,也没有"韬光养晦"的耐心。他看到因果关系最表面的现象,全力以赴,急于求成,往往起到适得其反的效果。

小布什2009年1月20日卸任离开白宫,给继任的奥巴马总统留下一个满目疮痍的烂摊子。根据2008年11月盖洛普民调显示,小布什是施政满意度最低的离任总统,支持率仅达27%,史无前例。他被认为是二战以来最糟糕的总统。

对于坚决的布什反对者,小布什的"罪行"可是罄竹难书!

9.11后,小布什真正地"子承父业",以销毁萨达姆拥有的大规模杀伤性武器和反恐为名,他增拨巨额军费,发动了伊拉克战争和阿富汗反恐战争,让美军在海外两线作战,耗费了大量的人力,财力和政治资源。结果,美军虽然占领了伊拉克,打败了塔利班,但却被拖入战争泥潭。扶持起来的伊拉克政权不稳,恐怖炸弹袭击频频,美军近10年不能撤出;由于找不到大规模杀伤性武器,小布什发动伊拉克战争的动机遭到质疑;美国飞机炸死平民,关塔那摩监狱美军的虐囚事件,阿富汗的北约和美军士兵伤亡数字上升,这些都把小布什弄得声名狼藉。当初,小布什喊着"根除恐怖主义"的口号发动战争。结果却适得其反,反恐战争反倒聚集了原本分散的伊斯兰原教旨主义反美情绪,世界反倒变得更不安全。在欧洲,亚洲和中东,局势更加不安定,美国的反恐战争反倒成了恐怖主义的温床。英国、俄国、西班牙、巴基斯坦、印尼、中国和埃及都相继遭到恐怖主义的袭击,2013年4月美国本土再次遭到恐怖炸弹袭击,波士顿马拉松的爆炸再次震惊了美国朝野。

美国经济倒退,小布什似乎也难辞其咎。庞大的反恐战争军费开支把克林顿政府的经济成果抵消殆尽;联邦政府财政赤字,国债,贸易赤字也再创新高。失业率上升,经济总量萎缩,银行倒闭,汽车工业几乎全面崩溃,更有甚者,股票市场走跌,房地产市场疲软,使得很多人手中的美元和养老金贬值。2008年盖洛普民调统计表明,高达80%的美国人认为,国家面临的重大问题是经济倒退,而不是反恐;90%认为工作难找,大多数人对未来经济前景悲观失望。这些都显示着,小布什的8年执政使美国经济是1929年经济大萧条以来的又一低谷。

严格说来,2007年美国次贷市场的崩溃也与小布什的经济政策有关。他坚持大规模减税,大肆借债,扩大财政赤字,却错过投资的大好机会;他放松金融监管,对风险投资缺乏管理,固执片面地追求自由市场经济,而且决策过程独断专行,听不得其他人的意见,这些所作所为都加快了金融危机的到来。具有讽刺意义的是,一方面,他奉行小政府政策,依靠资本主义自由市场调节,但金融风暴来临,政府却必须耗费大量精力和财力实行大公司和银行国有化;政府甚至花费巨额资金注入金融市场,以救银行坏账和流动资产,拯救衰败的大公司如通用汽车、福特公司等等。

21世纪初,大规模的政府干预市场早已被认为是过时之举,尤其经过了里根的右转,更是如此,克林顿也曾宣布大政府时代已经终结。但是,布什却反其道而行之,面临2007年的金融危机,小布什病急投医,提出7000亿美元的庞大救市计划,用纳税人的钱为金融坏账埋单。美国大众本来就对银行和企业高管的高薪和红包不满,小布什的救市也就导致3年以后的占领华尔街行动的发生。布什宣称,7000亿美元救市为的是"稳定金融市场,保护市场,而不是取代之"。此语等同自嘲而已,有如人称"美国特色的社会主义"一般。

不管怎么说,小布什政府治下的美国经济持续疲软,却是不争的事实。失业率仍维持在9%以上,导致贫困人口大量增加。美国人口普查局发布的报告显示,2010年美国贫困率为15.1%,贫困人口达到4620万人,为52年来最高。与此同时,社会财富高度向以华尔街为代表的少数富有的美国人集中。最富有的5%美国人拥有全国72%的财富。贫富差距进一步拉大,酝酿着深刻的社会危机。

其实,事到如今,非战之罪,势也。小布什能治一州,成效斐然,但要在全球化多边复杂的世界格局中治理美国这样一个超级大国,他还欠大国领袖的功力,加之时运不济,焉能不败?古语有云:"人贵有自知之明"。当年,孔子的学生子路才学卓然,志向高远,也只敢治理一个困于大国之间的"千乘之国",而且承诺,3年之后使之初见成效而已。对于这一点,小布什卸任后应该有所领悟。2012年7月,过着隐居生活,不问政治的他接受胡佛研究所的采访,不无感慨地说,他已经历过太多政治,"我从沼泽中爬出来,不想再爬回去。"对于才66岁的小布什来说,此话其实并不晚。

2002年6月1日,小布什来到西点军校,参加毕业典礼,会上发表了演讲。在美国发动伊拉克战争和阿富汗反恐战争前夕,这篇演讲象征着布什政府的战争动员令。布什在演说中告诉毕业军官们,9.11以后美国将进行一场特殊的反恐战争,美国的民主和自由面临的威胁不是大规模的军事行动,而是"激进主义和科技"的威胁,是少数掌握了"大规模杀伤性武器"的邪恶之人,花费区区几千美元就可以造成大规模的人员伤亡和财产损失的威胁。为此,美国必须超越冷战"遏制"和"威慑"的防御性思维模式,代之以先发制人的主动战争行动,动员所有的人力物力,与盟友一道,在世界范围内把恐怖主义扼杀在未然和计划之中。这就是所谓"布什主义"或"布什宣言"新思维。布什在演说中还为他提出的"反恐无中立立场","不是朋友就是敌人"的论断做了辩护,认为在道德的对与错之间不存在中间立场。同时,布什在演说中还不忘高扬美国自由民主的价值,号召通过反恐战争而实现和平和人权。

小布什的演讲风格别具一格。他往往出其不意,在严肃的话语中突降俏皮的玩笑,赞美的风格和通俗的话语相互映照,他甚至拿自己开玩笑,在宏大叙事和自嘲之中导出幽默感和戏剧性,以此始终抓住听众的注意力,演说现场总是充满欢笑和掌声。这是小布什可爱的地方,也是他的生活经历和性情的必然。

小布什操着得克萨斯西部的口音,有些音读不准,吞音现象则时常发生,比如"s"总读成"sh","nuclear"老念成"nucular"。白宫语音专家纠正多次,可是乡音难改,而且小布什也不想改。由于他每次都把"W"念成了"dubya",于是人们干脆送他一个绰号叫"Dubya"。他也欣然接受,用做笑料。

他还往往喜欢用词开玩笑,以至于无意识造出一些令人莫名其妙的单词。他的政敌借此批评他不学无术,发音不准确,常犯语法错误。这些批评为了政治目的,有些言过其实。依小布什的性情,有意出错,何尝不是玩笑,而且,这也是一种修辞手法。不过,有时玩笑过了头,或者是真犯了迷糊,那可真要误事,比如他把 tax barrier 说成 tax terrier,persevere 说成 preserve 倒也罢了,也许还博得观众一笑。但是如果把话说反了,或把外国元首的名字念错了,那就会出尽了洋相。更有甚者,如果有些要紧的词选用错了,那将会导致仇恨和冲突,比如用"crusade"指代反恐战争,用"infinite justice"指代阿富汗战争,这都是对穆斯林的极大侮辱,会激起宗教情绪的新仇旧恨,增加民族冲突。

1810年,那位"子承父业"的当选总统昆西·亚当斯出版了一本演讲修辞书,书名叫《修辞与口才讲演录》,其中纵论古今修辞,论证演讲对于多元国家的文化统一之重要。可惜小布什上任前没有好好读过,否则他的演讲就会更为精彩得多。

■ 演讲文(节选)

Commencement Address at the United States Military Academy at West Point

George W. Bush

...

Every West Point class is **commissioned** to the Armed Forces. Some West Point classes are also commissioned by history, to take part in a great new calling for their country. Speaking here to the class of 1942—six months after Pearl Harbor—**General Marshall** said, "We're determined that before the sun sets on this terrible struggle, our flag will be recognized throughout the world as a symbol of freedom on the

commence-ment: the graduation ceremony

commission: to make someone an officer in the armed forces

General Marshall: American general famous for the victories in WWII and Marshall plan for which he won Nobel Prize for Peace in 1953

one hand, and of overwhelming power on the other."

Officers graduating that year helped fulfill that mission, defeating Japan and Germany, and then reconstructing those nations as **allies**. West Point graduates of the 1940s saw the rise of a deadly new challenge—the challenge of imperial communism—and opposed it from Korea to Berlin, to Vietnam, and in the Cold War, from beginning to end. And as the sun set on their struggle, many of those West Point officers lived to see a world transformed.

History has also **issued** its call to your generation. In your last year, America was attacked by a **ruthless** and **resourceful** enemy. You graduate from this Academy in a time of war, taking your place in an American military that is powerful and is honorable. Our war on terror is only begun, but in Afghanistan it was begun well.

I am proud of the men and women who have fought on my **orders**. America is profoundly grateful for all who serve the cause of freedom, and for all who have given their lives in its defense. This nation respects and trusts our military, and we are confident in your victories to come.

This war will take many **turns** we cannot predict. Yet I am certain of this: Wherever we carry it, the American flag will stand not only for our power, but for freedom. Our nation's cause has always been larger than our nation's defense. We fight, as we always fight, for a just peace—a peace that favors human liberty. We will defend the peace against threats from terrorists and tyrants. We will **preserve** the peace by building good relations among the great powers. And we will extend the peace by encouraging free and open societies on every continent.

Building this just peace is America's opportunity, and America's duty. From this day forward, it is your challenge, as well, and we will meet this challenge together. You will wear the uniform of a great and unique country. America has no empire to extend or **utopia** to establish. We wish for others only what we wish for ourselves—safety from violence, the rewards of liberty, and the hope for a better life.

In defending the peace, we face a threat with no **precedent**. Enemies in the past needed great armies and great industrial capabilities to endanger the American people and our nation. The attacks of September the 11th required a few hundred thousand dollars in the hands of a few dozen evil and **deluded** men. All of the chaos and suffering they caused came at much less than the cost of a single **tank**. The dangers have not passed. This government and the American people are **on watch**, we are ready, because we know the terrorists have more money and more men and more plans.

allies: countries bound by agreement to work together in a war

issue: announce; make known
ruthless: pitiless and cruel
resourceful: well prepared; thoughtful

order: instruction (the President is also the commander-in-chief of the military
turn: (here) unexpected difficulty

preserve: keep something whole

utopia: imagined land; unreal country

precedent: example from history
deluded: believing in something which is not true
on watch: alert; on guard against

The gravest danger to freedom lies at the **perilous** crossroads of **radicalism** and technology. When the spread of chemical and biological and nuclear weapons, along with **ballistic** missile technology —when that occurs, even weak states and small groups could attain a **catastrophic** power to strike great nations. Our enemies have declared this very intention, and have been caught seeking these terrible weapons. They want the capability to **blackmail** us, or to harm us, or to harm our friends—and we will oppose them with all our power.

For much of the last century, America's defense relied on the Cold War doctrines of **deterrence** and **containment**. In some cases, those strategies still apply. But new threats also require new thinking. Deterrence —the promise of massive **retaliation** against nations—means nothing against shadowy terrorist networks with no nation or citizens to defend. Containment is not possible when unbalanced dictators with weapons of mass destruction can deliver those weapons on missiles or secretly provide them to terrorist allies.

We cannot defend America and our friends by hoping for the best. We cannot put our faith in the word of tyrants, who solemnly sign non-**proliferation** treaties, and then systemically break them. If we wait for threats to fully materialize, we will have waited too long.

Homeland defense and missile defense are part of stronger security, and they're essential **priorities** for America. Yet the war on terror will not be won on the defensive. We must take the battle to the enemy, disrupt his plans, and confront the worst threats before they emerge. In the world we have entered, the only path to safety is the path of action. And this nation will act.

Our security will require the best **intelligence**, to reveal threats hidden in caves and growing in laboratories. Our security will require modernizing domestic agencies such as the **FBI**, so they're prepared to act, and act quickly, against danger. Our security will require transforming the military you will lead—a military that must be ready to strike **at a moment's notice** in any dark corner of the world. And our security will require all Americans to be forward-looking and resolute, to be ready for **preemptive** action when necessary to defend our liberty and to defend our lives.

The work ahead is difficult. The choices we will face are complex. We must uncover terror **cells** in 60 or more countries, using every tool of finance, intelligence and law enforcement. Along with our friends and allies, we must oppose proliferation and confront **regimes** that

---

perilous: dangerous
radicalism: belief in violent change
ballistic: able to travel long distance at fast speed
catastrophic: massively destructive
blackmail: take money by threatening to tell secrets
deterrence: threat
containment: controlling
retaliation: fighting back as revenge

proliferation: sudden increase in number or amount (of nuclear weapons)
priority: preference; something more important than others

intelligence: military of economic information
FBI: Federal Bureau of Investigation
at a moment's notice: at any moment of order
preemptive: preventive of the enemy attack

cell: secret camp or group
regime: (here) totalitarian government

sponsor terror, as each case requires. Some nations need military training to fight terror, and we'll provide it. Other nations oppose terror, but tolerate the hatred that leads to terror—and that must change. We will send diplomats where they are needed, and we will send you, our soldiers, where you're needed.

All nations that decide for **aggression** and terror will pay a price. We will not leave the safety of America and the peace of the planet at the mercy of a few mad terrorists and tyrants. We will lift this dark threat from our country and from the world.

...

Some worry that it is somehow **undiplomatic** or impolite to speak the language of right and wrong. I disagree. Different circumstances require different methods, but not different moralities. Moral truth is the same in every culture, in every time, and in every place. Targeting innocent **civilians** for murder is always and everywhere wrong. **Brutality** against women is always and everywhere wrong. There can be no neutrality between justice and cruelty, between the innocent and the guilty. We are in a conflict between good and evil, and America will **call evil by its name**. By confronting evil and lawless regimes, we do not create a problem, we reveal a problem. And we will lead the world in opposing it.

...

Competition between great nations is inevitable, but armed conflict in our world is not. More and more, civilized nations find ourselves on the same side—united by common dangers of terrorist violence and chaos. America has, and intends to keep, military strengths beyond challenge, **thereby**, making the **destabilizing** arms races of other eras pointless, and limiting rivalries to trade and other pursuits of peace.

Today the great powers are also increasingly united by common values, instead of divided by conflicting ideologies. The United States, Japan and our Pacific friends, and now all of Europe, share a deep commitment to human freedom, **embodied** in strong alliances such as NATO. And the tide of liberty is rising in many other nations.

Generations of West Point officers planned and practiced for battles with Soviet Russia. I've just returned from a new Russia, now a country reaching toward democracy, and our partner in the war against terror. Even in China, leaders are discovering that economic freedom is the only lasting source of national wealth. **In time**, they will find that social and political freedom is the only true source of national greatness.

When the great powers share common values, we are better able

---

aggression: attacking for gain

undiplomatic: too straightforward as to appear rude
civilian: people who are not soldiers and police in a war
brutality: cruelty; violence
call evil by its name: fight the evil as it is

thereby: because of this
destabilizing: problematic; troublesome

embody: show in reality; realization of an ideal

in time: soon

to confront serious regional conflicts together, better able to cooperate in preventing the spread of violence or economic chaos. In the past, great power rivals **took sides** in difficult regional problems, making divisions deeper and more complicated. Today, from the Middle East to South Asia, we are gathering broad international **coalitions** to increase the pressure for peace. We must build strong and great power relations when times are good; to help manage crisis when times are bad. America needs partners to preserve the peace, and we will work with every nation that shares this noble goal.

...

America has a greater objective than controlling threats and containing **resentment**. We will work for a just and peaceful world beyond the war on terror.

The **bicentennial** class of West Point now enters this drama. With all in the United States Army, you will stand between your fellow citizens and grave danger. You will help establish a peace that allows millions around the world to live in liberty and to grow in prosperity. You will face times of calm, and times of crisis. And every test will find you prepared—because you're the men and women of West Point. You leave here marked by the character of this Academy, carrying with you the highest ideals of our nation.

Toward the end of his life, **Dwight Eisenhower** recalled the first day he stood on the plain at West Point. "The feeling came over me," he said, "that the expression 'the United States of America' would now and henceforth mean something different than it had ever before. From here on, it would be the nation I would be serving, not myself."

Today, your last day at West Point, you begin a life of service in a **career** unlike any other. You've answered a calling to hardship and purpose, to risk and honor. At the end of every day you will know that you have faithfully done your duty. May you always bring to that duty the high standards of this great American **institution**. May you always be worthy of the **long gray line** that stretches two centuries behind you.

On behalf of the nation, I congratulate each one of you for the commission you've earned and for the credit you bring to the United States of America. May God bless you all.

---

take sides: (here) find different allies

coalition: temporary union of different groups agreeing to work together for shared aim

resentment: hard felling; discontent

bicentennial: of two hundred years

Dwight Eisenhower: American general, the commander-in-chief of the allied force during the WWII; later elected president of USA

career: a job or a series of job related to one's profession

institution: system of government and society

long gray line: all the graduates from the Military Academy at West Point

■ 重点学习点评和提示

1. West Point graduates of the 1940s saw the rise of a deadly new challenge—the challenge of imperial communism—and opposed it from Korea to Berlin, to Vietnam, and in the Cold War, from beginning to end. And as the sun set on their struggle, many of those West Point officers lived to see a world transformed.

    世界格局的确发生了巨大的变化和重组,但不是因为东西方冷战的对抗,而是因为苏联的解体和冷战的消融。小布什在这里重提美国军人在冷战中的英勇表现,固然是应景的需要,但也在无意识中延续了冷战的思维。事实上,在小布什在此段落中提到的这 3 个美军参战的地点,柏林是绝对的冷战对峙,最后以柏林墙的倒塌结束;朝鲜战争则与对手打成平局,而在越战中则遭到了完全的失败。

2. The attacks of September the 11th required a few hundred thousand dollars in the hands of a few dozen evil and deluded men. All of the chaos and suffering they caused came at much less than the cost of a single tank.

    这是对恐怖主义袭击极为形象的描述。邪恶的恐怖分子在暗处发动袭击,以价值一辆坦克的代价,造成大规模的死伤和恐慌。这是一场完全不同性质的战争,预示着美国反恐战争的艰巨性和不确定性。

3. The gravest danger to freedom lies at the perilous crossroads of radicalism and technology. When the spread of chemical and biological and nuclear weapons, along with ballistic missile technology—when that occurs, even weak states and small groups could attain a catastrophic power to strike great nations.

    小布什意识到,"激进主义"(即宗教极端主义情绪)和高科技的结合是恐怖主义的源泉,大国核讹诈的时代已经终结。这是明智的判断,但是以摧毁伊拉克大规模杀伤性武器为由,猛烈地空袭和大兵团地面部队进攻一个主权国家,则不是对付在暗处的恐怖分子的最好办法。而且,萨达姆和拉登本人的死亡,也并没有根除恐怖主义。在此意义上,布什的反恐战争自然被反对者们说成是一场"没有必要的战争"。

4. For much of the last century, America's defense relied on the Cold War doctrines of deterrence and containment. In some cases, those strategies still apply. But new threats also require new thinking.

    的确,冷战结束,美国应该反思长期以来遏制共产主义和核威胁的政策,制定一种在新的全球格局中处理大国关系的新政策。但是如果以霸权主义的傲慢思考和行事,则结果只有一个,那就是奉行单边主义,在世界范围内主动干预,推行美国的自由民主价值观念,制造出亚冷战状态。这就是小布什的新思维。

5. We must take the battle to the enemy, disrupt his plans, and confront the worst before they emerge. In the world we have entered, the only path to safety is the path of action. And this nation will act.

   这是小布什先发制人的反恐战争的宣言,也是一场"猫捉老鼠"的反恐战争的开端。观念上继承了里根主义"主动出击"的冷战思维,措辞上模仿了小罗斯福的风格,结果是小布什单边霸权主义的形成,后果是美国在伊拉克和阿富汗陷入战争泥淖,而且由于大规模战争中误伤平民和虐囚事件,反而引起宗教和民族仇恨。

6. Some worry that it is somehow undiplomatic or impolite to speak the language of right and wrong. I disagree. Different circumstances require different methods, but not different moralities. Moral truth is the same in every culture, in every time, and in every place.

   这就是小布什反恐战争中非此即彼的逻辑思维:"不是美国的朋友,就是美国的敌人"的道德辩护。其实,恐怖主义的产生和发展都是一个极为复杂的过程,其中涉及历史地理,宗教文化和经济众多的因素,需要具体情况具体分析,采取不同的对策。针对无辜平民生命和财产的死亡袭击是邪恶的行为,这毋庸置疑。但以复仇的心态对某个可能藏有恐怖分子的主权国家的军事打击又会产生新的道德问题。这种治标不治本的思维和行为已被证明是无济于事的。

7. Today the great powers are also increasingly united by common values, instead of divided by conflicting ideologies.

   小布什在此意识到,冷战后的世界格局发生了巨大变化,世界由两极走向多级多元。但在美国民主的傲慢心态中,这种变化还是被纳入冷战思维的框架。下文中,小布什眼中的世界还是意识形态冲突的场所,不同的社会制度无法调和,还是非此即彼的判断。

8. When the great powers share common values, we are better able to confront serious regional conflicts together, better able to cooperate in preventing the spread of violence or economic chaos.

   抛弃意识形态偏见,构建新的大国关系,共同维护世界和平与安全,共享经济发展。这应是新时代的潮流。可惜的是,小布什心目中的"具有共识的大国"并不包括中国这样的社会主义国家,他在竞选中把中国定位为"战略竞争对手",执政后在中美南海撞机事件、对台军售等一系列事件中表现出对中国的强硬态度,都表明美国遏制中国政策的延续。

■ 思考及讨论题

1. What are some important issues during the 2000 presidential campaign?
2. In what ways did the terrorist attack of 9.11 change American foreign policies?
3. What was George W. Bush's strategy in the War on Terror?
4. How did President George W. Bush handle the financial crisis of 2007—2009?

■ 阅读书目

1. Edwards, George C. *The Polarized Presidency of George W. Bush*. New York: Oxford University Press, 2007.
2. Zelizer, Julian E. ed. *The Presidency of George W. Bush: A First Historical Assessment*. Princeton: Princeton University Press, 2010.
3. Fred, Greenstein. "The Contemporary Presidency: The Changing Leadership of George W. Bush: A Pre-and Post-9/11 Comparison" in *Presidential Studies Quarterly*, June 2002.
4. Dervin, Dan. "George W. Bush's Second Term: Saving the World, Saving the Country" in *The Journal of Psychohistory*, Fall 2005.

后记/AFTERWORD

书稿写完,夜已深沉。历史仿佛像这星光闪烁的夜空,偶尔一颗星星划过,留下一道灿烂美丽的曲线,不待仔细看过,消逝了,一切又归于静穆和神秘。我们的语言是这么的无力,它无法让我们回到那多事而又精彩的政治历史境遇之中。我们如果能够捕捉到历史的瞬间,追溯政治历史人物生命的轨迹,正如这天边一刹那的辉煌和灿烂,那么我们所能感受到的与其说是历史的真实,倒不如说是历史赠予我们现实生活的意义和乐趣。过去的人类精神轨迹让我们感受到我们此刻的存在和欢娱,这应该就是历史馈赠吧。对于政治,对于历史,不能言说的,让我们保持沉默,就像这静穆而又神秘的夜空一样。

回到现实中,却有诸多有关这本书的师生情谊和友情需要表达。愿达意尽情。

1995年—1998年,我受业北京大学著名学者,西方语言文化大师李赋宁先生,攻读博士学位。一次,李先生邀我登香山,路上向我讲起他在美国耶鲁大学念书期间的感受,末了谆谆教我:"术业有专攻,但基础要广博。对英语国家,特别是美国的政治历史和人文的知识也要有广泛的涉猎,用辩证唯物主义和历史唯物主义的观点进行综合和分析,这对研究文学有好处。"寥寥数语,出自李先生感言,我终生不忘,刻意笃行。转眼间,李先生仙逝已近10年,学生谨以此书深切缅怀恩师李赋宁先生。

2007年起,我在北京大学开设了人文通选课"美国政治演说中的历史文化评析",6年多来共有约400名学生,特别是有志赴美继续攻读学位的学生参与了这一课程。同学们都反映这门课内容丰富,功夫愈大,所学愈多。这本书在原来分章讲义的基础上,在教学过程中不断得以充实完善,今日得以出版,当是这门课6年来师生共同努力的结果。也惟愿这本书未来使更多的学生和读者受益。

本书是北京大学教材建设委员会和北京大学出版社2011年的立项出版项目。作者借本书付梓出版之机,向上述部门的领导和专家表示感谢。由于作者写作进度迟缓,致使交稿时间一再拖延,在此深表歉意。

最后,我要感谢北京大学出版社外语编辑部的领导,感谢责编黄瑞明女士精心的策划和编辑,感谢黄浩女士颇具创意的书封装帧设计,她们的专业奉献精神和技能为本书陡然增色,让这本书能够及时呈现在广大学生和读者面前。

黄必康
2013年8月3日于
北京大学燕北园